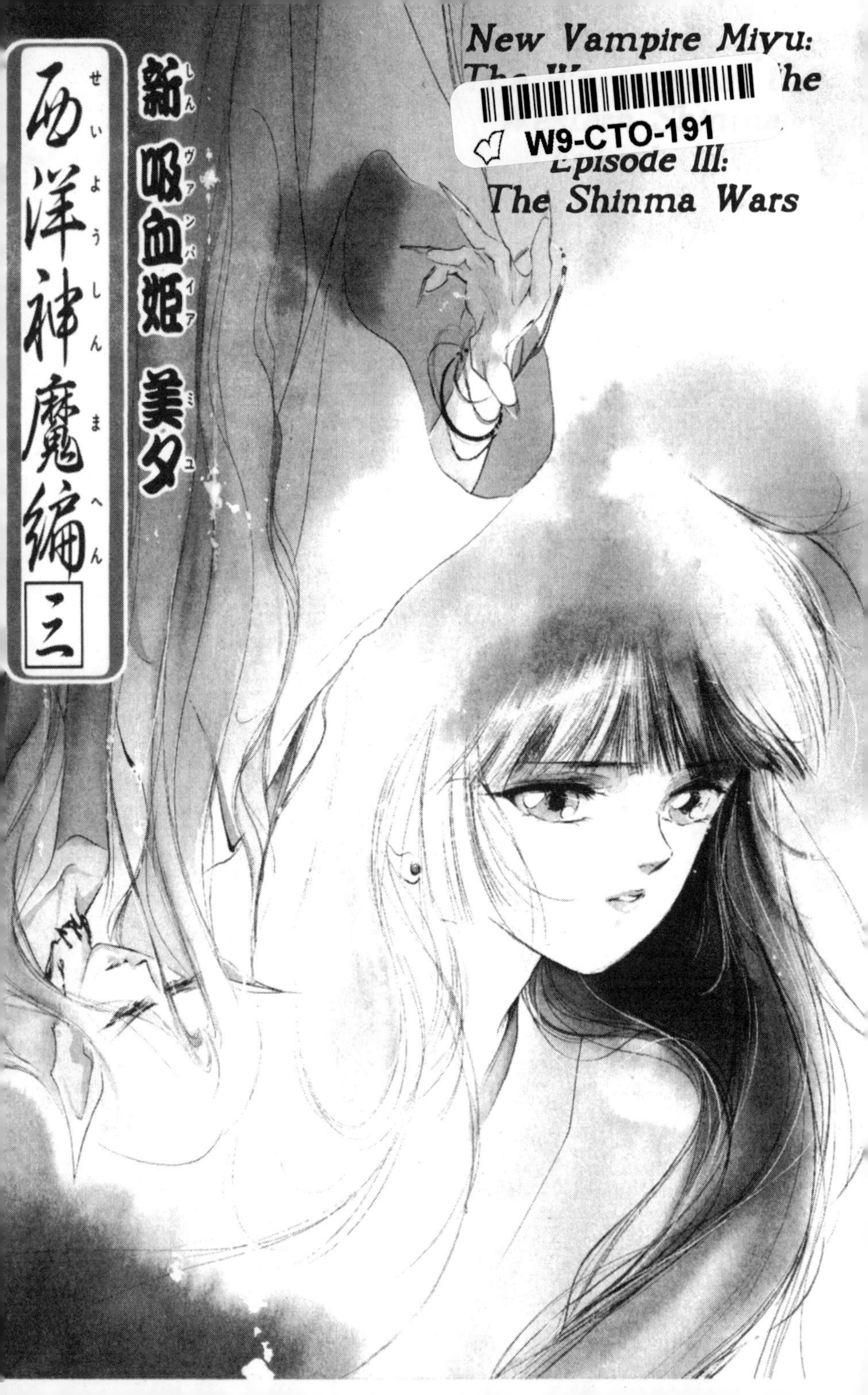
新吸血姫 美夕
西洋神魔編 二
New Vampire Miyu:
The
he
Episode III:
The Shinma Wars

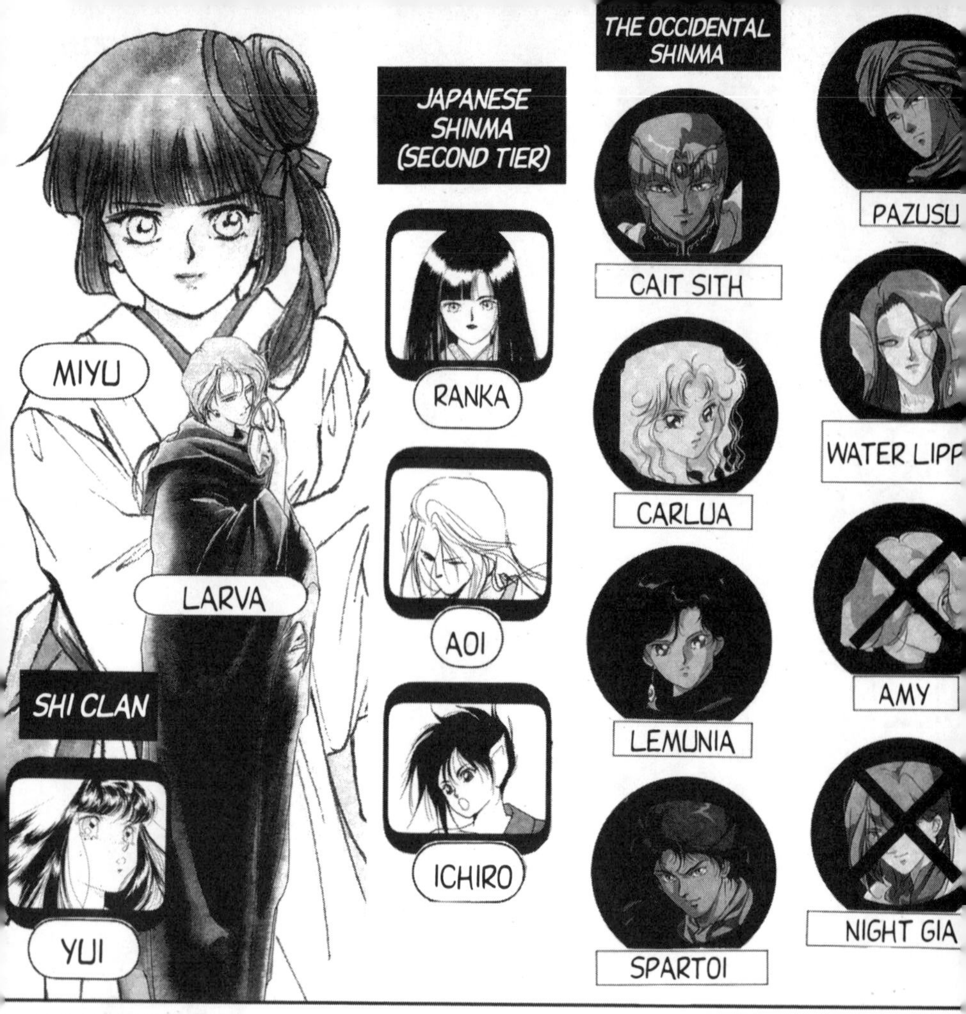

THE OCCIDENTAL SHINMA
JAPANESE SHINMA (SECOND TIER)
MIYU
LARVA
SHI CLAN
YUI
RANKA
AOI
ICHIRO
CAIT SITH
CARLUA
LEMUNIA
SPARTOI
PAZUSU
WATER LIPP
AMY
NIGHT GIA

THE STORY THUS FAR:

AN EERIE GHOST SHIP APPEARED IN THE SEA OF JAPAN WITH EIGHT OCCIDENTAL SHINMA ON BOARD. UPON REACHING THE SHORE, THEY SPLIT UP INTO TWO PARTIES. ONE GROUP WENT TO DESTROY THE GATE TO THE SHINMA REALM WHILE THE OTHER WENT TO ASSAULT MIYU, THE WATCHER OF DARKNESS. MIYU WAS DECEIVED BY "THE DREAM USER" NIGHT GIA WHILE THE GATE AND THE ELDER OF THE FIRST LAYER OF THE JAPANESE SHINMA WERE DESTROYED. THE OCCIDENTAL SHINMA'S OTHER OBJECTIVE WAS TO RETRIEVE THEIR FORMER COMRADE LARVA. THE "SURGERY OF DARKNESS" WOULD BE THE ONLY WAY TO RELEASE LARVA FROM THE CONTROL OF MIYU'S BLOOD. SOON AFTER MIYU BARELY DEFEATED NIGHT GIA AND WHILE SHE WAS STILL WEAK, SHE WAS ATTACKED BY MORE OCCIDENTAL SHINMA. IN THE ENSUING BATTLE, LARVA WAS DEFEATED AND MIYU ESCAPED FROM HER ENEMIES. THE OCCIDENTAL SHINMA THEN TOOK LARVA BACK TO THEIR SHIP AND PERFORMED THE SURGERY. WITH PAZUSU'S MAGIC POWER AND CARLUA'S BLOOD, MIYU'S CURSE WAS REMOVED FROM LARVA AND HE REJOINED THEM IN THEIR BATTLE AGAINST MIYU. AFTER MIYU DEFEATED AMY, MIYU WAS ATTACKED BY LARVA AND THE OCCIDENTAL SHINMA AND THEN KILLED!

NOW, THE REST OF THE JAPANESE SHINMA WORLD IS SHAKING...

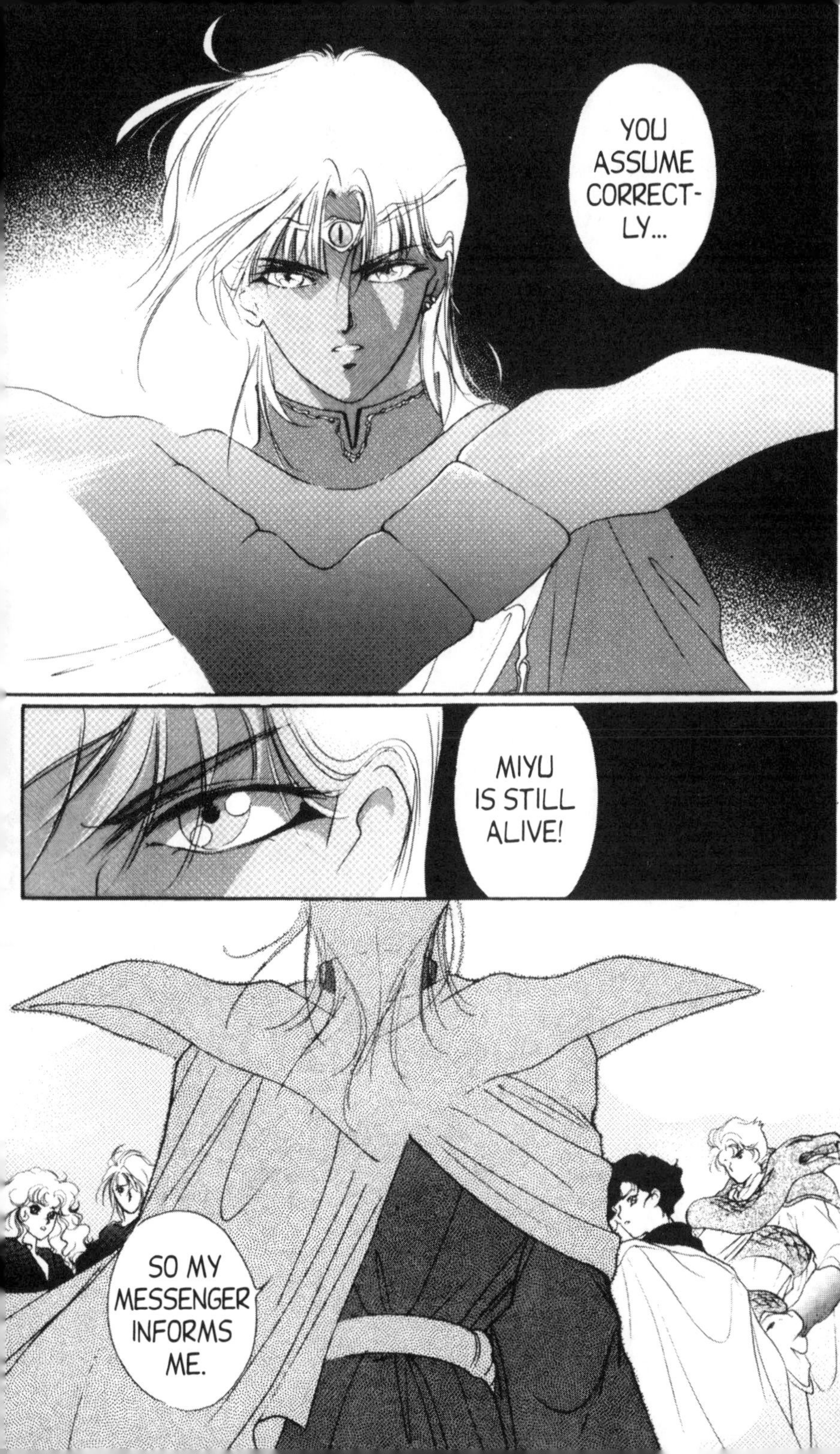
YOU ASSUME CORRECT-LY...
MIYU IS STILL ALIVE!
SO MY MESSENGER INFORMS ME.

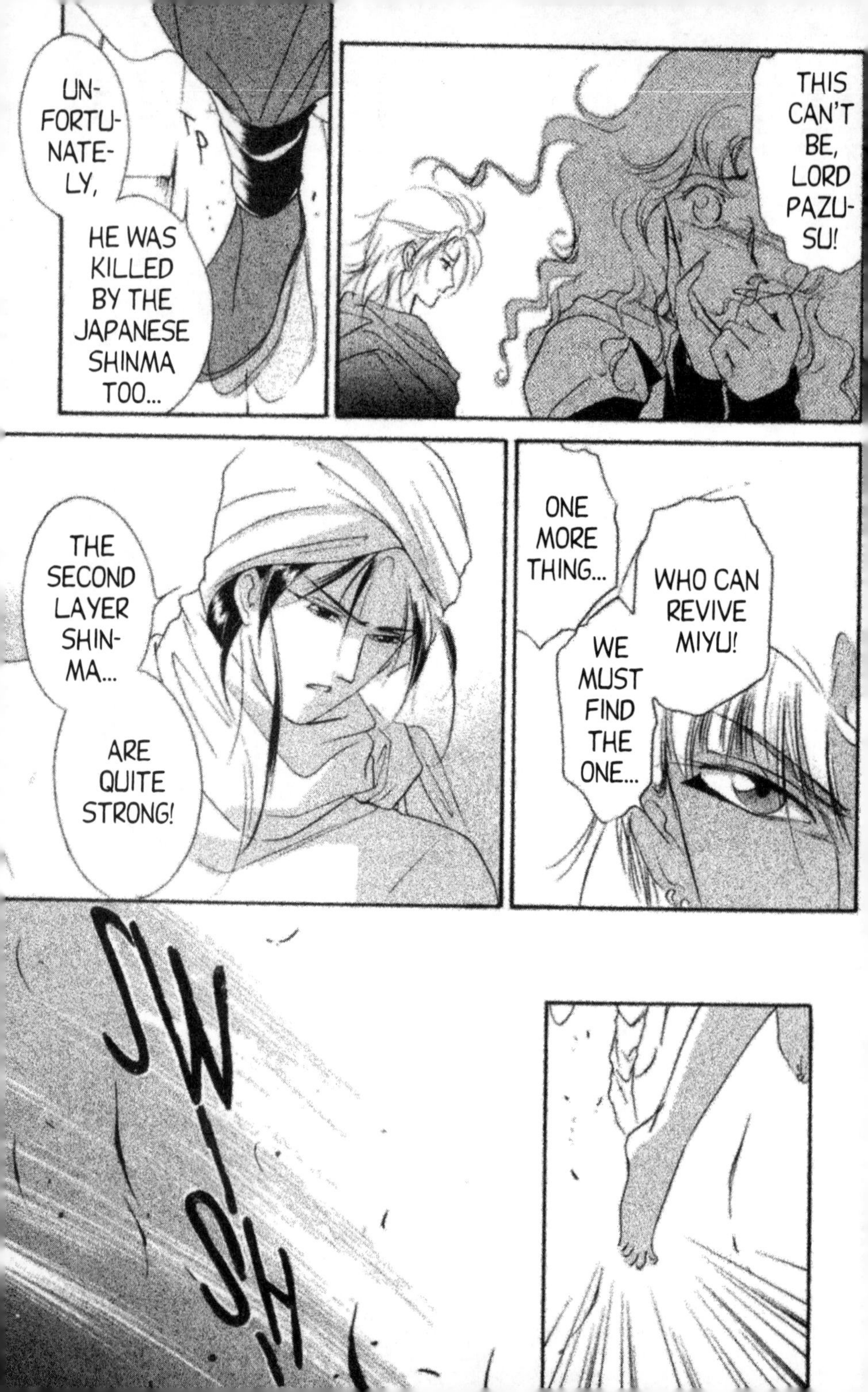
THIS CAN'T BE, LORD PAZUSU!
UNFORTUNATELY,
HE WAS KILLED BY THE JAPANESE SHINMA TOO...
ONE MORE THING...
WE MUST FIND THE ONE...
WHO CAN REVIVE MIYU!
THE SECOND LAYER SHINMA...
ARE QUITE STRONG!
SW-SH

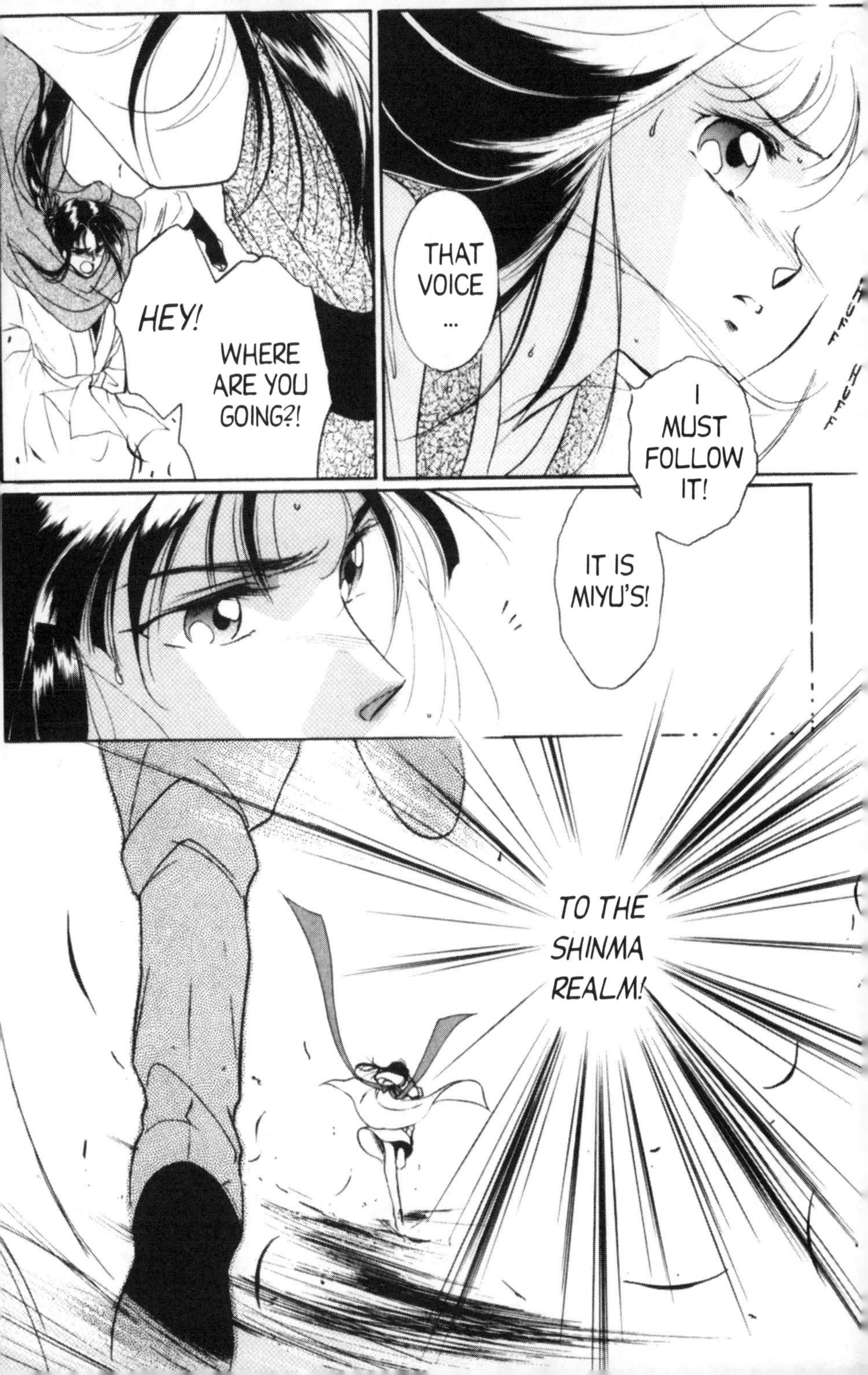
THAT VOICE ...
I MUST FOLLOW IT!
HEY!
WHERE ARE YOU GOING?!
IT IS MIYU'S!
TO THE SHINMA REALM!

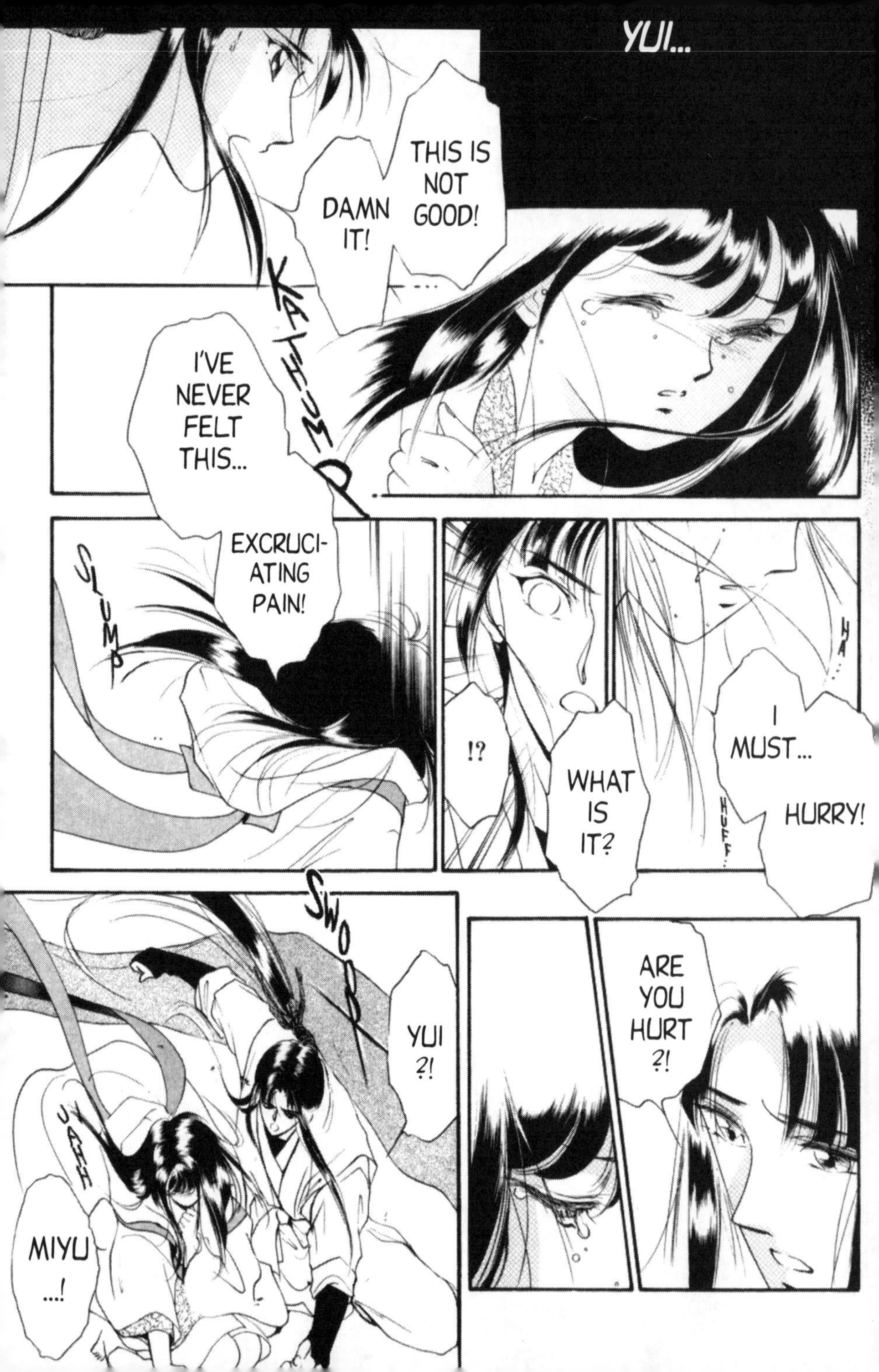
YUI...
THIS IS NOT GOOD!
DAMN IT!
KATHUMP
I'VE NEVER FELT THIS...
EXCRUCIATING PAIN!
SLUMP
I MUST...
HURRY!
HUFF...
WHAT IS IT?
!?
SWOOP
YUI ?!
MIYU ...!
ARE YOU HURT ?!

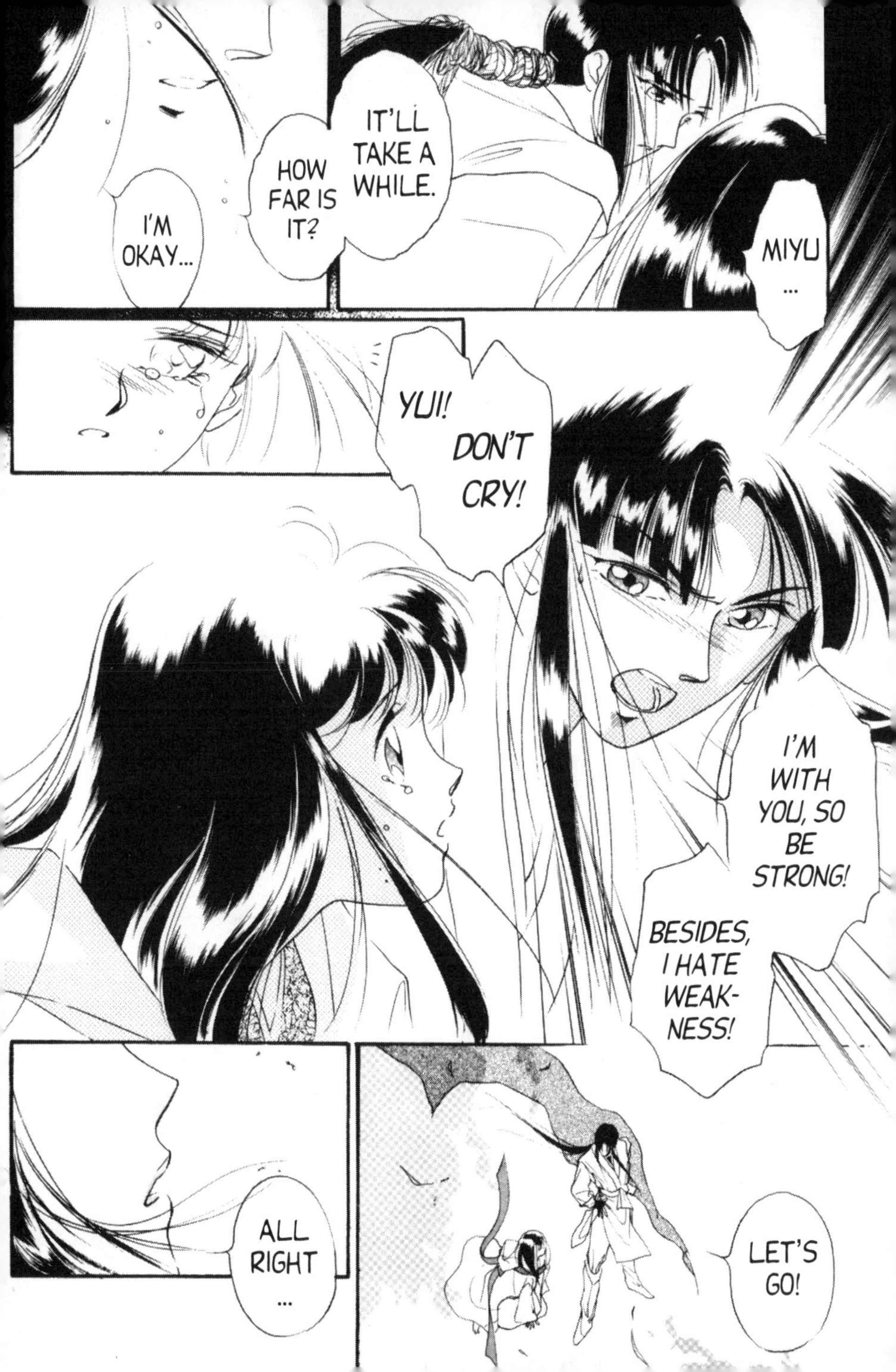
MIYU ...
I'M OKAY...
HOW FAR IS IT?
IT'LL TAKE A WHILE.
YUI! DON'T CRY!
I'M WITH YOU, SO BE STRONG!
BESIDES, I HATE WEAK-NESS!
LET'S GO!
ALL RIGHT ...

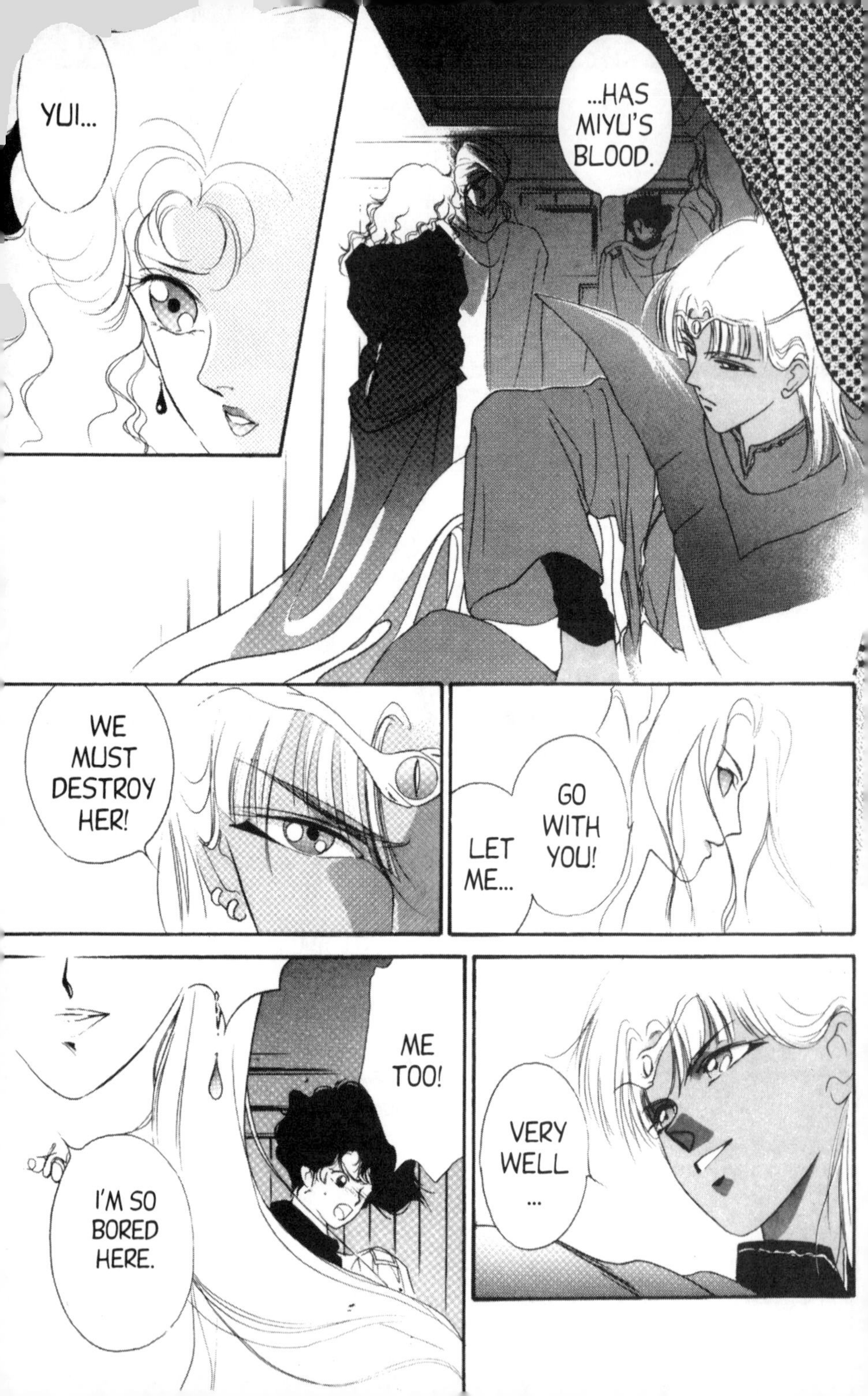

YUI...
...HAS MIYU'S BLOOD.
WE MUST DESTROY HER!
LET ME... GO WITH YOU!
ME TOO!
I'M SO BORED HERE.
VERY WELL ...

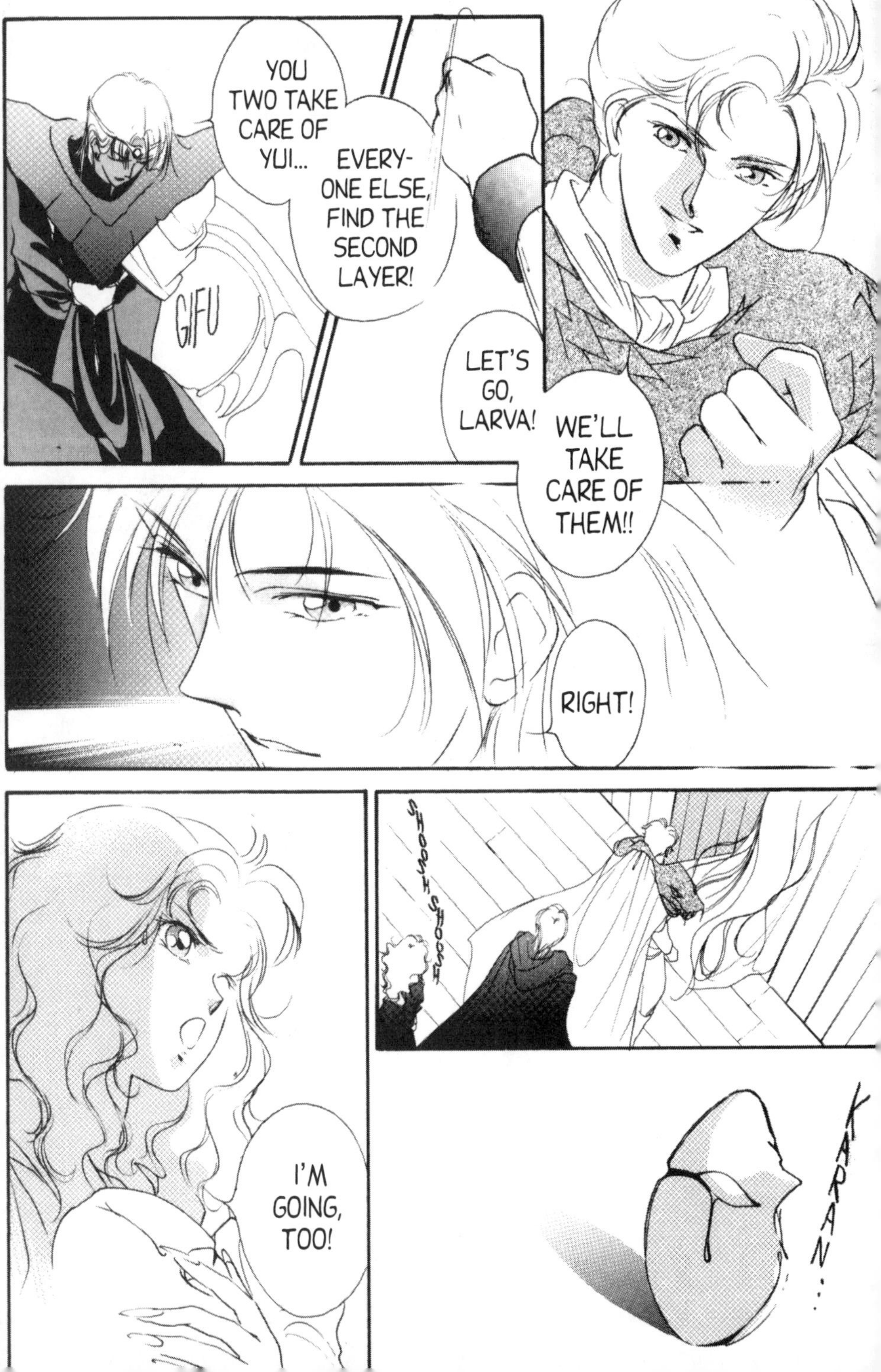
YOU TWO TAKE CARE OF YUI...
EVERY-ONE ELSE, FIND THE SECOND LAYER!
GIFU
LET'S GO, LARVA!
WE'LL TAKE CARE OF THEM!!
RIGHT!
I'M GOING, TOO!
SHOOSH SHOOSH
KARAN...

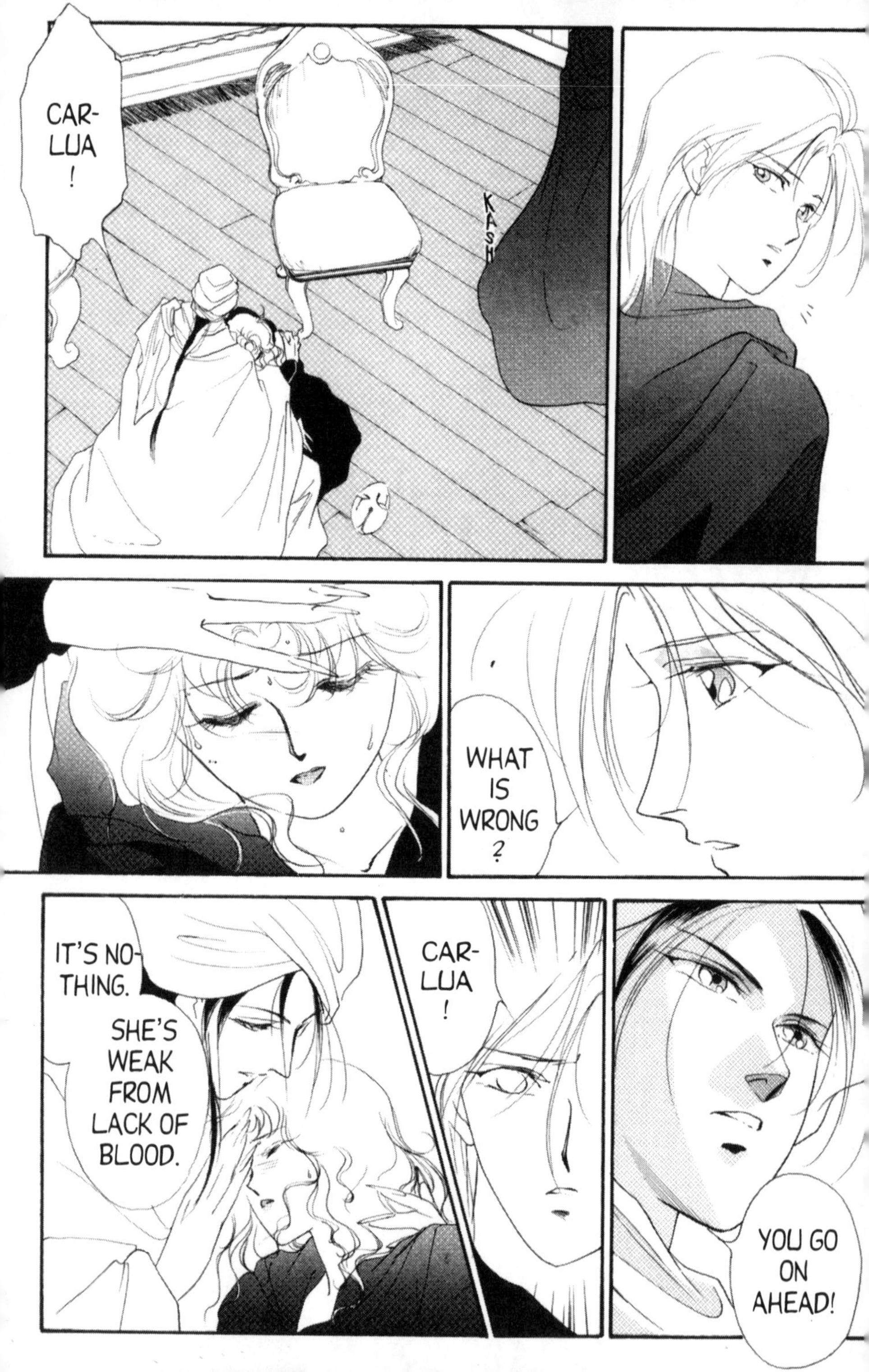
KASH
CAR-LUA!
WHAT IS WRONG?
YOU GO ON AHEAD!
CAR-LUA!
IT'S NO-THING.
SHE'S WEAK FROM LACK OF BLOOD.

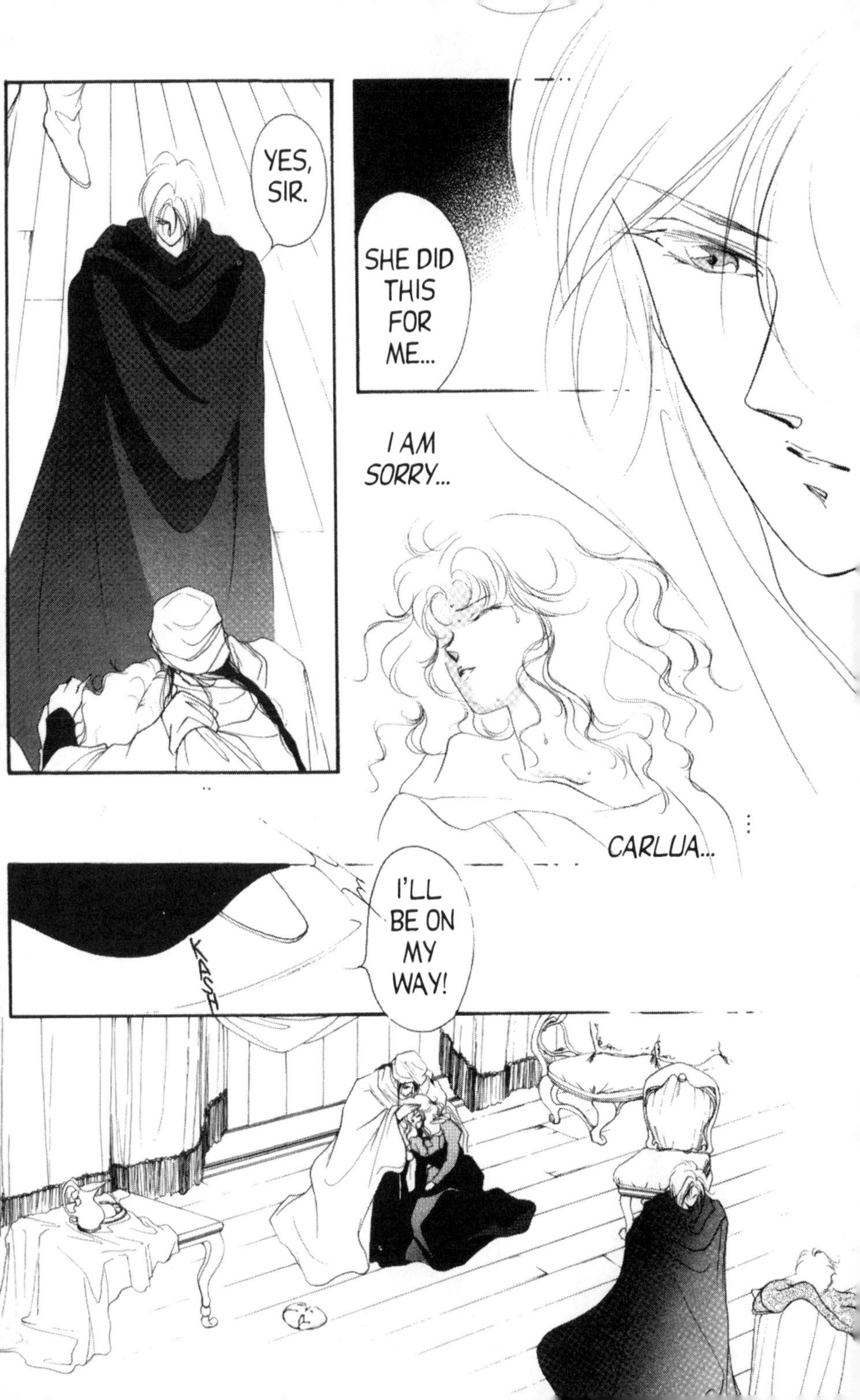
YES, SIR.
SHE DID THIS FOR ME...
I AM SORRY...
CARLUA...
I'LL BE ON MY WAY!
KASH

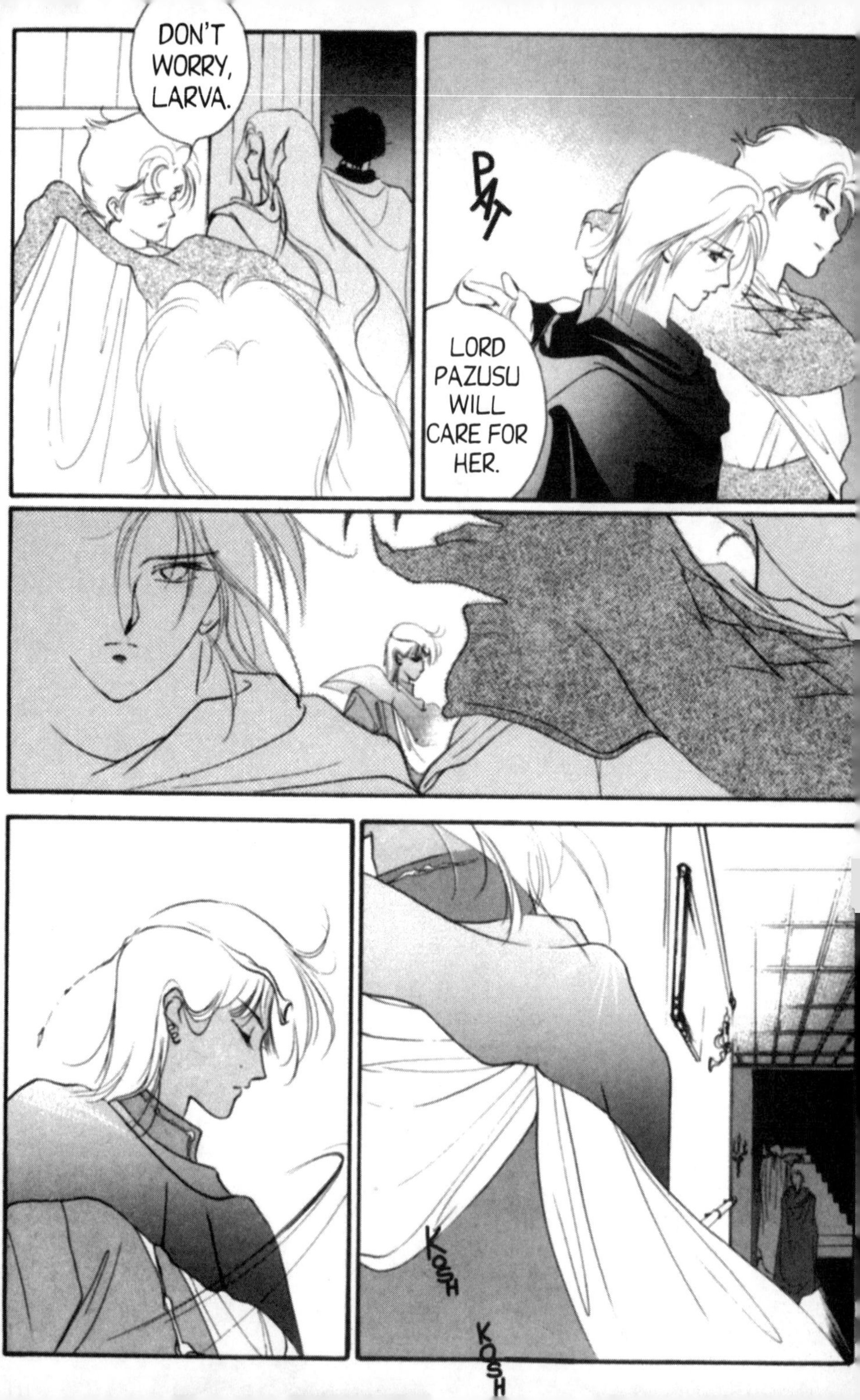

DON'T WORRY, LARVA.
PAT
LORD PAZUSU WILL CARE FOR HER.
KOSH
KOSH

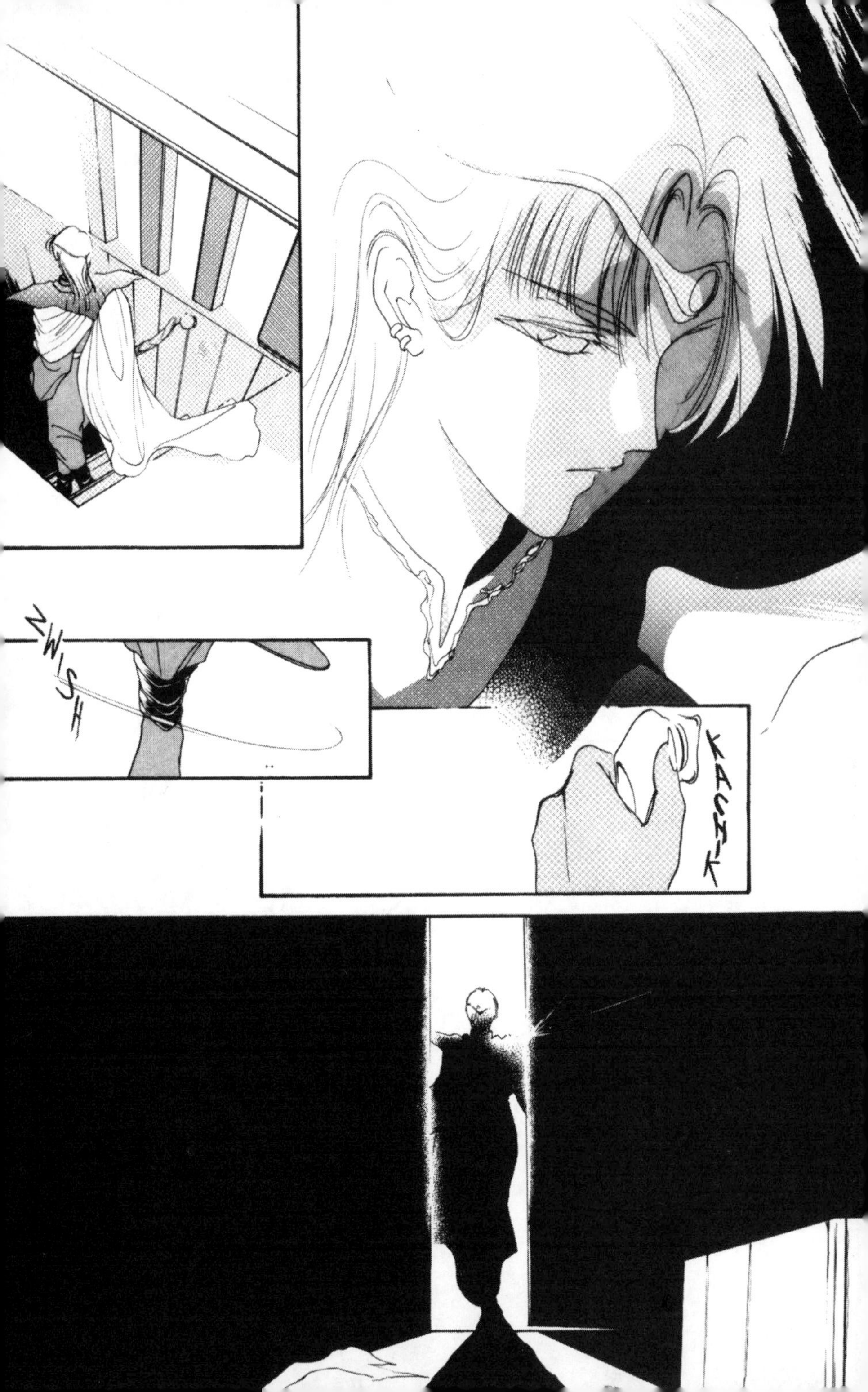
ZWISH
KACHIK

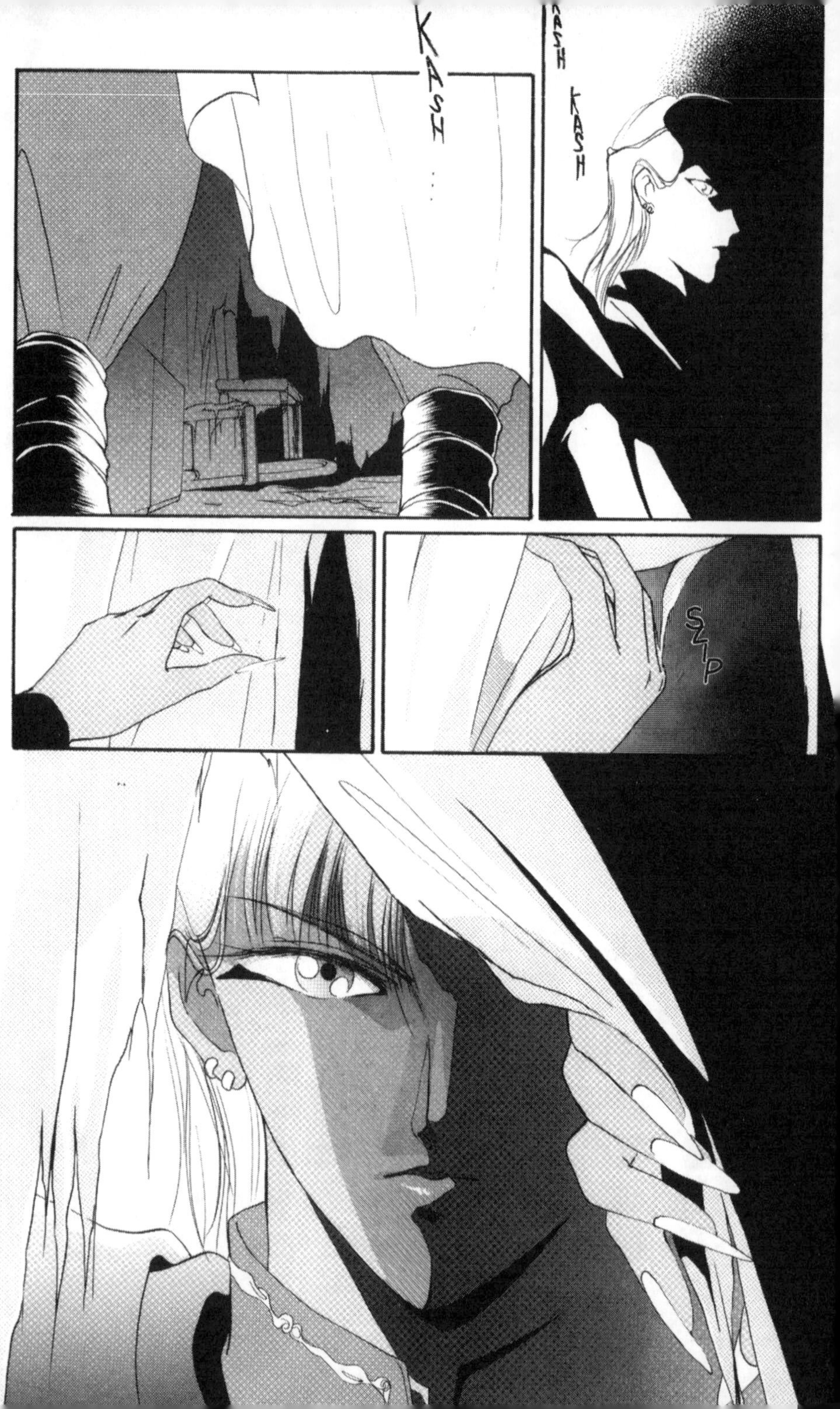

KASH
KASH KASH ...
SLIP

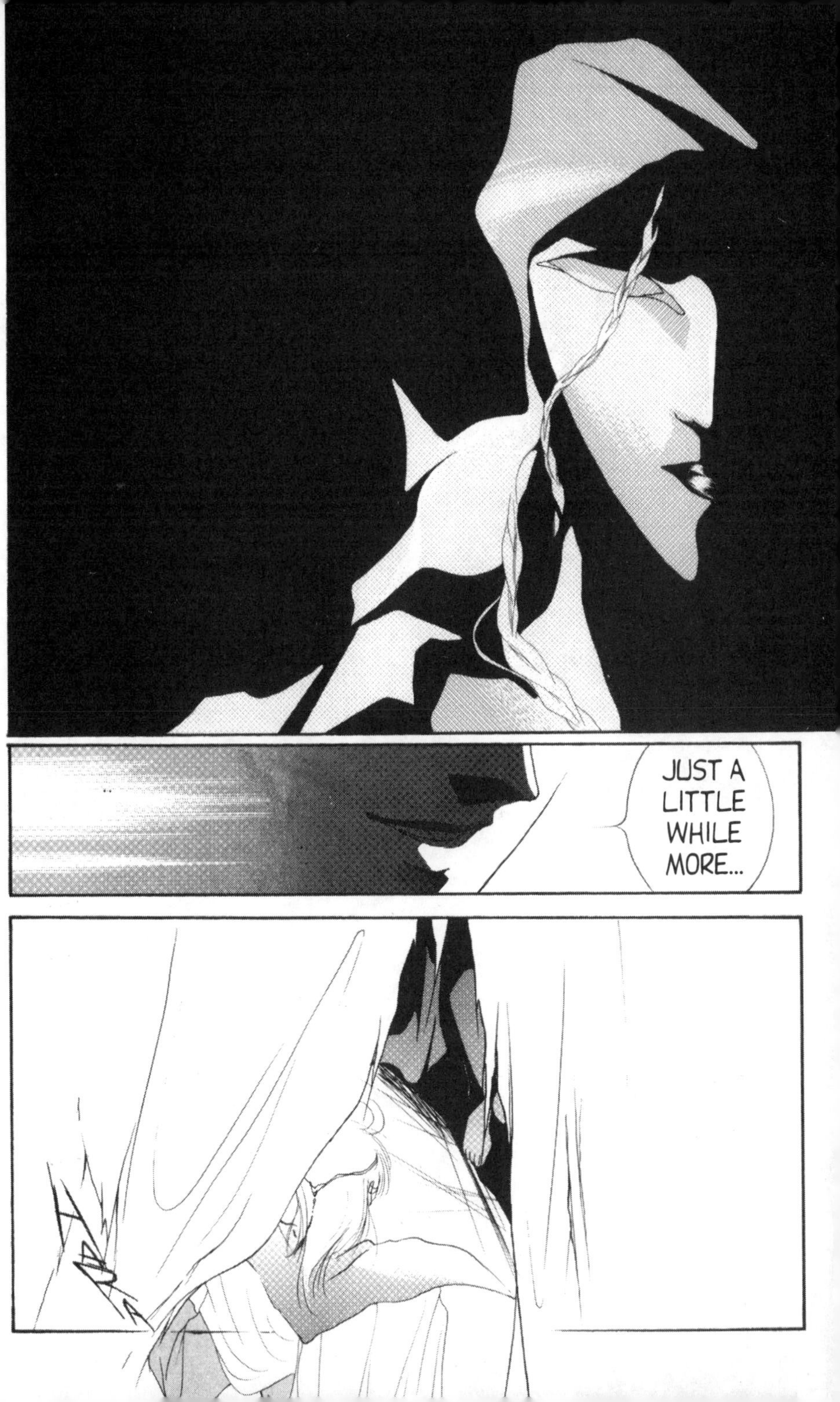
JUST A LITTLE WHILE MORE...

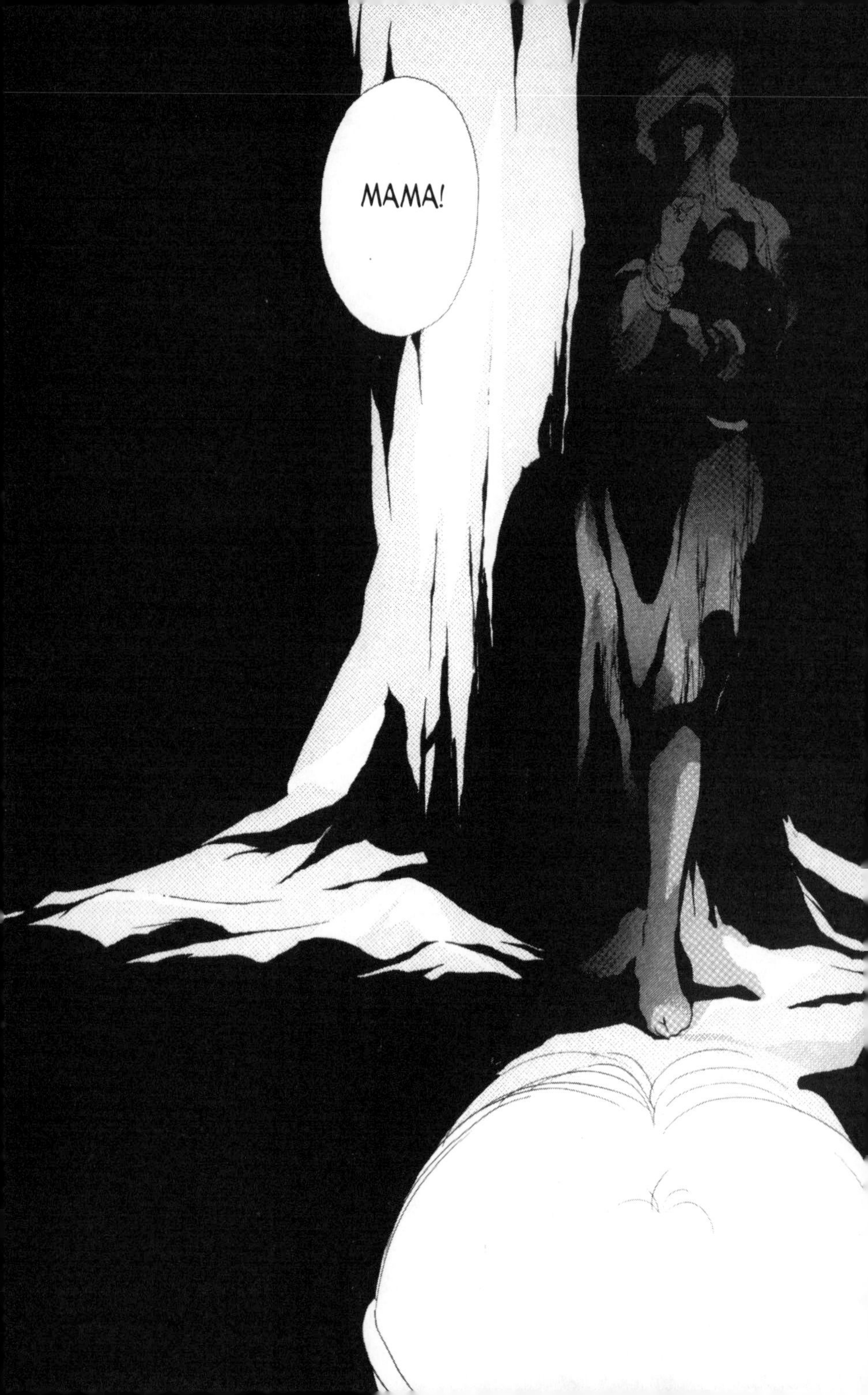
MAMA!

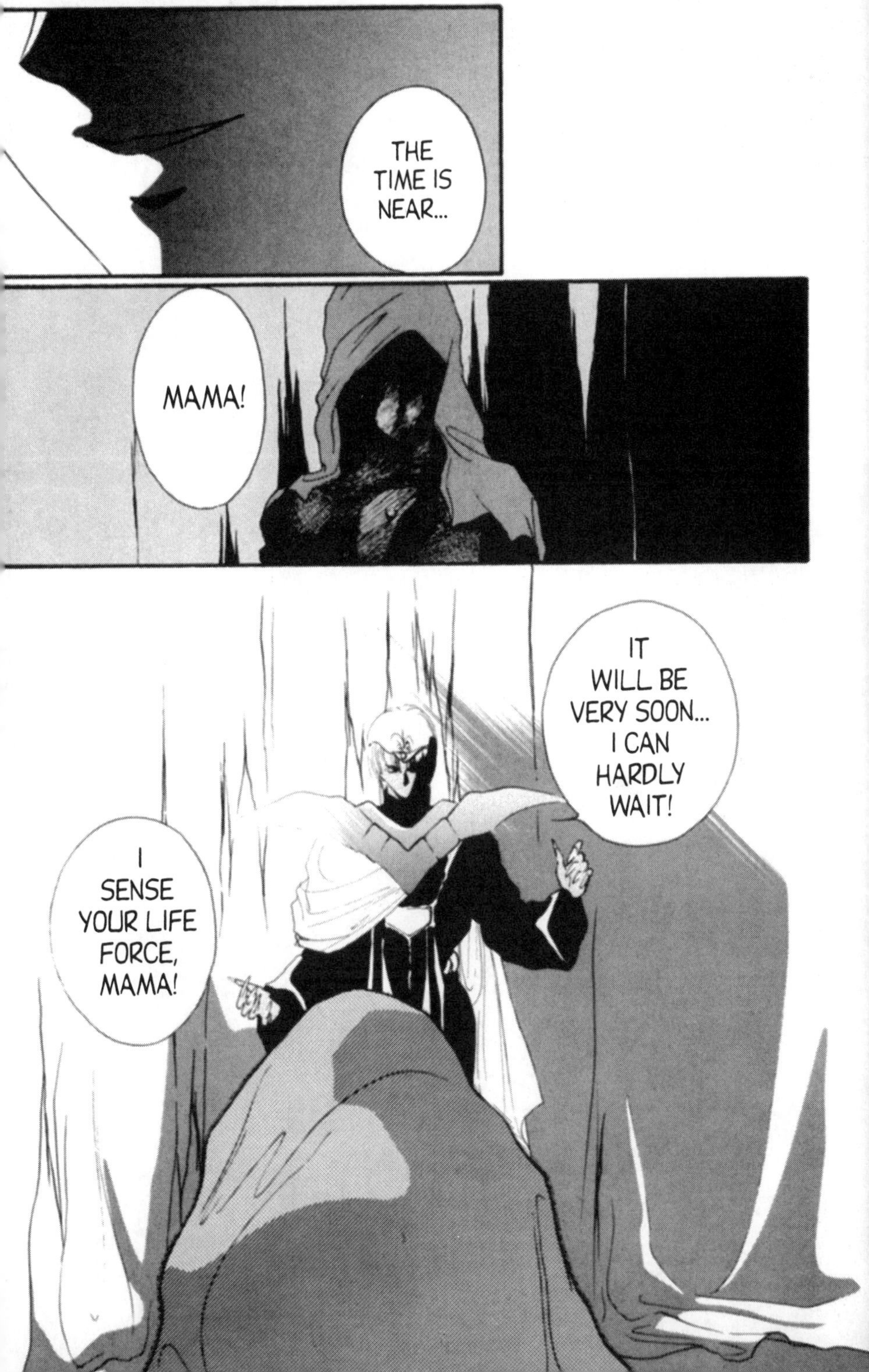
THE TIME IS NEAR...
MAMA!
IT WILL BE VERY SOON... I CAN HARDLY WAIT!
I SENSE YOUR LIFE FORCE, MAMA!

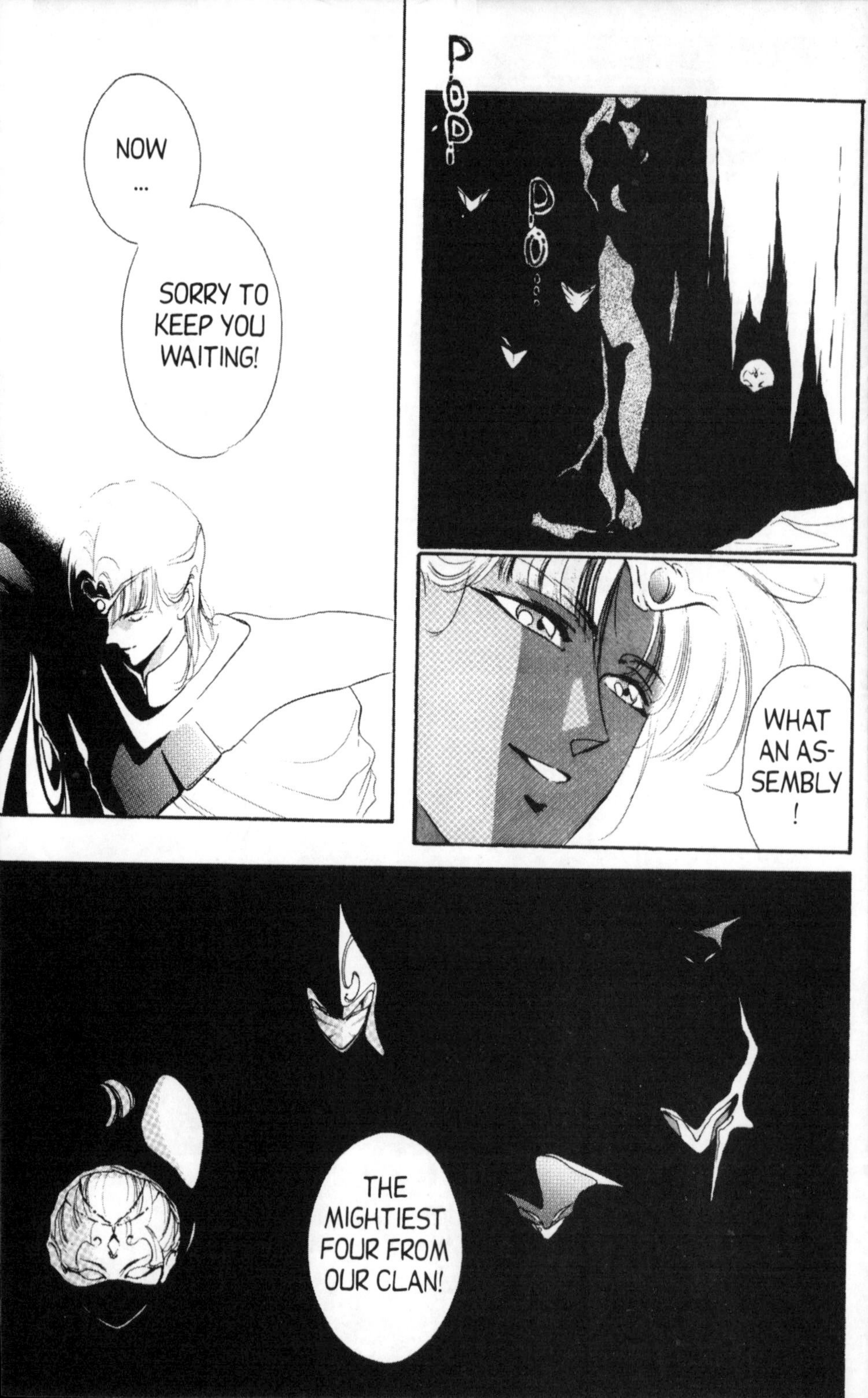

NOW ...
SORRY TO KEEP YOU WAITING!
PO PO
WHAT AN AS- SEMBLY !
THE MIGHTIEST FOUR FROM OUR CLAN!

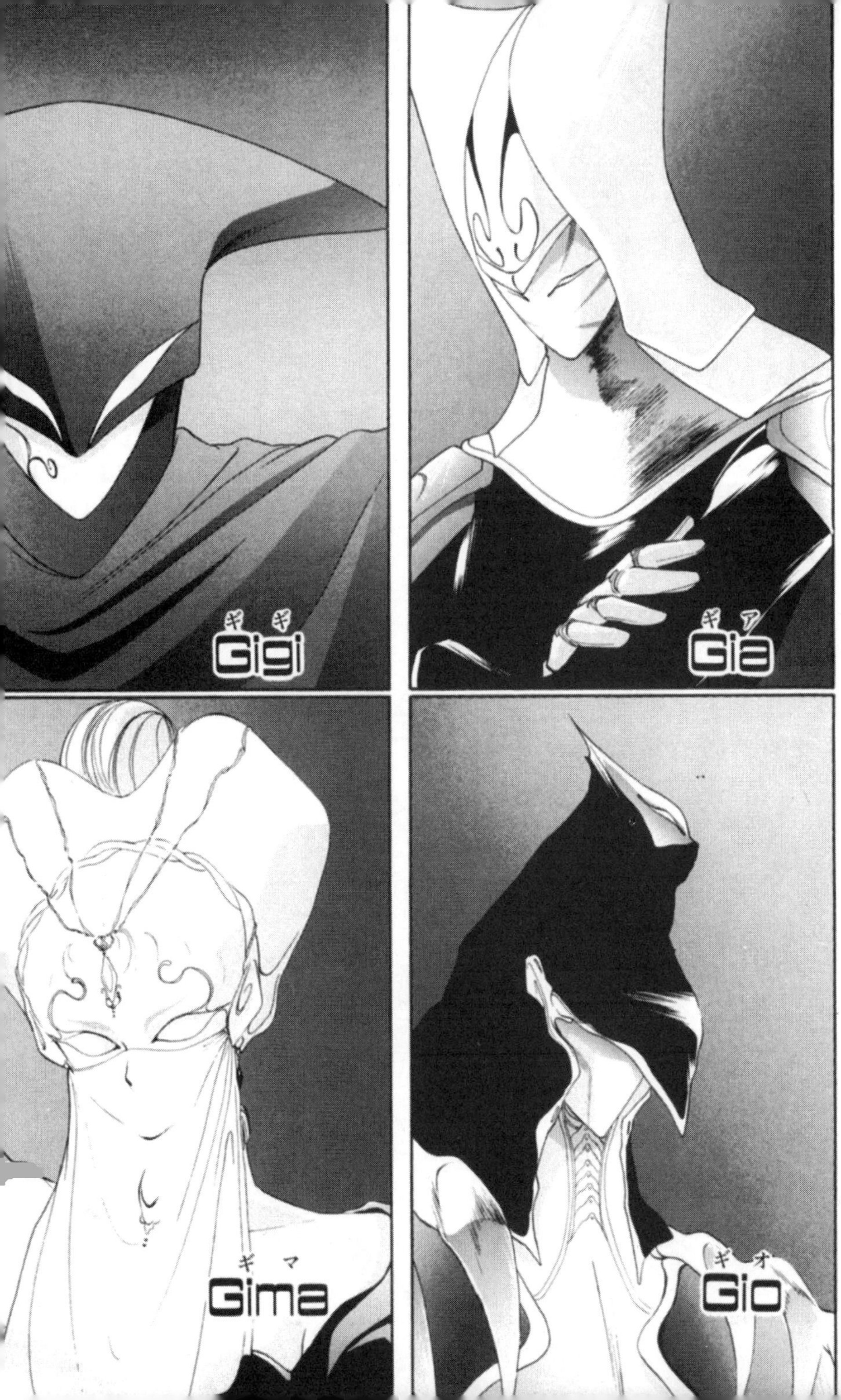
ギア
Gia
ギギ
Gigi
ギオ
Gio
ギマ
Gima

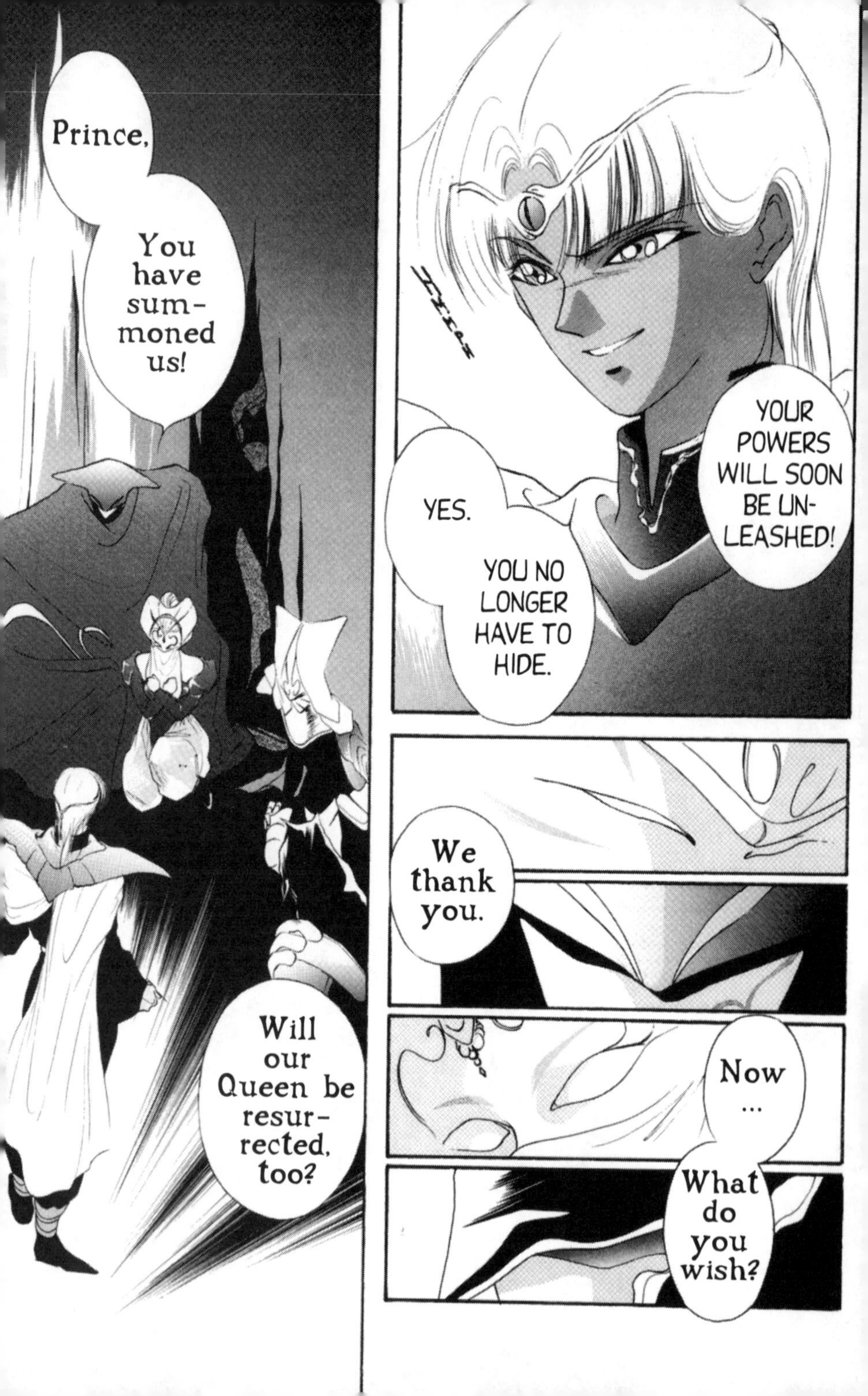
Prince,
You have summoned us!
Will our Queen be resurrected, too?
YES.
YOU NO LONGER HAVE TO HIDE.
YOUR POWERS WILL SOON BE UNLEASHED!
We thank you.
Now ...
What do you wish?

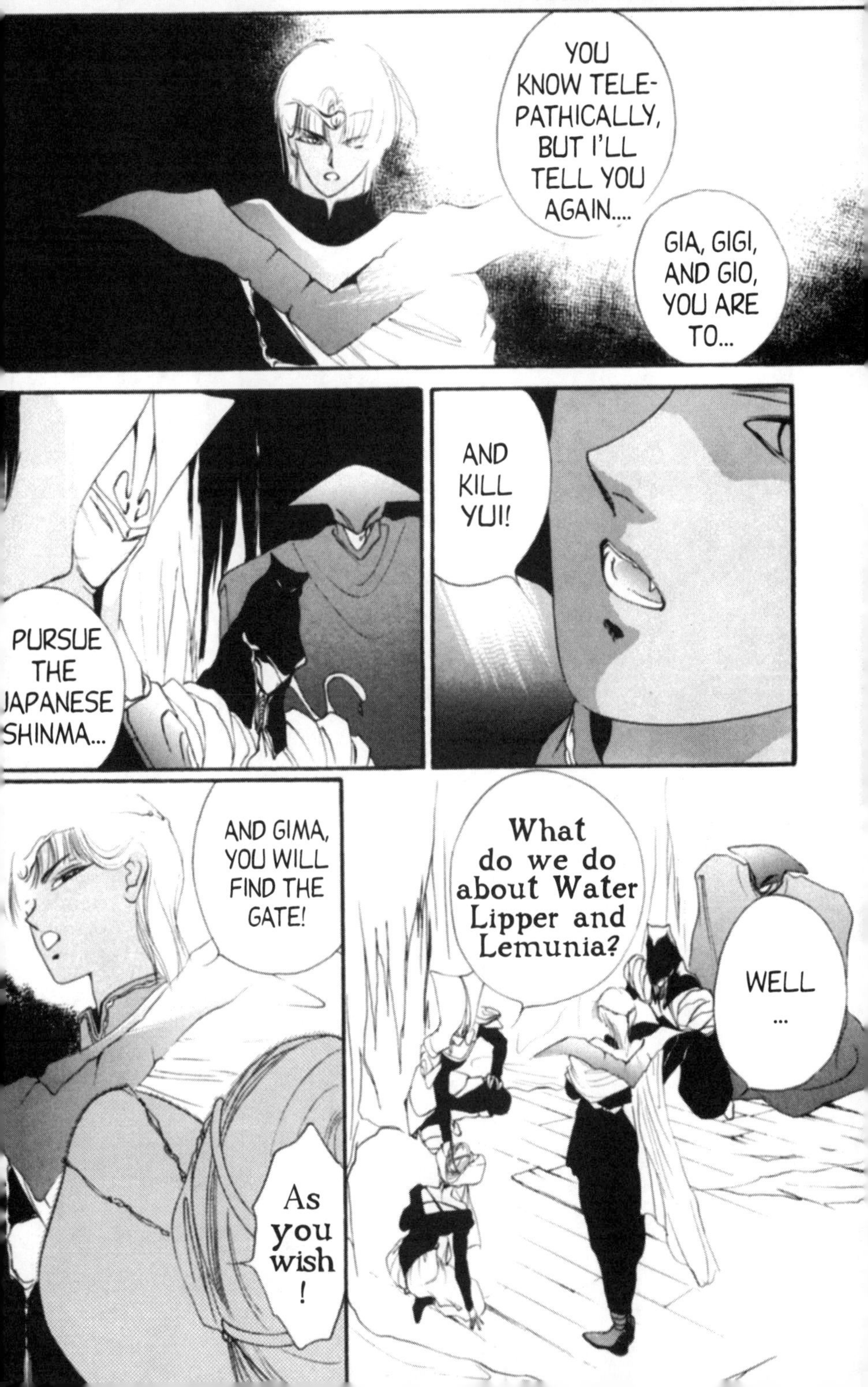
YOU KNOW TELE-PATHICALLY, BUT I'LL TELL YOU AGAIN....
GIA, GIGI, AND GIO, YOU ARE TO...
PURSUE THE JAPANESE SHINMA...
AND KILL YUI!
AND GIMA, YOU WILL FIND THE GATE!
As you wish!
What do we do about Water Lipper and Lemunia?
WELL ...

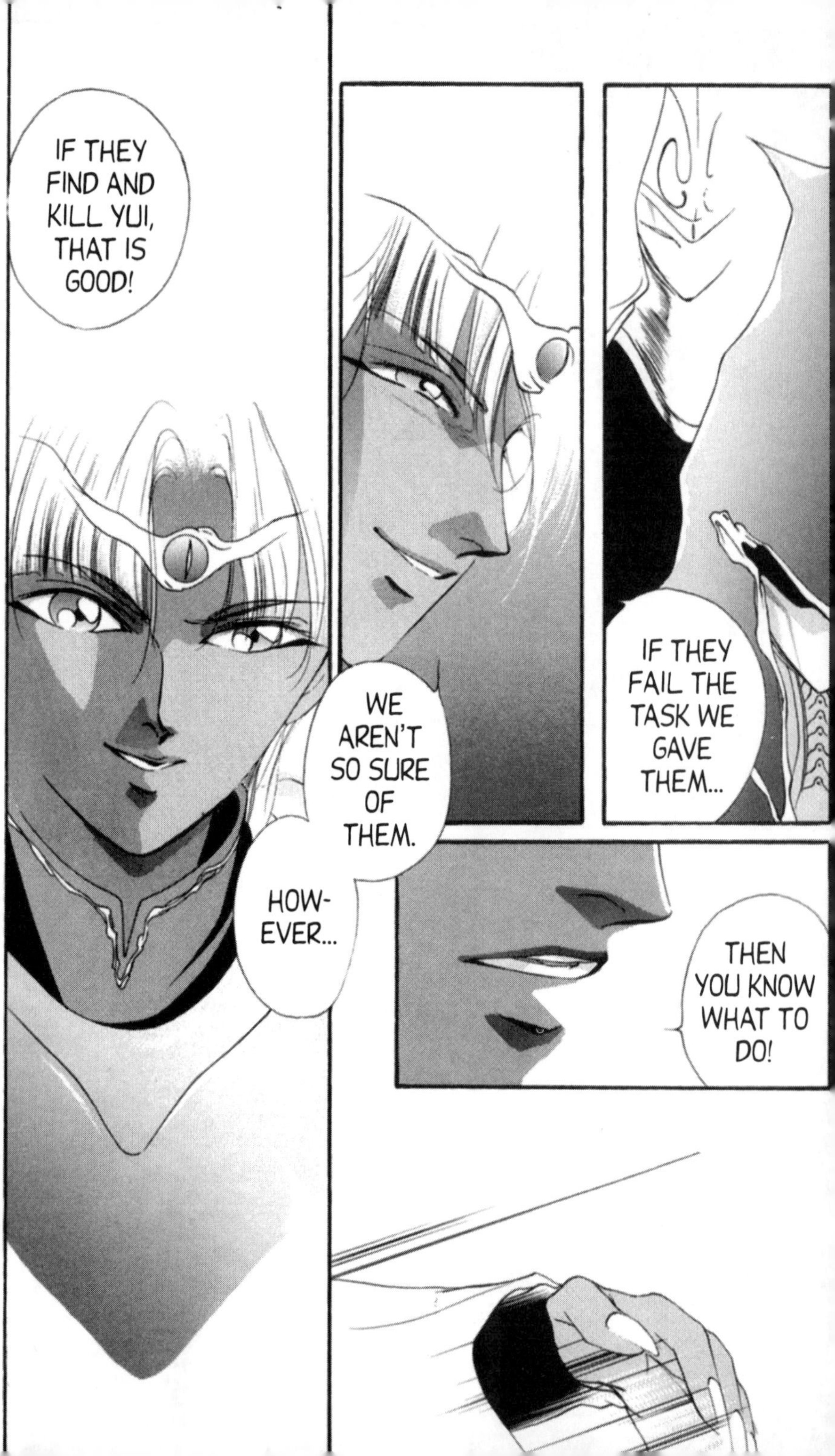
IF THEY FIND AND KILL YUI, THAT IS GOOD!
HOW-EVER...
WE AREN'T SO SURE OF THEM.
IF THEY FAIL THE TASK WE GAVE THEM...
THEN YOU KNOW WHAT TO DO!

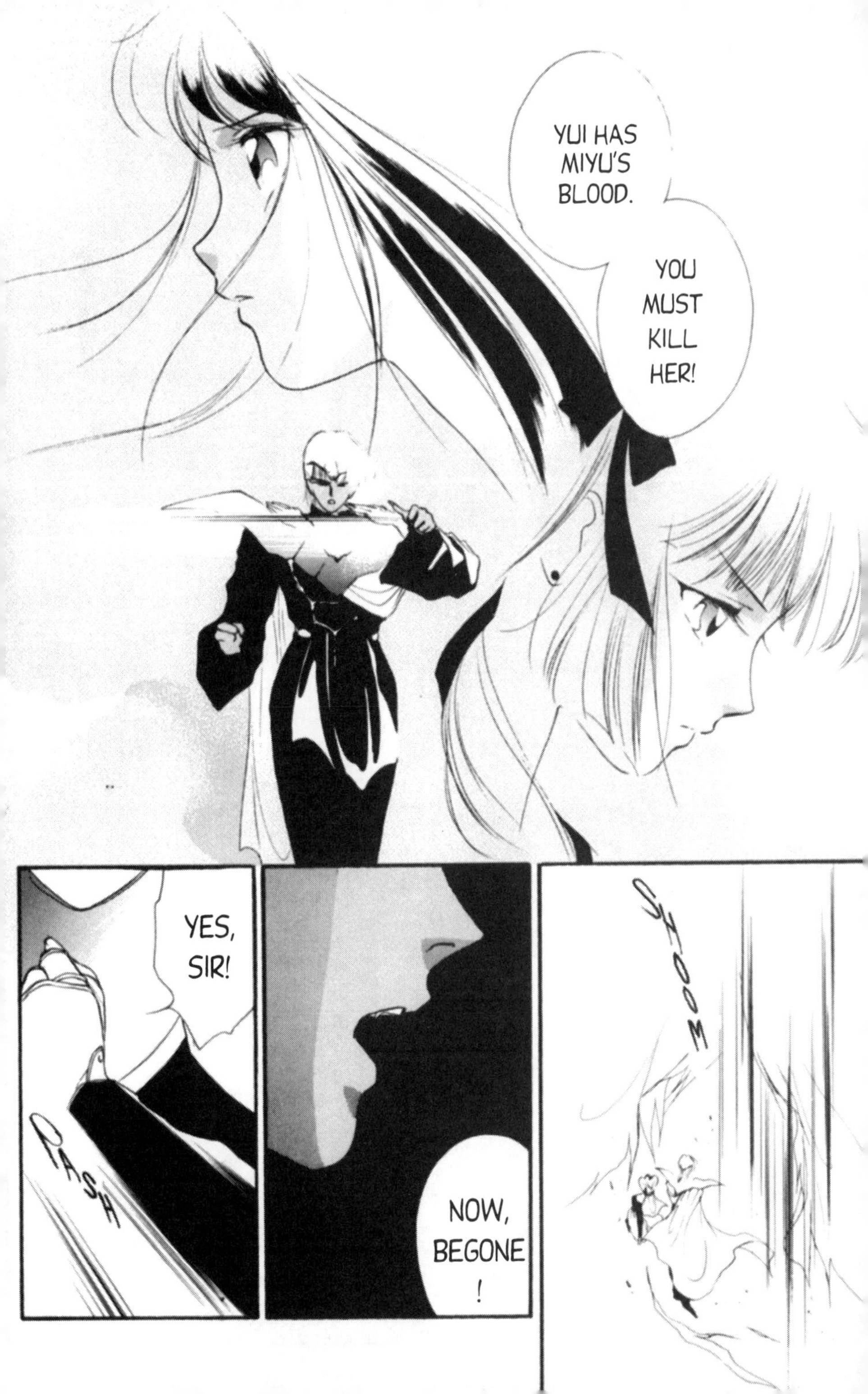
YUI HAS MIYU'S BLOOD.
YOU MUST KILL HER!
SHOOM
NOW, BEGONE!
YES, SIR!
RASH

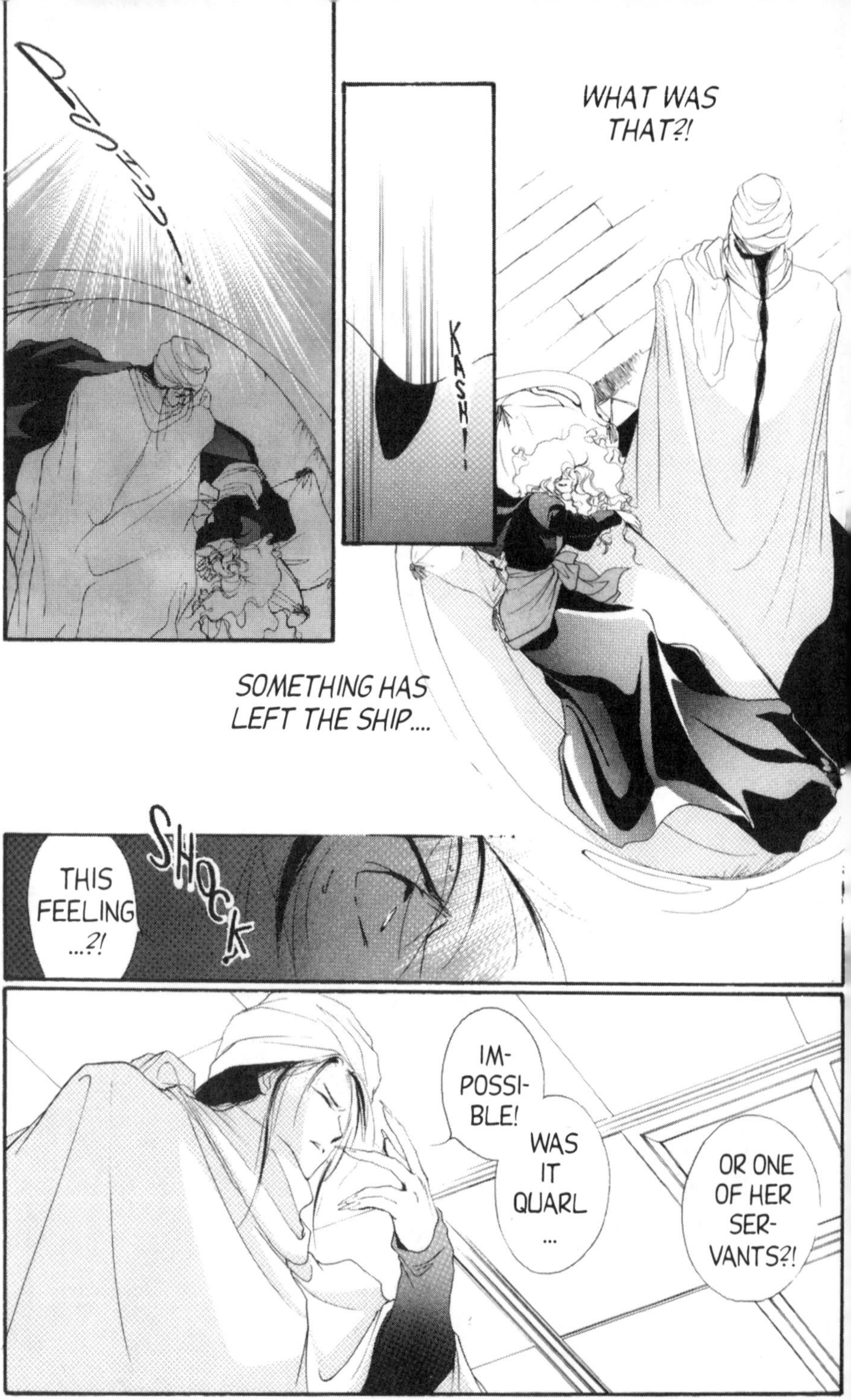
WHAT WAS THAT?!
KASH!!
SOMETHING HAS LEFT THE SHIP....
SHOCK
THIS FEELING ...?!
IM-POSSI-BLE!
WAS IT QUARL ...
OR ONE OF HER SER-VANTS?!

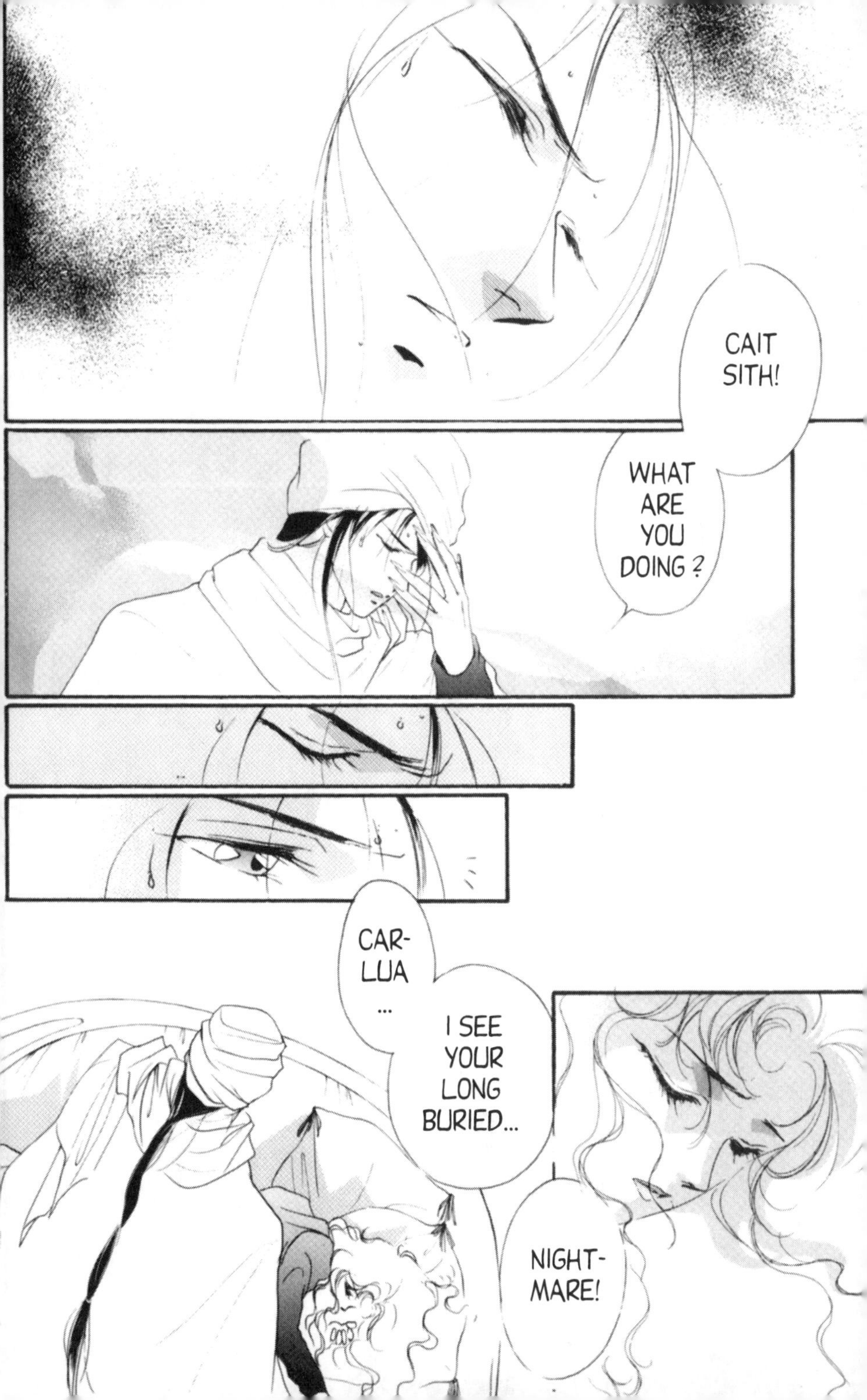
CAIT SITH!
WHAT ARE YOU DOING?
CAR-LUA ...
I SEE YOUR LONG BURIED...
NIGHT-MARE!

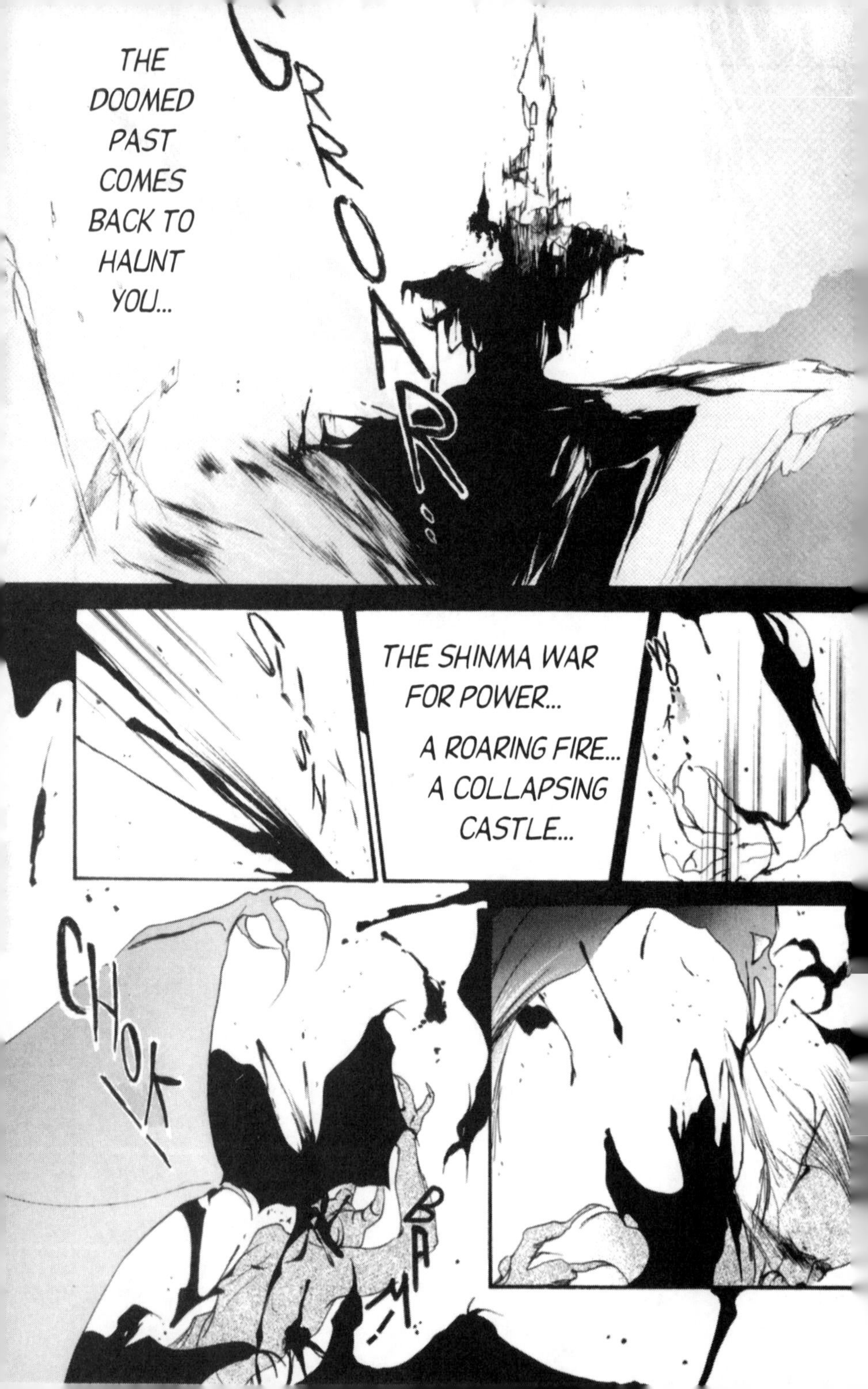
THE DOOMED PAST COMES BACK TO HAUNT YOU...
GRRROAR...
THE SHINMA WAR FOR POWER...
A ROARING FIRE...
A COLLAPSING CASTLE...
CHOK
BAM

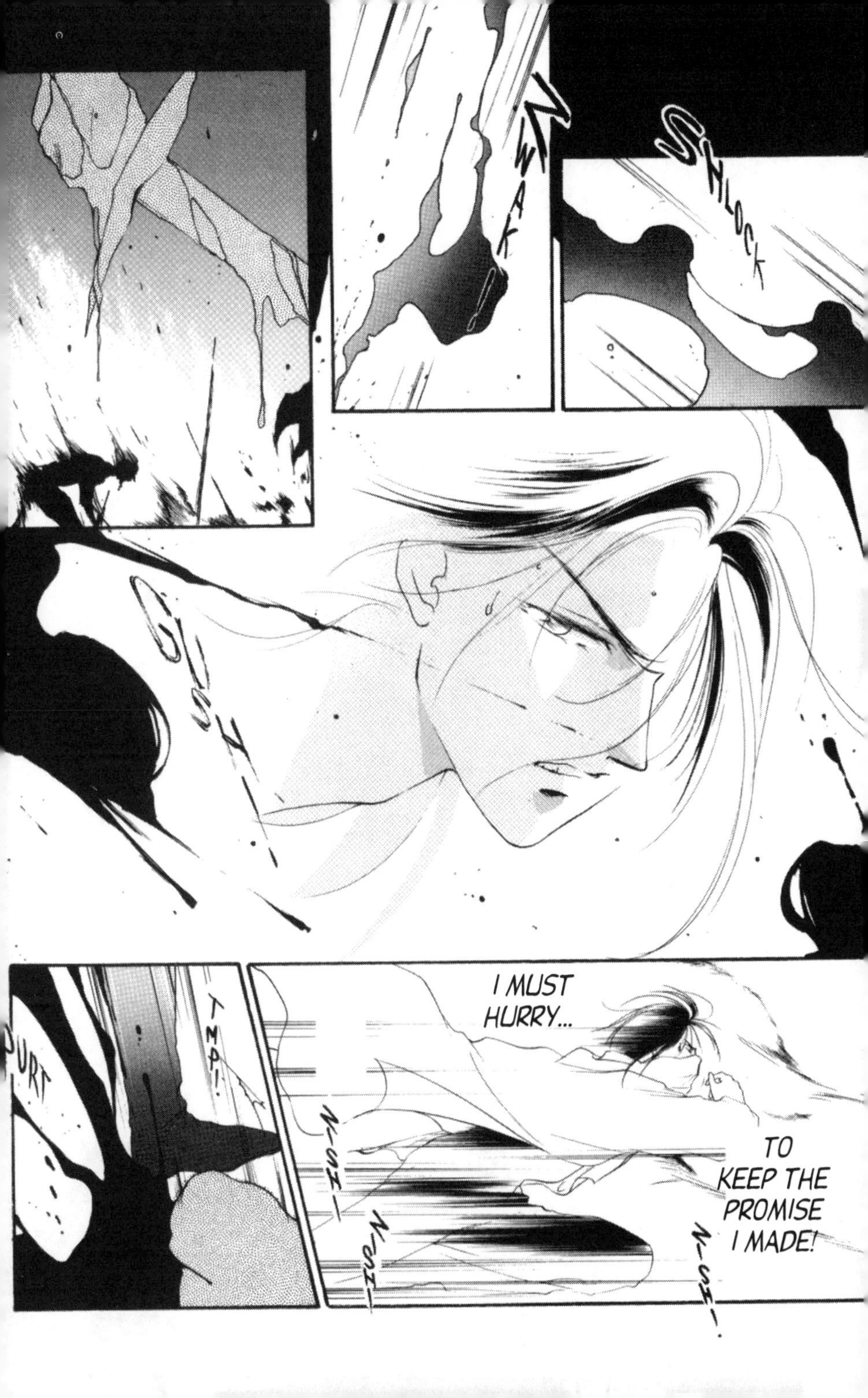
SHLOCK
ZWAK
I MUST HURRY...
TO KEEP THE PROMISE I MADE!
TMP!

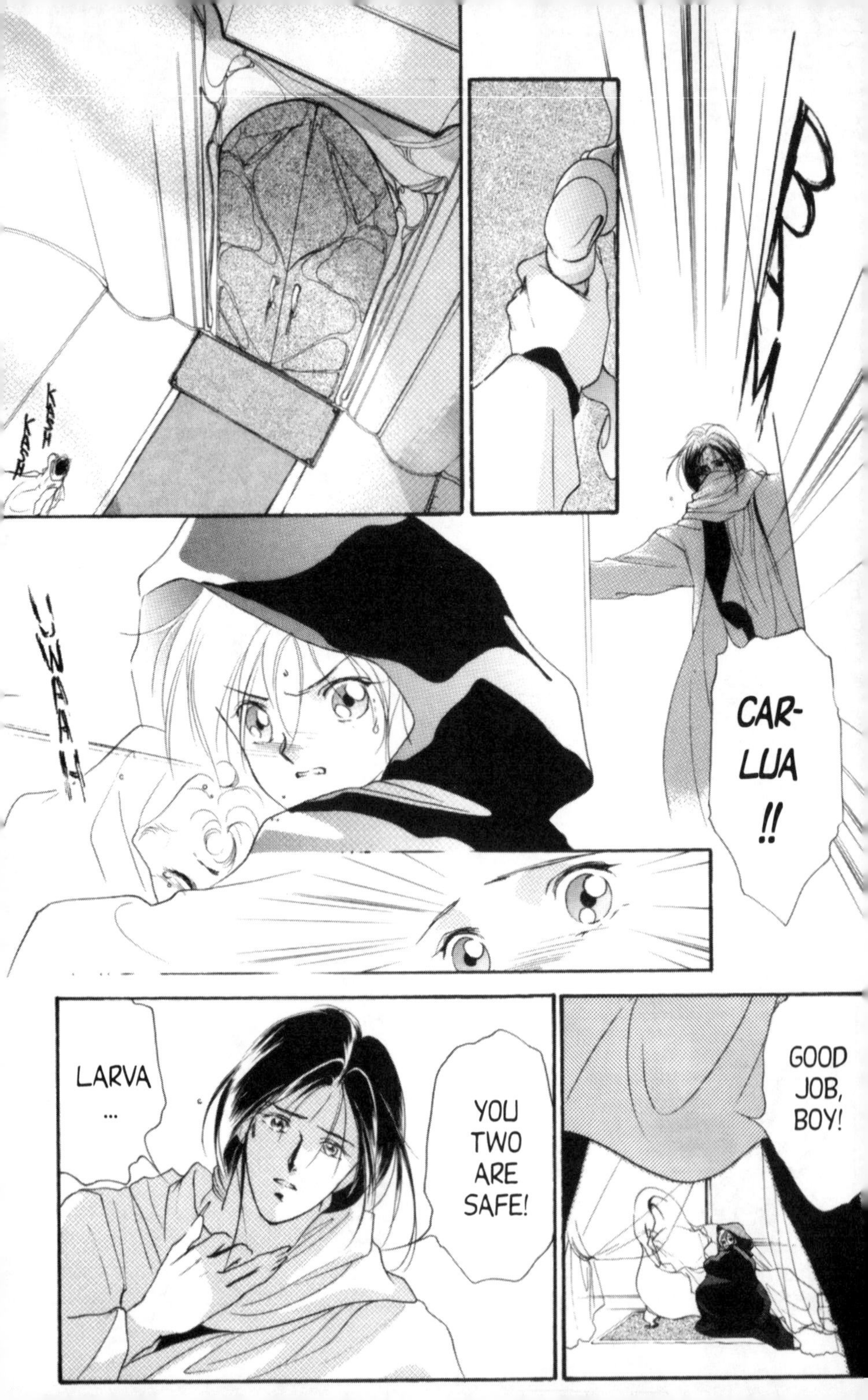
BRAM
KASH KASH
CAR-LUA!!
UWAAAH!
GOOD JOB, BOY!
YOU TWO ARE SAFE!
LARVA ...

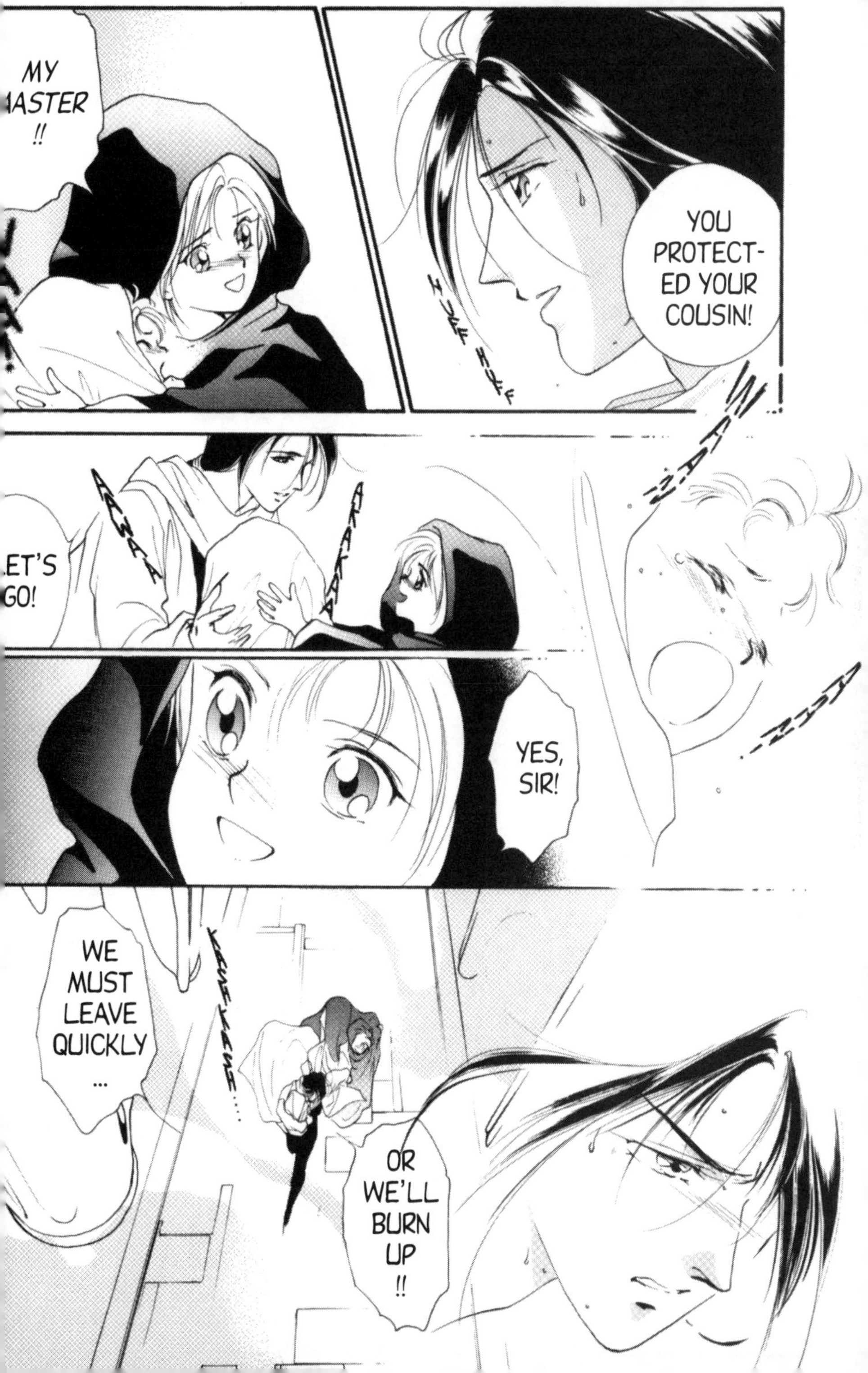
YOU PROTECTED YOUR COUSIN!
HUFF HUFF
MY MASTER !!
LET'S GO!
YES, SIR!
WE MUST LEAVE QUICKLY ...
OR WE'LL BURN UP !!

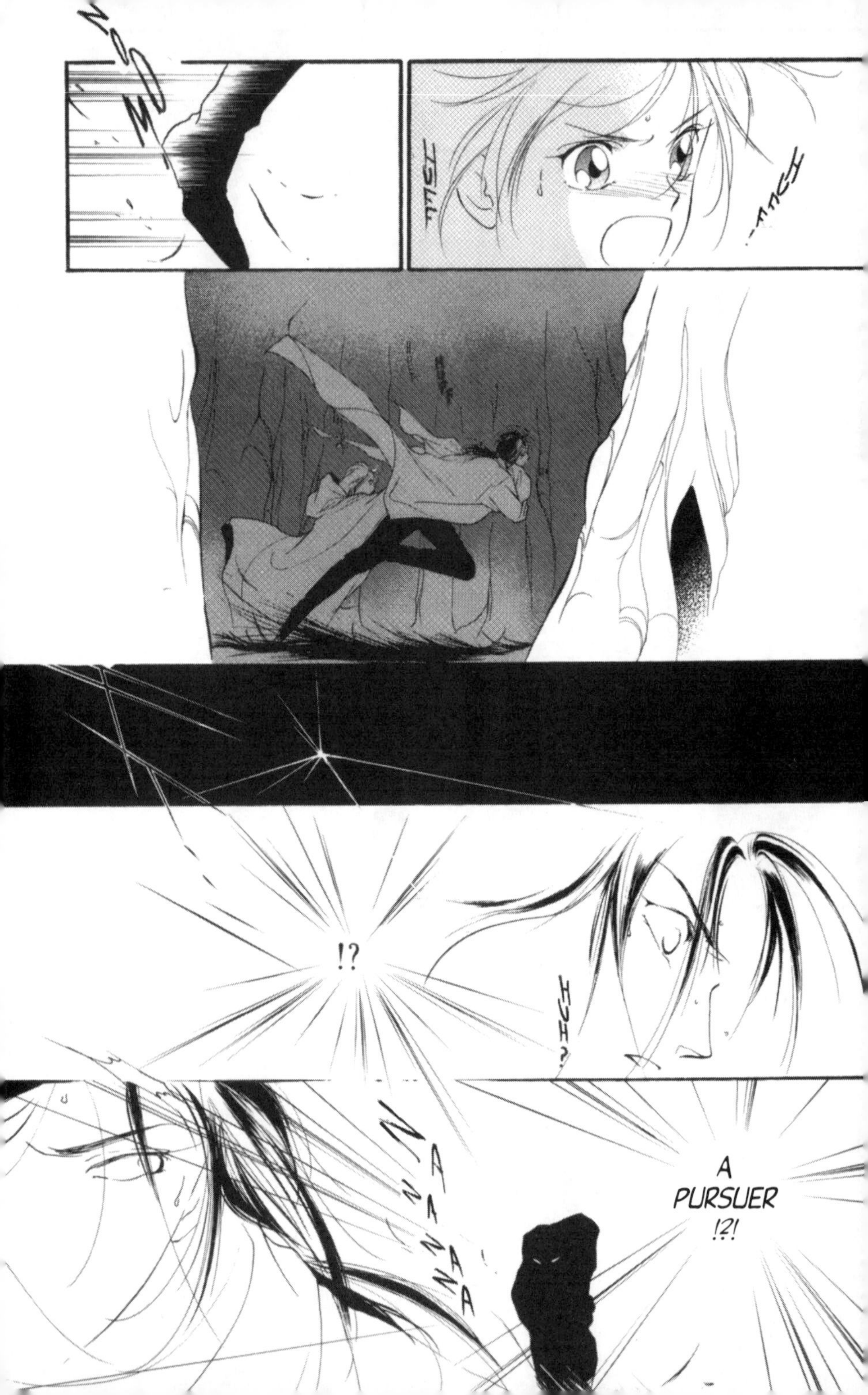

ZOOM
!?
HUH?
A PURSUER !?!

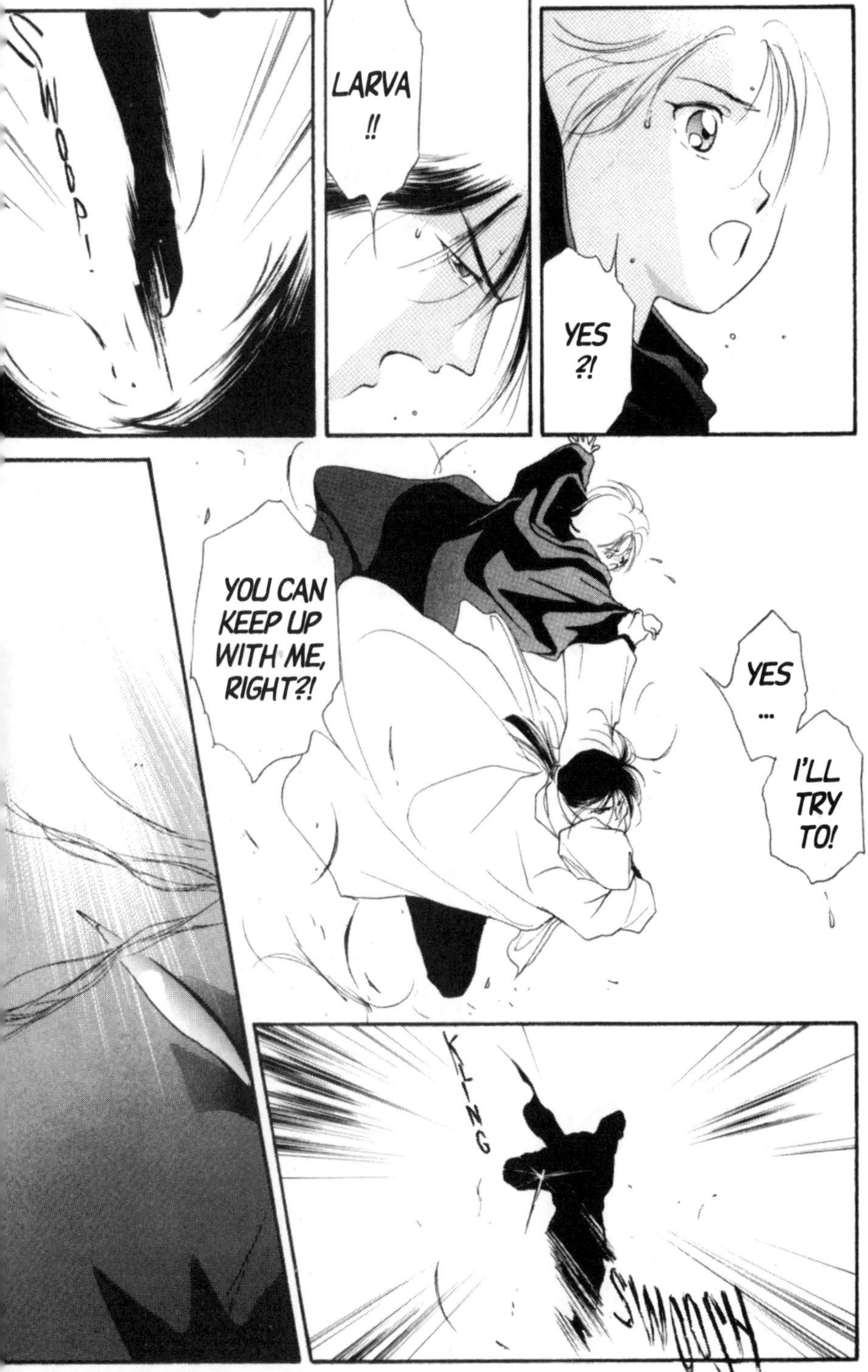
YES ?!
LARVA !!
SWOOP!
YOU CAN KEEP UP WITH ME, RIGHT?!
YES ... I'LL TRY TO!
KLING
SWOOSH

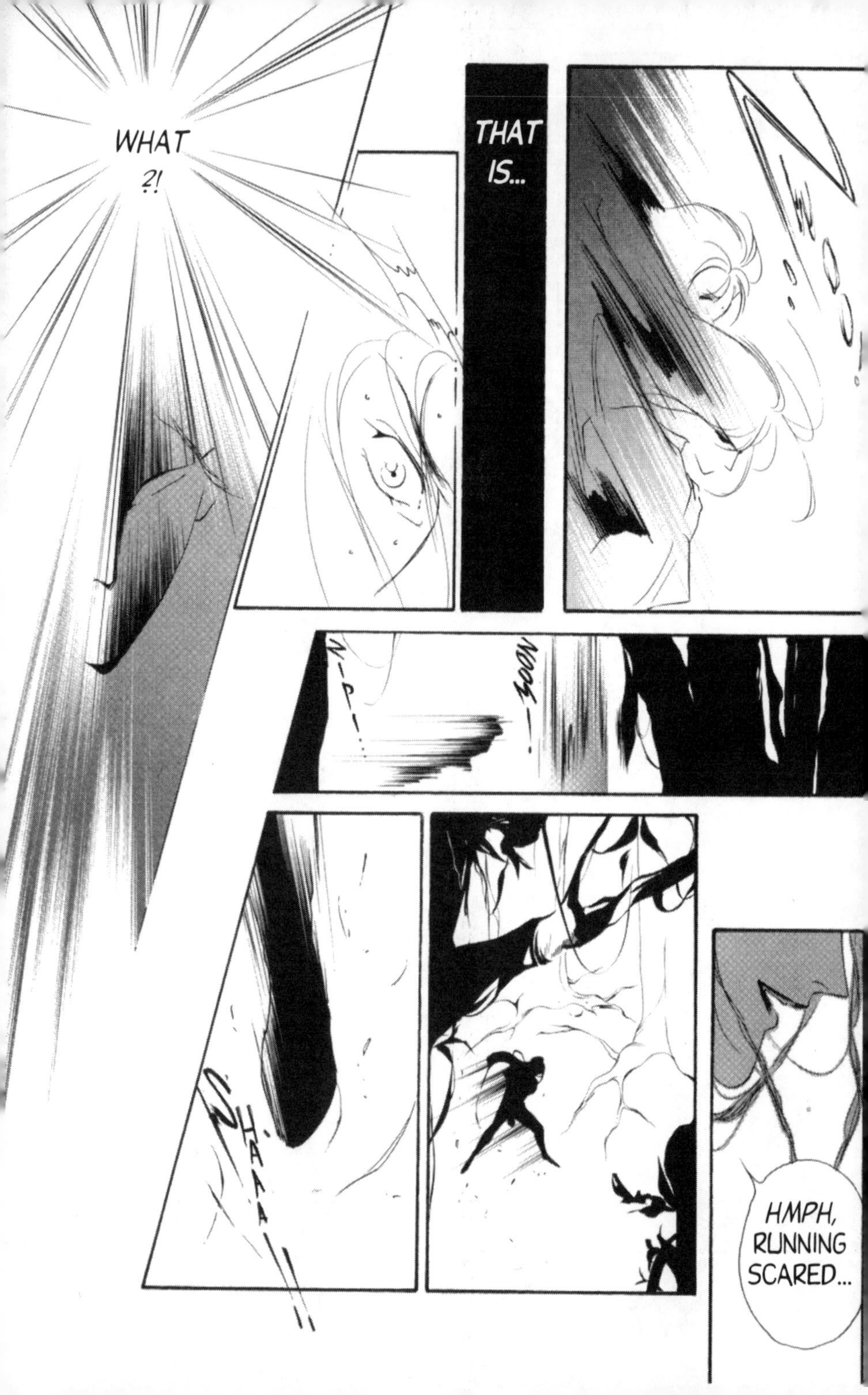
THAT IS...
WHAT ?!
HMPH, RUNNING SCARED...

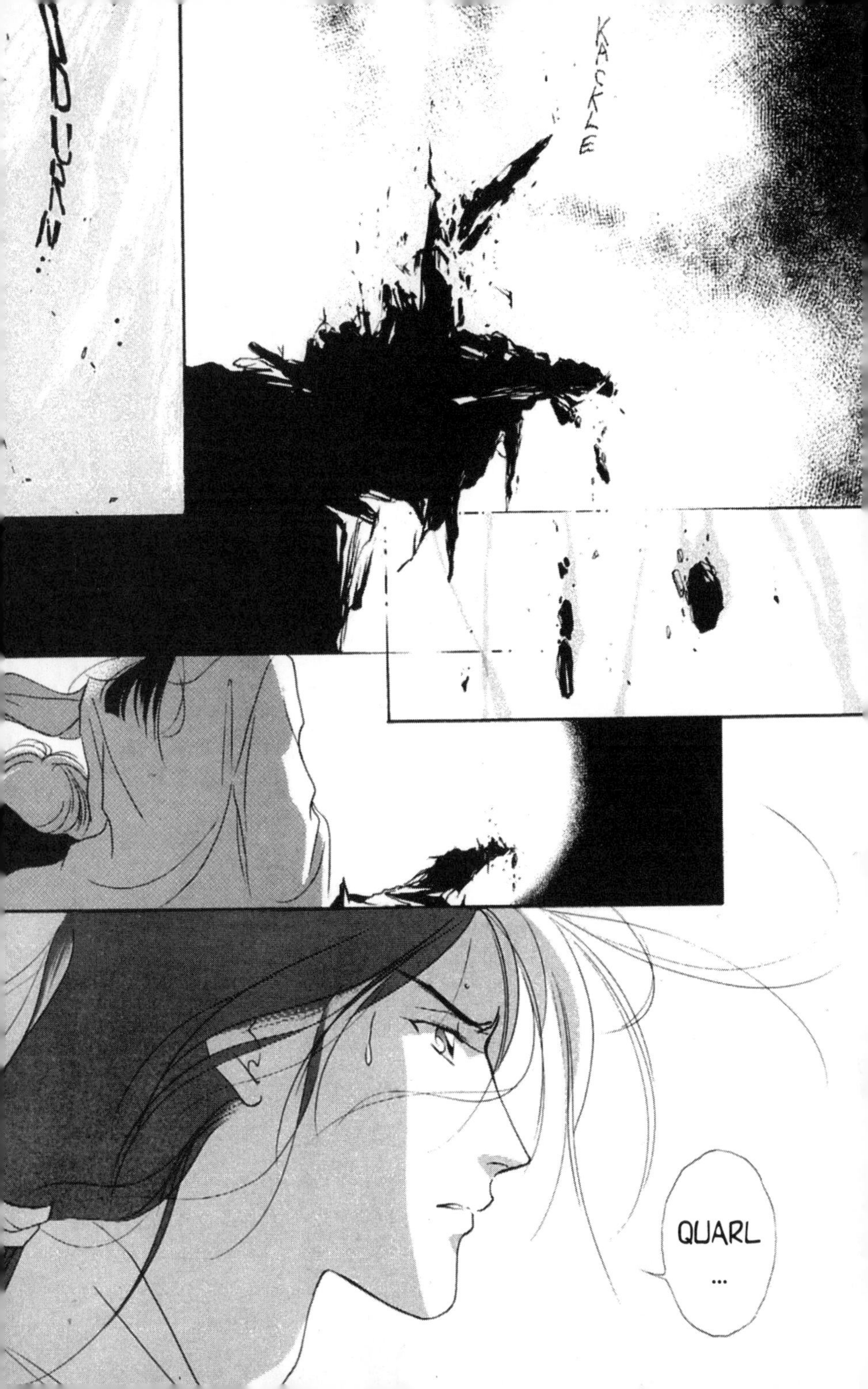
KACKLE
QUARL …

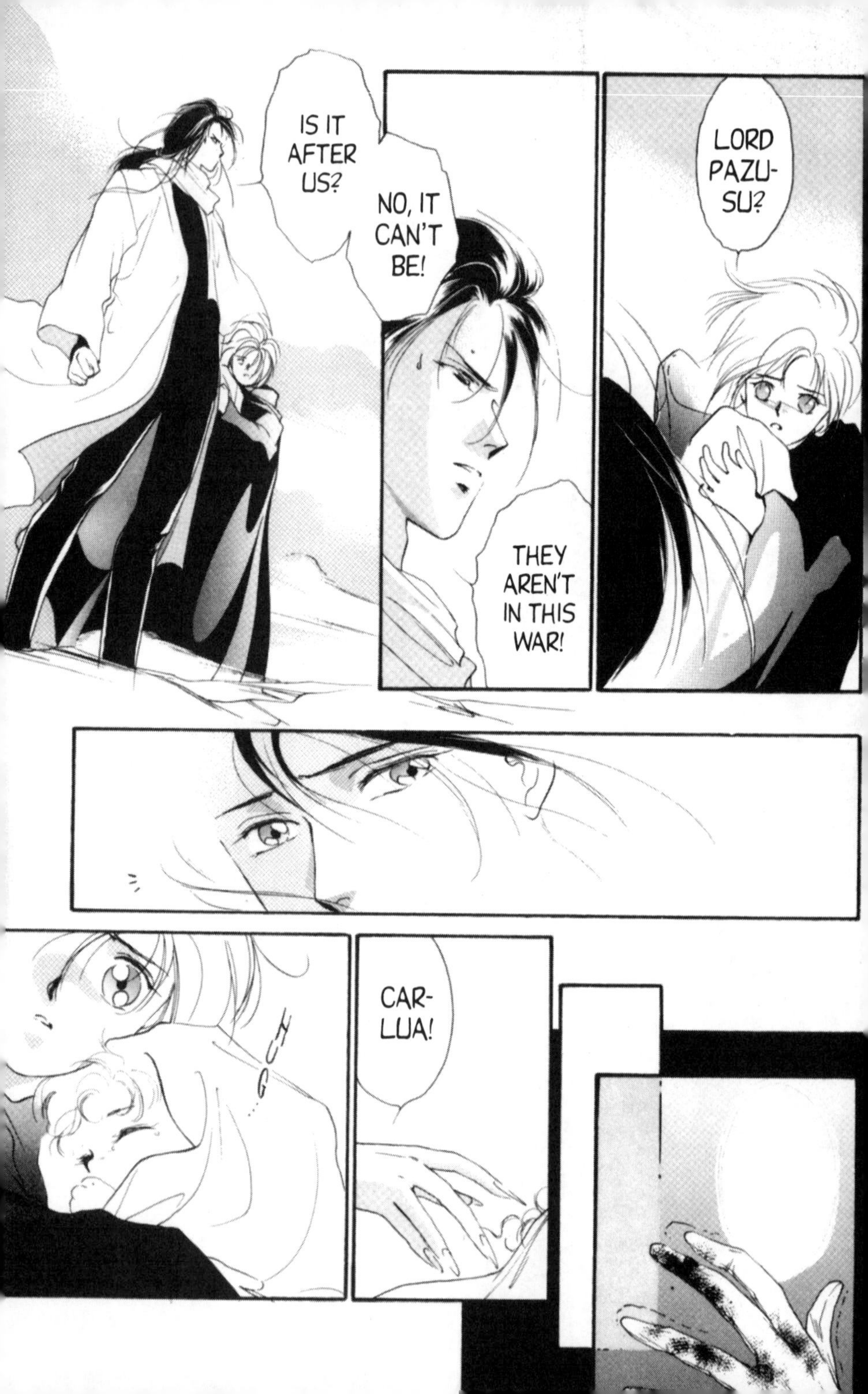
IS IT AFTER US?
NO, IT CAN'T BE!
THEY AREN'T IN THIS WAR!
LORD PAZUSU?
CARLUA!

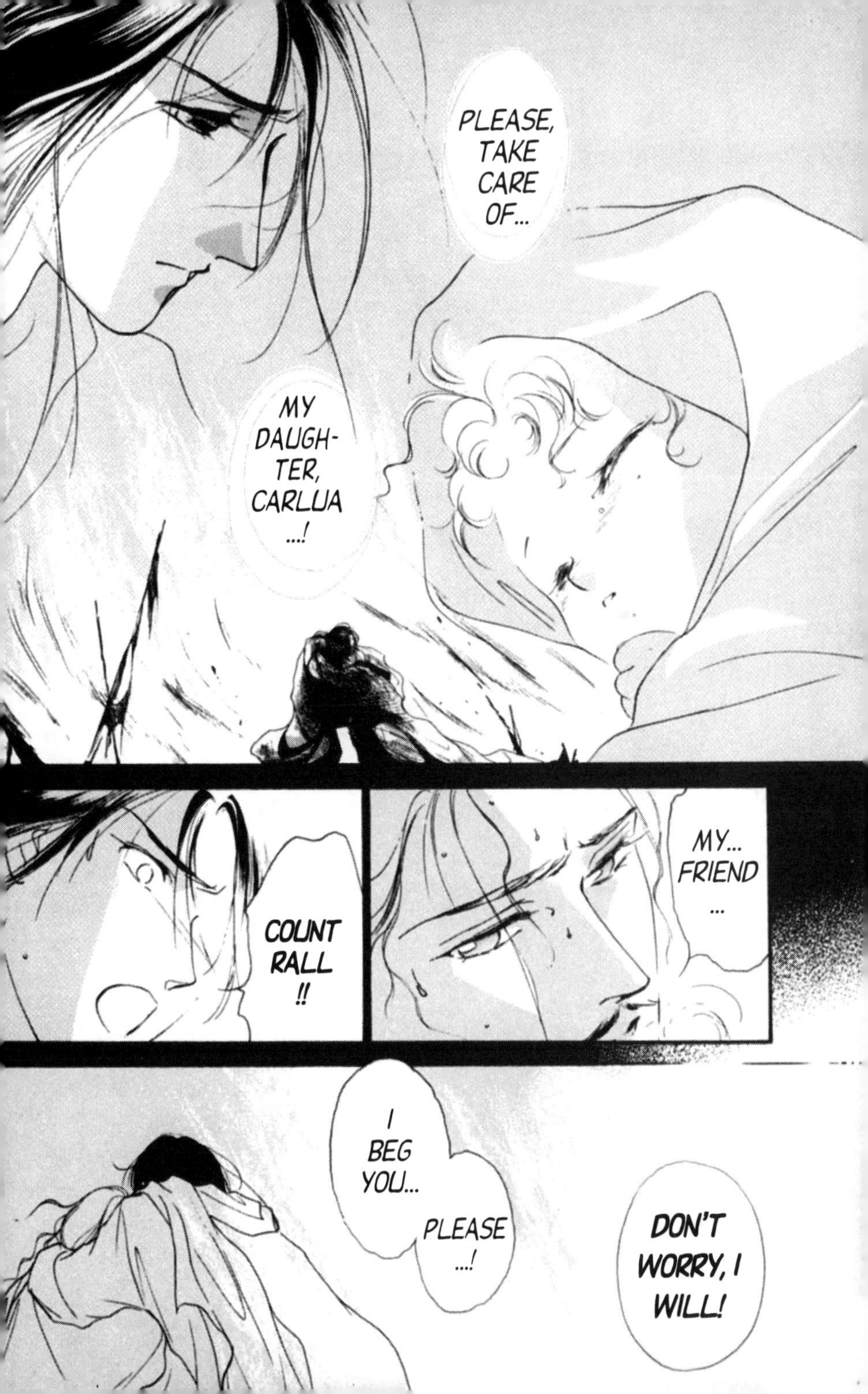
PLEASE, TAKE CARE OF...
MY DAUGHTER, CARLUA ...!
MY... FRIEND ...
COUNT RALL !!
I BEG YOU...
PLEASE ...!
DON'T WORRY, I WILL!

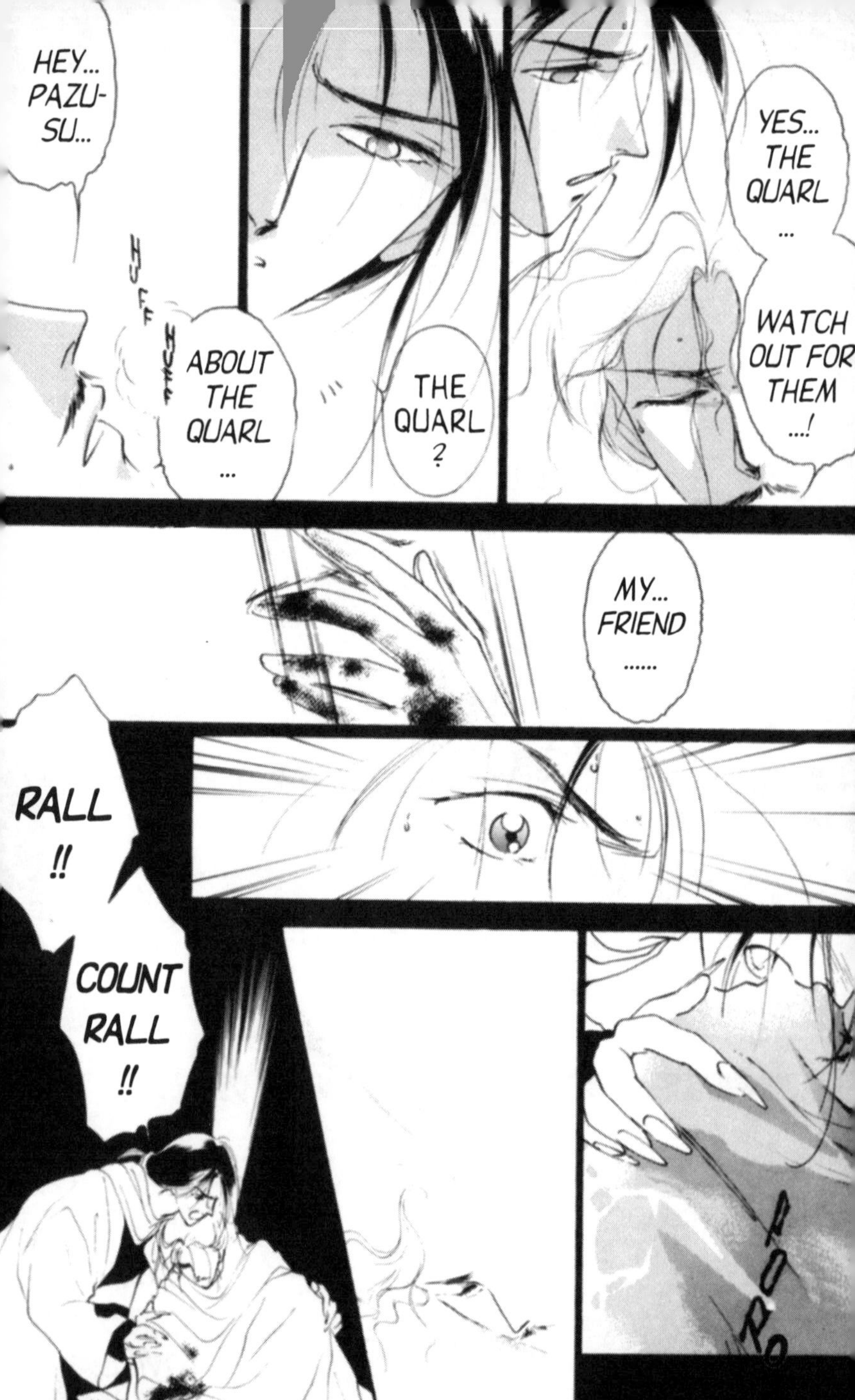
HEY... PAZU-SU...
HUFF HUFF
ABOUT THE QUARL ...
THE QUARL ?
YES... THE QUARL ...
WATCH OUT FOR THEM ...!
MY... FRIEND ......
RALL !!
COUNT RALL !!
PORO

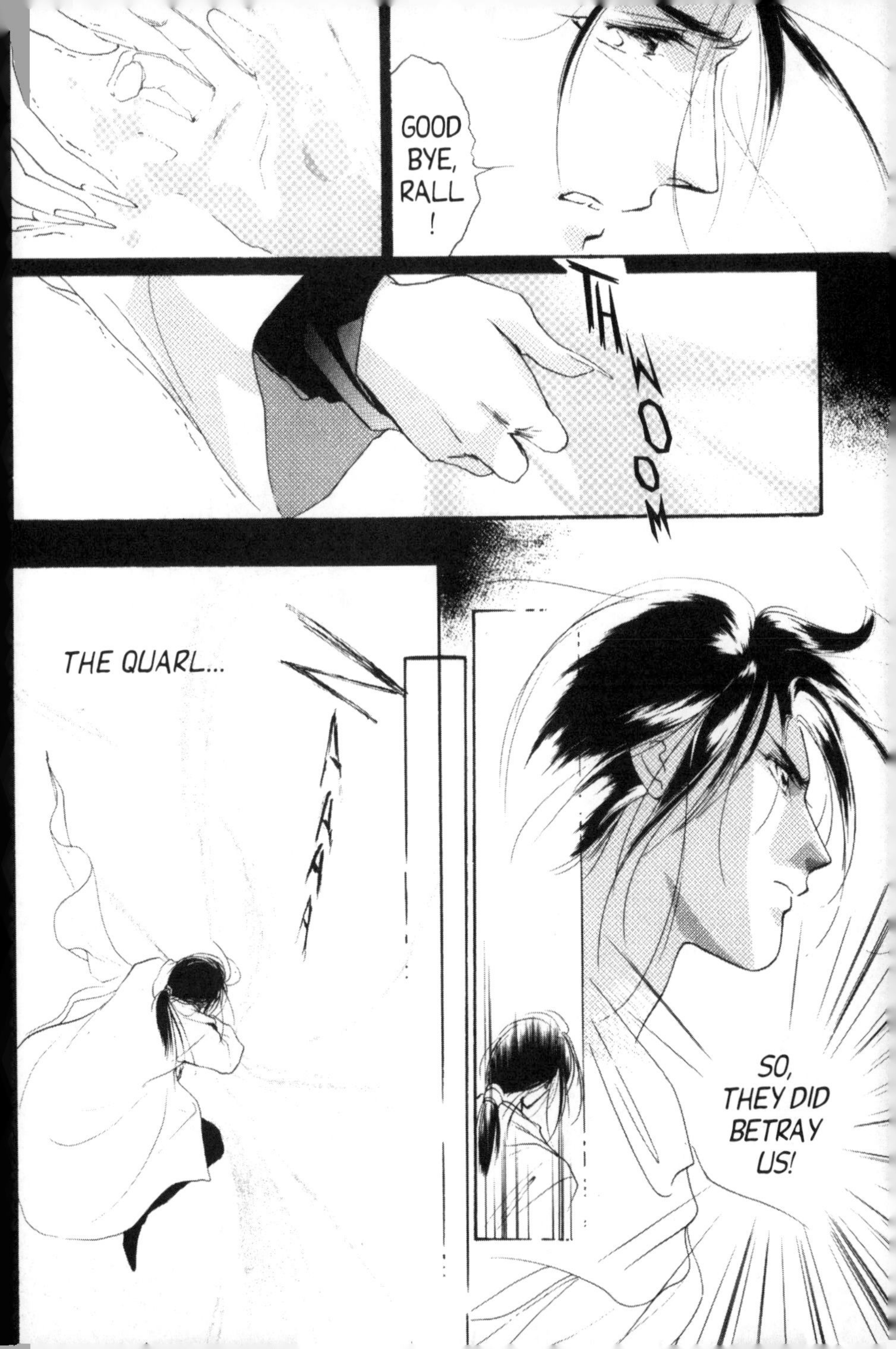
GOOD BYE, RALL!
THWOOM
THE QUARL...
SO, THEY DID BETRAY US!

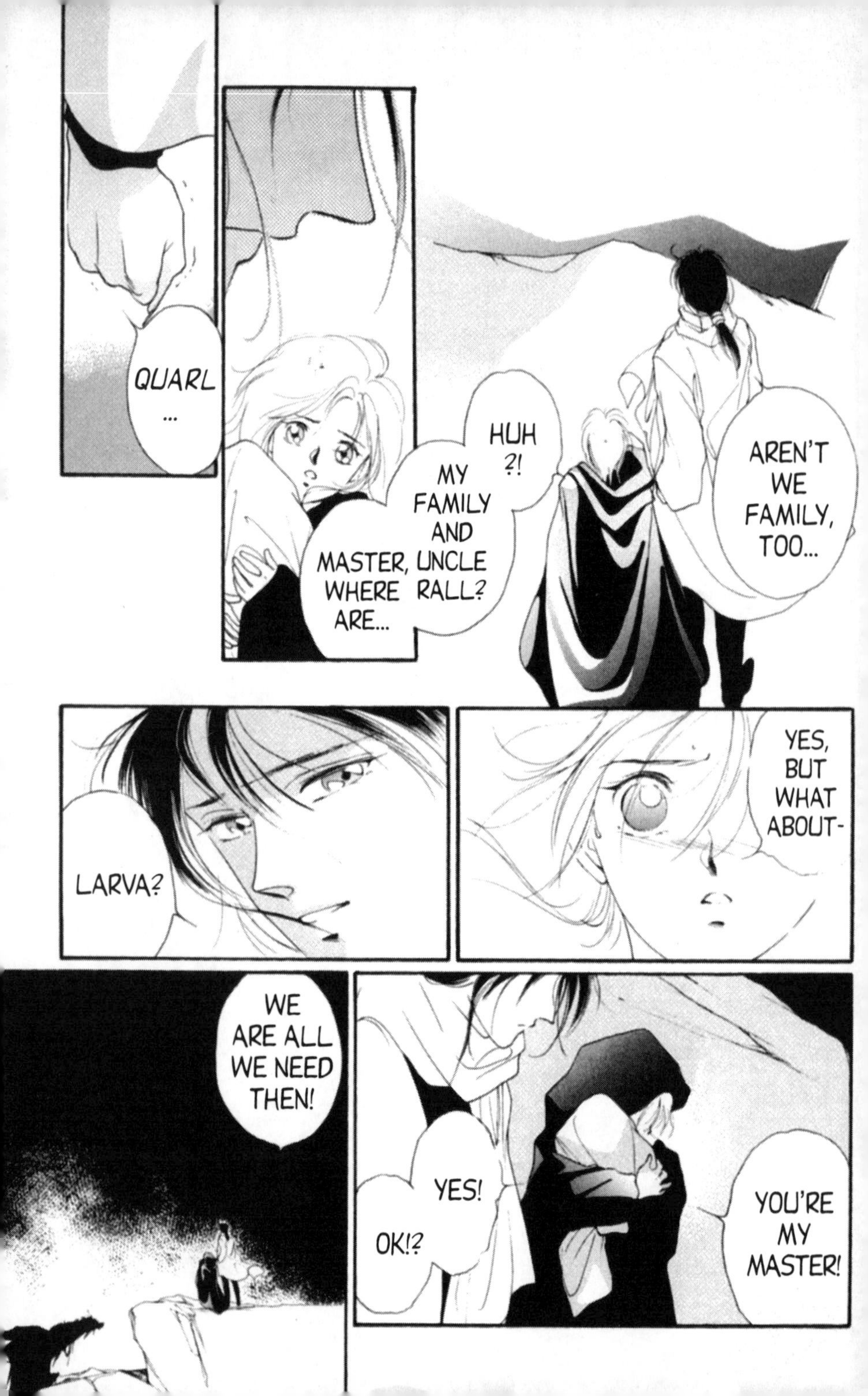
QUARL ...
MASTER, WHERE ARE... MY FAMILY AND UNCLE RALL?
HUH ?!
AREN'T WE FAMILY, TOO...
LARVA?
YES, BUT WHAT ABOUT-
WE ARE ALL WE NEED THEN!
YOU'RE MY MASTER!
OK!?
YES!

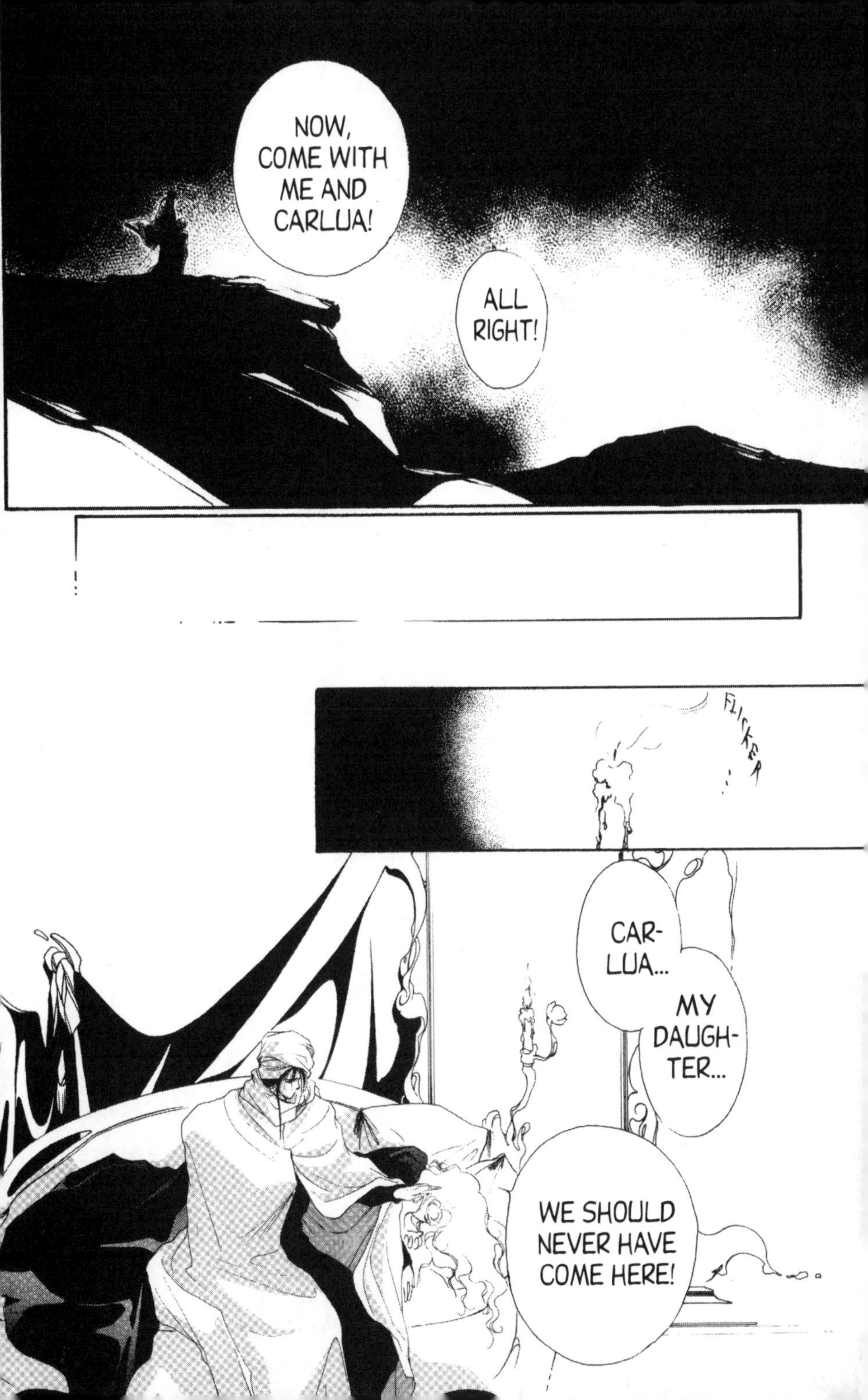
NOW, COME WITH ME AND CARLUA!
ALL RIGHT!
FLICKER
CAR-LUA...
MY DAUGH-TER...
WE SHOULD NEVER HAVE COME HERE!

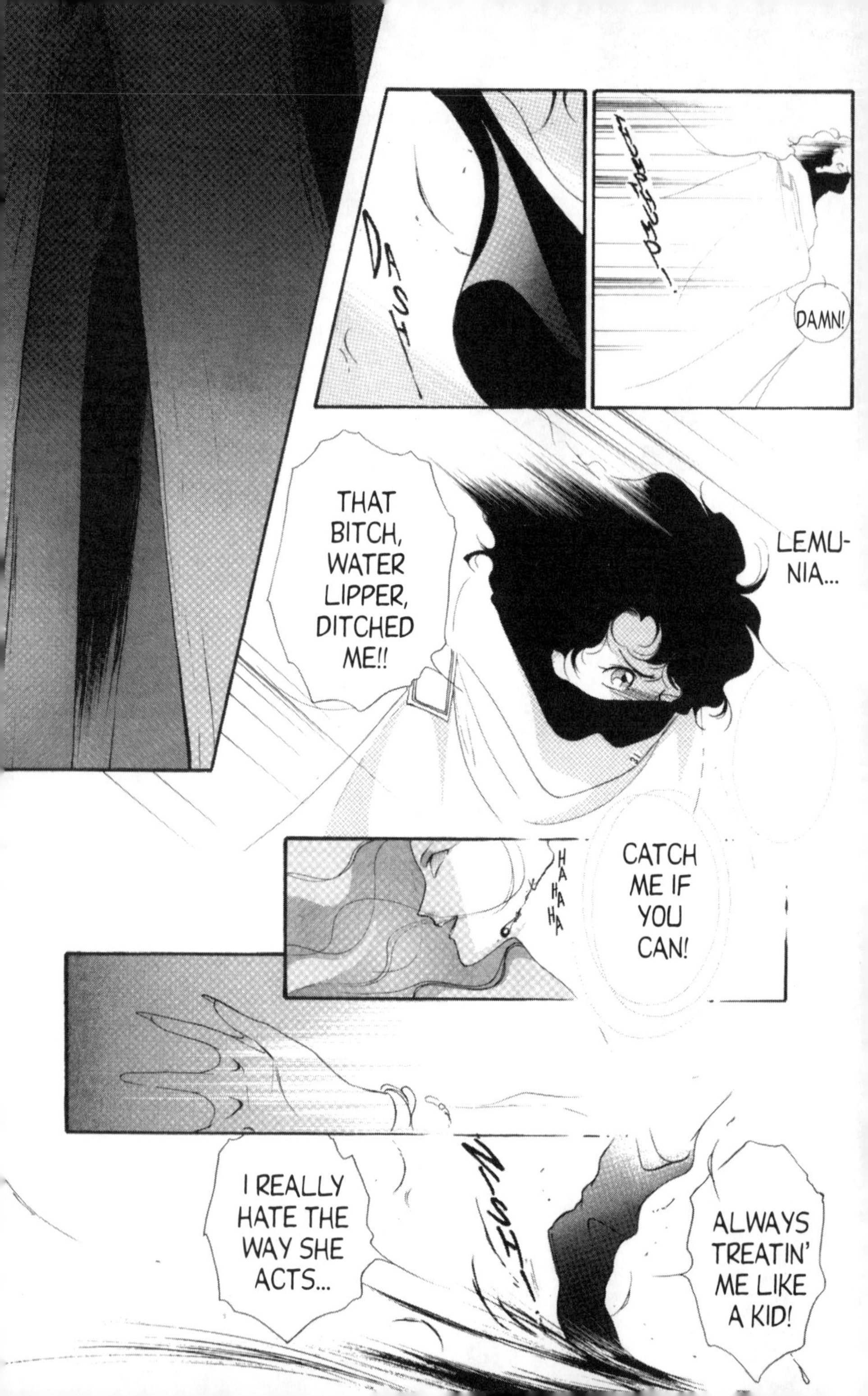

DAMN!
DASH
LEMU-NIA...
THAT BITCH, WATER LIPPER, DITCHED ME!!
CATCH ME IF YOU CAN!
HA HA HA HA
ALWAYS TREATIN' ME LIKE A KID!
I REALLY HATE THE WAY SHE ACTS...

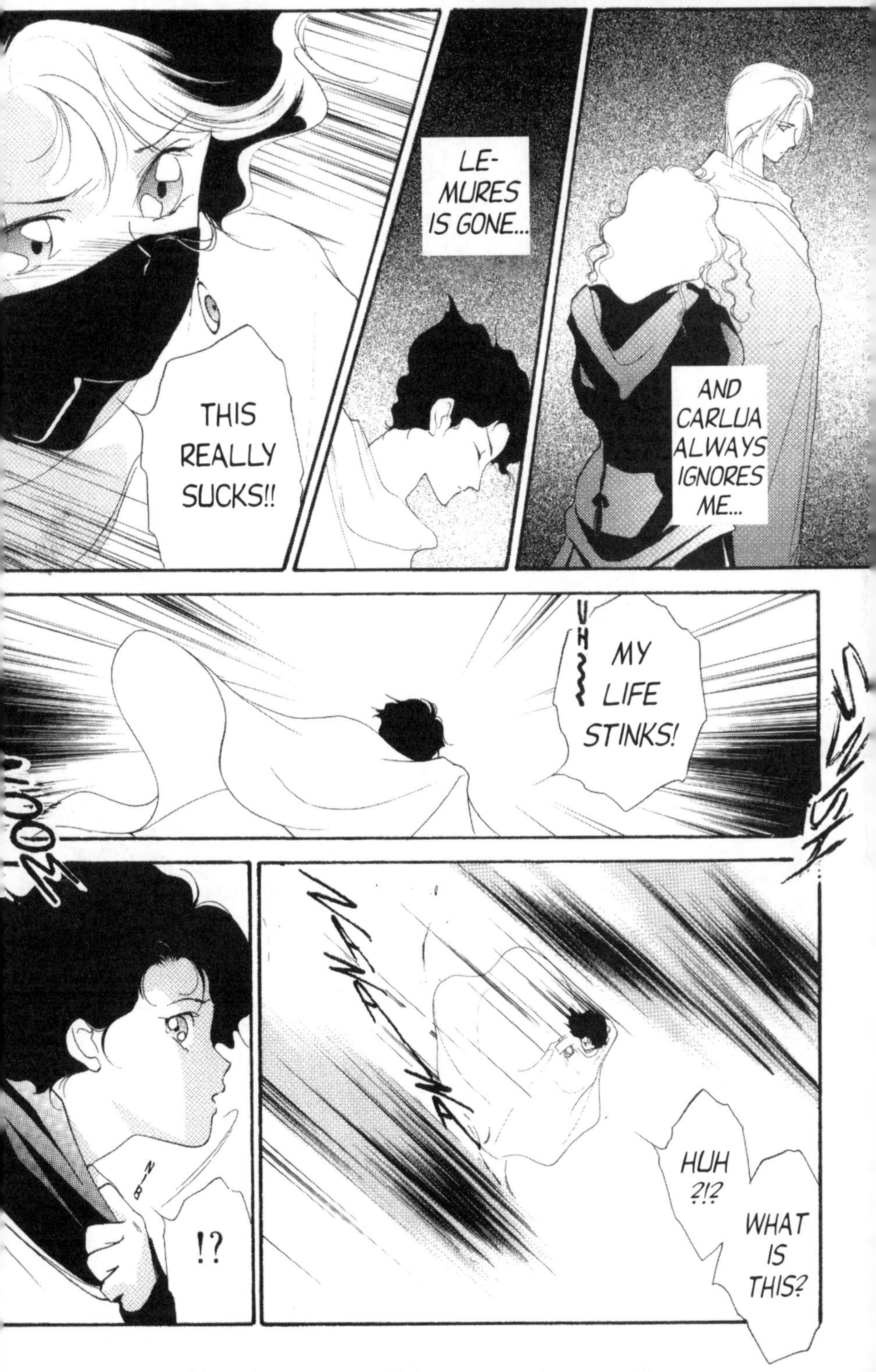
LE-MURES IS GONE...
AND CARLUA ALWAYS IGNORES ME...
THIS REALLY SUCKS!!
SWISH
UHM~
MY LIFE STINKS!
ZOOM!!
HUH?!? WHAT IS THIS?
NIB
!?

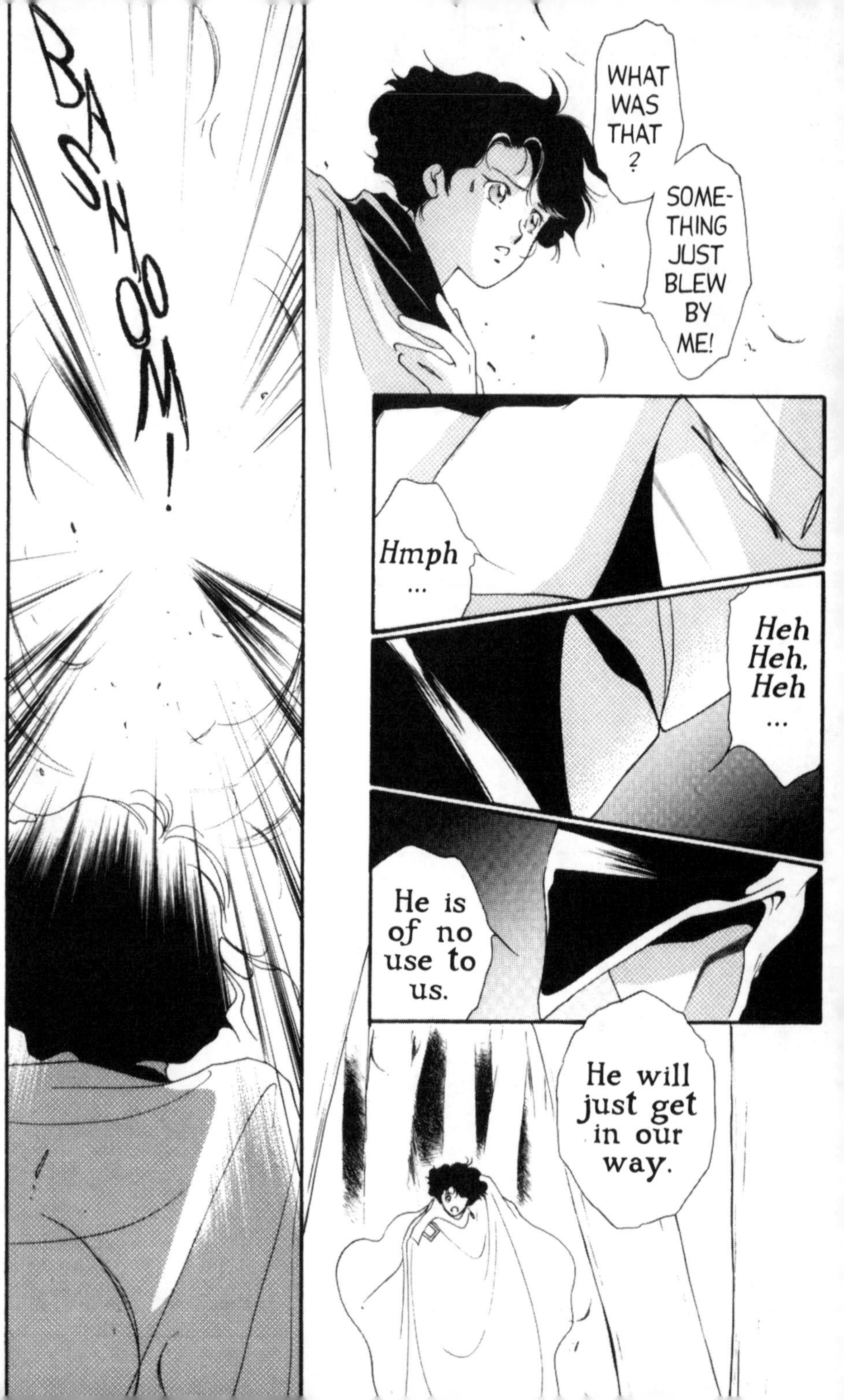
BASHOOM!
WHAT WAS THAT?
SOMETHING JUST BLEW BY ME!
Hmph ...
Heh Heh, Heh ...
He is of no use to us.
He will just get in our way.

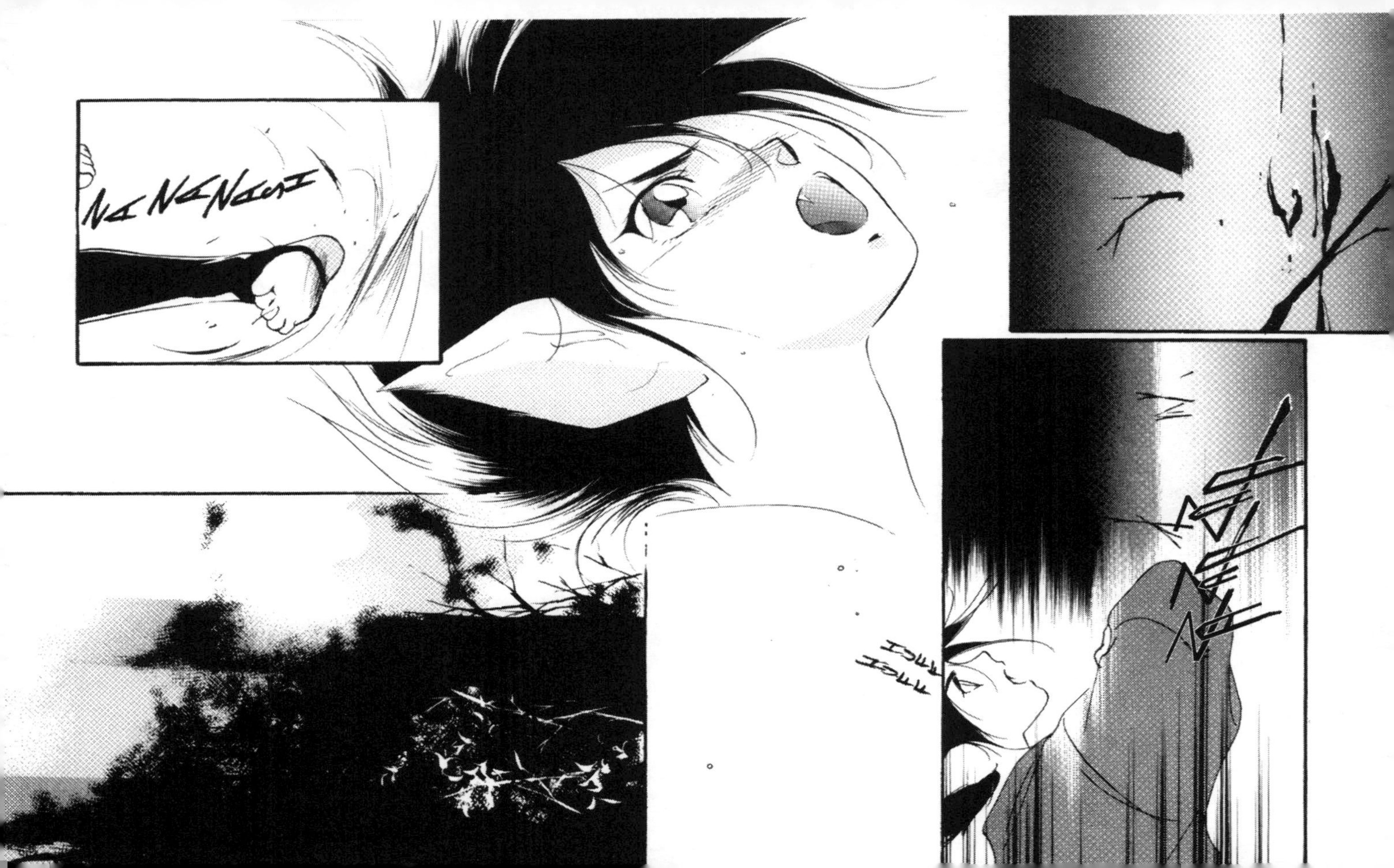

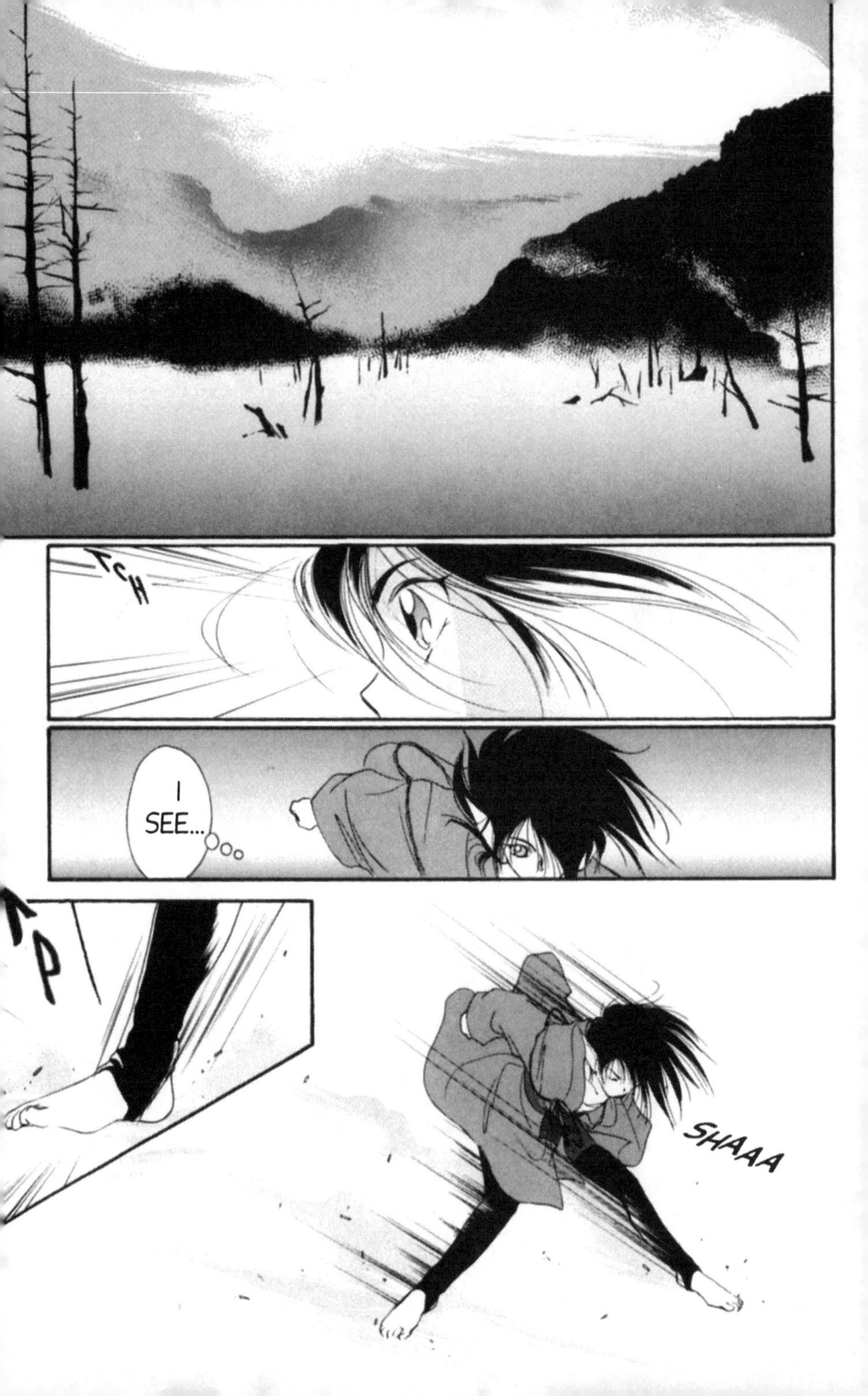
TCH
I SEE...
TP
SHAAA

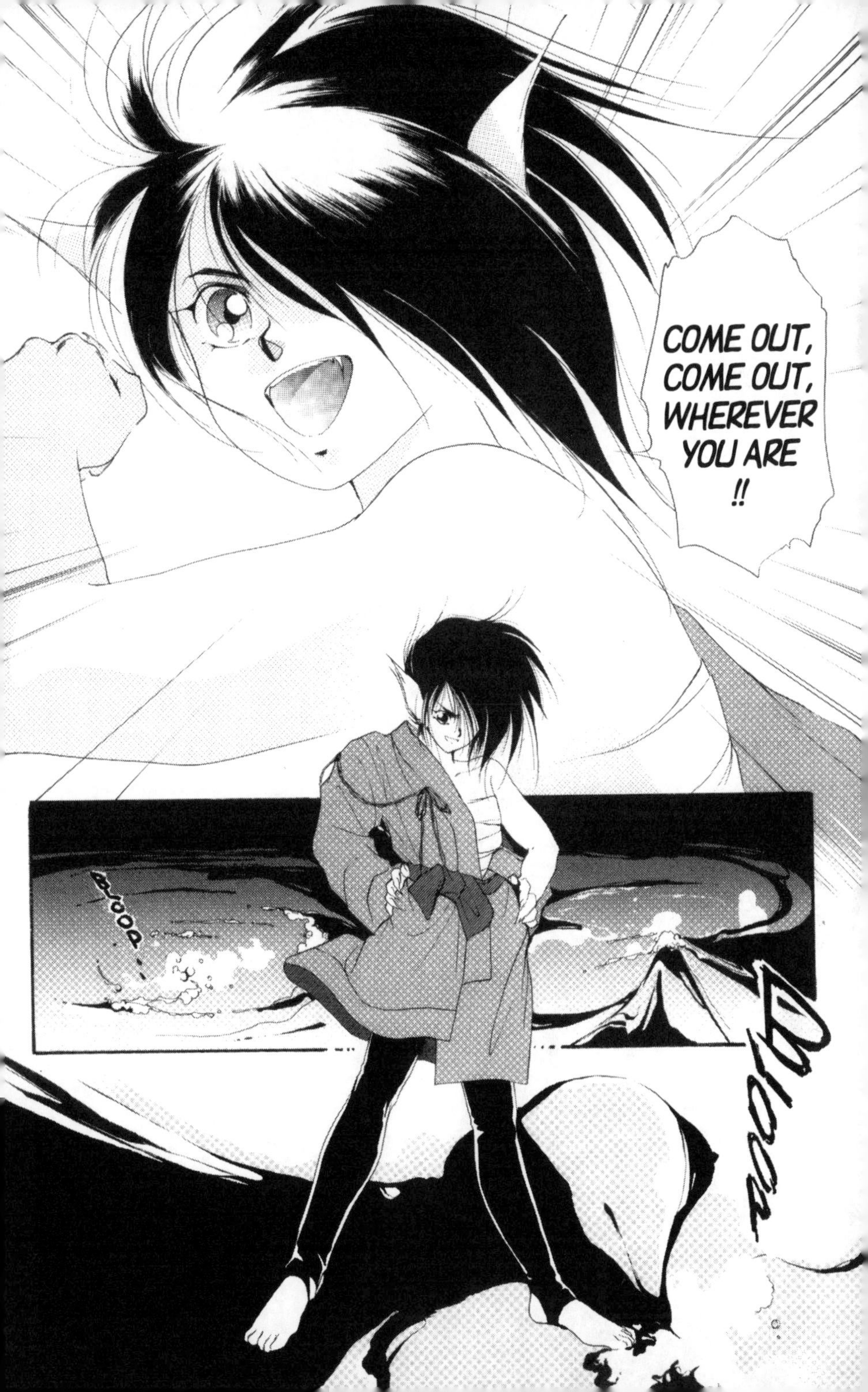
COME OUT, COME OUT, WHEREVER YOU ARE !!
BLOOP...

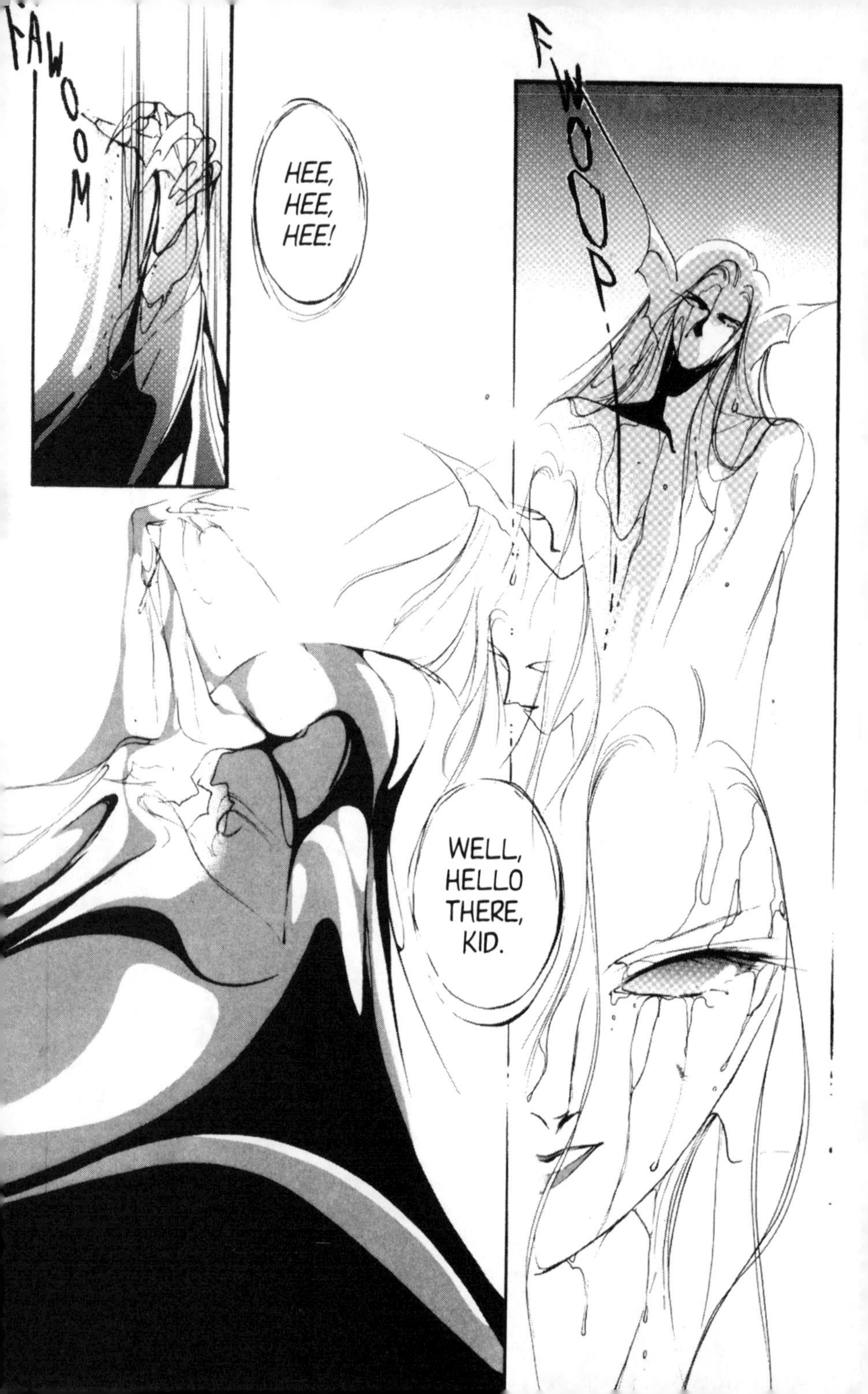
FWOOP
FAWOOM
HEE, HEE, HEE!
WELL, HELLO THERE, KID.

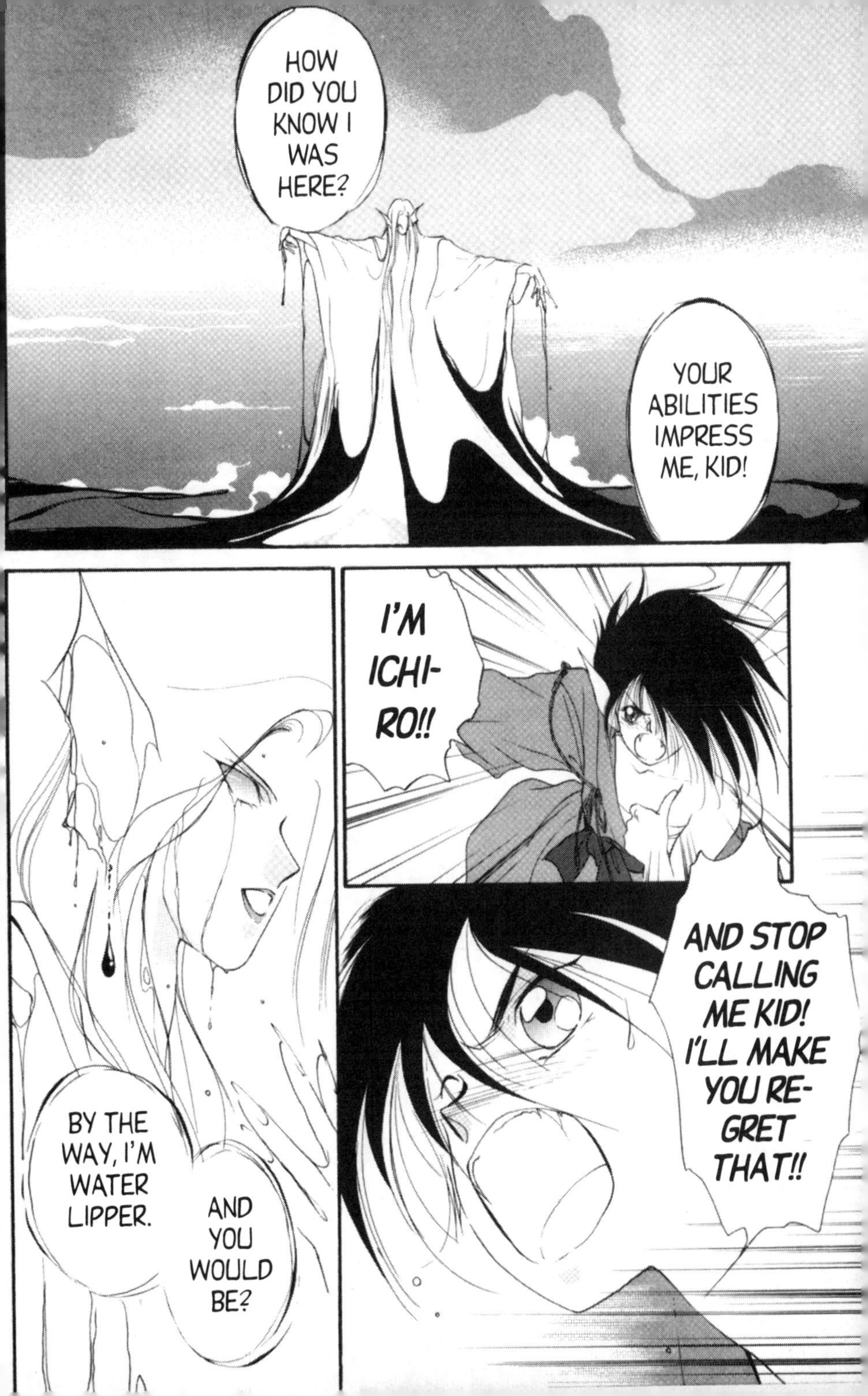

YOUR ABILITIES IMPRESS ME, KID!
HOW DID YOU KNOW I WAS HERE?
I'M ICHI-RO!!
AND STOP CALLING ME KID! I'LL MAKE YOU RE-GRET THAT!!
AND YOU WOULD BE?
BY THE WAY, I'M WATER LIPPER.

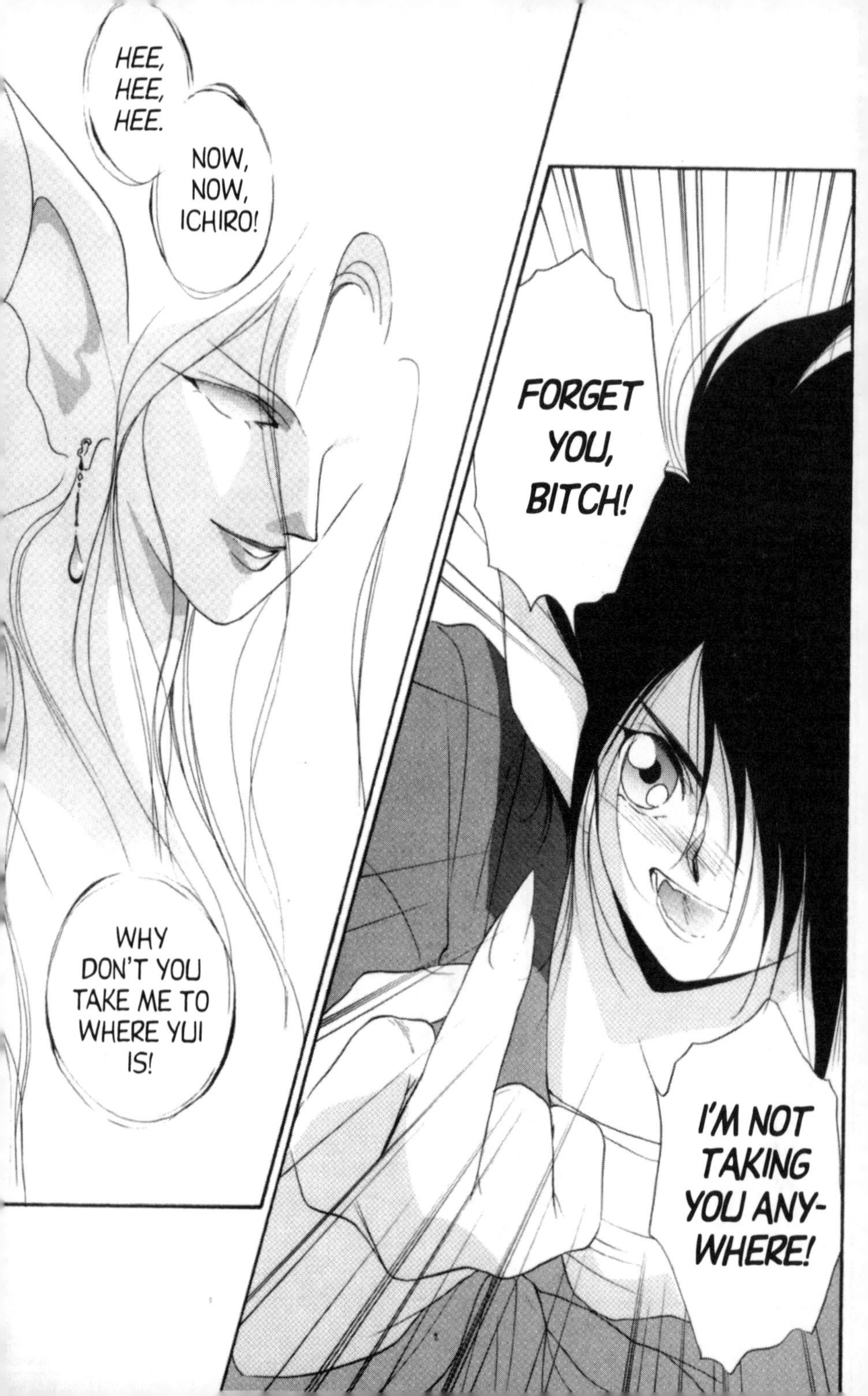
HEE, HEE, HEE.
NOW, NOW, ICHIRO!
WHY DON'T YOU TAKE ME TO WHERE YUI IS!
FORGET YOU, BITCH!
I'M NOT TAKING YOU ANY-WHERE!

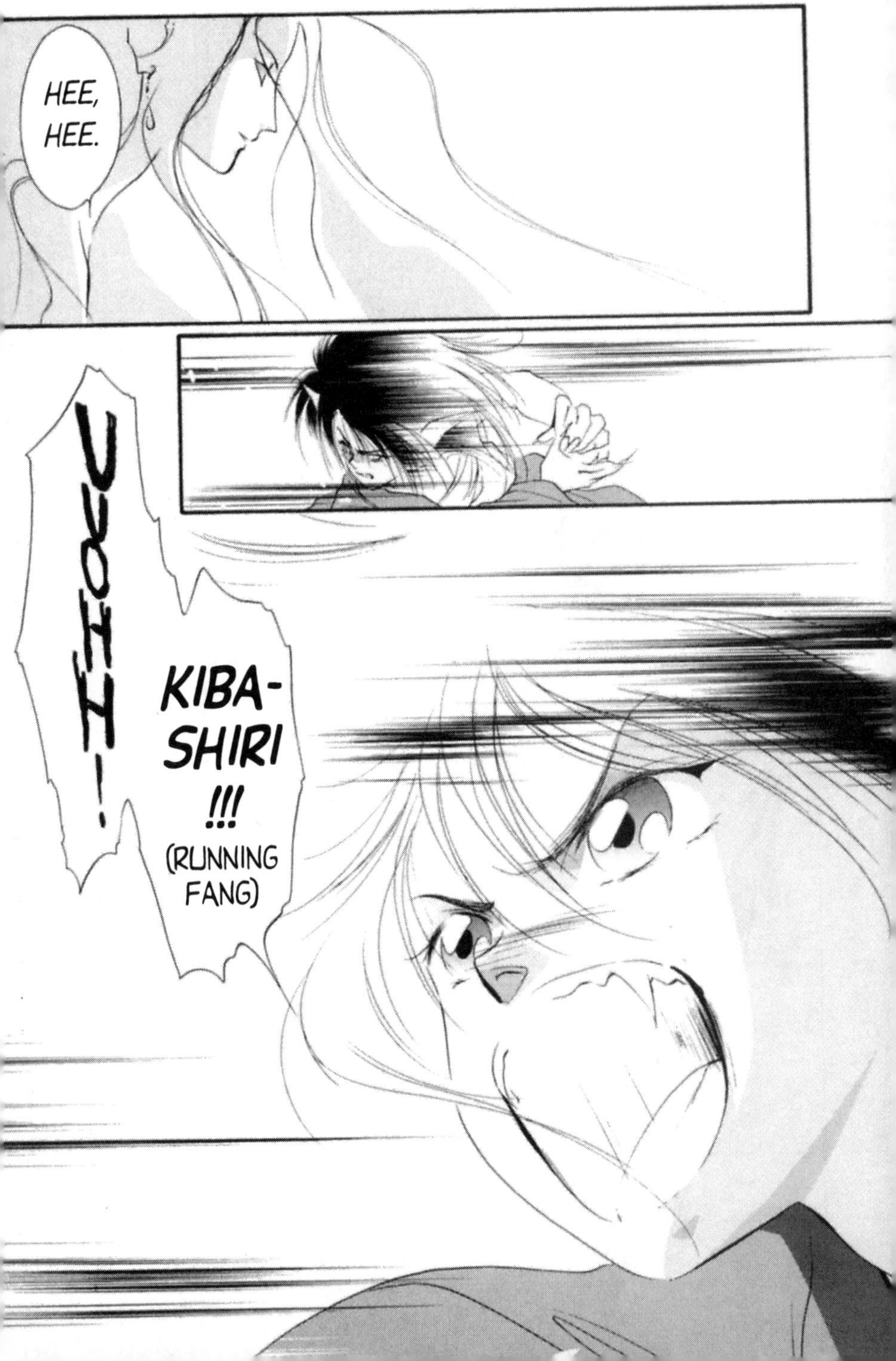

HEE, HEE.
KIBA-SHIRI!!! (RUNNING FANG)

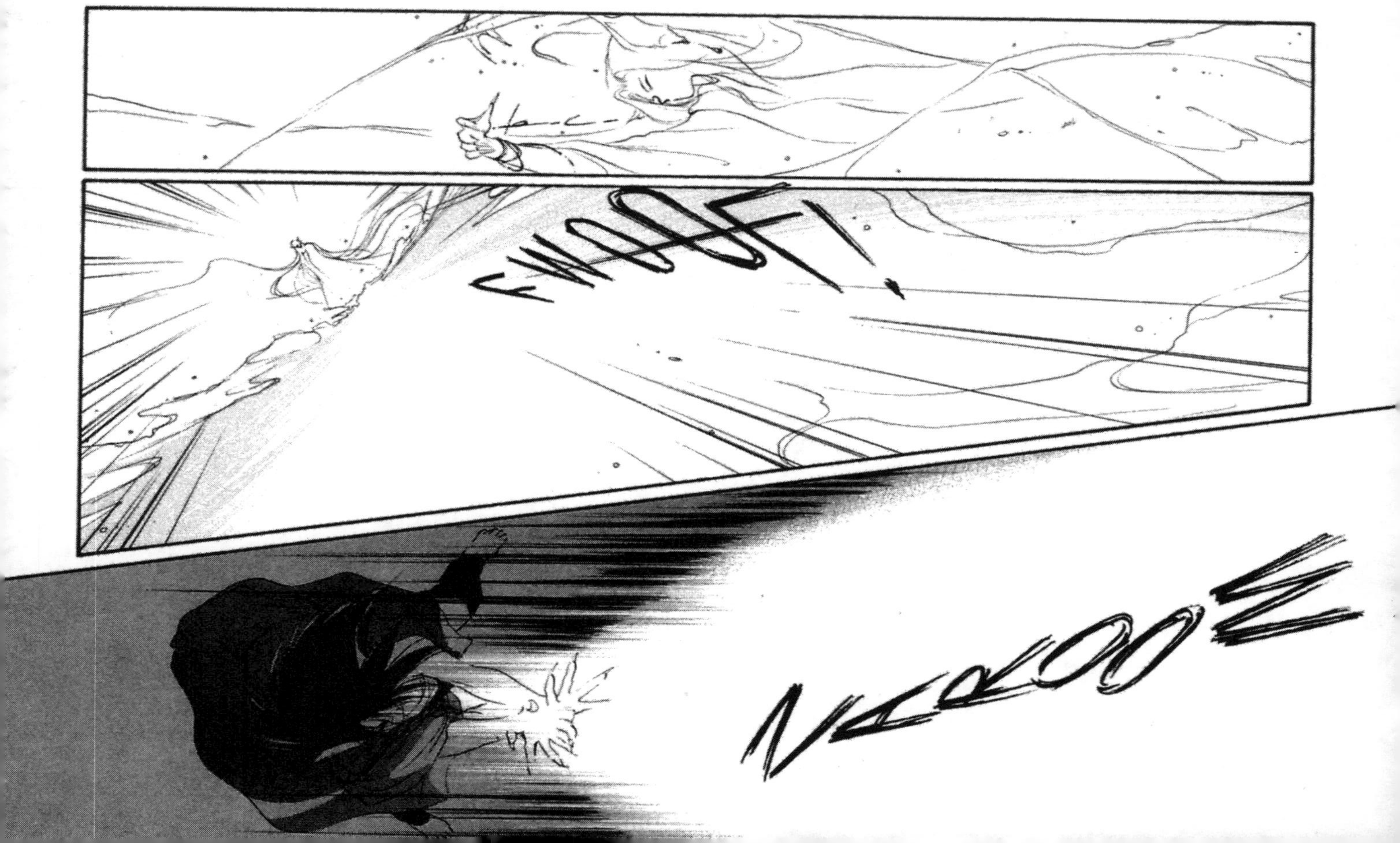
FWOOSH!
VROOM

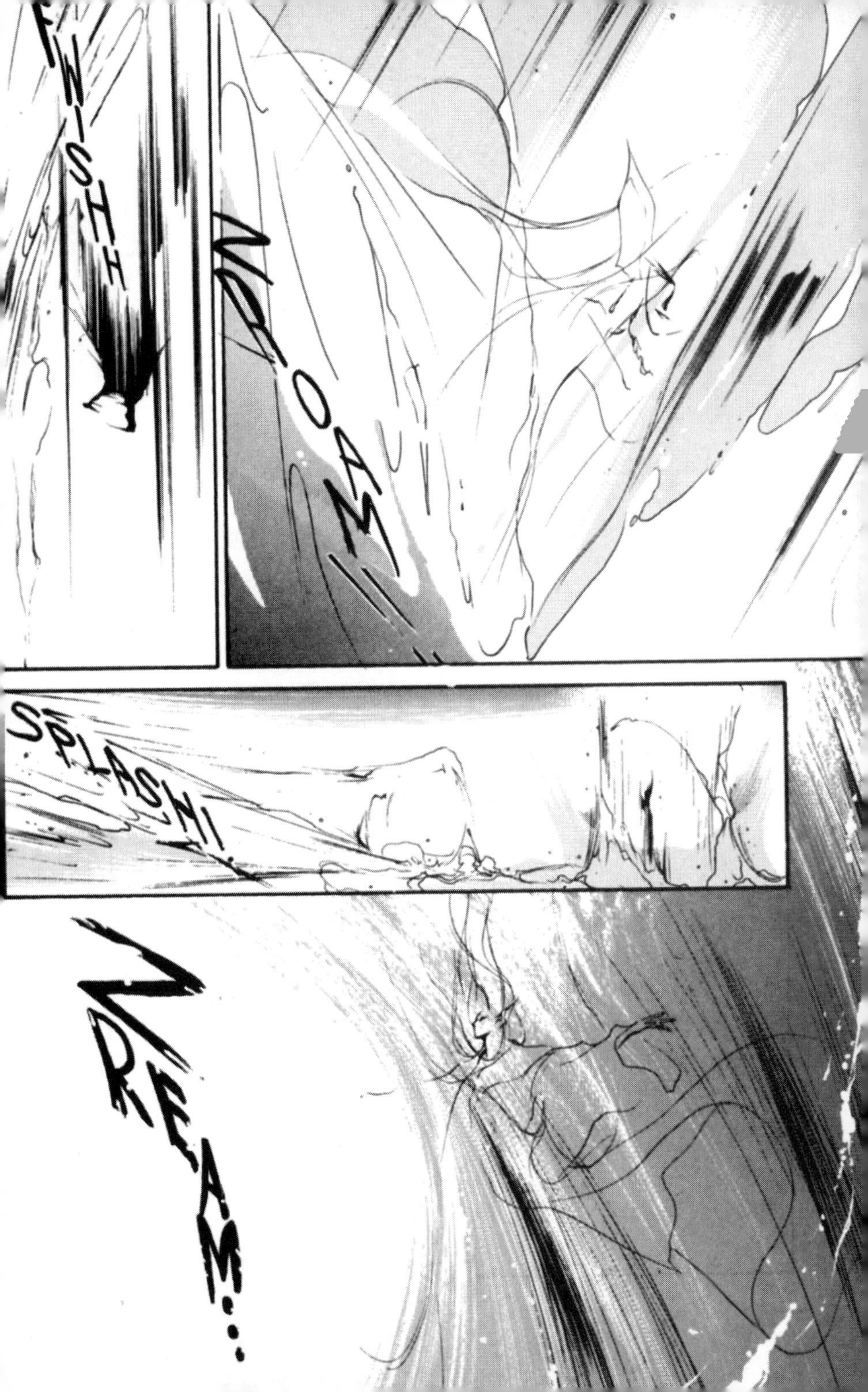
FWISHH
SPLASH!
ZREAM...

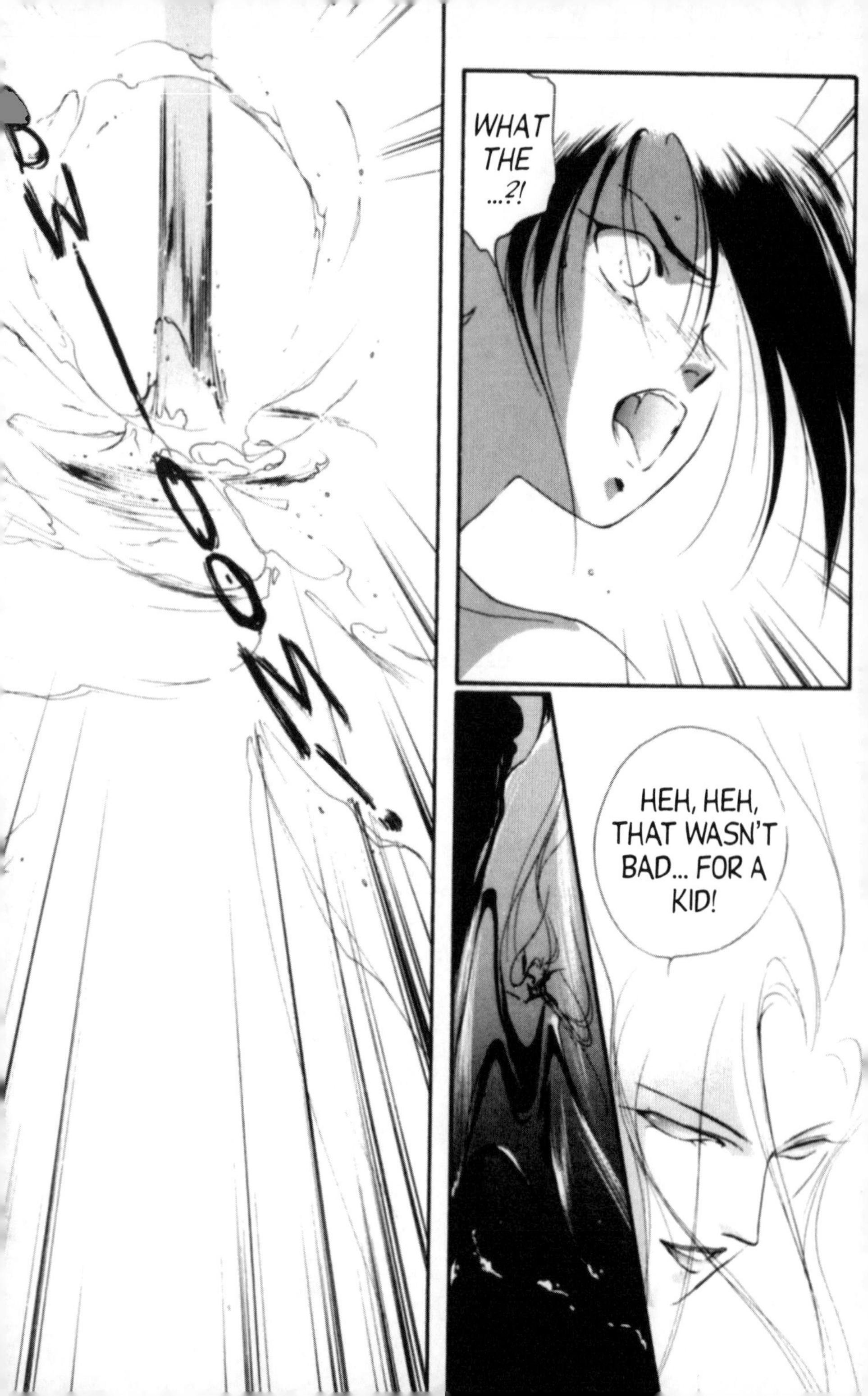
WHAT THE ...?!
HEH, HEH, THAT WASN'T BAD... FOR A KID!
BWOOOM!

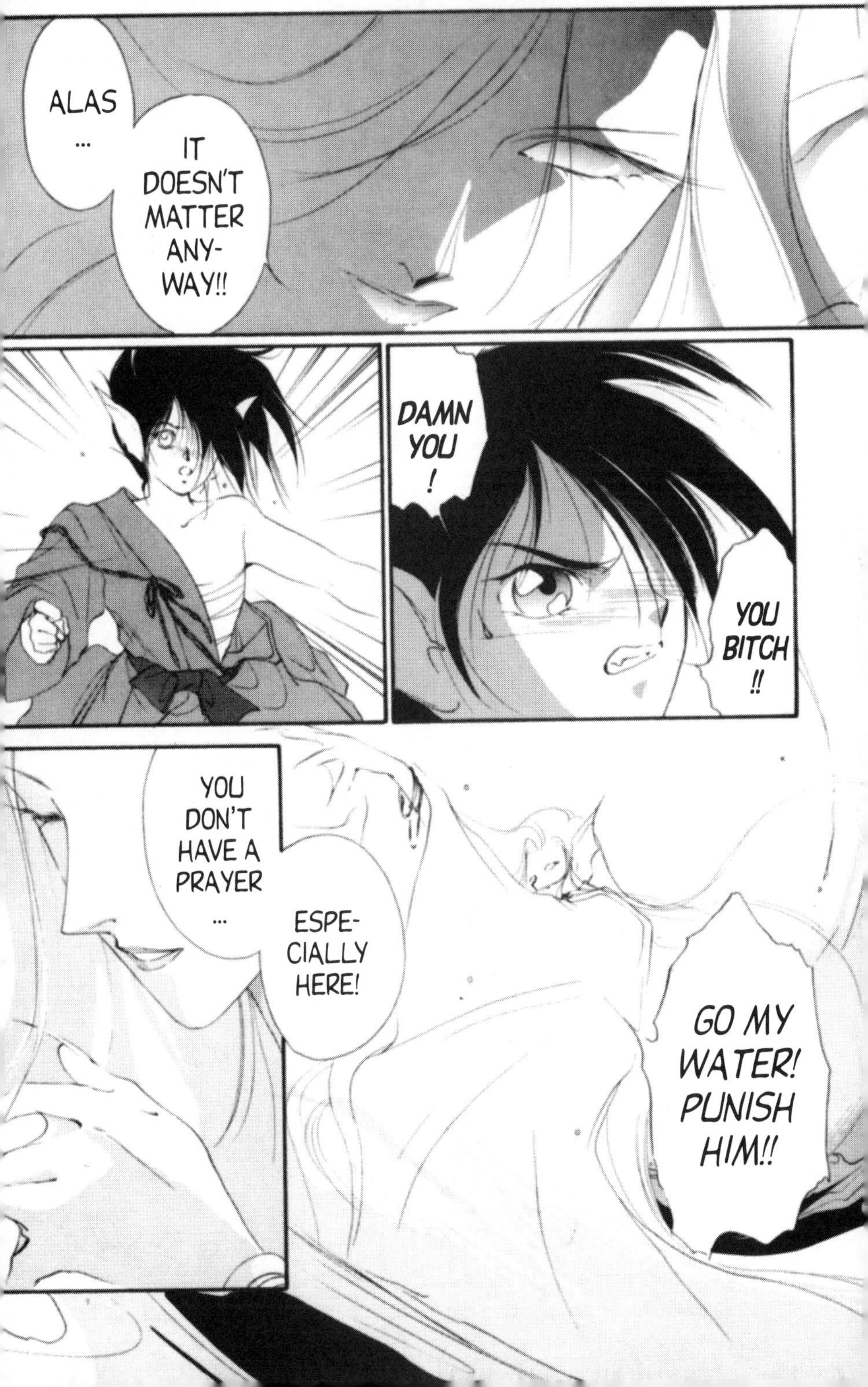
ALAS ...
IT DOESN'T MATTER ANY-WAY!!
DAMN YOU !
YOU BITCH !!
YOU DON'T HAVE A PRAYER ...
ESPE-CIALLY HERE!
GO MY WATER! PUNISH HIM!!

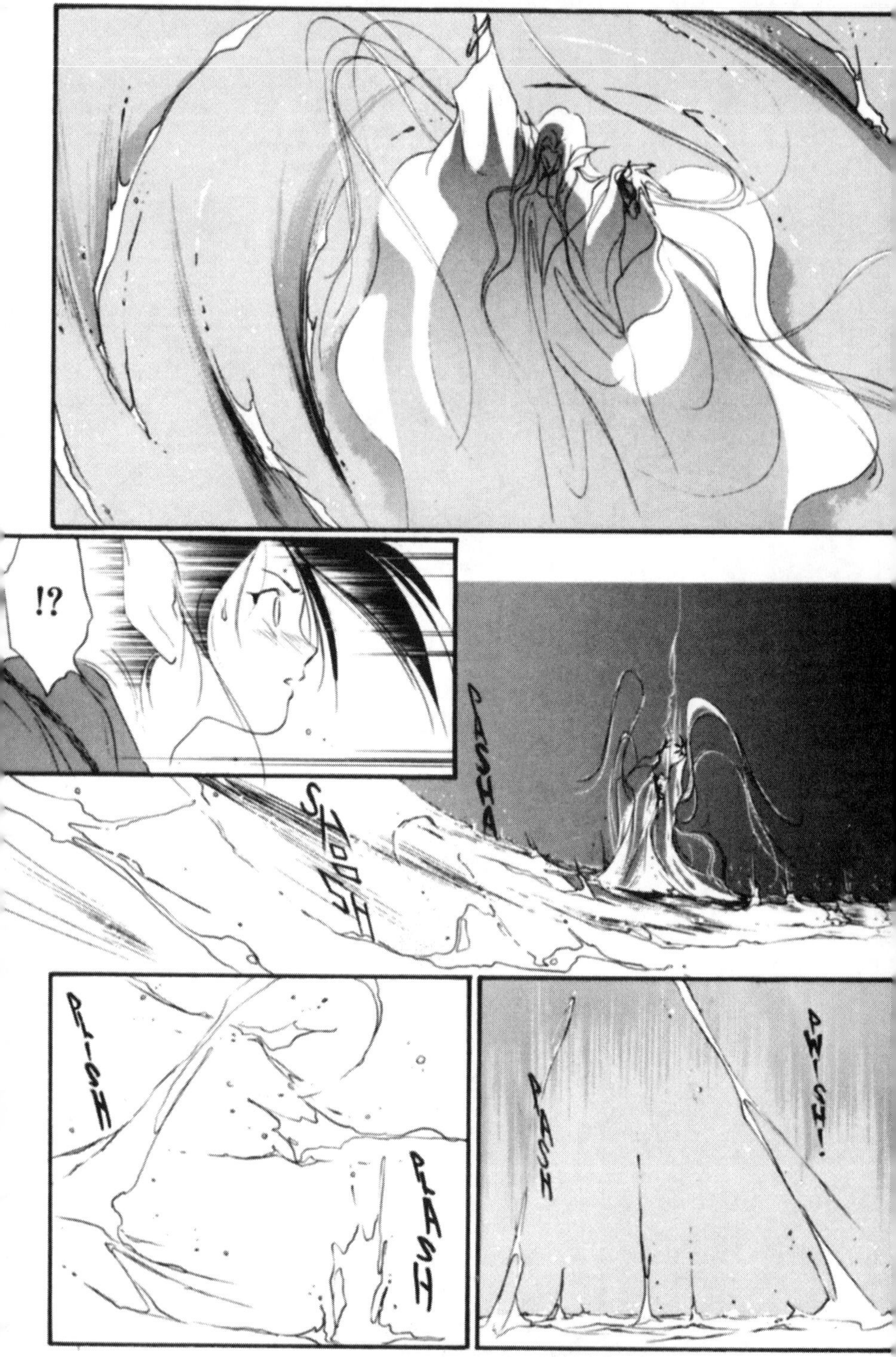

!?
CASHA
SWISH!

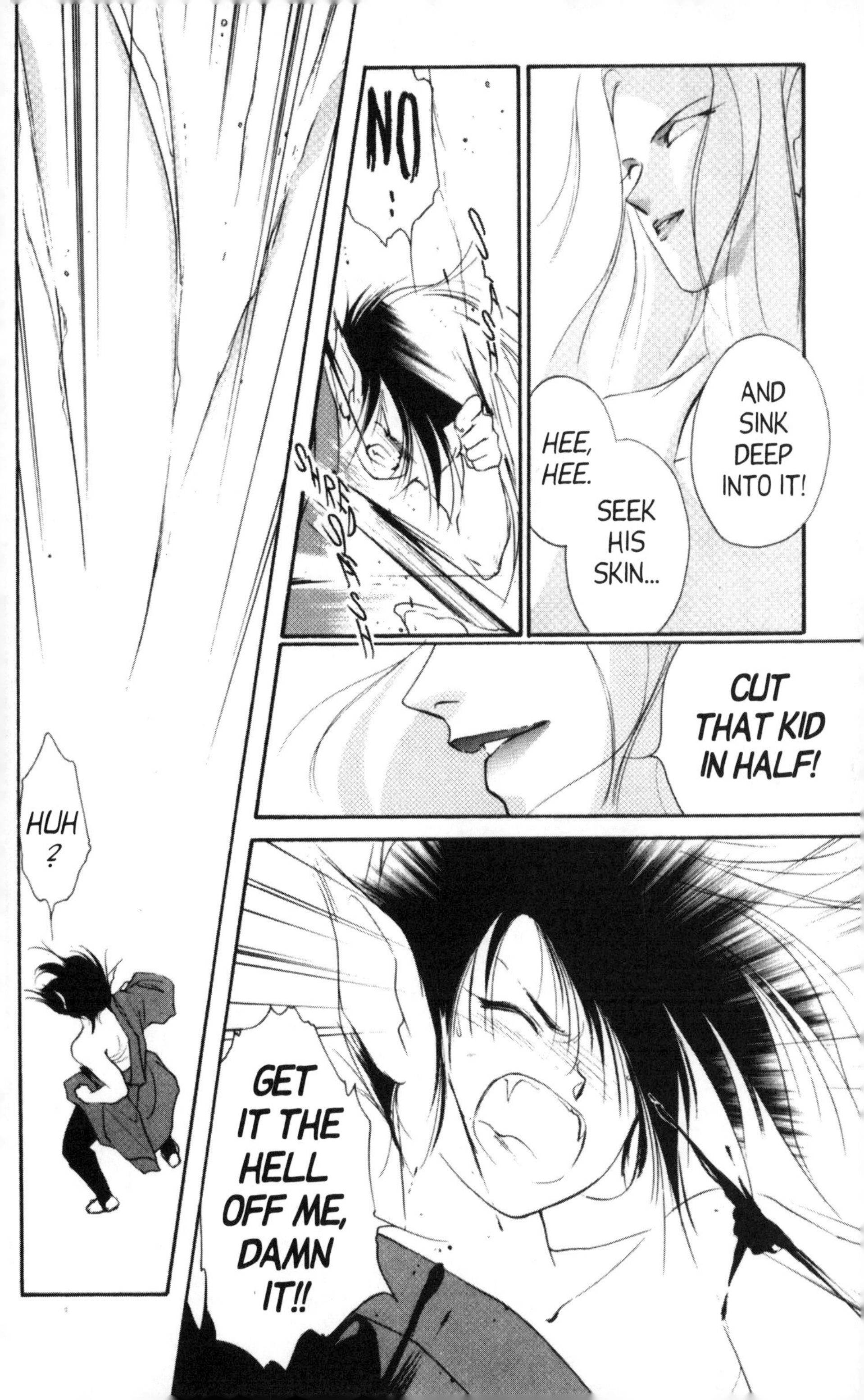

AND SINK DEEP INTO IT!
HEE, HEE.
SEEK HIS SKIN...
NO...
CUT THAT KID IN HALF!
HUH?
GET IT THE HELL OFF ME, DAMN IT!!

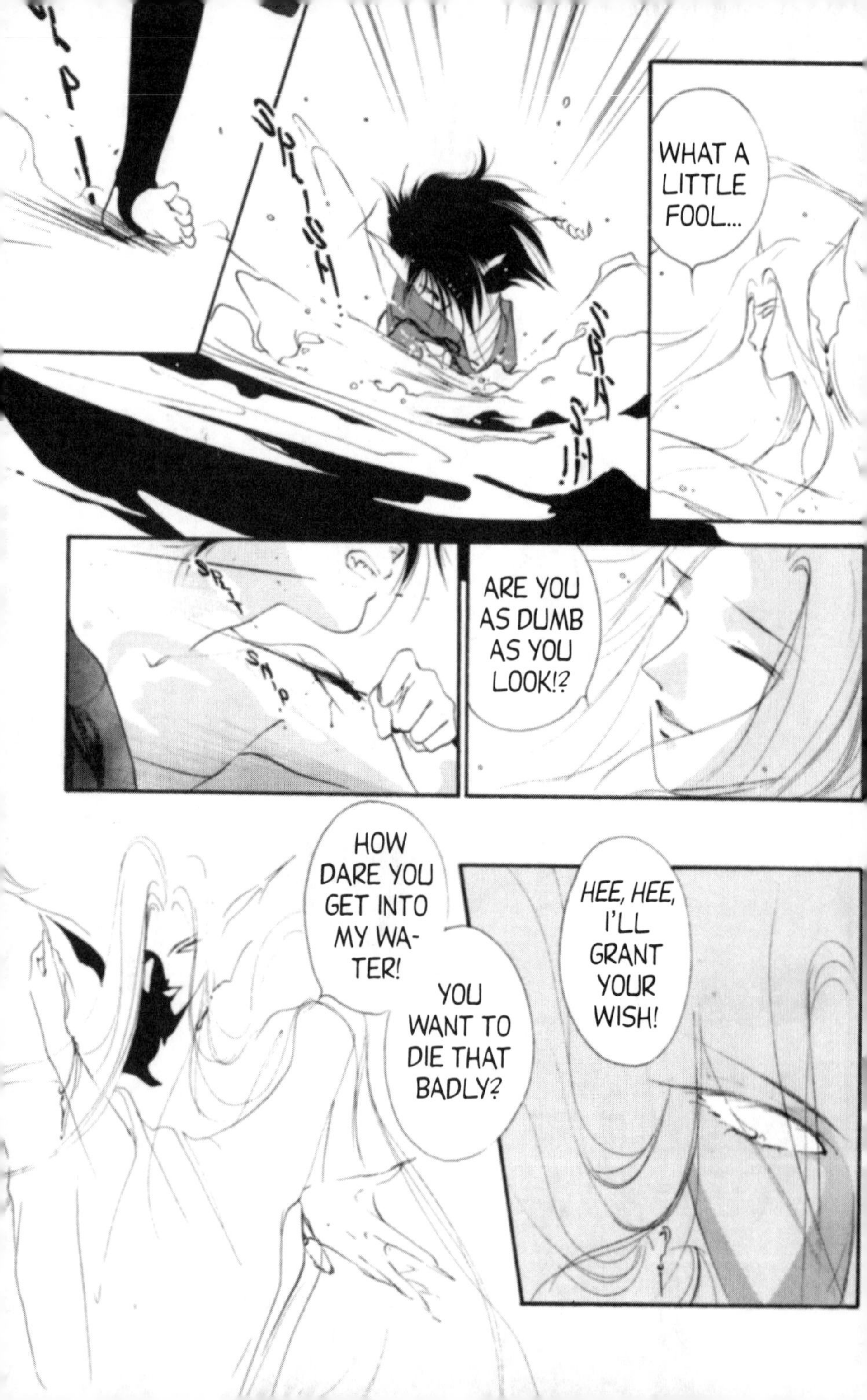
WHAT A LITTLE FOOL...
SPLISH
ARE YOU AS DUMB AS YOU LOOK!?
HEE, HEE, I'LL GRANT YOUR WISH!
HOW DARE YOU GET INTO MY WA-TER!
YOU WANT TO DIE THAT BADLY?

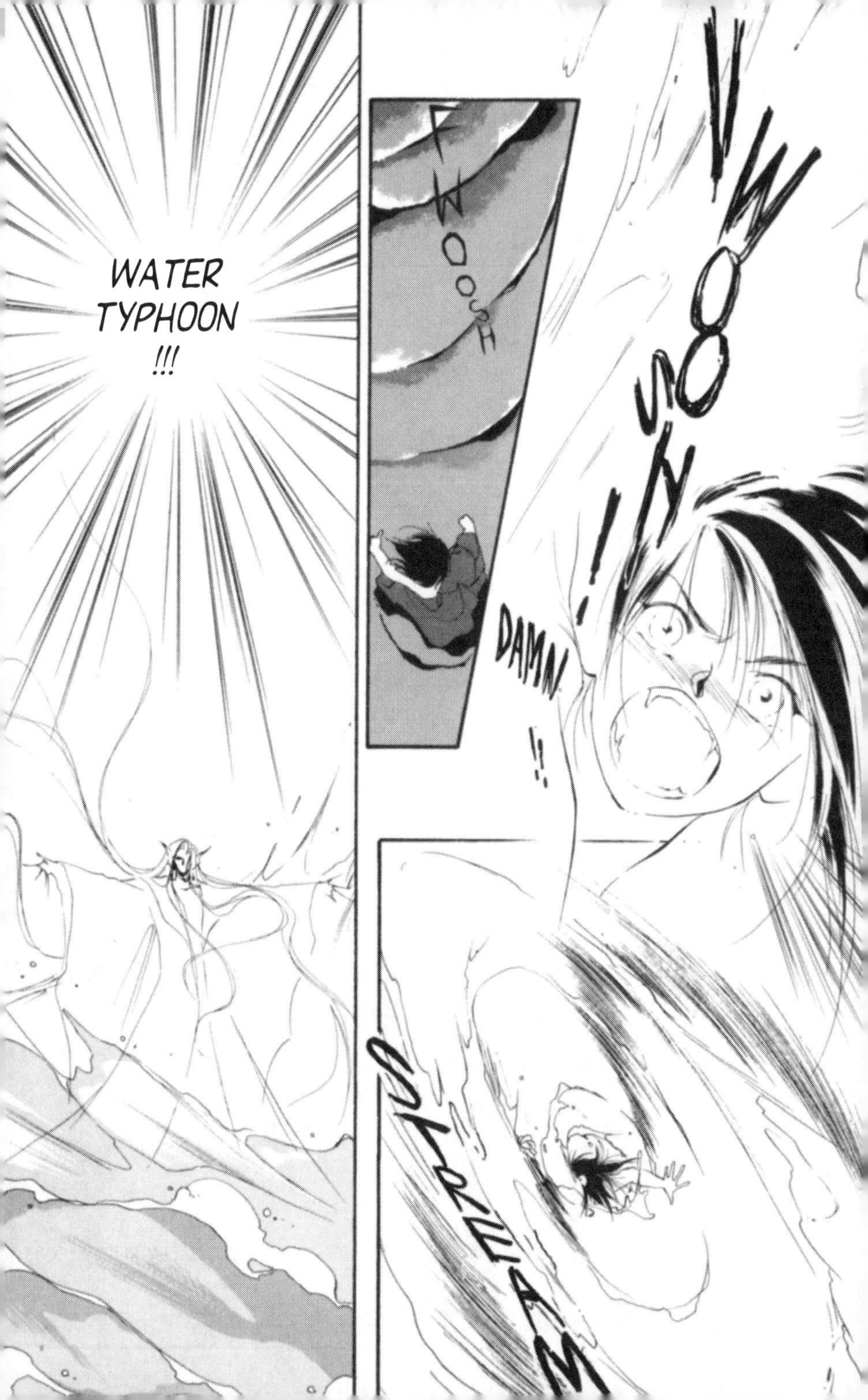

VWOOSH!!
WOOSH
DAMN!!!
WATER TYPHOON !!!

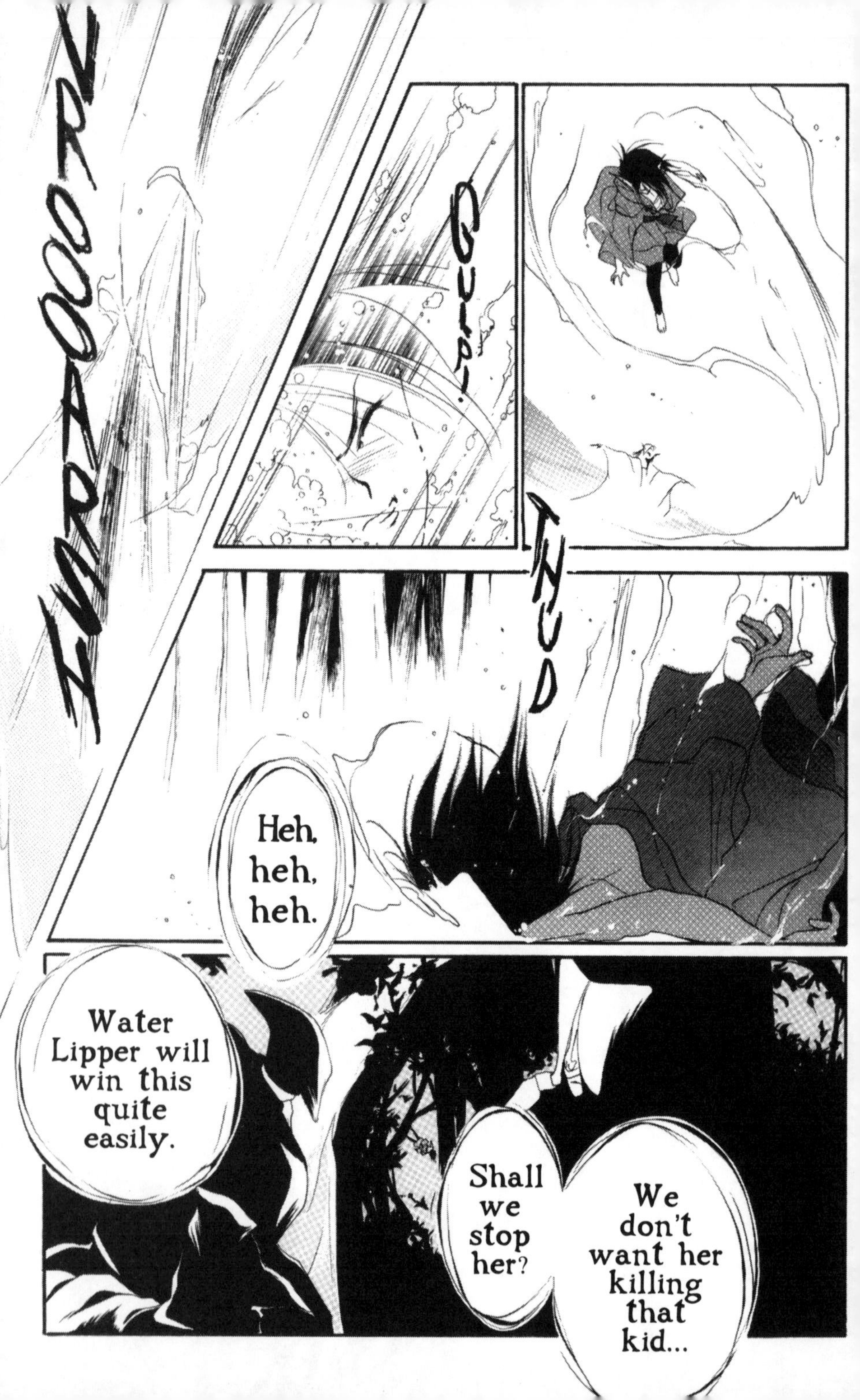
VROOOARSH
GULP!
THUD
Heh, heh, heh.
Water Lipper will win this quite easily.
Shall we stop her?
We don't want her killing that kid...

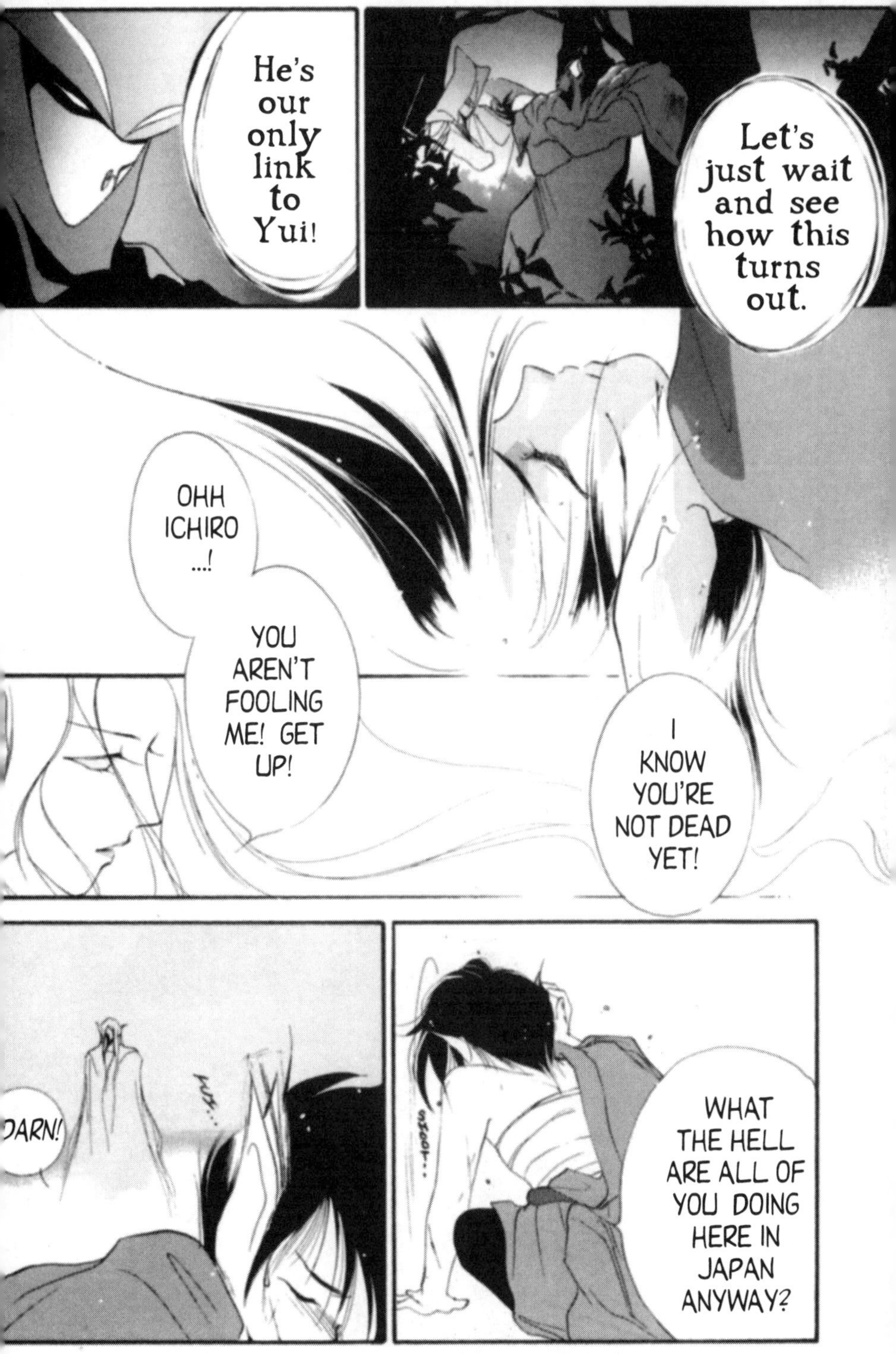
Let's just wait and see how this turns out.
He's our only link to Yui!
OHH ICHIRO ...!
YOU AREN'T FOOLING ME! GET UP!
I KNOW YOU'RE NOT DEAD YET!
WHAT THE HELL ARE ALL OF YOU DOING HERE IN JAPAN ANYWAY?
DARN!

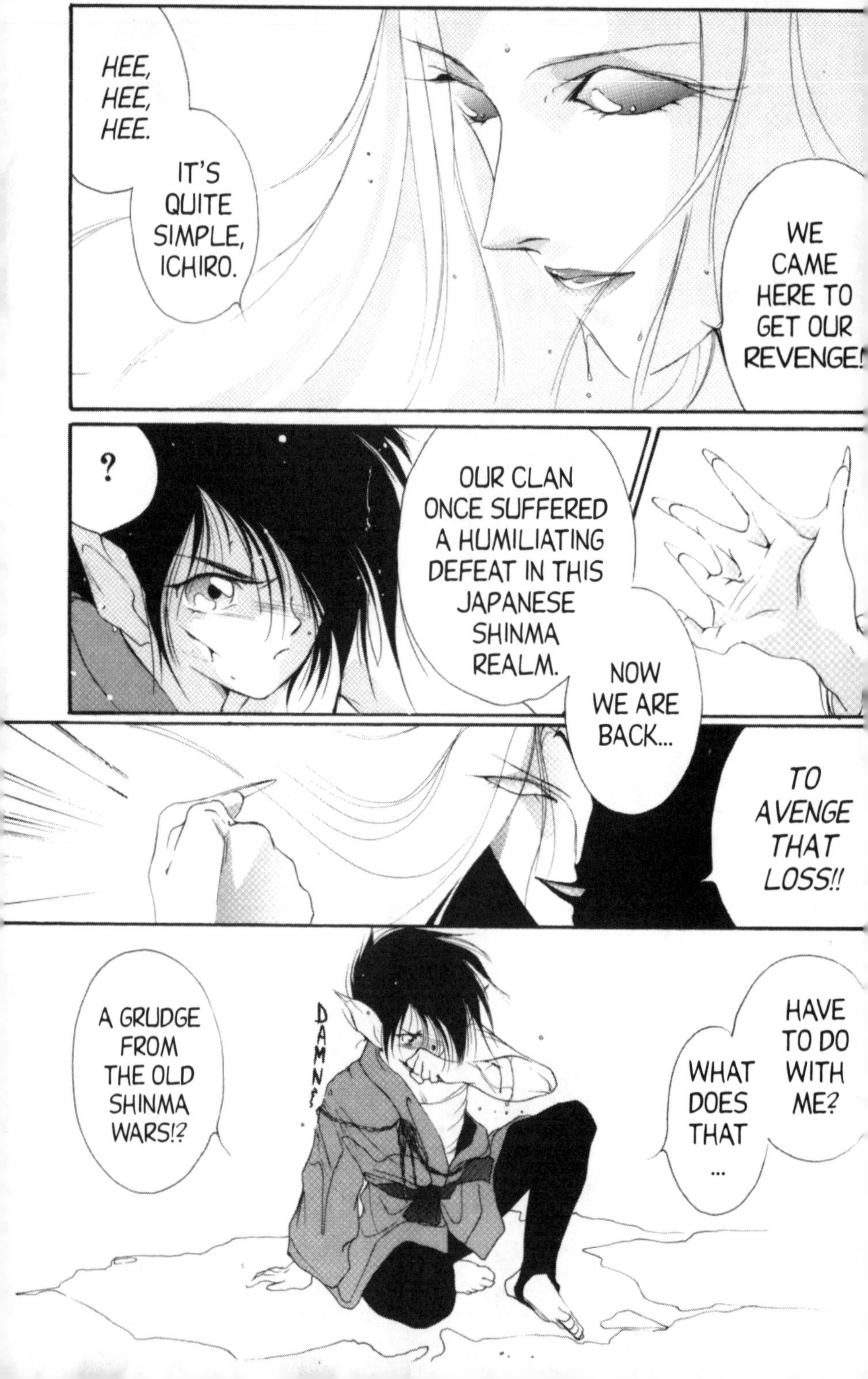
HEE, HEE, HEE.
IT'S QUITE SIMPLE, ICHIRO.
WE CAME HERE TO GET OUR REVENGE!
?
OUR CLAN ONCE SUFFERED A HUMILIATING DEFEAT IN THIS JAPANESE SHINMA REALM.
NOW WE ARE BACK...
TO AVENGE THAT LOSS!!
A GRUDGE FROM THE OLD SHINMA WARS!?
DAMN?
WHAT DOES THAT...
HAVE TO DO WITH ME?

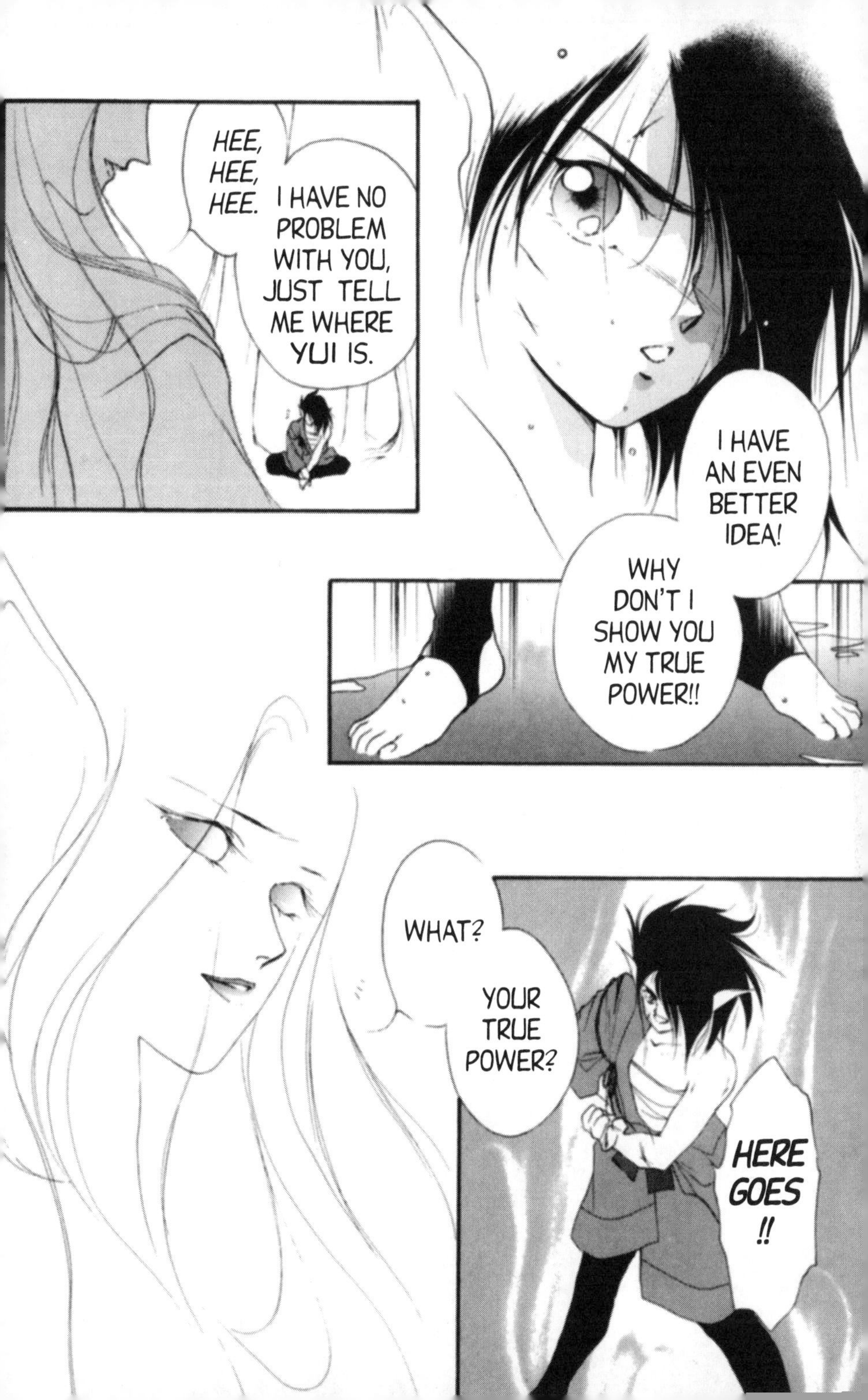
HEE, HEE, HEE.
I HAVE NO PROBLEM WITH YOU, JUST TELL ME WHERE YUI IS.
I HAVE AN EVEN BETTER IDEA!
WHY DON'T I SHOW YOU MY TRUE POWER!!
WHAT?
YOUR TRUE POWER?
HERE GOES !!

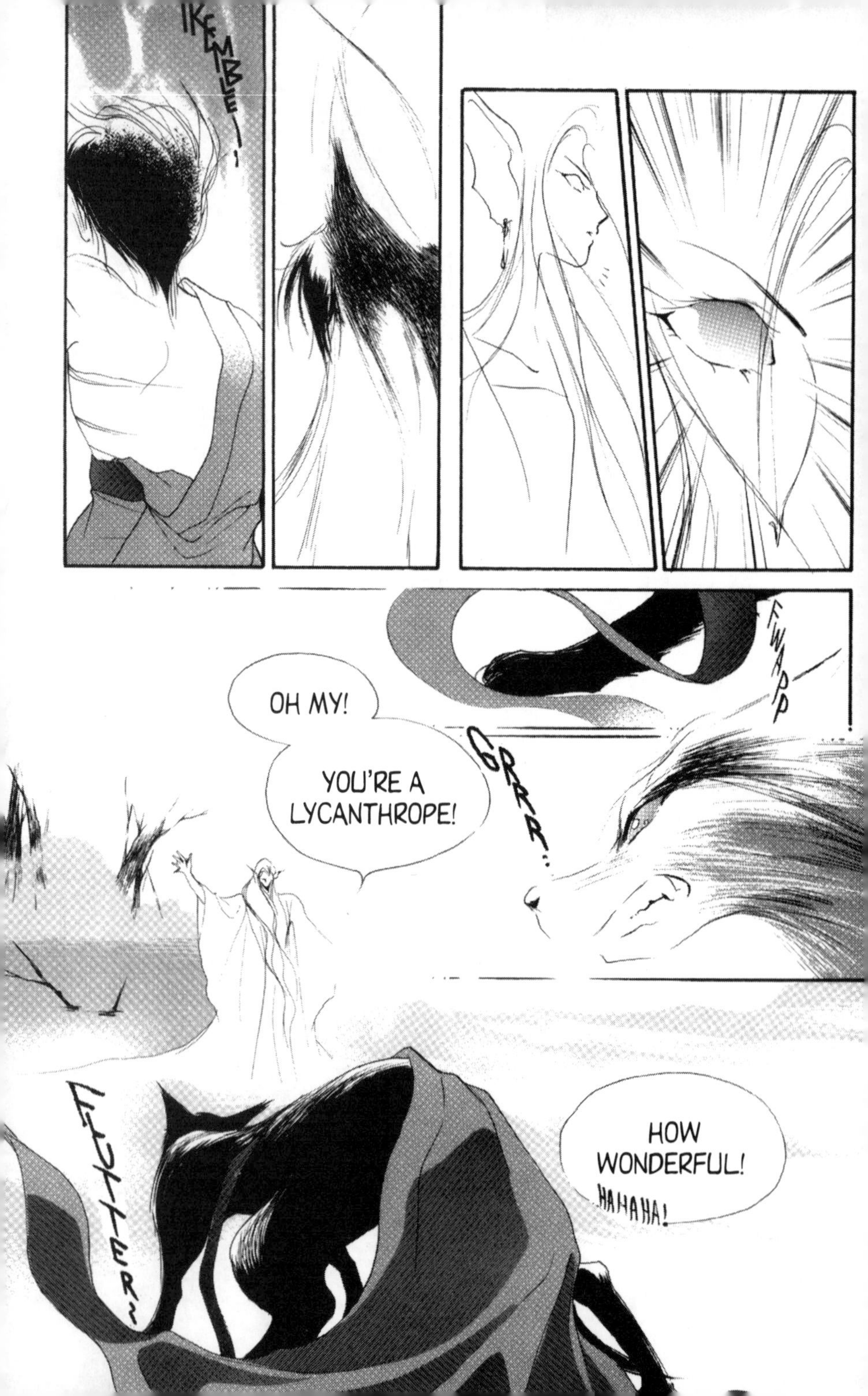
TREMBLE!!
FWAPP
OH MY!
YOU'RE A LYCANTHROPE!
GRRR..
HOW WONDERFUL!
HAHAHA!
FLUTTER~

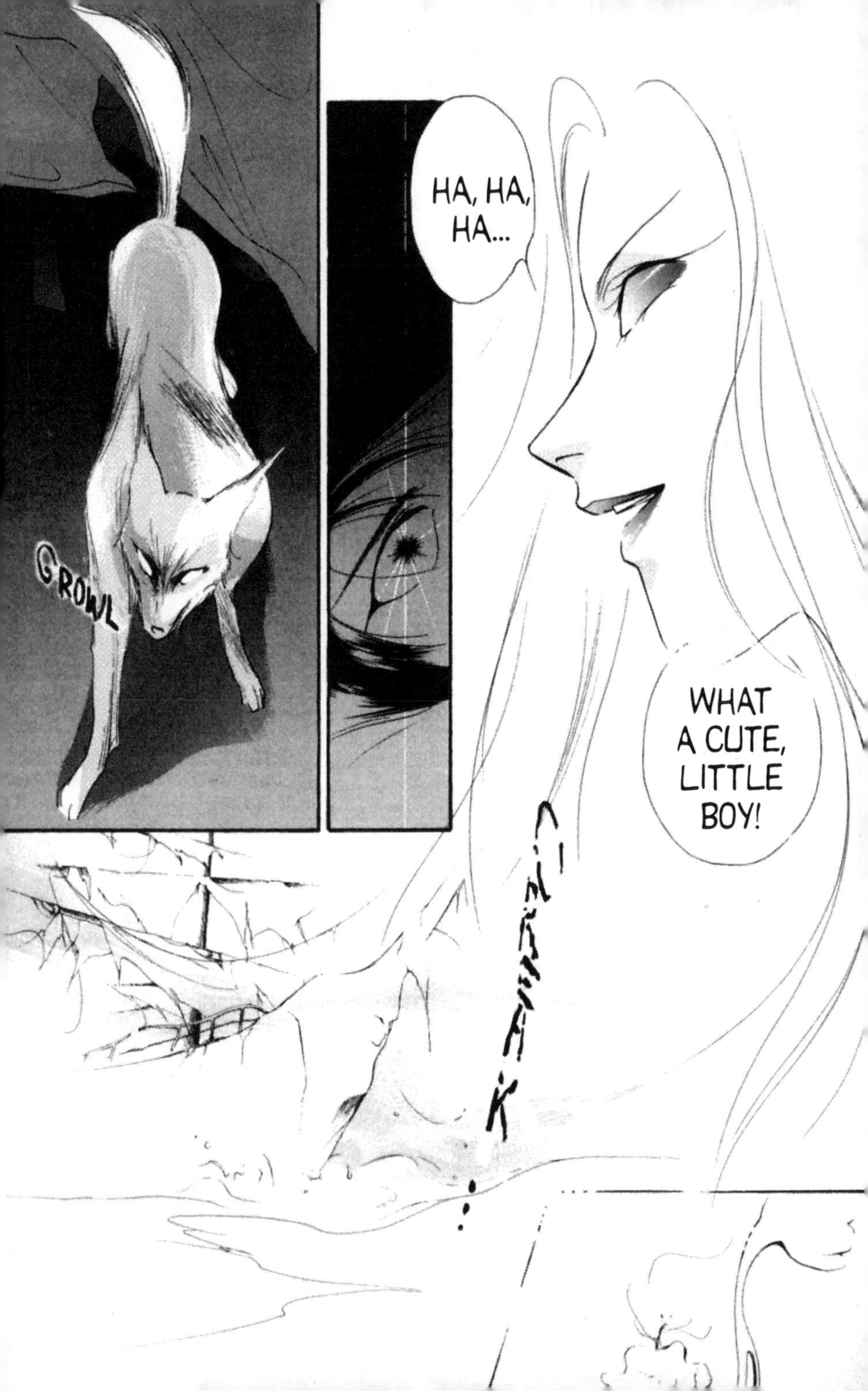
HA, HA, HA...
GROWL
WHAT A CUTE, LITTLE BOY!
CLENNNK
...

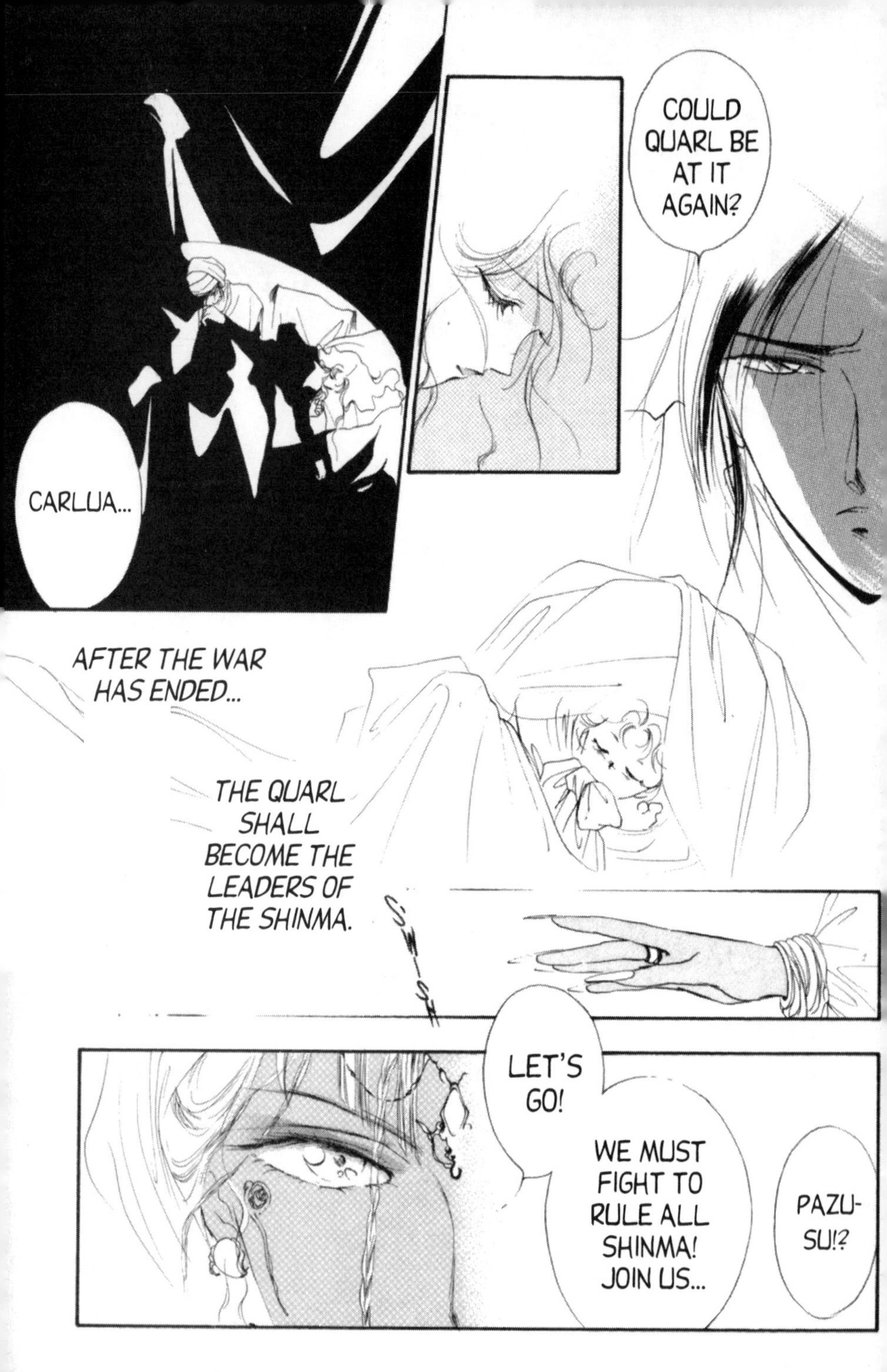
COULD QUARL BE AT IT AGAIN?
CARLUA...
AFTER THE WAR HAS ENDED...
THE QUARL SHALL BECOME THE LEADERS OF THE SHINMA.
LET'S GO!
WE MUST FIGHT TO RULE ALL SHINMA! JOIN US...
PAZU-SU!?

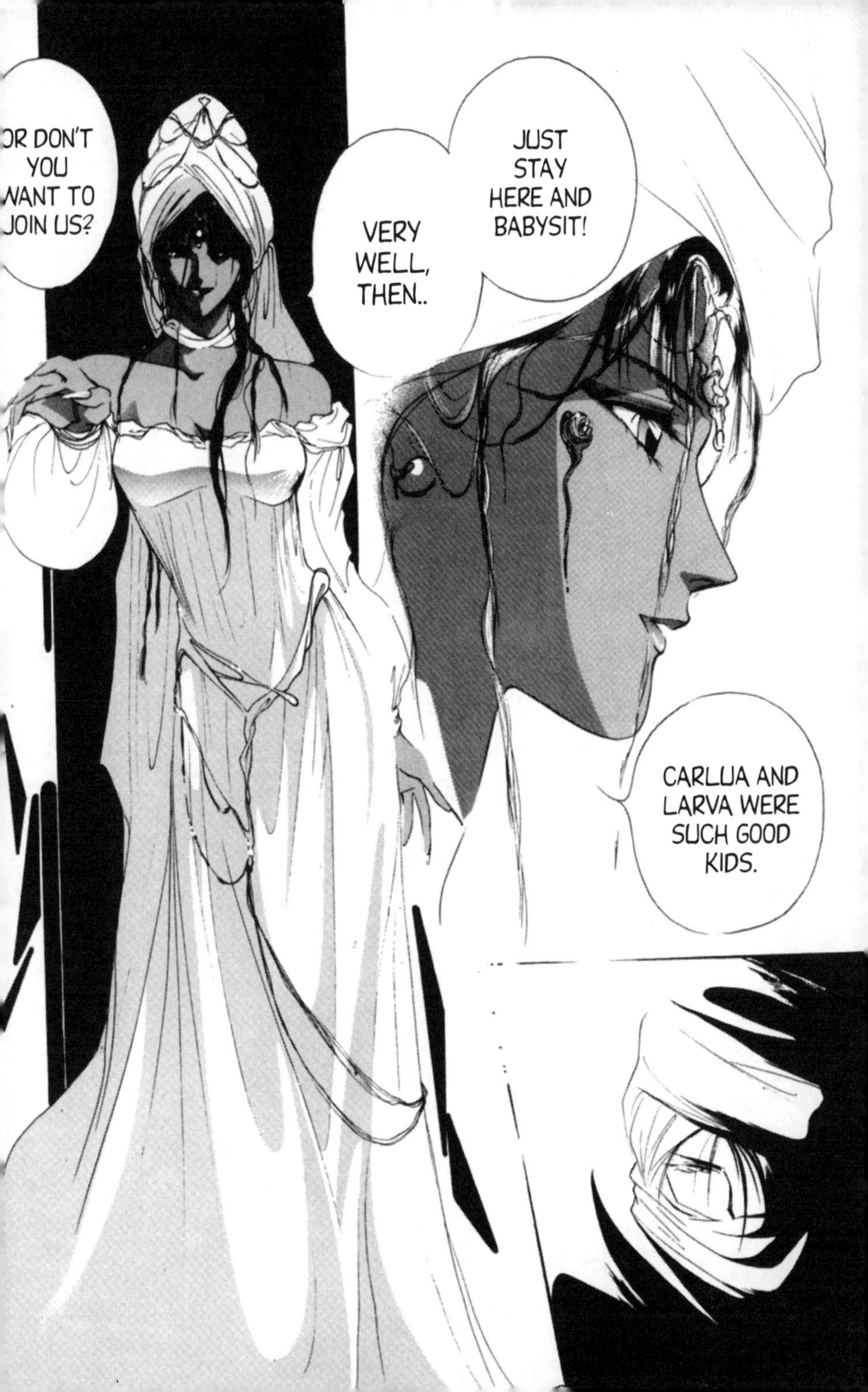
JUST STAY HERE AND BABYSIT!
VERY WELL, THEN..
OR DON'T YOU WANT TO JOIN US?
CARLUA AND LARVA WERE SUCH GOOD KIDS.

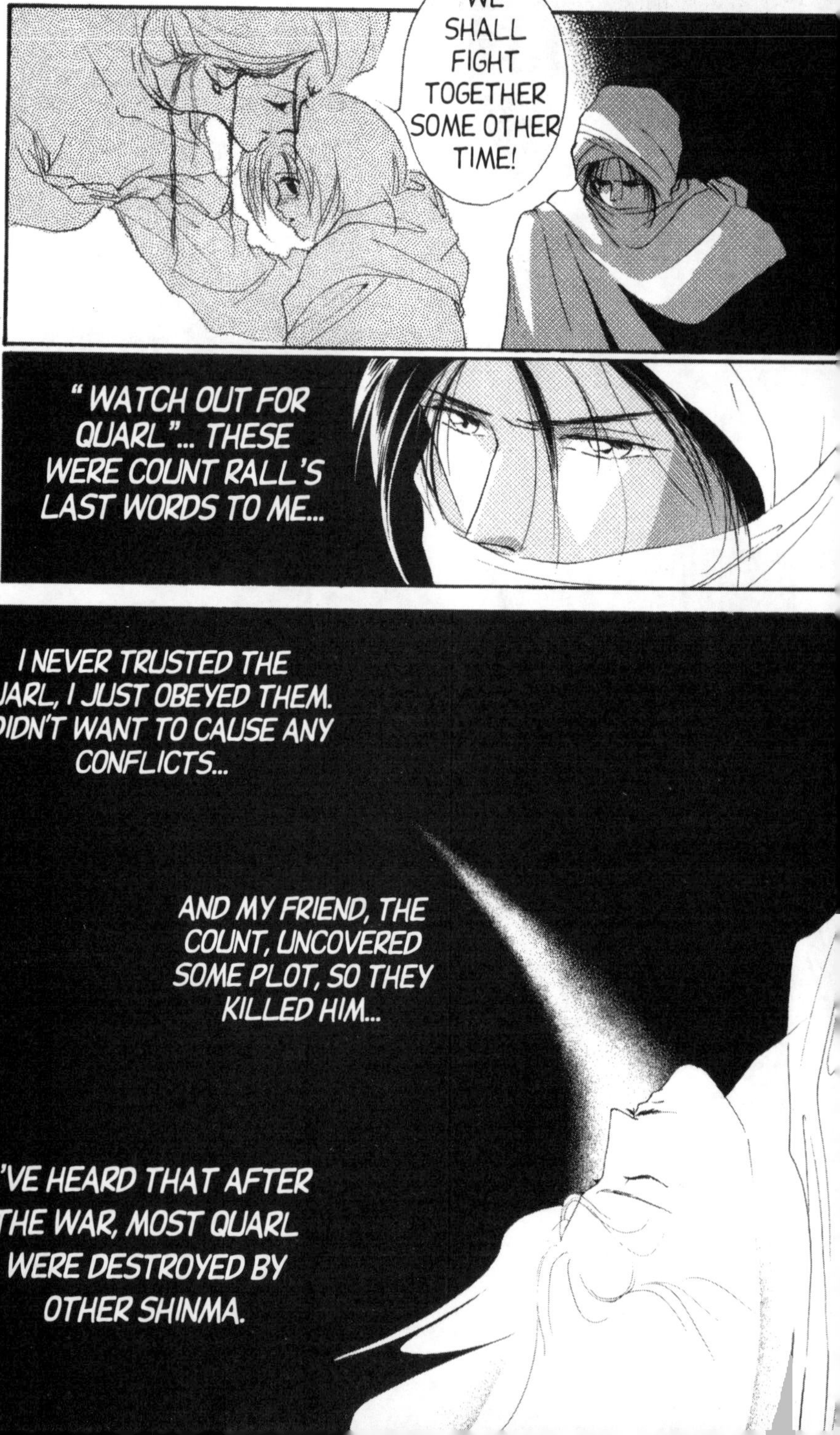
WE SHALL FIGHT TOGETHER SOME OTHER TIME!
"WATCH OUT FOR QUARL"... THESE WERE COUNT RALL'S LAST WORDS TO ME...
I NEVER TRUSTED THE QUARL, I JUST OBEYED THEM. I DIDN'T WANT TO CAUSE ANY CONFLICTS...
AND MY FRIEND, THE COUNT, UNCOVERED SOME PLOT, SO THEY KILLED HIM...
I'VE HEARD THAT AFTER THE WAR, MOST QUARL WERE DESTROYED BY OTHER SHINMA.

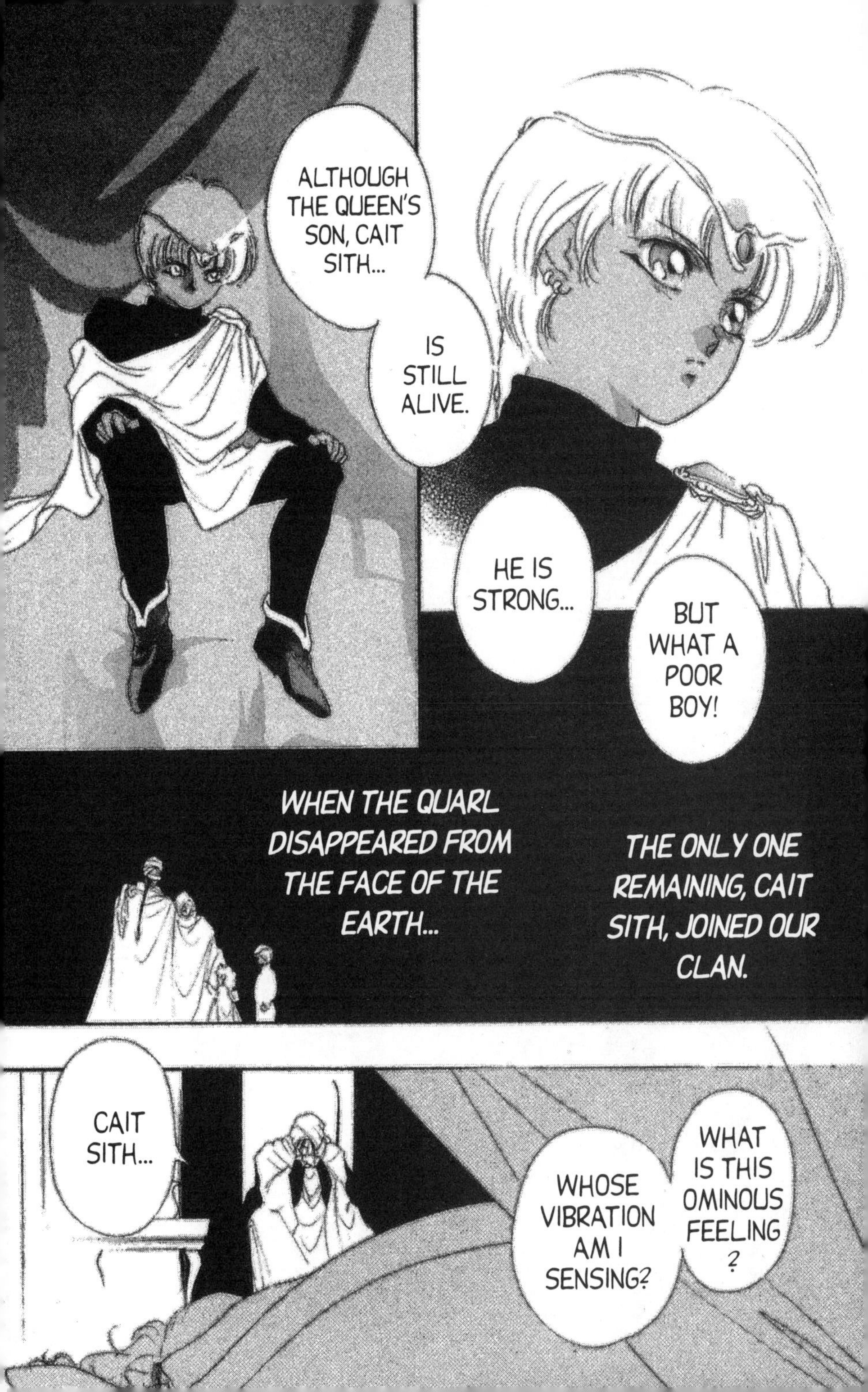

ALTHOUGH THE QUEEN'S SON, CAIT SITH...
IS STILL ALIVE.
HE IS STRONG...
BUT WHAT A POOR BOY!
WHEN THE QUARL DISAPPEARED FROM THE FACE OF THE EARTH...
THE ONLY ONE REMAINING, CAIT SITH, JOINED OUR CLAN.
CAIT SITH...
WHAT IS THIS OMINOUS FEELING?
WHOSE VIBRATION AM I SENSING?

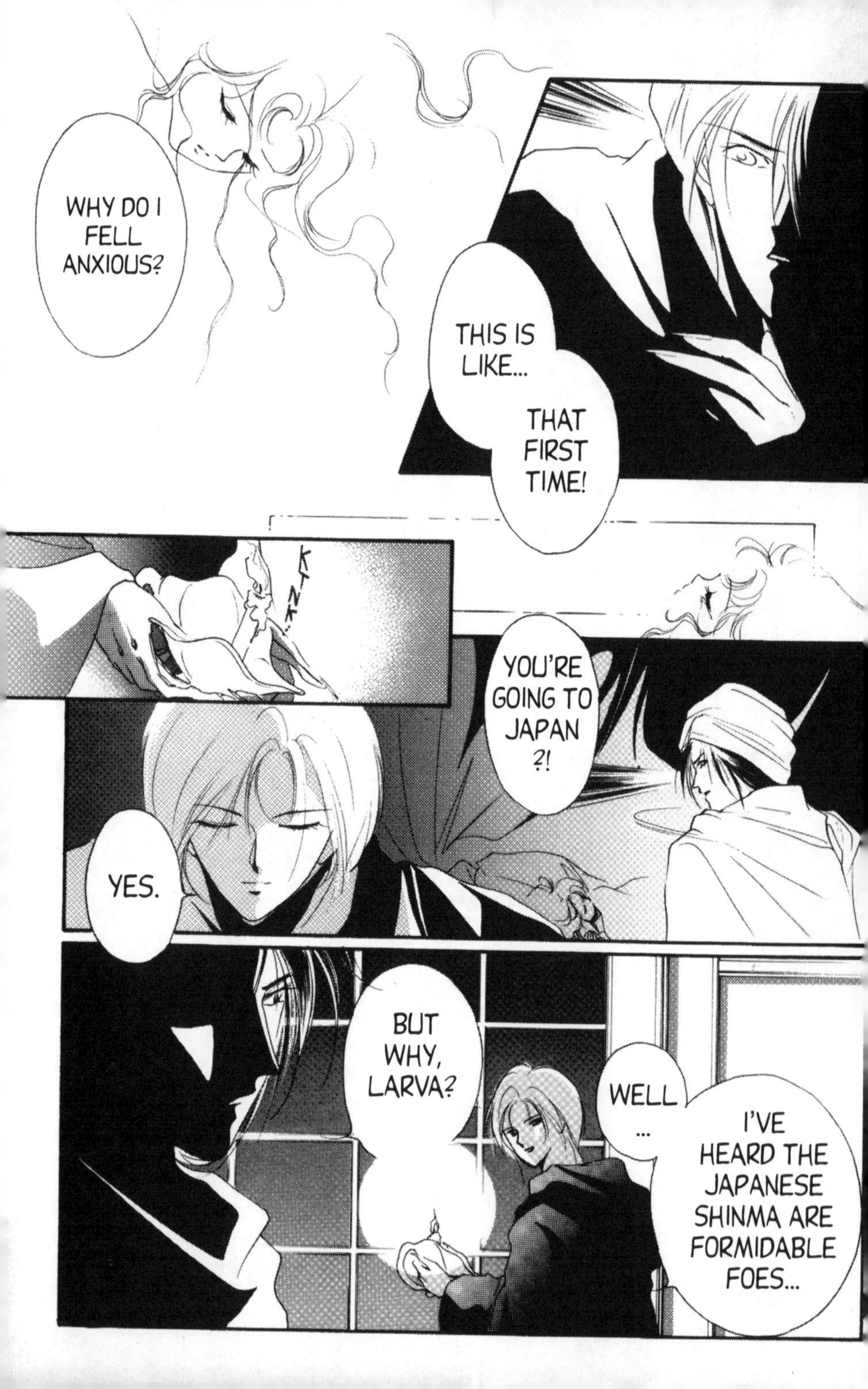
THIS IS LIKE...
THAT FIRST TIME!
WHY DO I FELL ANXIOUS?
YOU'RE GOING TO JAPAN?!
YES.
BUT WHY, LARVA?
WELL...
I'VE HEARD THE JAPANESE SHINMA ARE FORMIDABLE FOES...

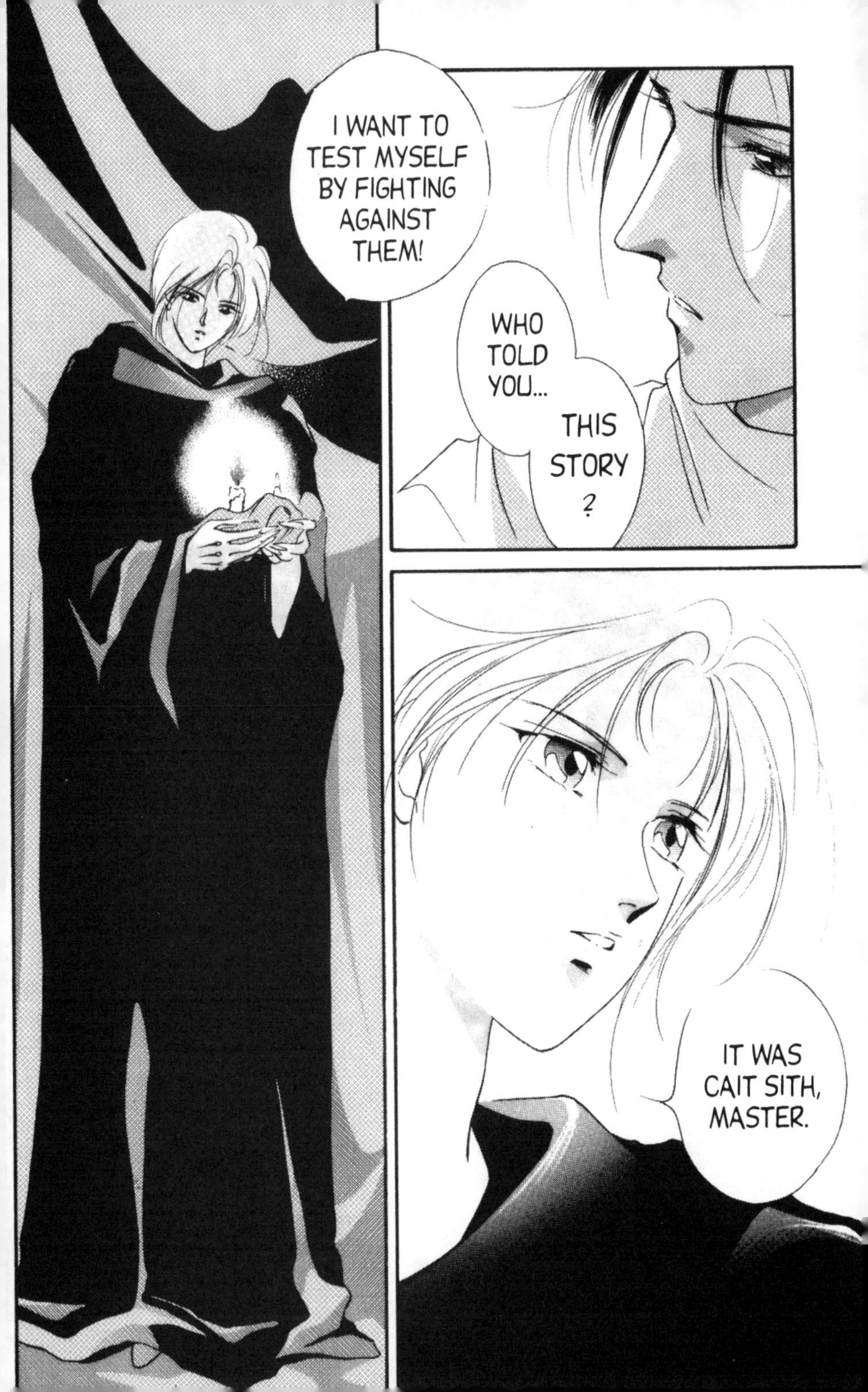
I WANT TO TEST MYSELF BY FIGHTING AGAINST THEM!
WHO TOLD YOU...
THIS STORY ?
IT WAS CAIT SITH, MASTER.

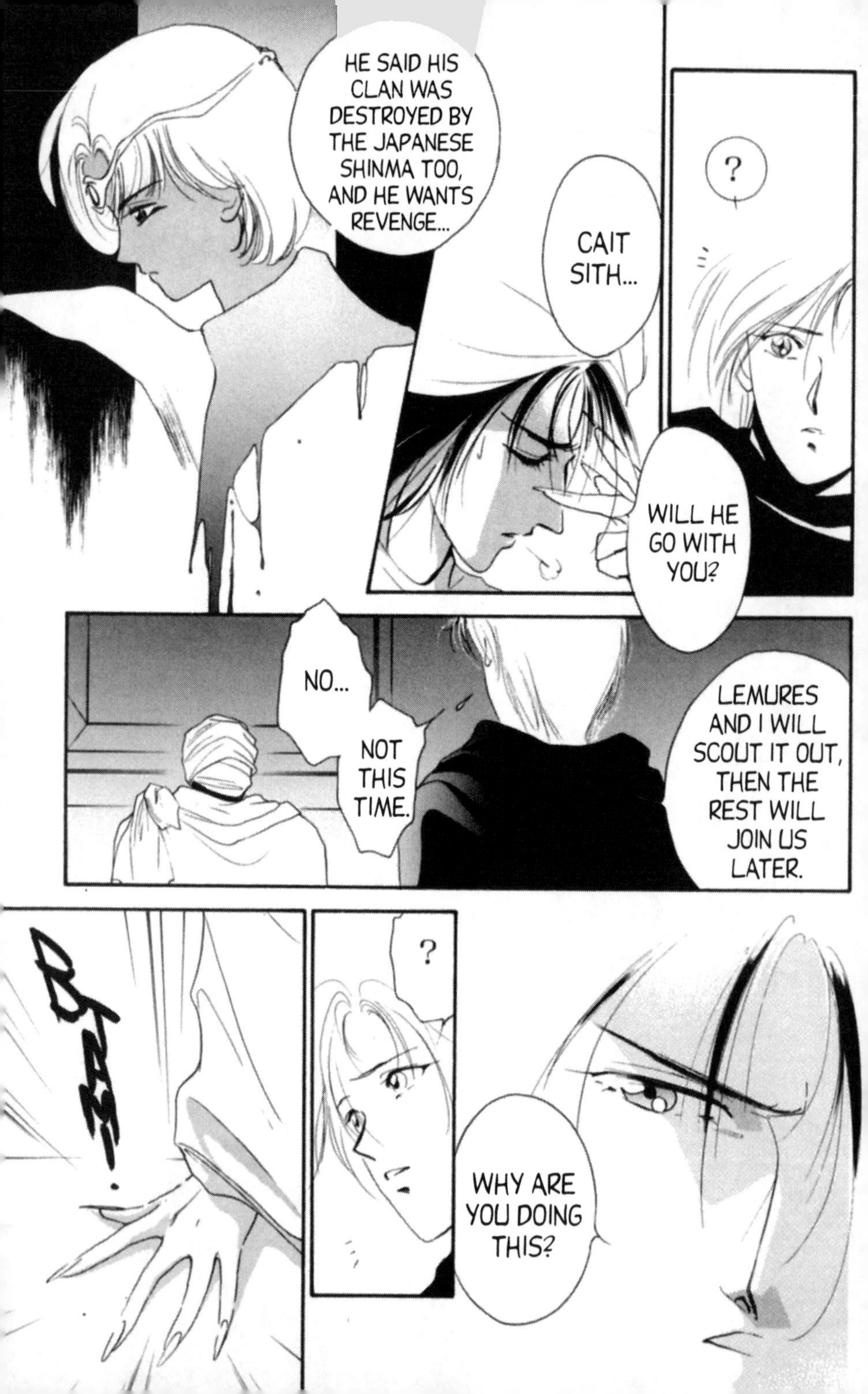
HE SAID HIS CLAN WAS DESTROYED BY THE JAPANESE SHINMA TOO, AND HE WANTS REVENGE...
CAIT SITH...
?
WILL HE GO WITH YOU?
NO...
NOT THIS TIME.
LEMURES AND I WILL SCOUT IT OUT, THEN THE REST WILL JOIN US LATER.
?
WHY ARE YOU DOING THIS?

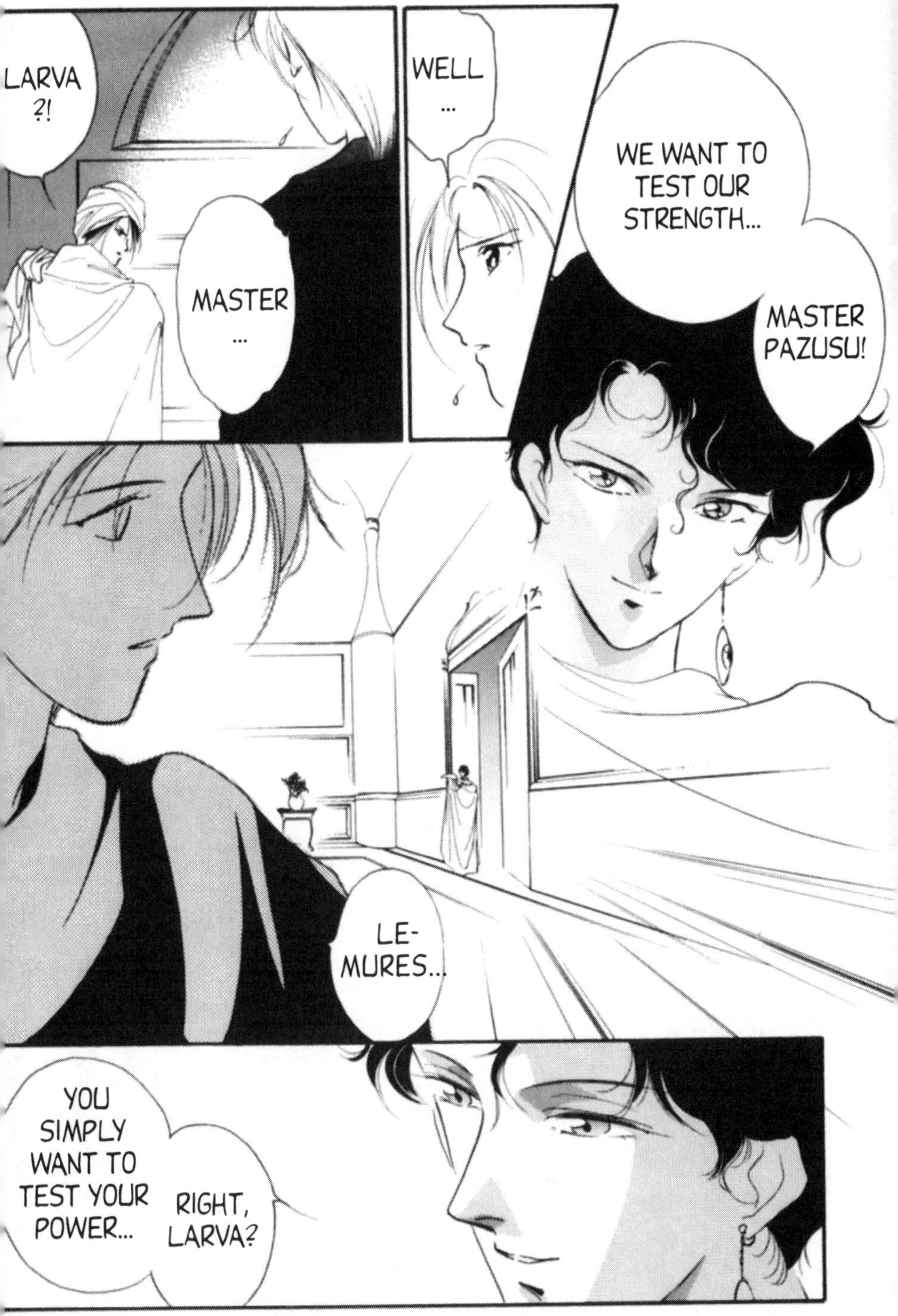
LARVA ?!
MASTER ...
WELL ...
WE WANT TO TEST OUR STRENGTH...
MASTER PAZUSU!
LE-MURES...
YOU SIMPLY WANT TO TEST YOUR POWER...
RIGHT, LARVA?

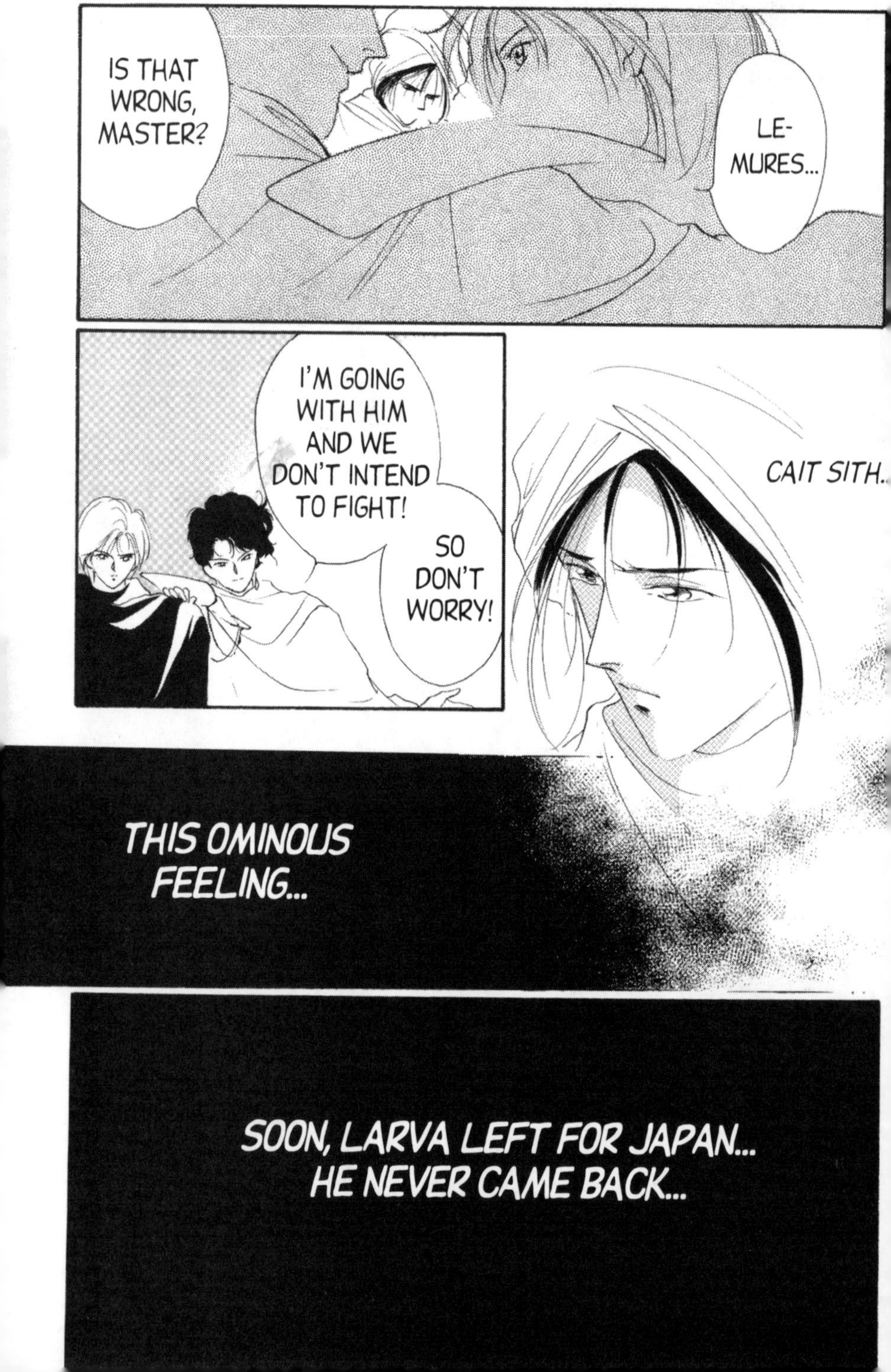
LE-MURES...
IS THAT WRONG, MASTER?
CAIT SITH...
I'M GOING WITH HIM AND WE DON'T INTEND TO FIGHT!
SO DON'T WORRY!
THIS OMINOUS FEELING...
SOON, LARVA LEFT FOR JAPAN... HE NEVER CAME BACK...

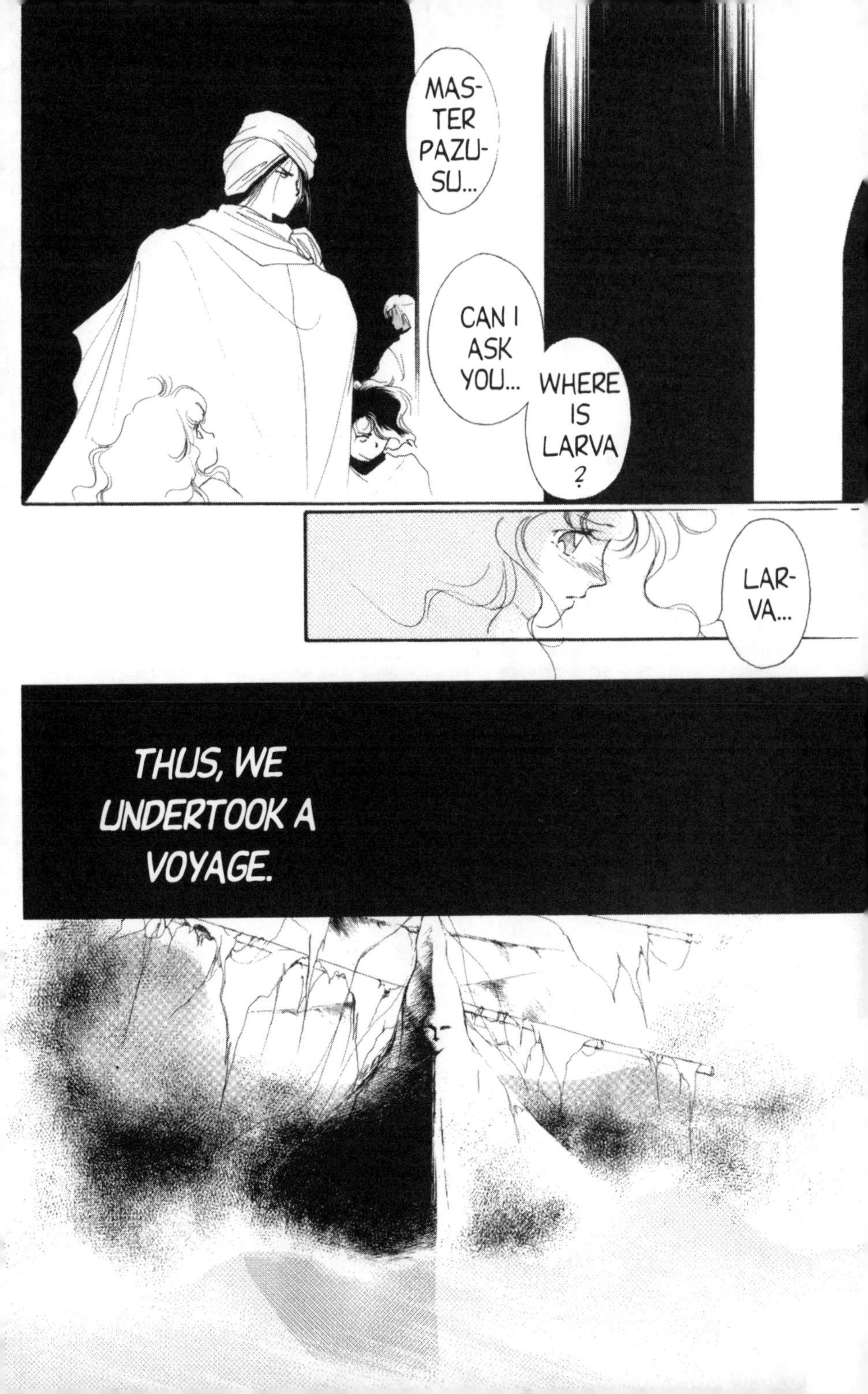
MAS-TER PAZU-SU...
CAN I ASK YOU...
WHERE IS LARVA?
LAR-VA...
THUS, WE UNDERTOOK A VOYAGE.

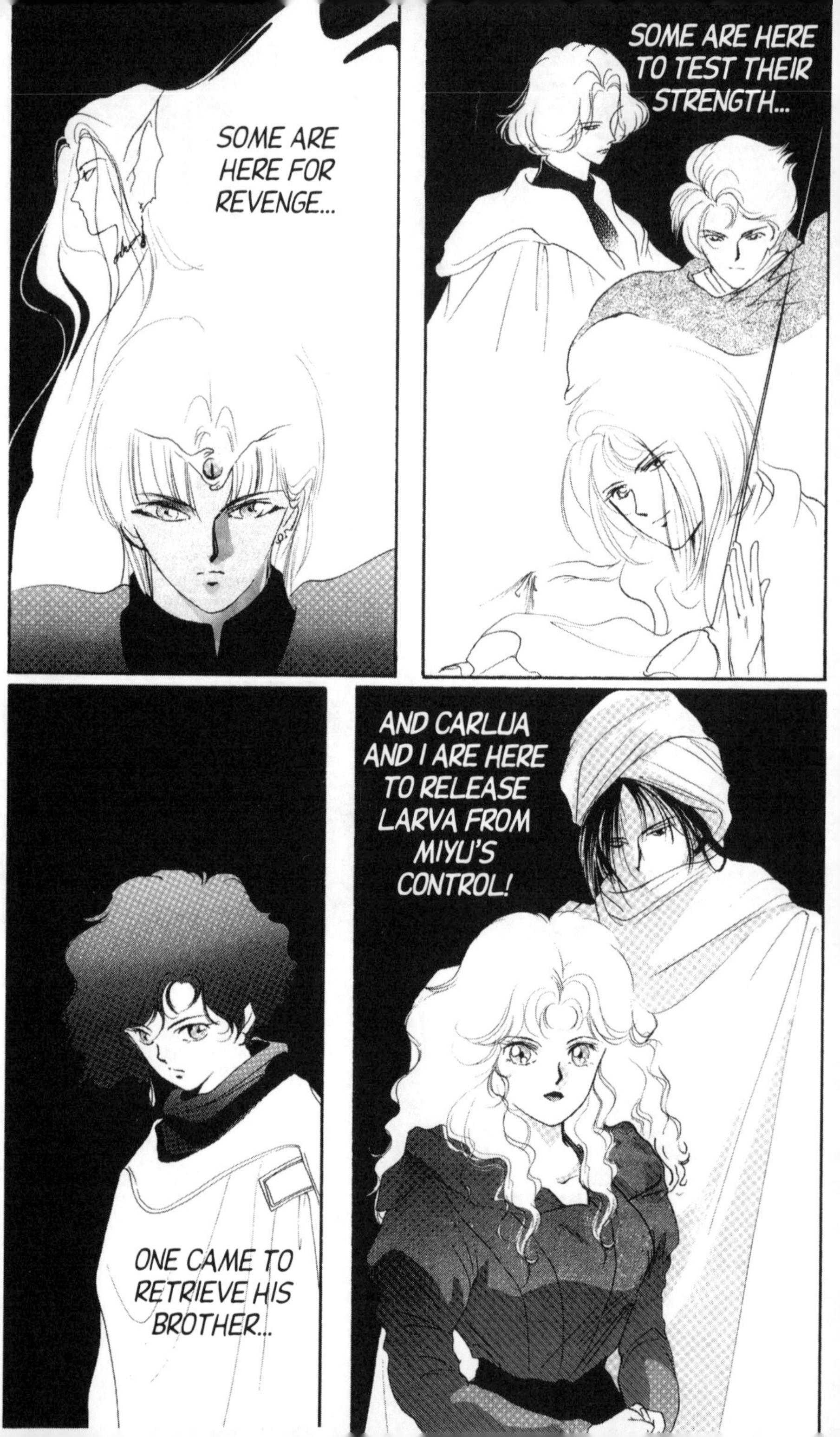
SOME ARE HERE TO TEST THEIR STRENGTH...
SOME ARE HERE FOR REVENGE...
AND CARLUA AND I ARE HERE TO RELEASE LARVA FROM MIYU'S CONTROL!
ONE CAME TO RETRIEVE HIS BROTHER...

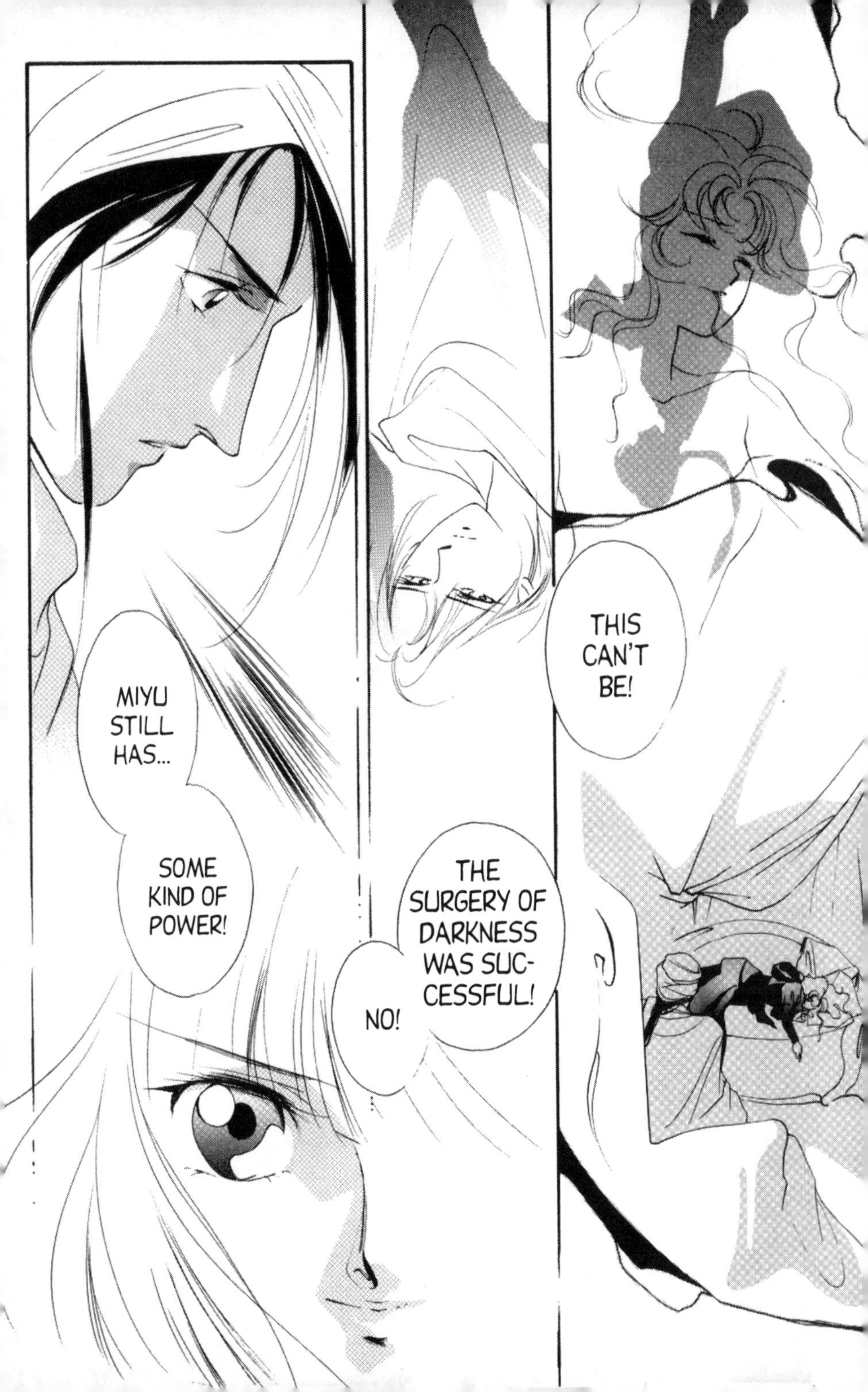
THIS CAN'T BE!
THE SURGERY OF DARKNESS WAS SUC-CESSFUL!
NO!
MIYU STILL HAS...
SOME KIND OF POWER!

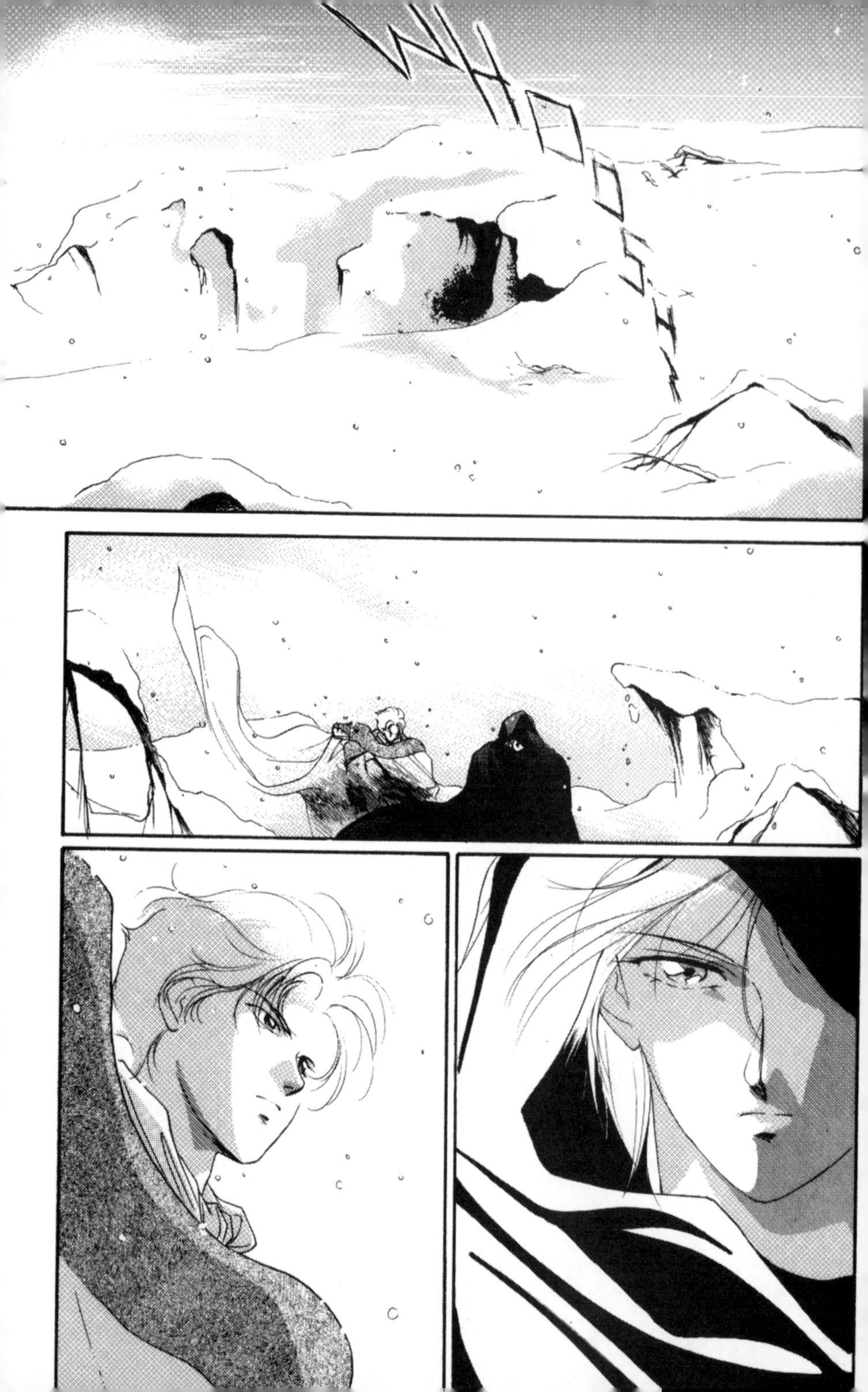
WHOOSH

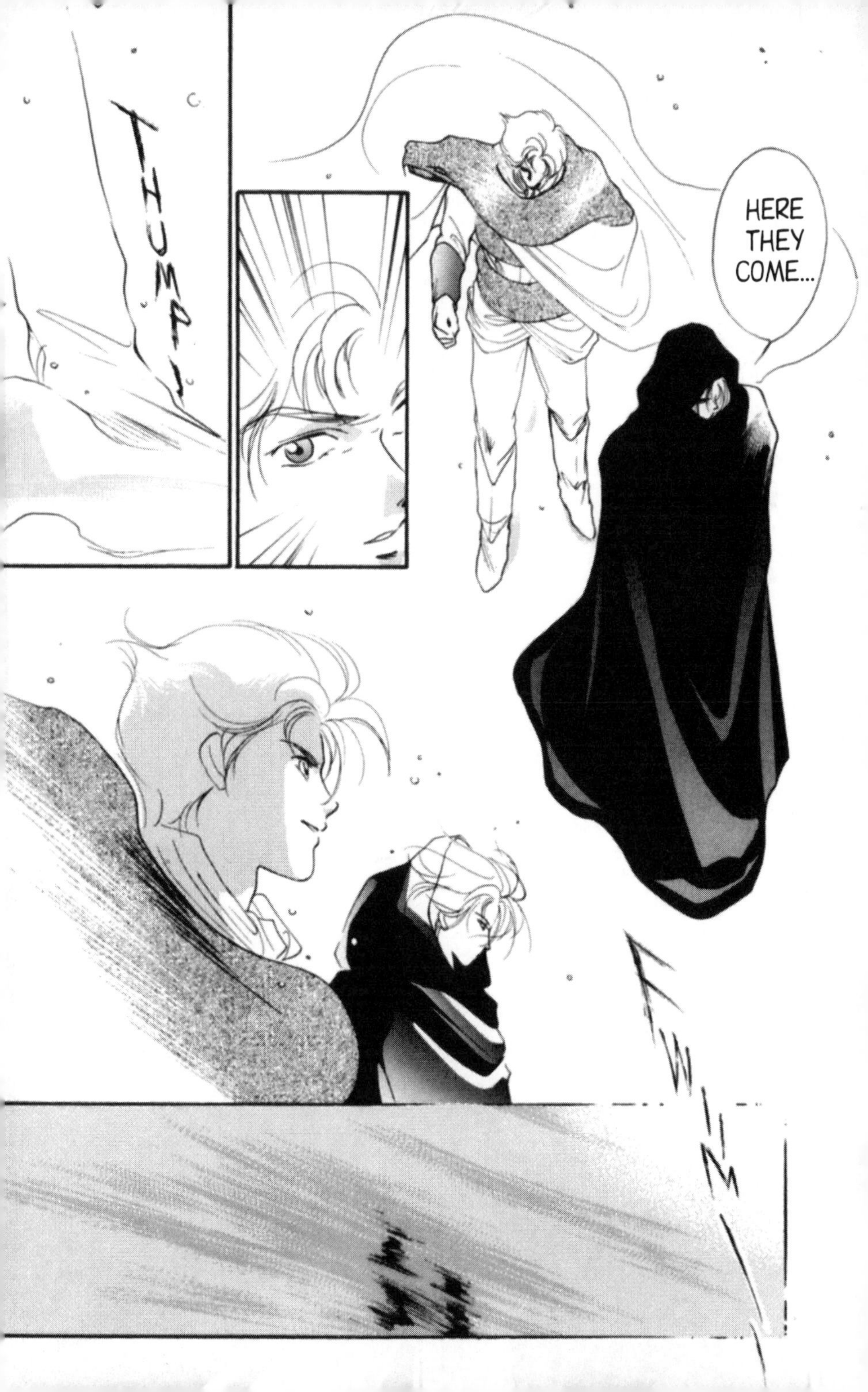
THUMP
HERE THEY COME...

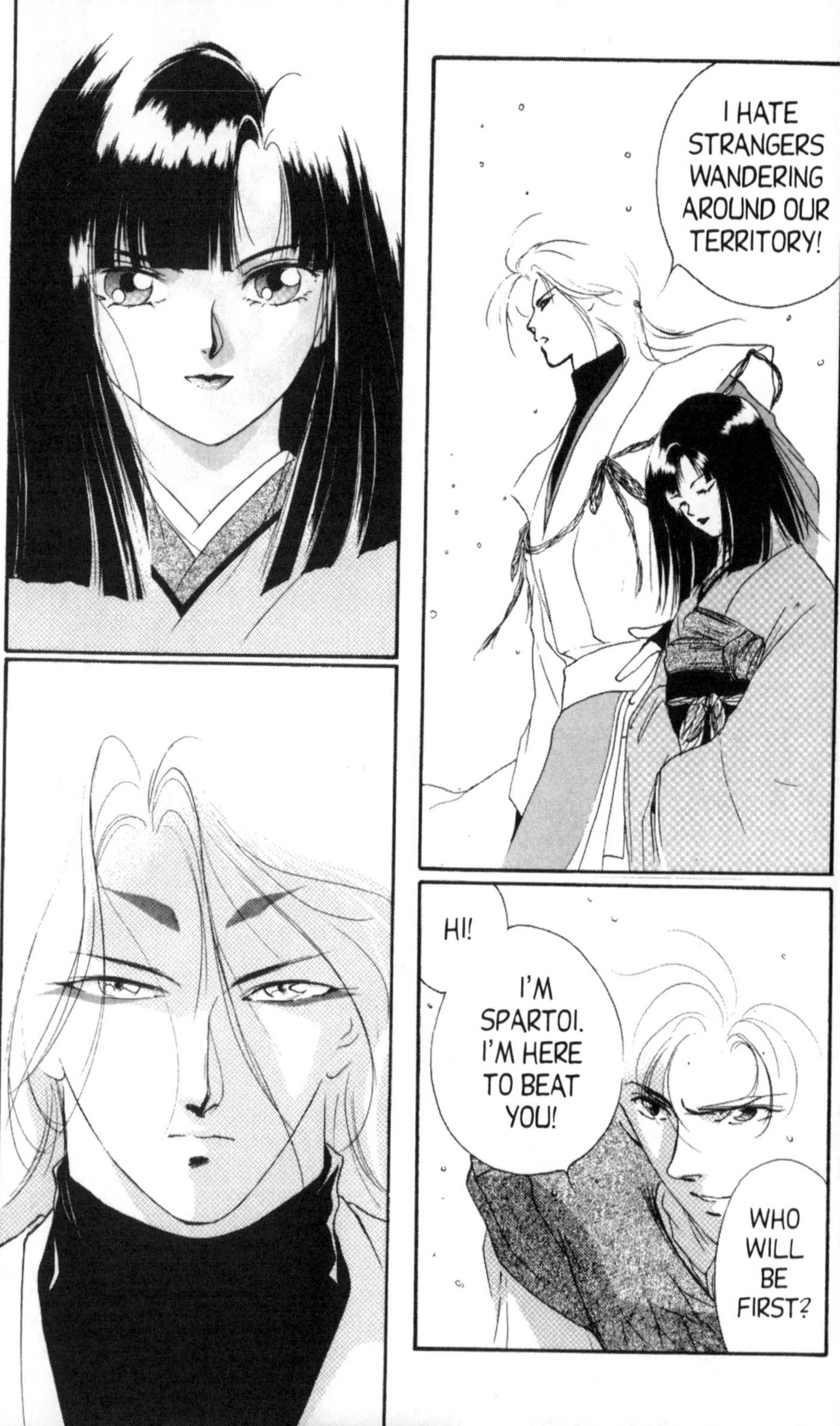
I HATE STRANGERS WANDERING AROUND OUR TERRITORY!
HI!
I'M SPARTOI. I'M HERE TO BEAT YOU!
WHO WILL BE FIRST?

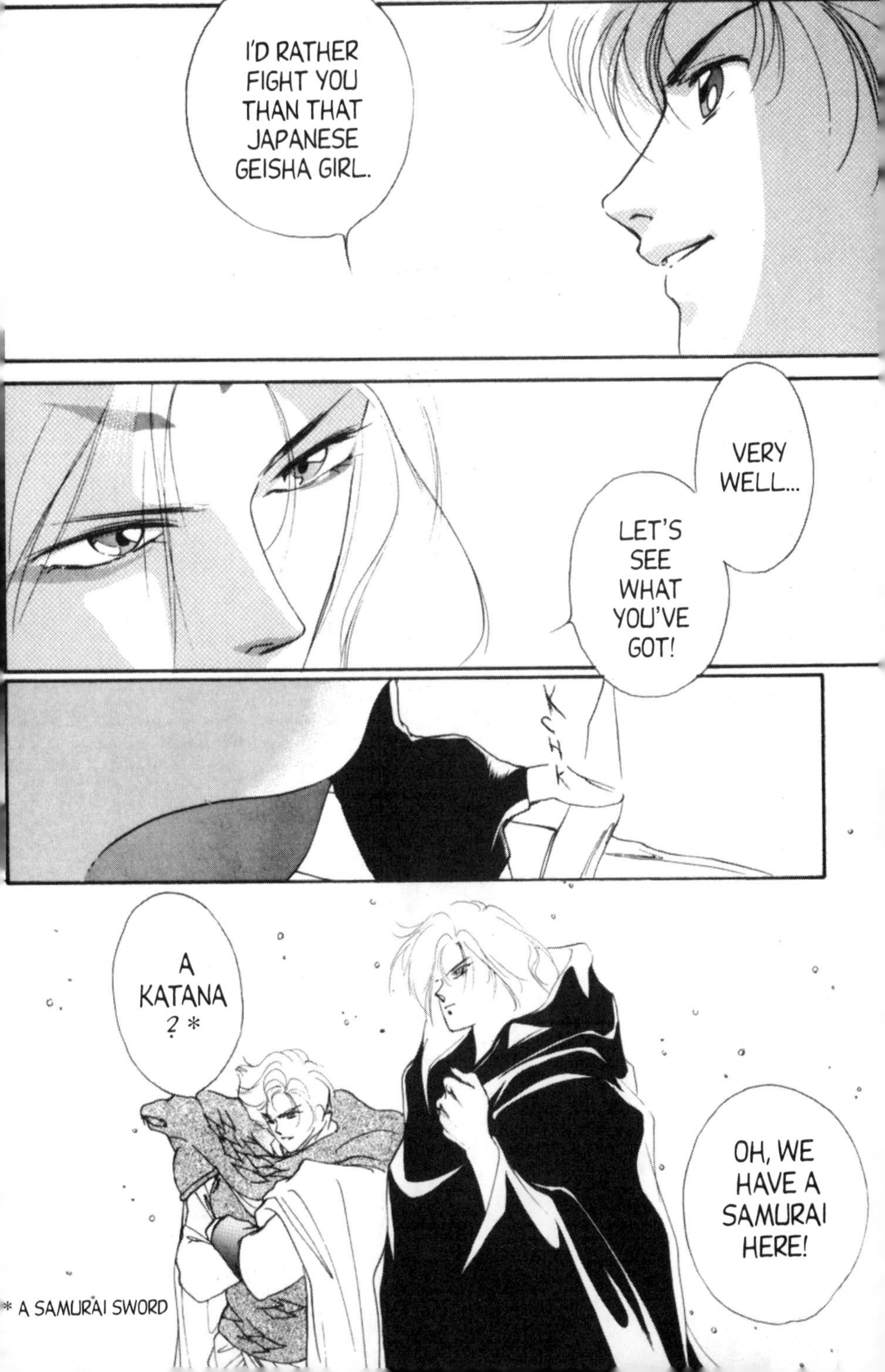
I'D RATHER FIGHT YOU THAN THAT JAPANESE GEISHA GIRL.
VERY WELL...
LET'S SEE WHAT YOU'VE GOT!
A KATANA?*
OH, WE HAVE A SAMURAI HERE!
* A SAMURAI SWORD

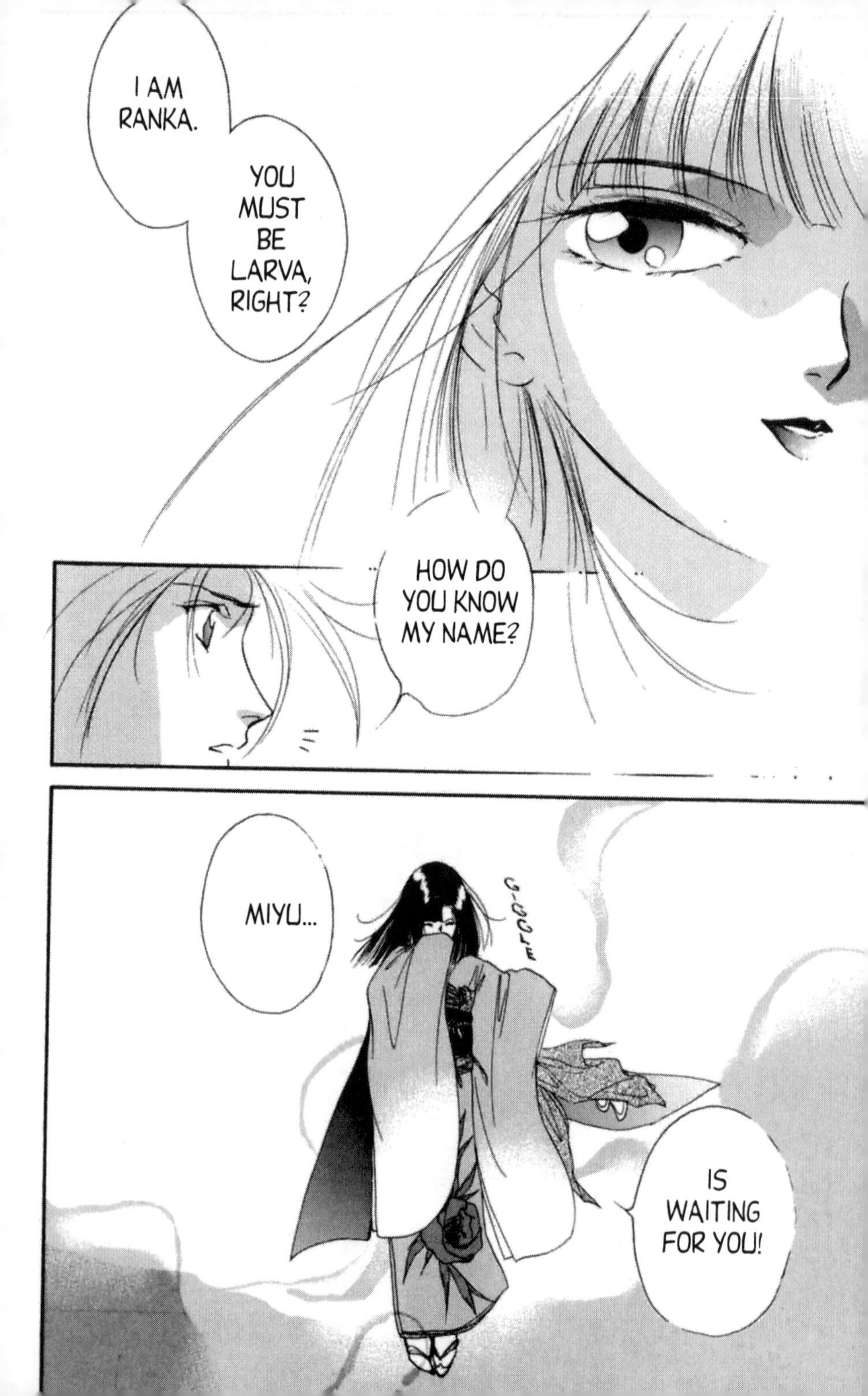
I AM RANKA.
YOU MUST BE LARVA, RIGHT?
HOW DO YOU KNOW MY NAME?
MIYU...
IS WAITING FOR YOU!

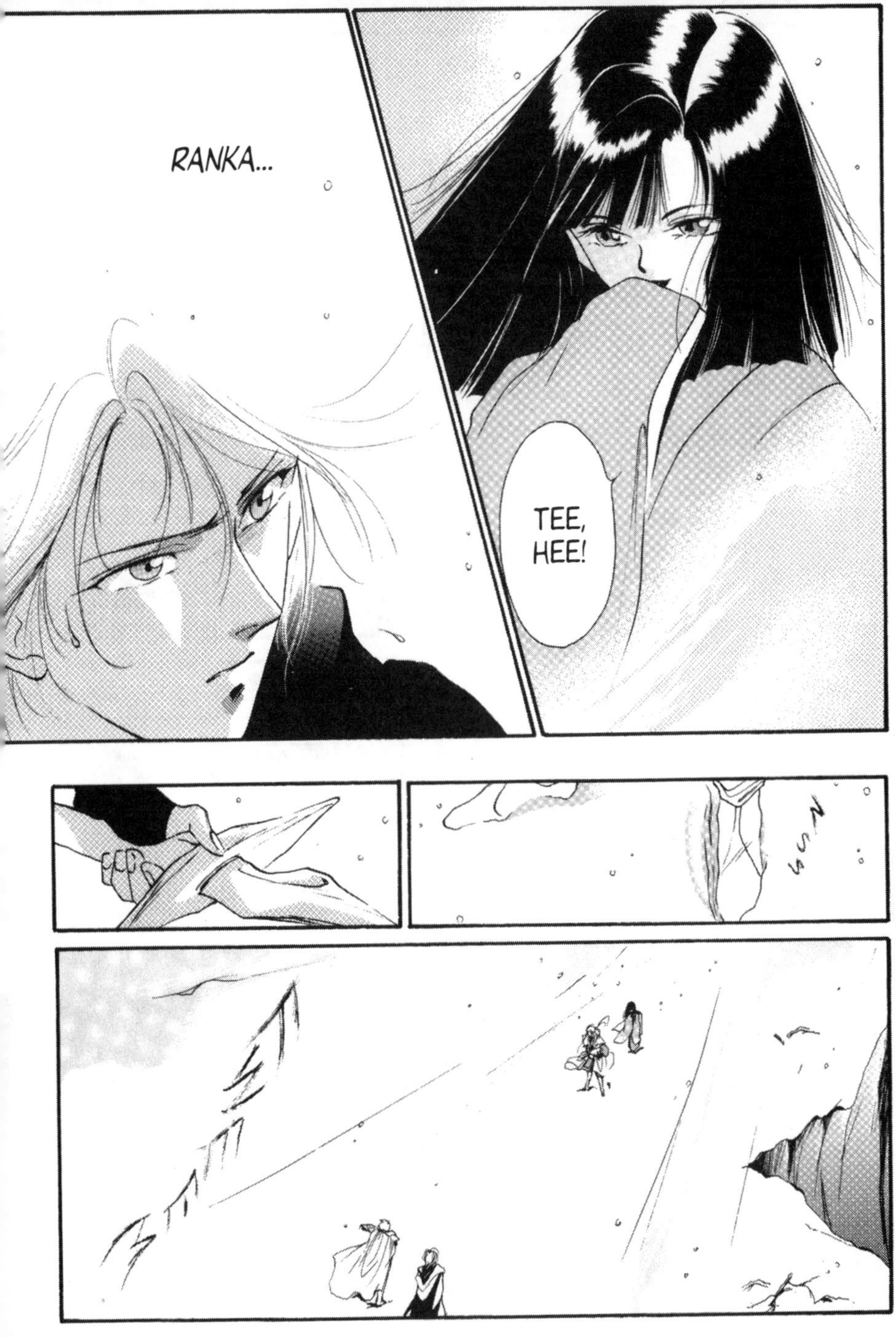
TEE, HEE!
RANKA...

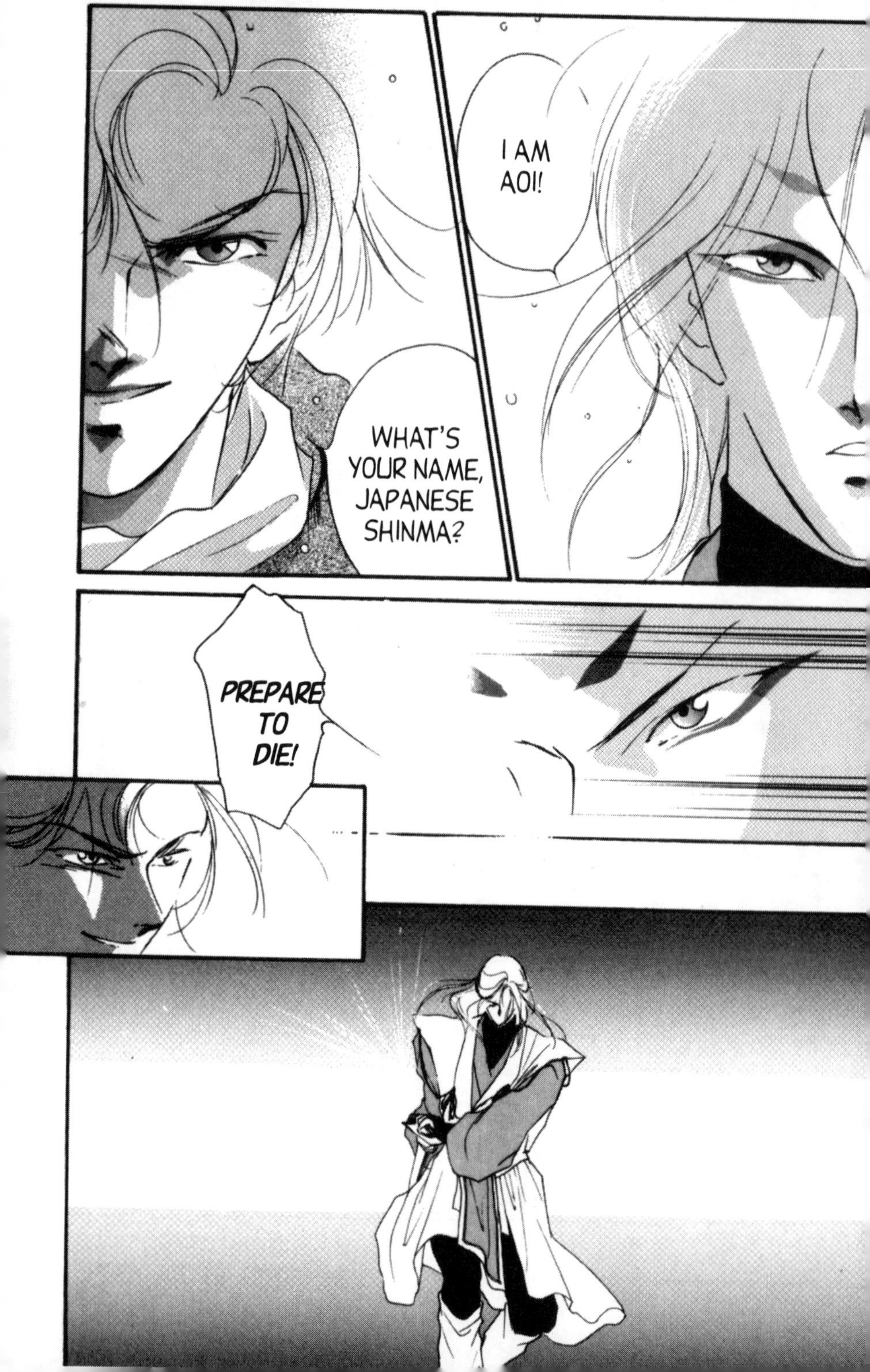
I AM AOI!
WHAT'S YOUR NAME, JAPANESE SHINMA?
PREPARE TO DIE!

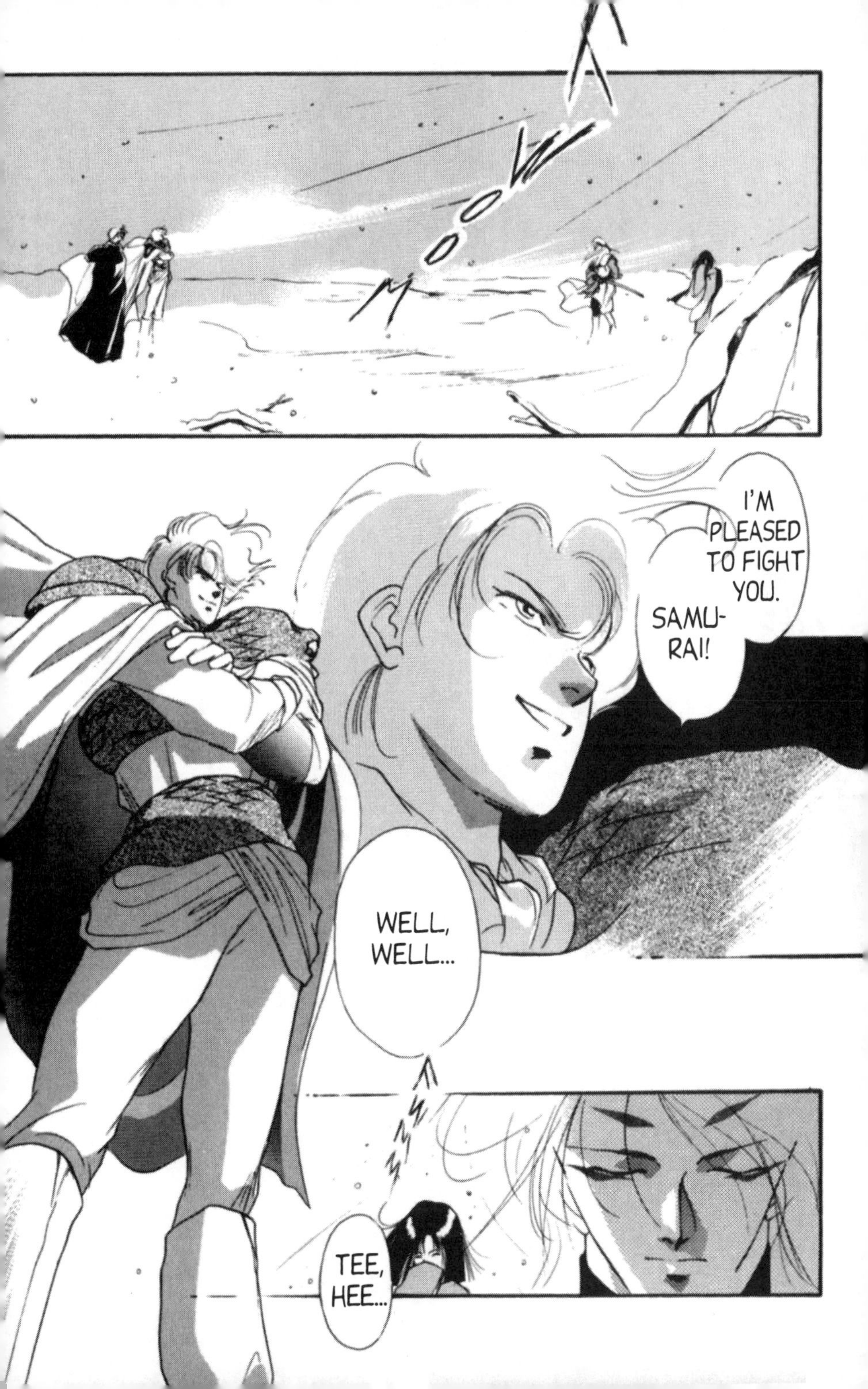

I'M PLEASED TO FIGHT YOU.
SAMU-RAI!
WELL, WELL...
TEE, HEE...

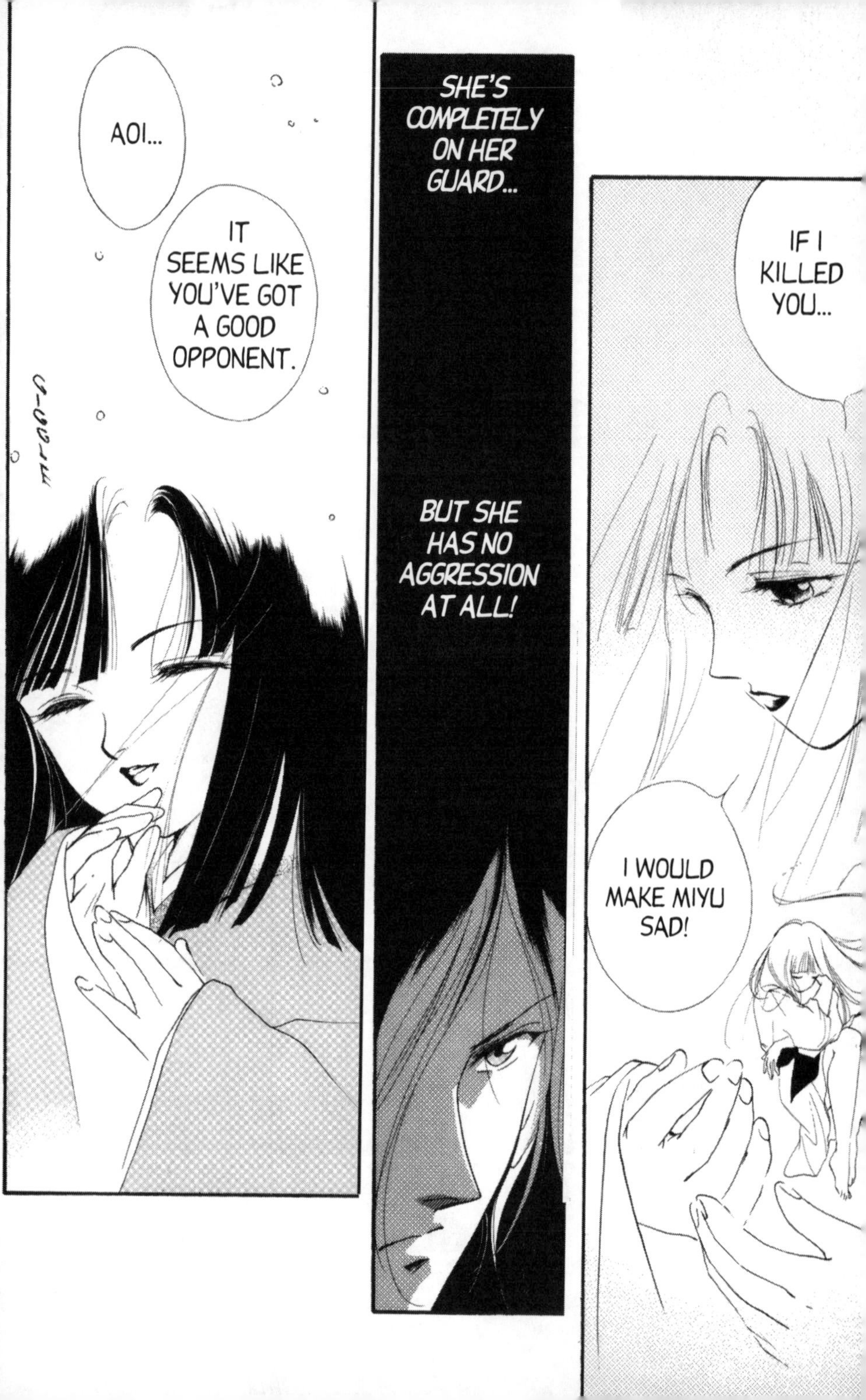
IF I KILLED YOU...
I WOULD MAKE MIYU SAD!
SHE'S COMPLETELY ON HER GUARD...
BUT SHE HAS NO AGGRESSION AT ALL!
AOI...
IT SEEMS LIKE YOU'VE GOT A GOOD OPPONENT.

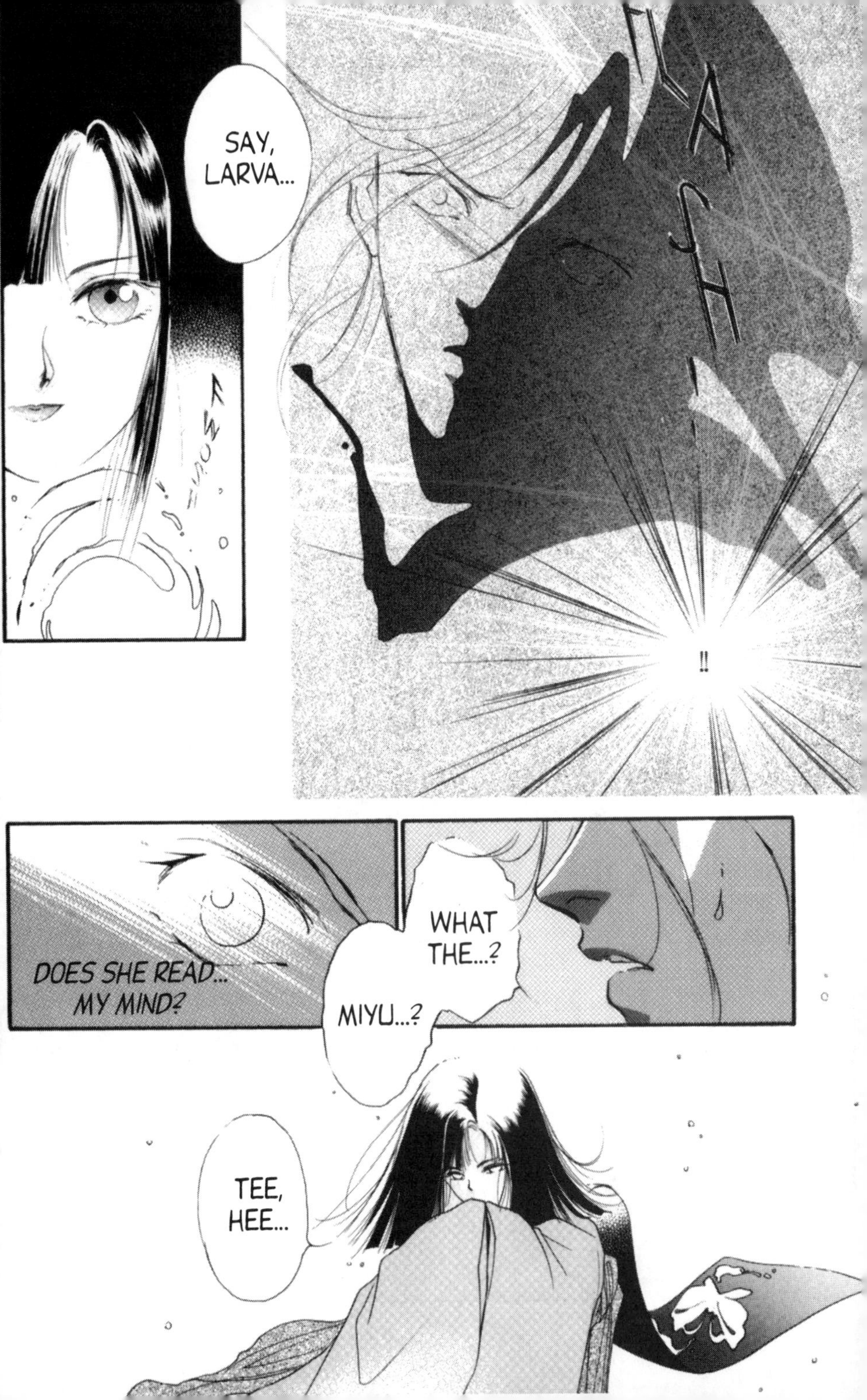
FLASH
SAY, LARVA...
FWOOSH!!
!!
WHAT THE...?
MIYU...?
DOES SHE READ... MY MIND?
TEE, HEE...

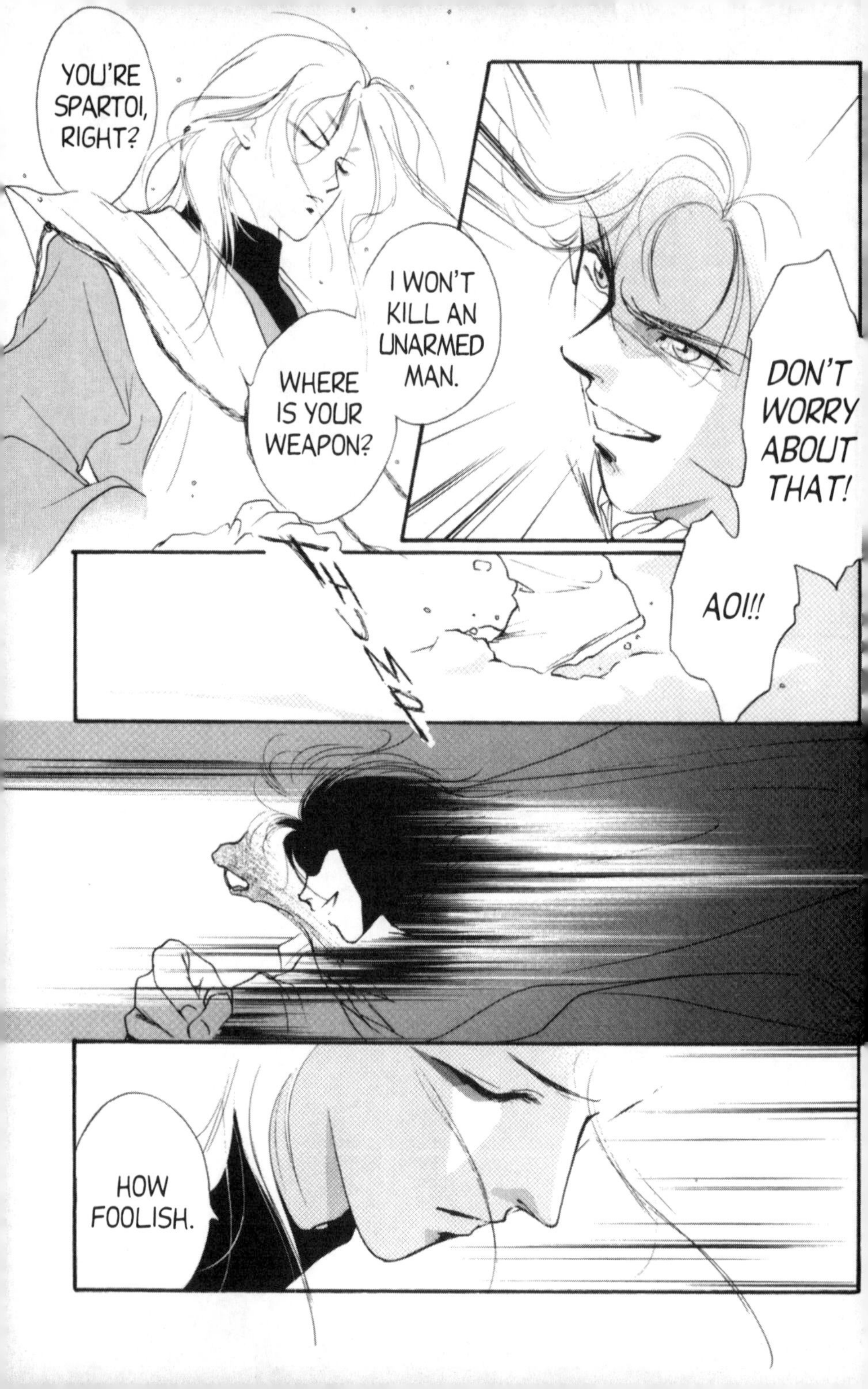
YOU'RE SPARTOI, RIGHT?
I WON'T KILL AN UNARMED MAN.
WHERE IS YOUR WEAPON?
DON'T WORRY ABOUT THAT!
AOI!!
HOW FOOLISH.

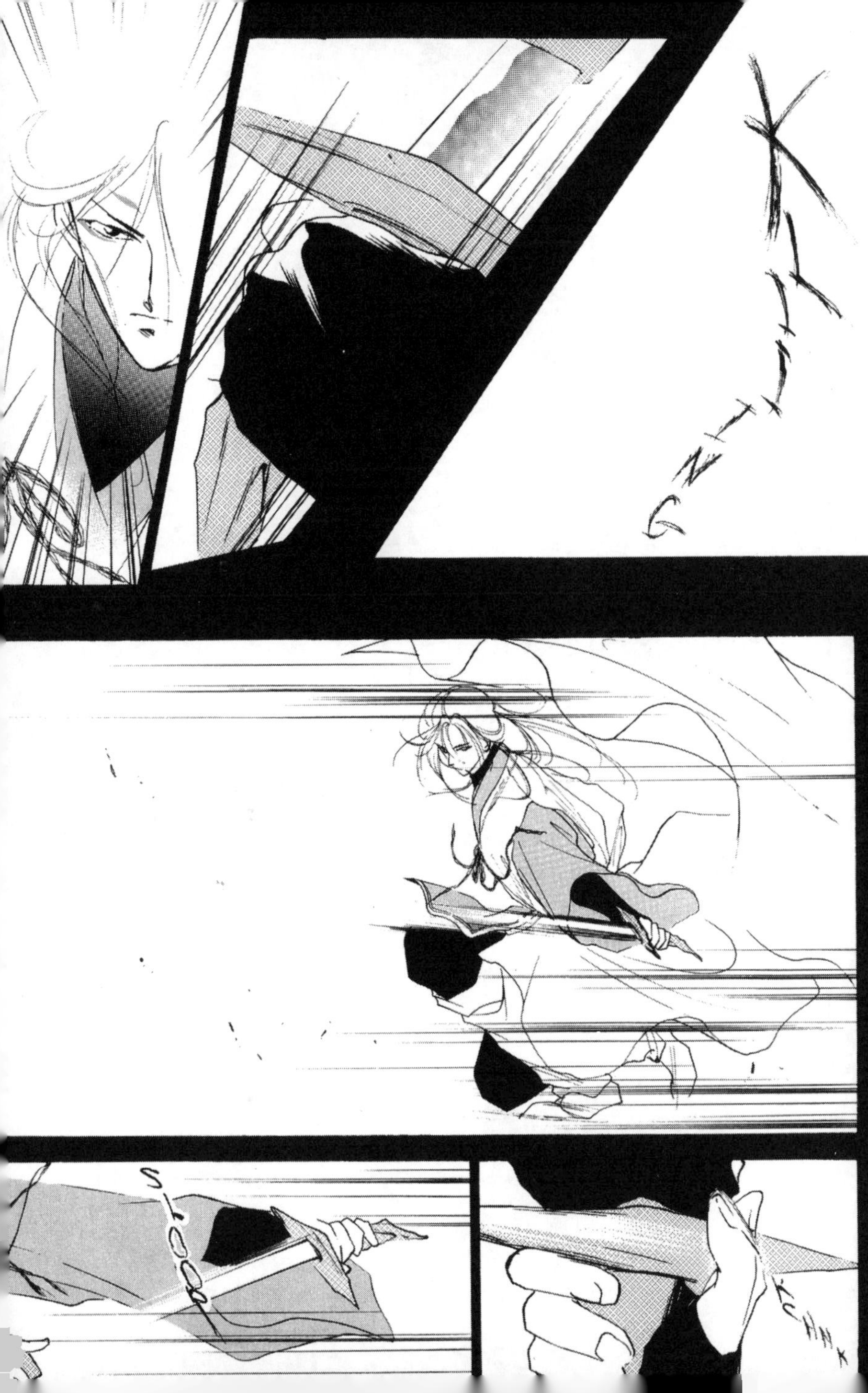
KIIIING
SHOOP
KCHNK

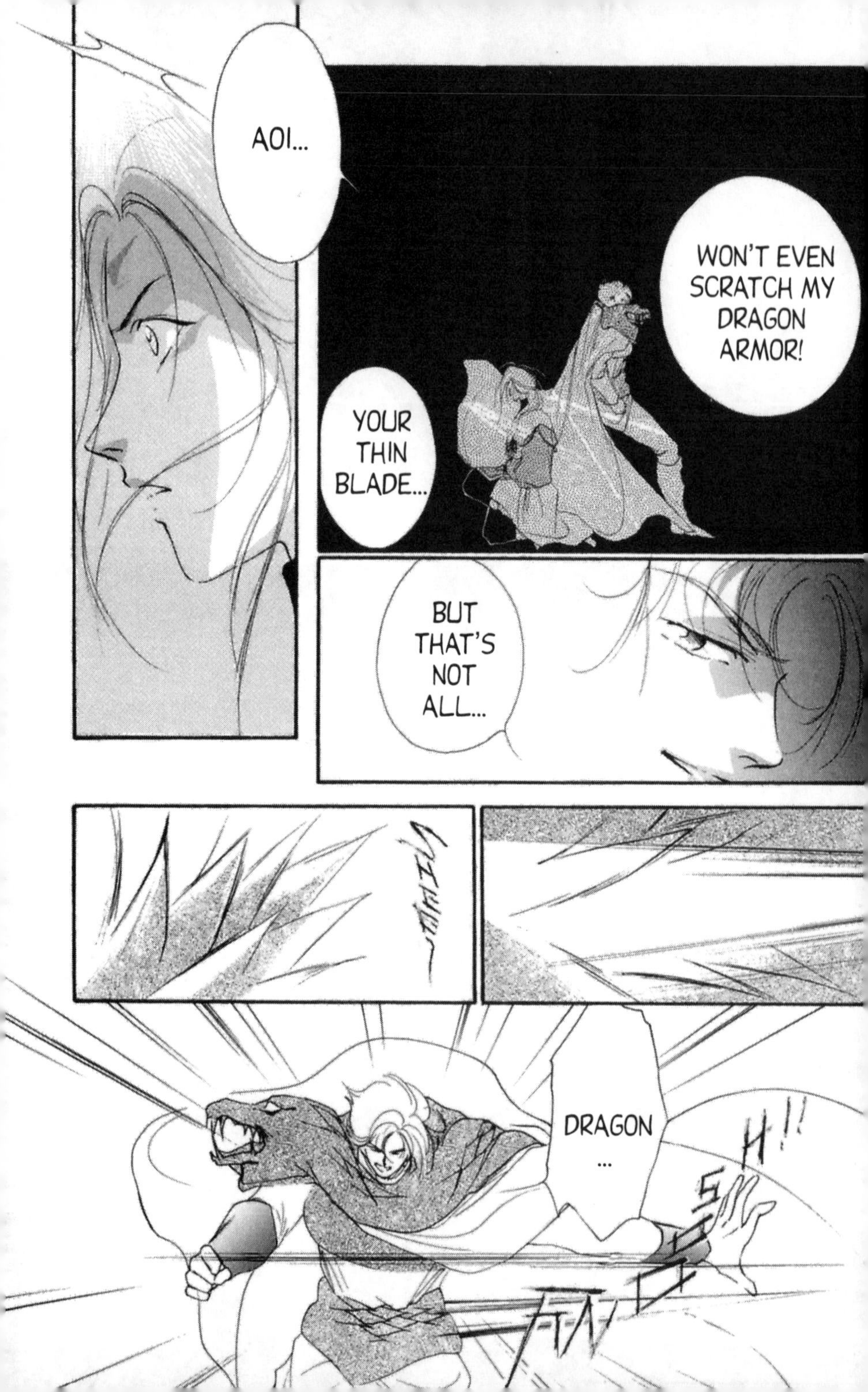
YOUR THIN BLADE...
WON'T EVEN SCRATCH MY DRAGON ARMOR!
BUT THAT'S NOT ALL...
AOI...
DRAGON ...
FWIIISH!!

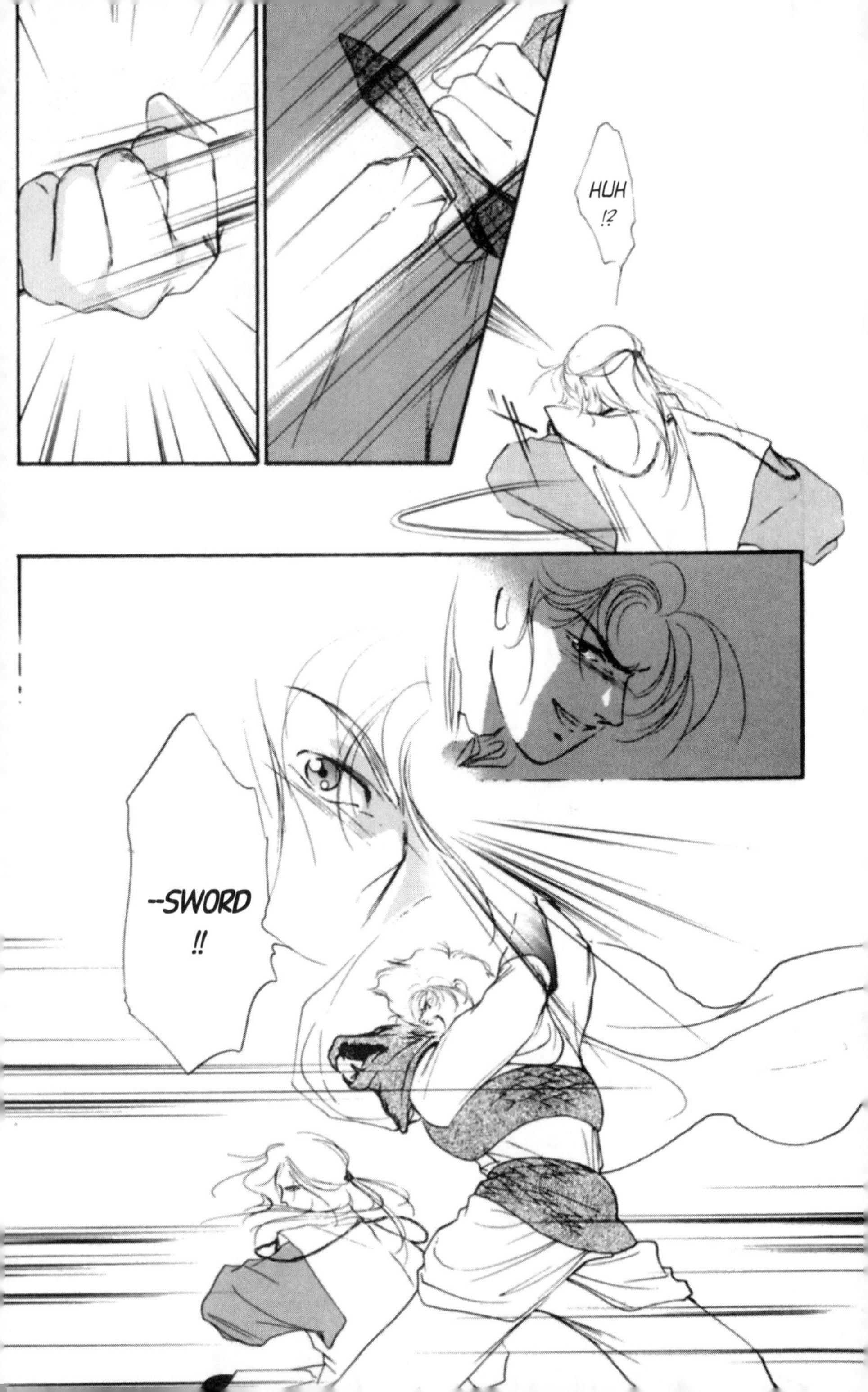
HUH !?
--SWORD !!

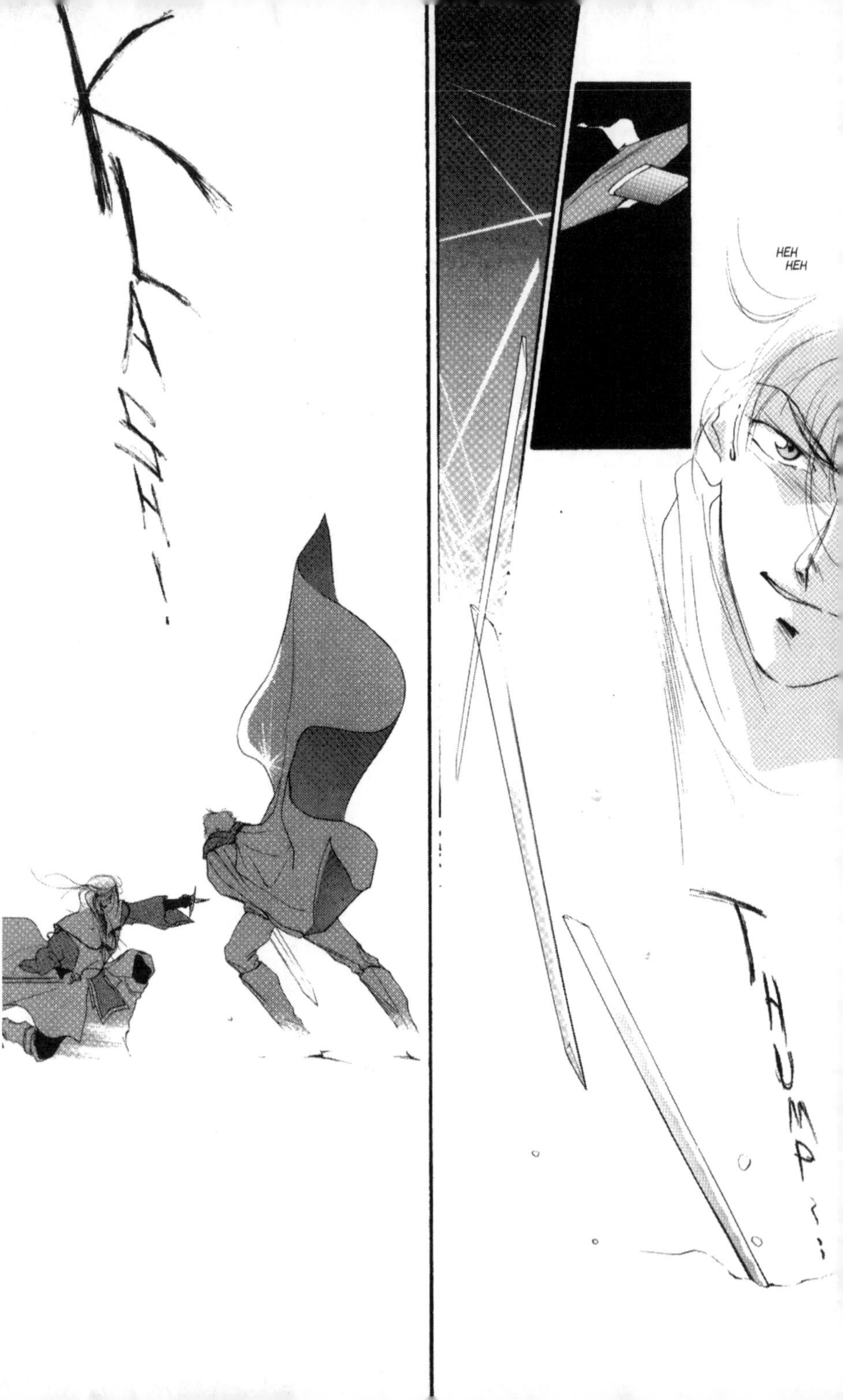
HEH HEH
THUMP...
KLANG!

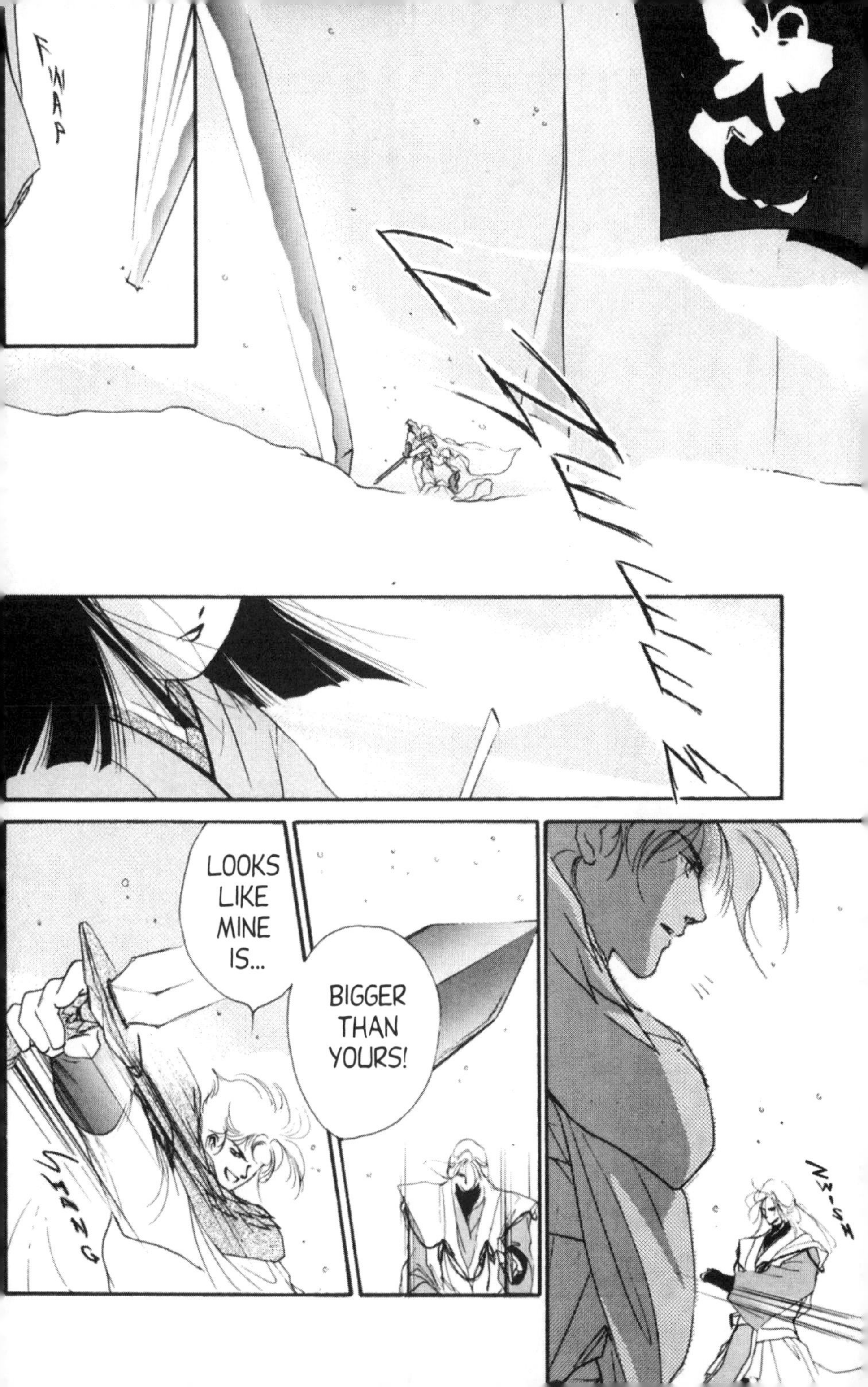
LOOKS LIKE MINE IS...
BIGGER THAN YOURS!

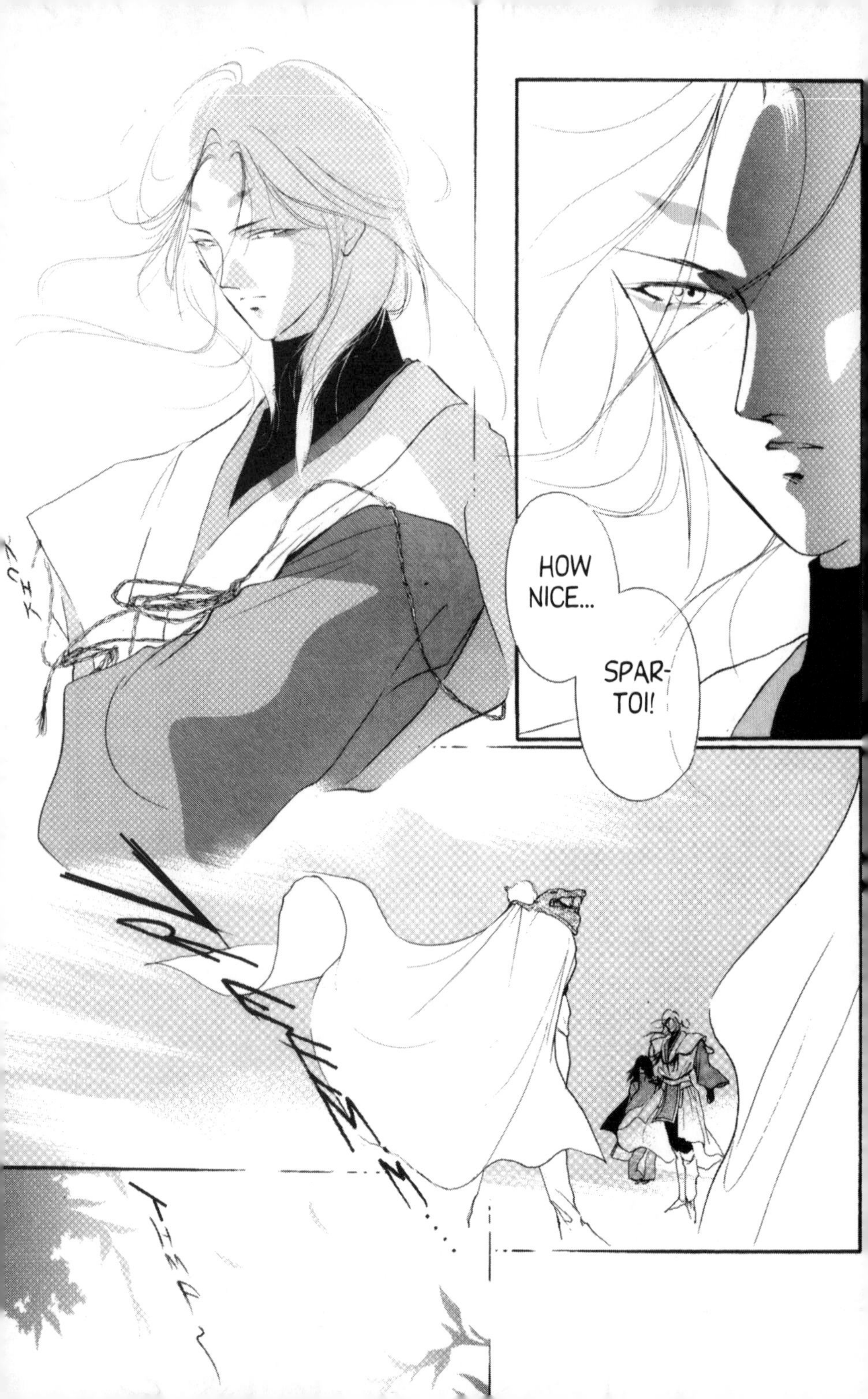
HOW NICE...
SPAR-TOI!

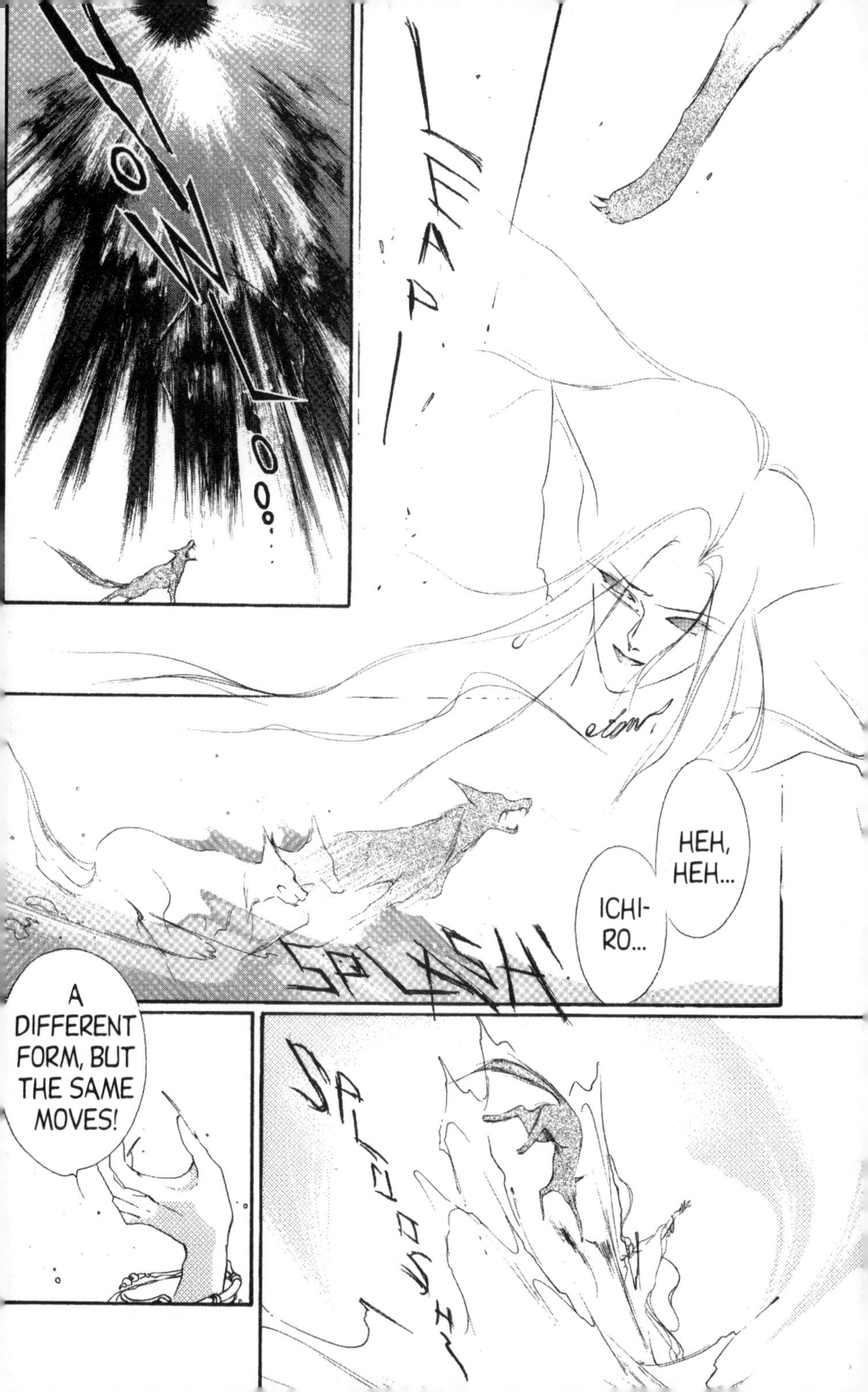
LEAP
HOWLOOOO...
HEH, HEH...
ICHI-RO...
SPLASH!
SPLOOSH
A DIFFERENT FORM, BUT THE SAME MOVES!

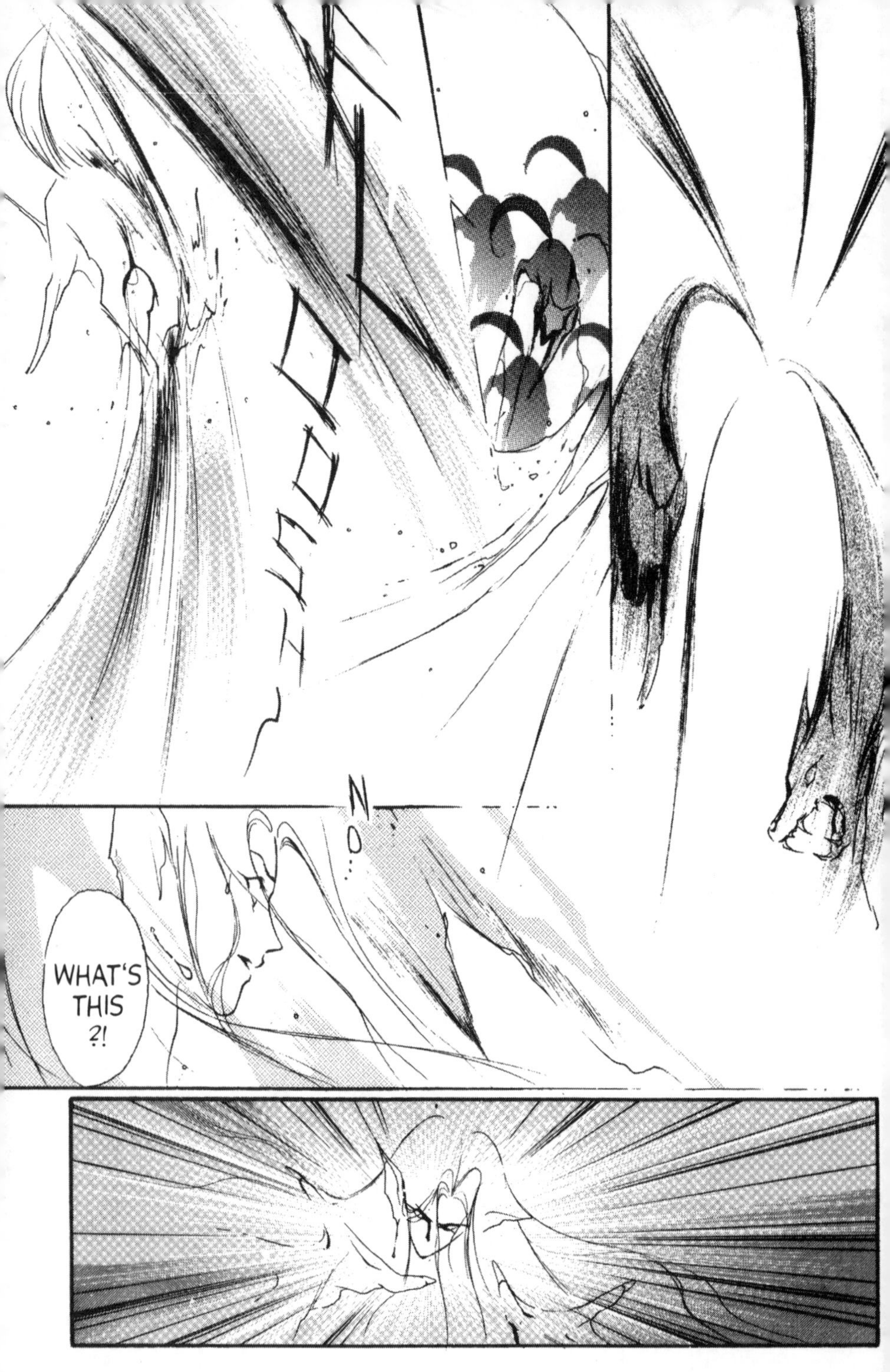
NO...
WHAT'S THIS ?!

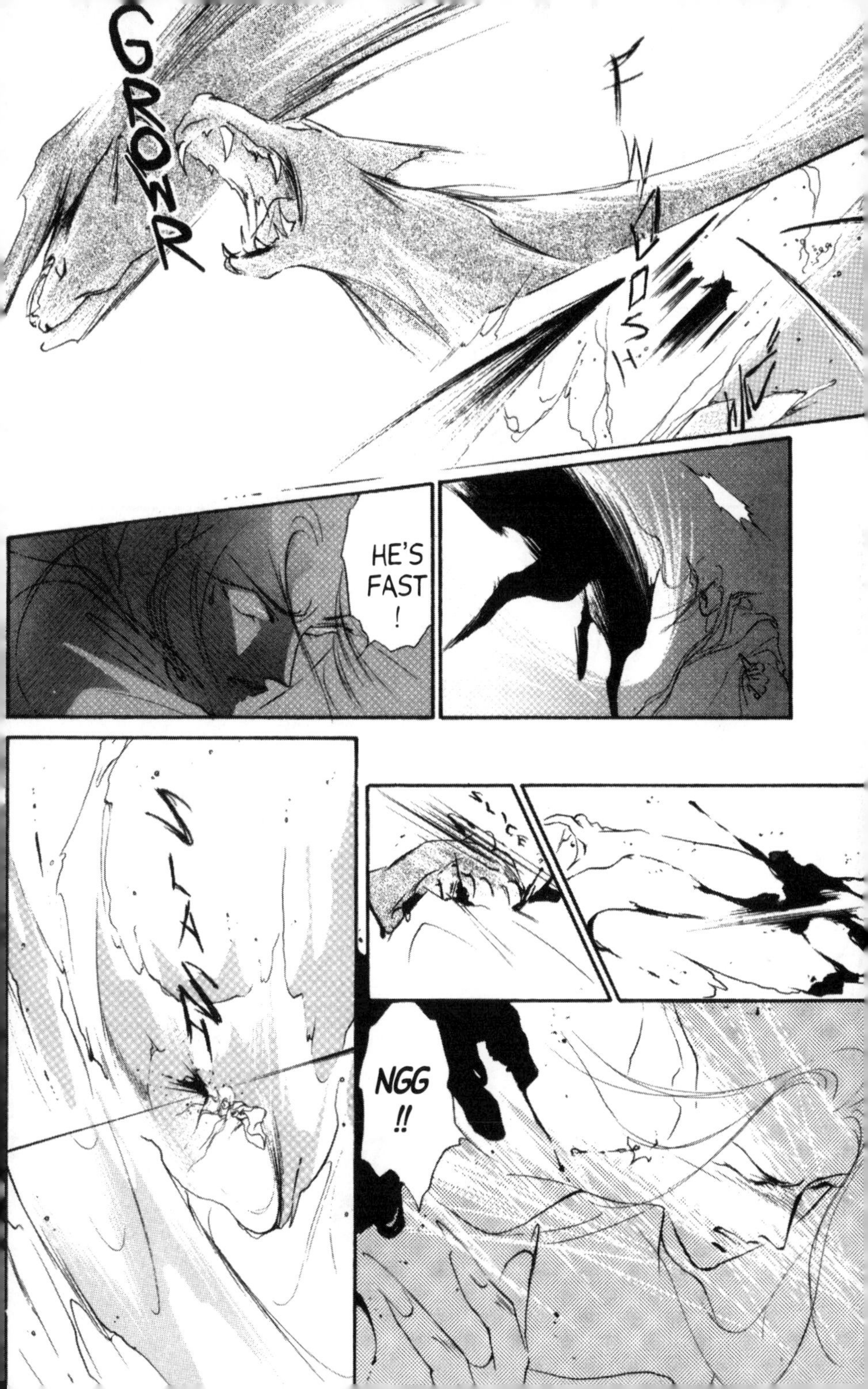
GROWR
FWOOSH
HE'S FAST!
SLASH
SLICE
NGG!!

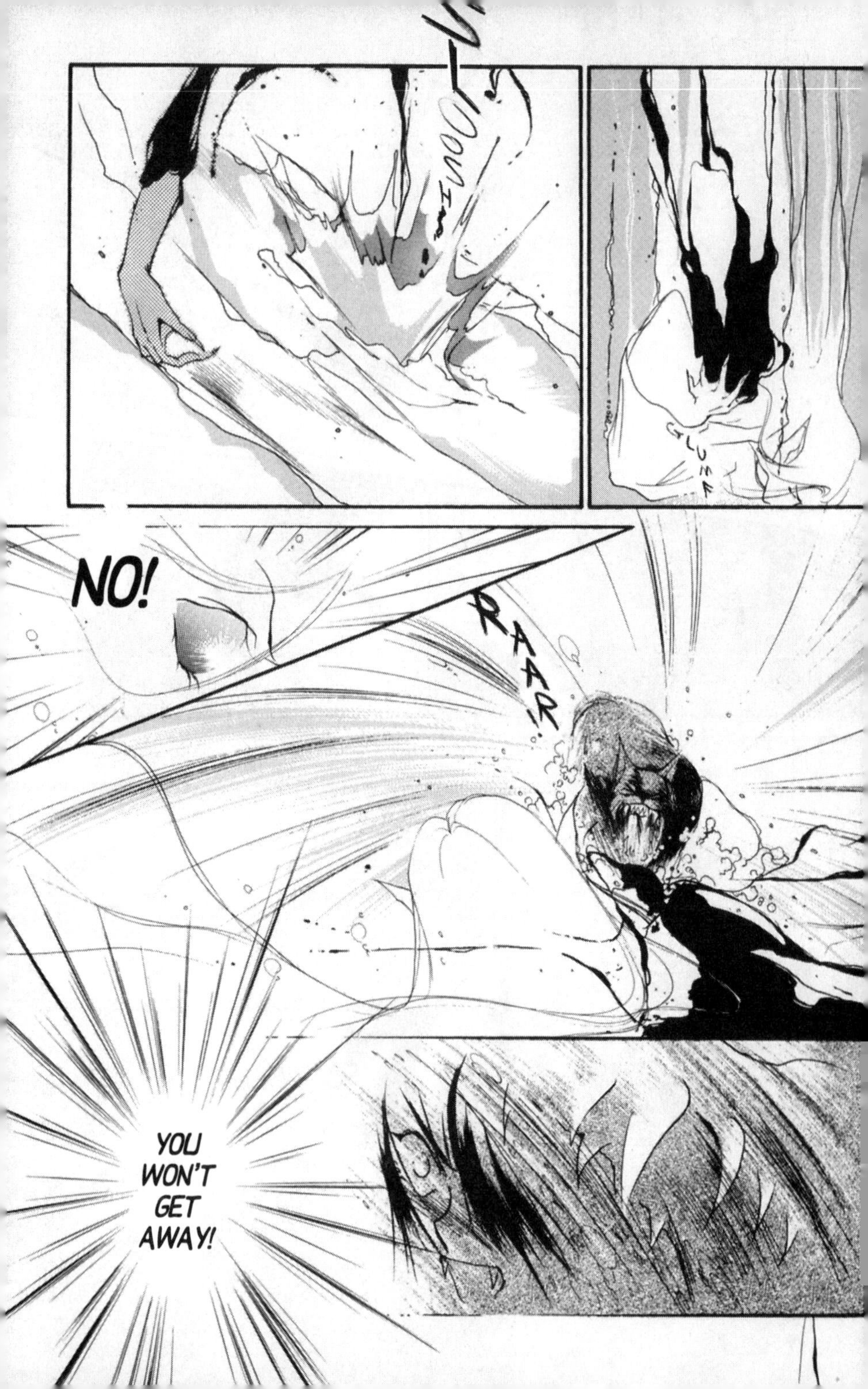
GLUMF
NO!
RAAR!
YOU WON'T GET AWAY!

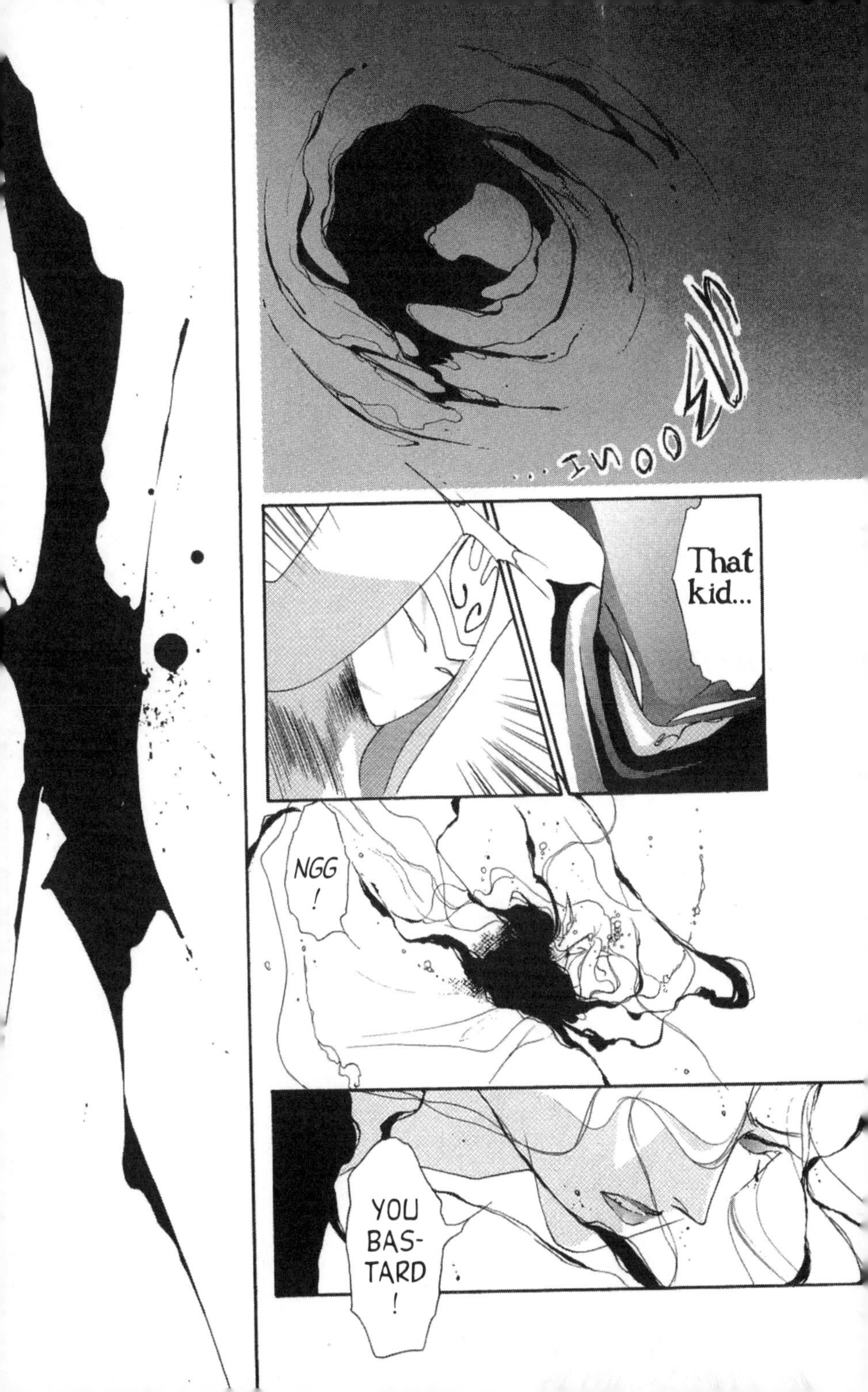

ZOON!...
That kid...
NGG!
YOU BAS-TARD!

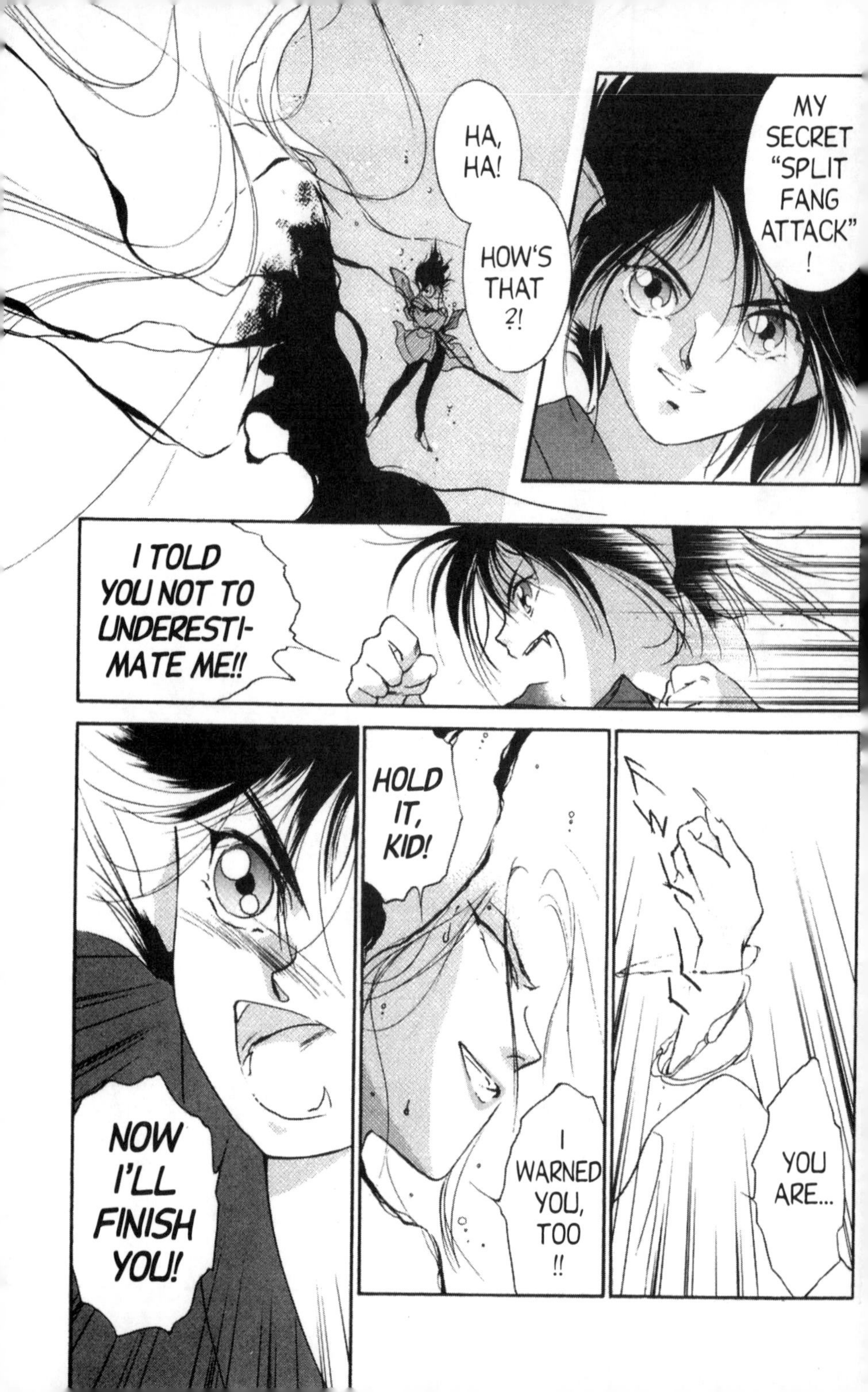
MY SECRET "SPLIT FANG ATTACK"!
HA, HA!
HOW'S THAT?!
I TOLD YOU NOT TO UNDERESTI-MATE ME!!
HOLD IT, KID!
NOW I'LL FINISH YOU!
YOU ARE...
I WARNED YOU, TOO!!

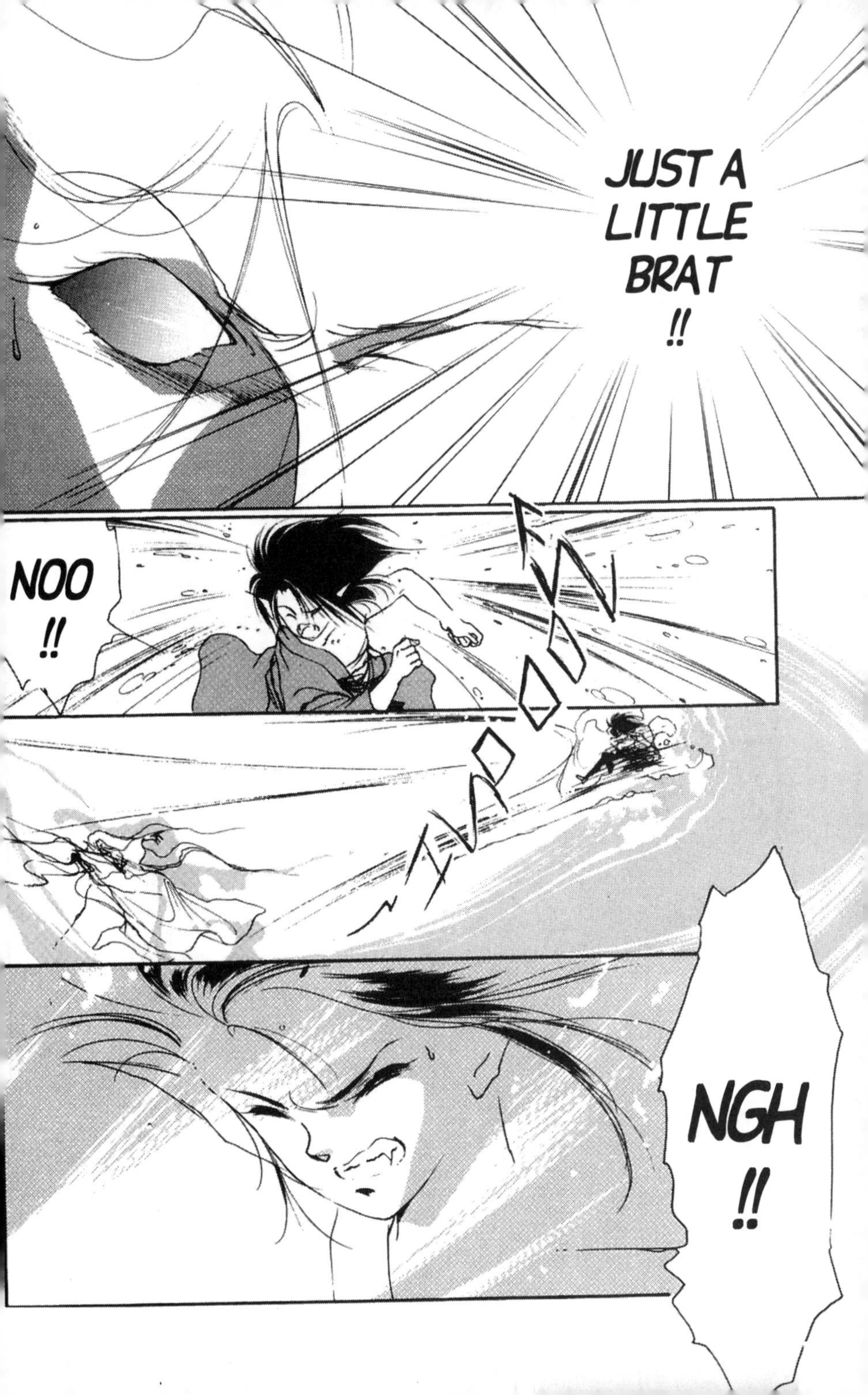
JUST A LITTLE BRAT !!
NOO !!
NGH !!

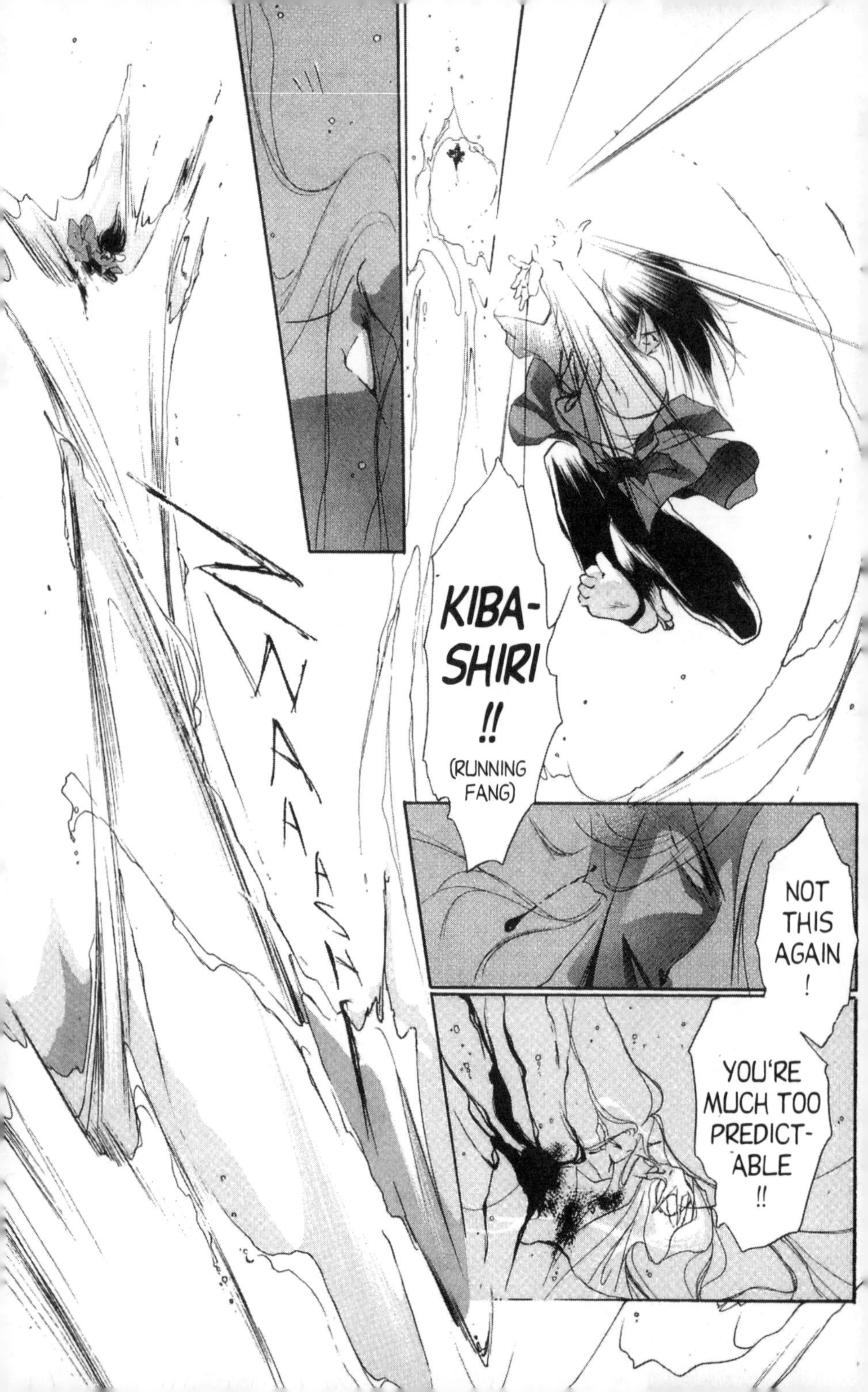
ZWAASH
KIBA-SHIRI!!
(RUNNING FANG)
NOT THIS AGAIN!
YOU'RE MUCH TOO PREDICT-ABLE!!

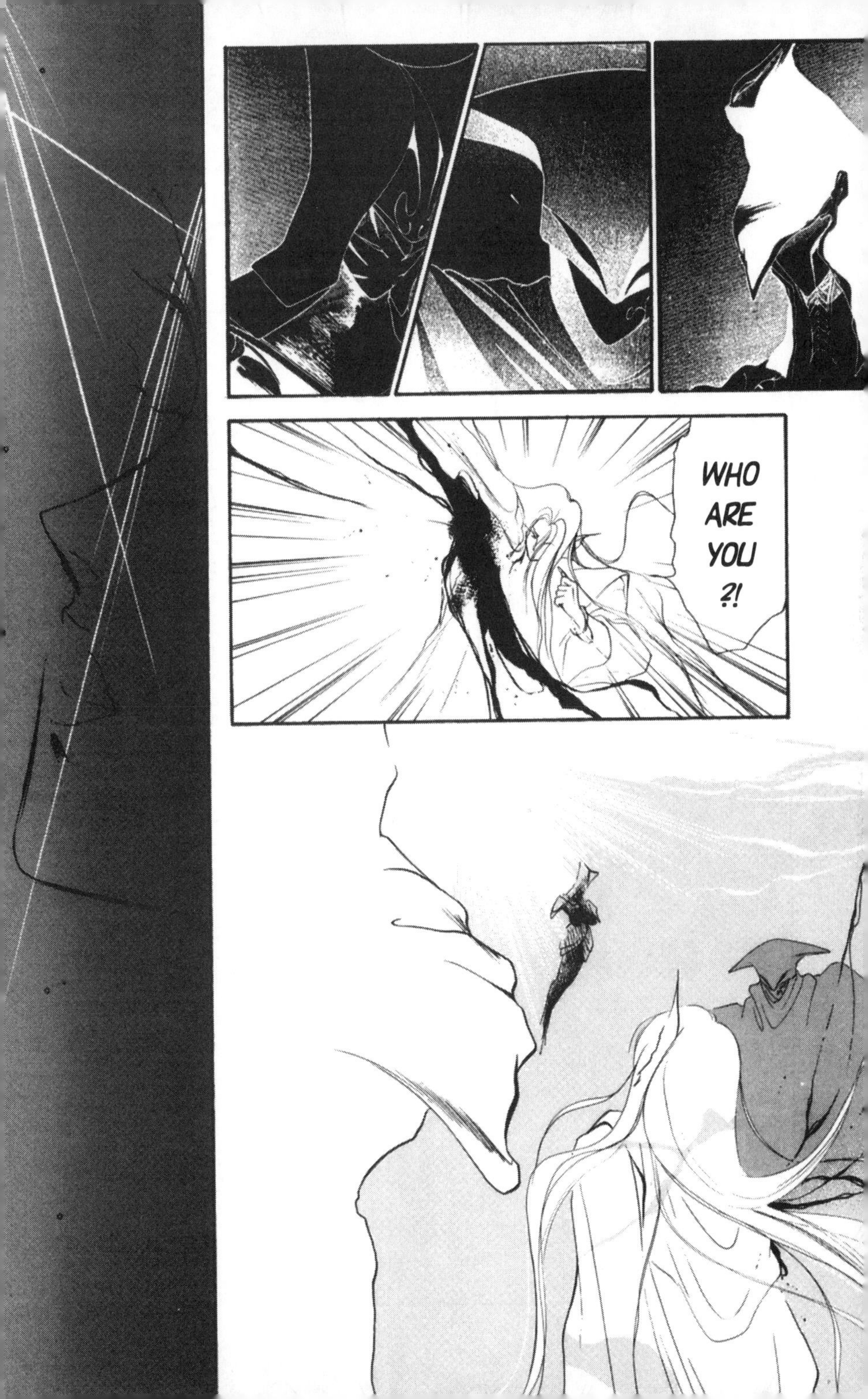
WHO ARE YOU ?!

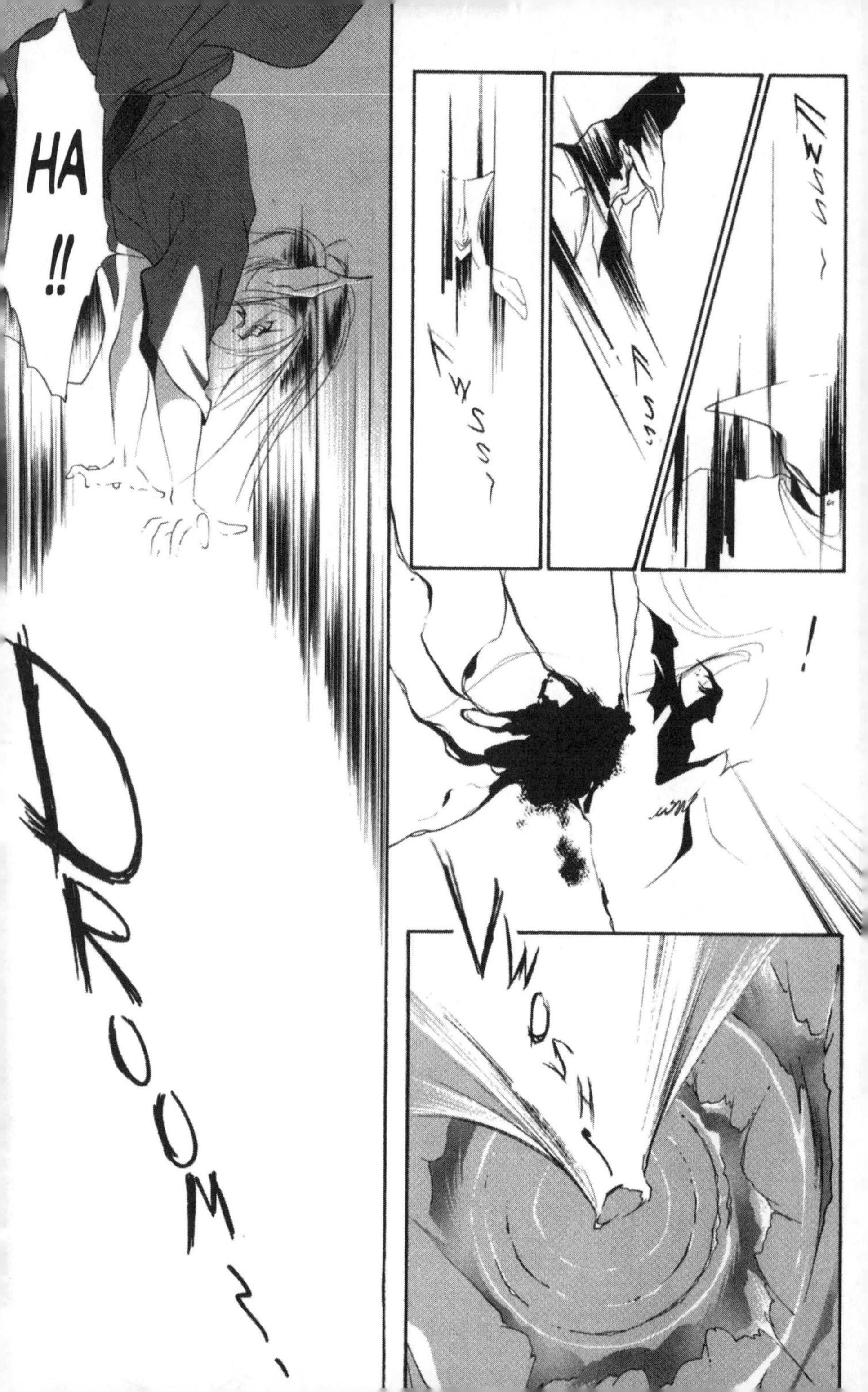
!
VWOSH
HA !!
DROOM~..

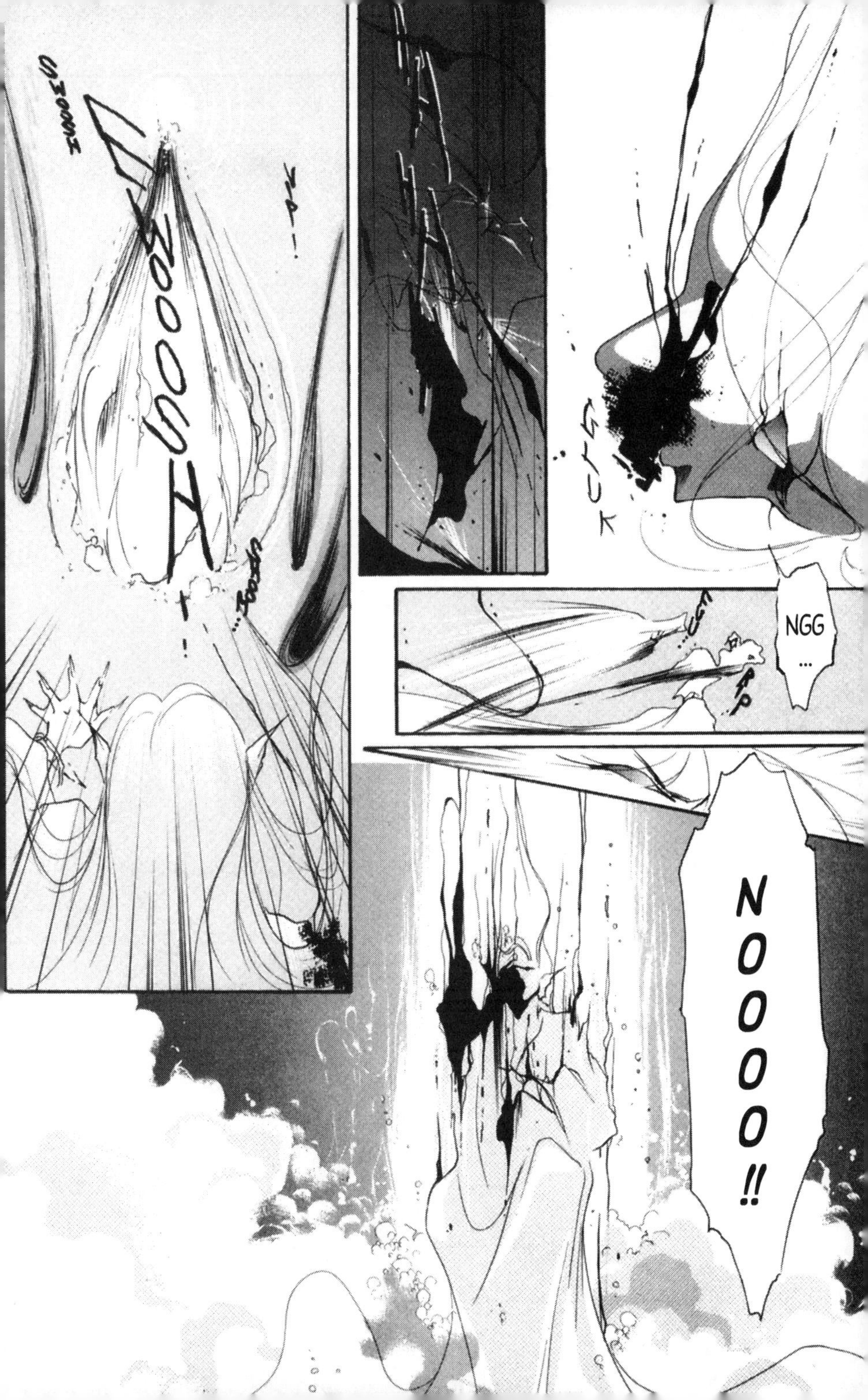
WHOOOSH!!
NGG ...
NOOOOO!!

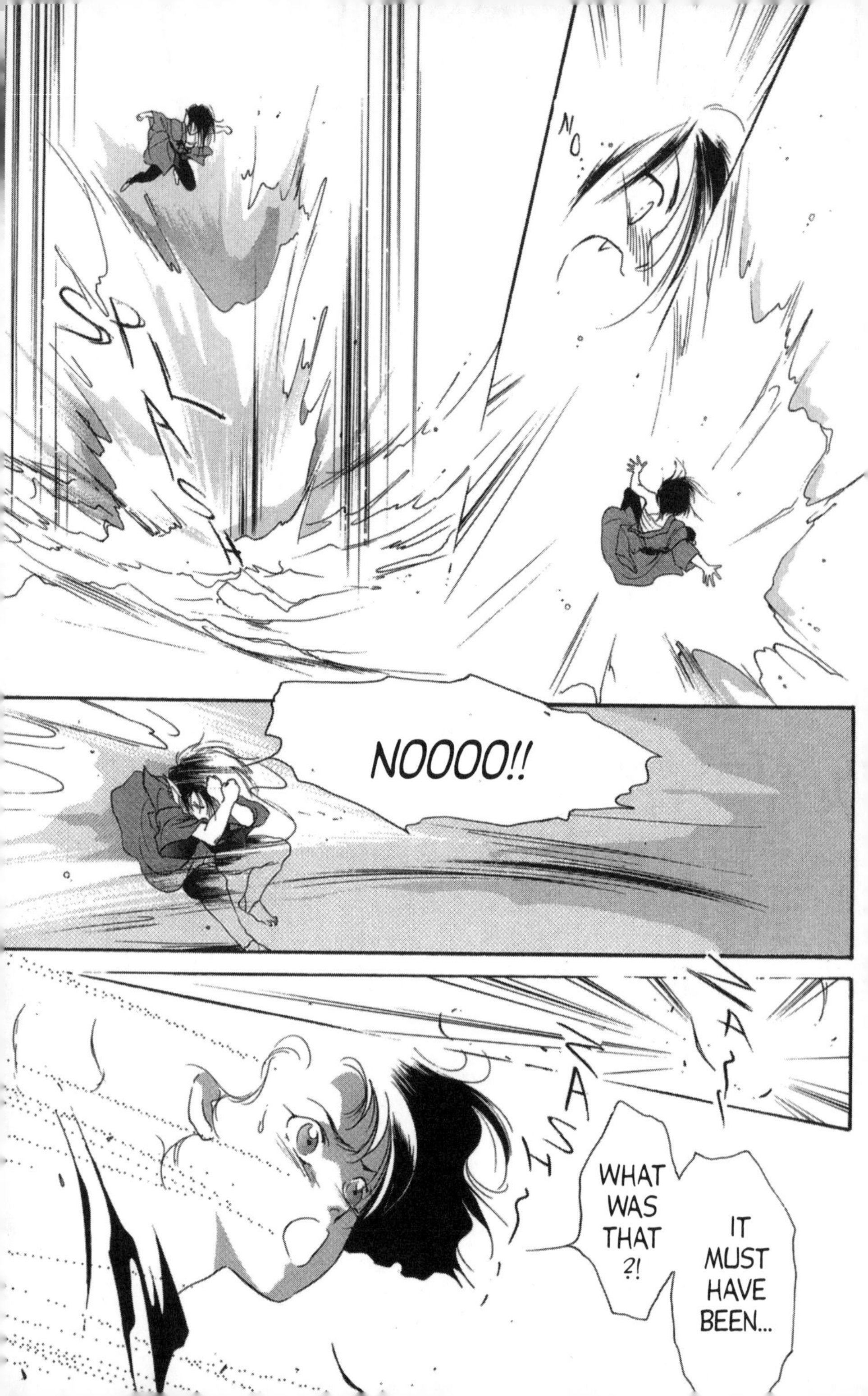
NO...
SPLASH
NOOOO!!
ZAAAH
IT MUST HAVE BEEN...
WHAT WAS THAT?!

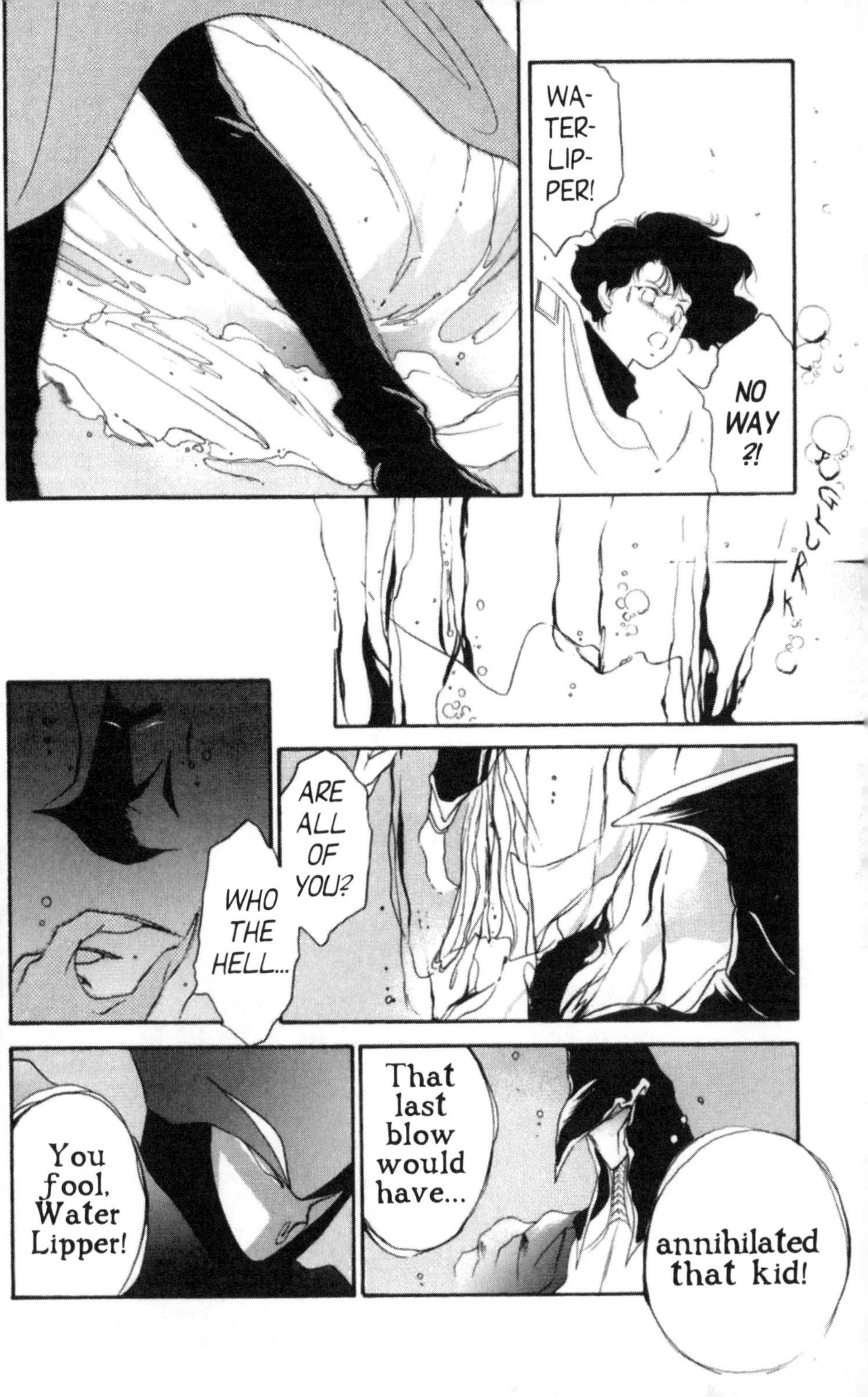
WATER-LIPPER!
NO WAY?!
WHO THE HELL...
ARE ALL OF YOU?
You fool, Water Lipper!
That last blow would have...
annihilated that kid!

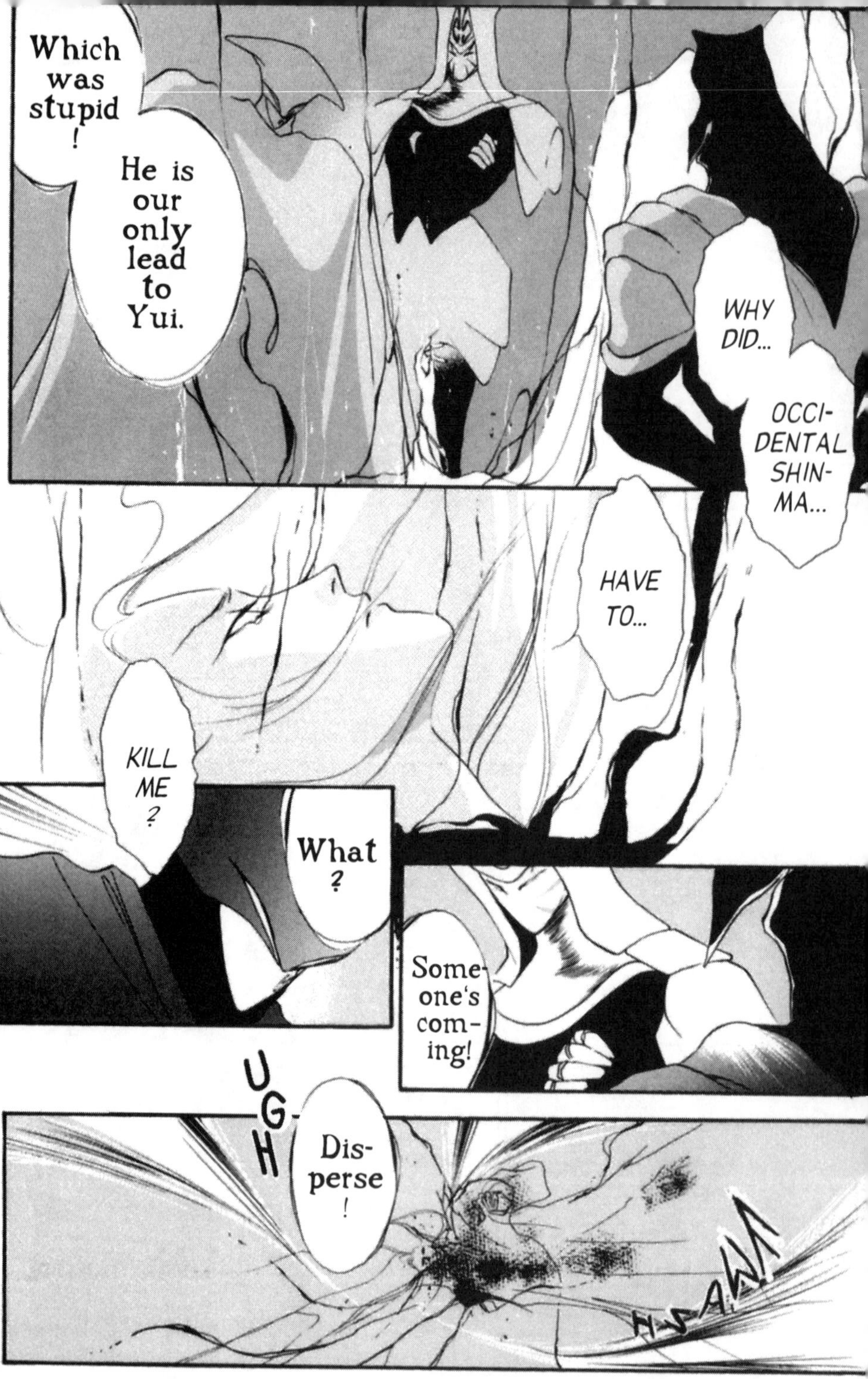
Which was stupid!
He is our only lead to Yui.
WHY DID... OCCI-DENTAL SHIN-MA...
HAVE TO...
KILL ME?
What?
Some-one's com-ing!
UGH
Dis-perse!
HSAAA

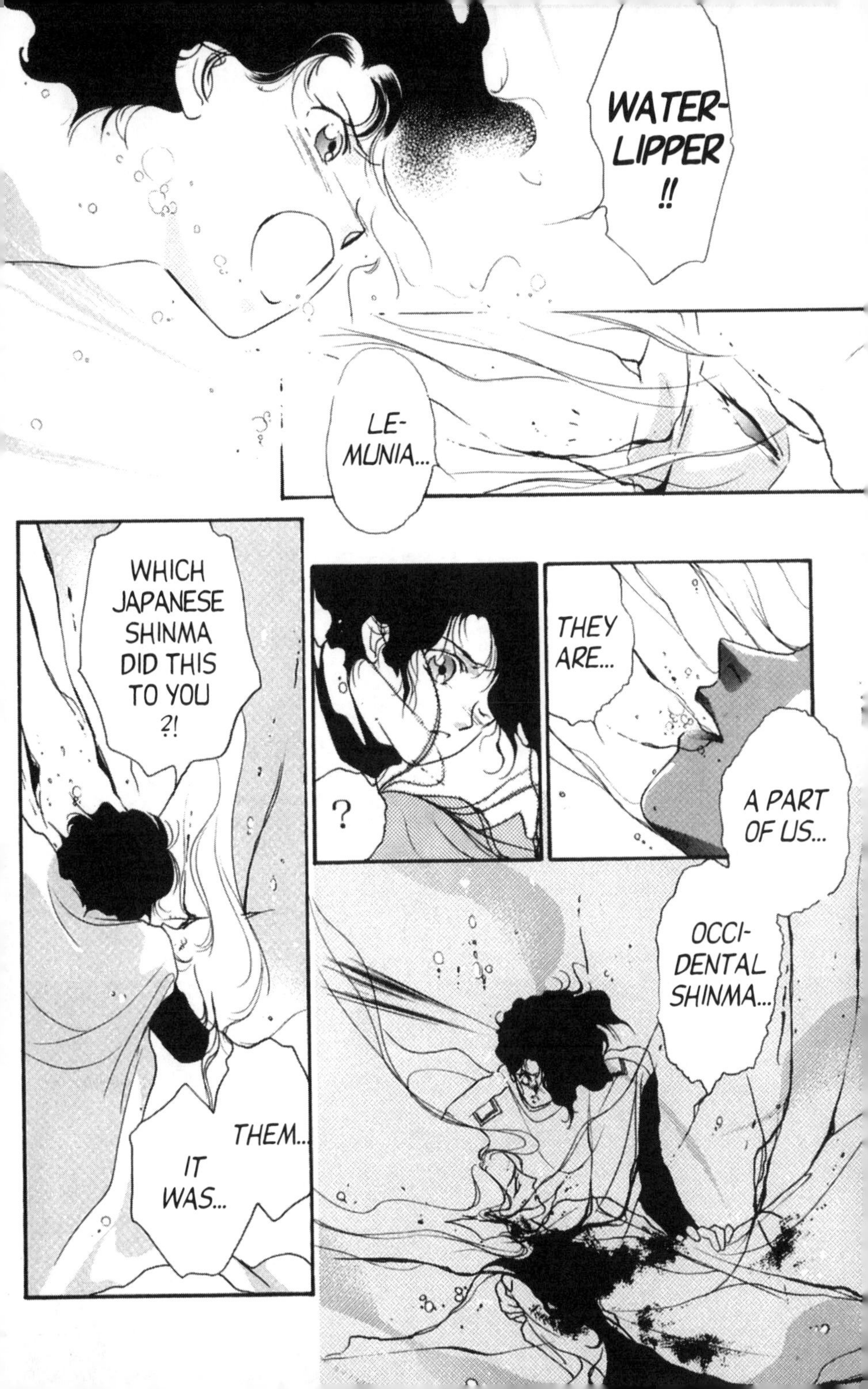

WATER-LIPPER!!
LE-MUNIA...
WHICH JAPANESE SHINMA DID THIS TO YOU?!
IT WAS...
THEM...
?
THEY ARE...
A PART OF US...
OCCI-DENTAL SHINMA...

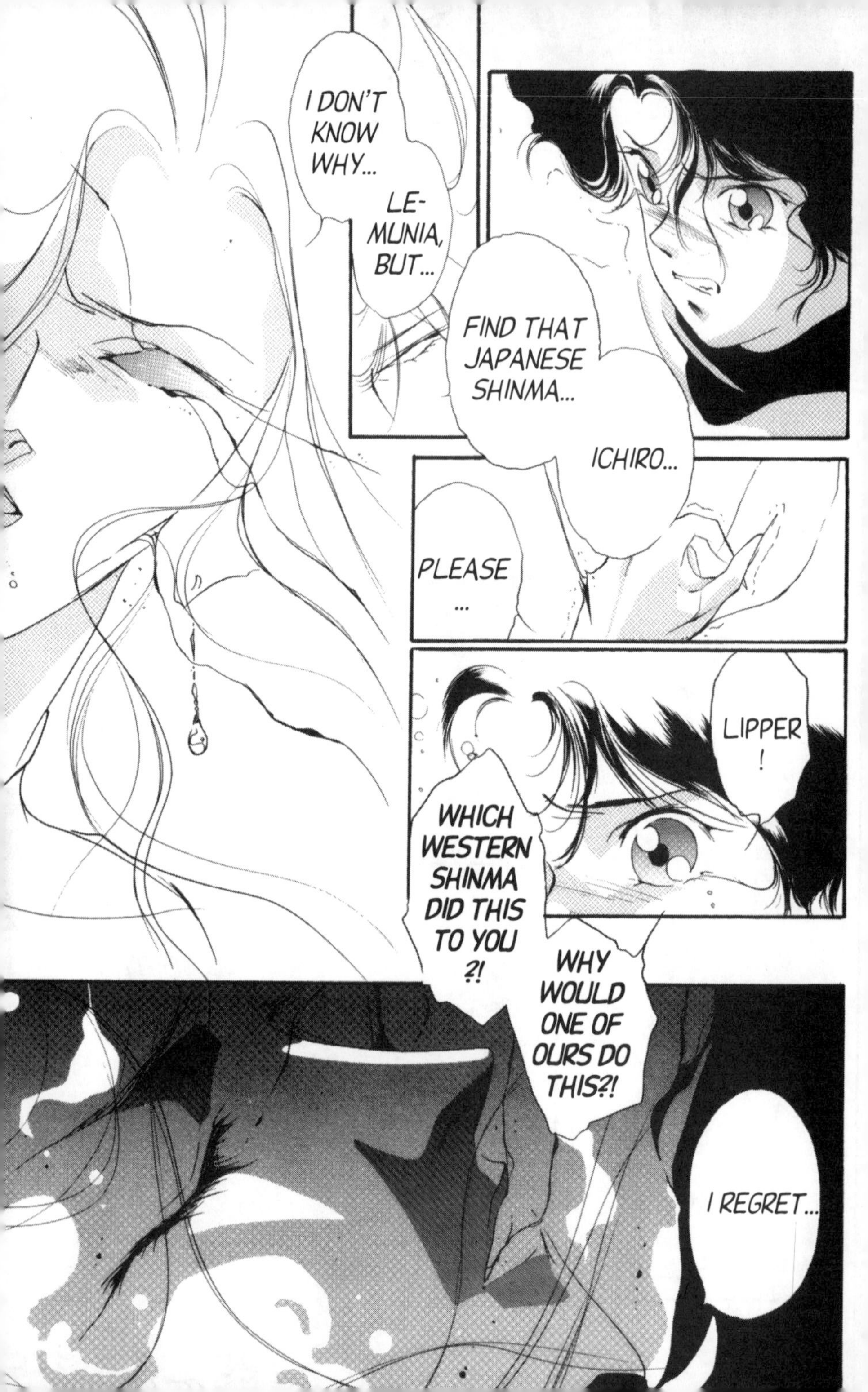
I DON'T KNOW WHY...
LE-MUNIA, BUT...
FIND THAT JAPANESE SHINMA...
ICHIRO...
PLEASE ...
LIPPER !
WHICH WESTERN SHINMA DID THIS TO YOU ?!
WHY WOULD ONE OF OURS DO THIS?!
I REGRET...

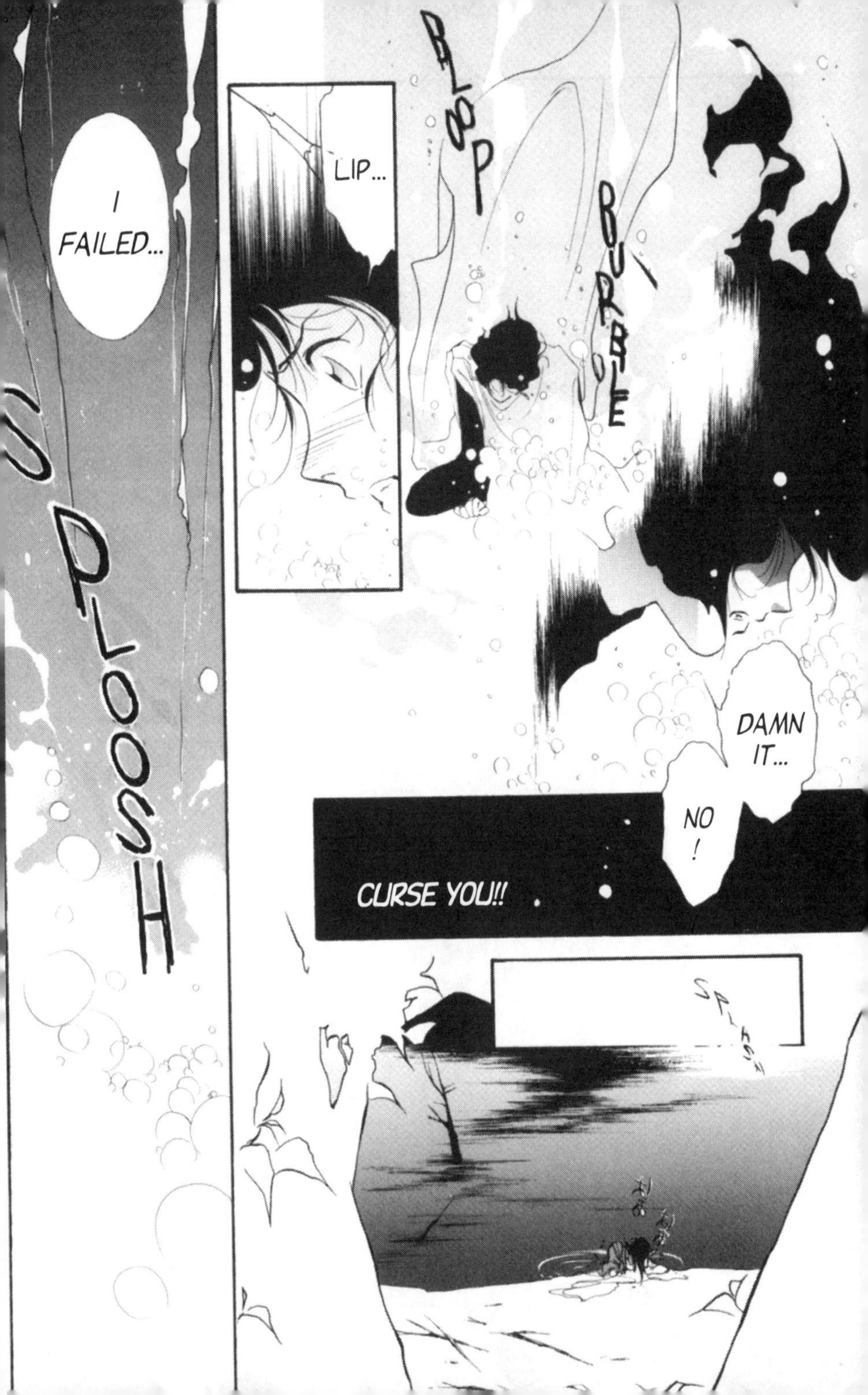
BLOOP
BUBBLE
LIP...
DAMN IT...
NO!
CURSE YOU!!
SPLASH
I FAILED...
SPLOOSH

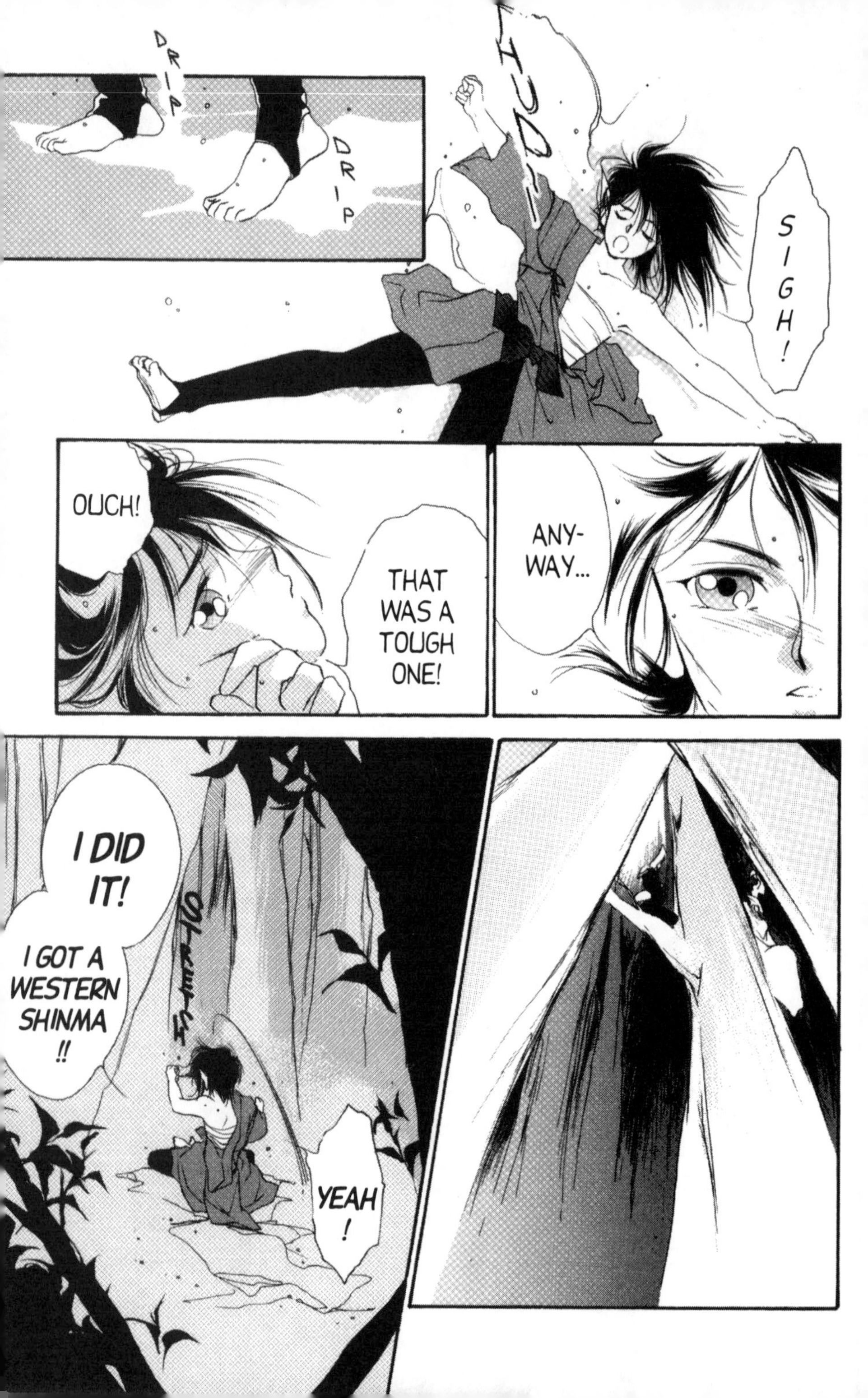
THUD!!
SIGH!
DRIP
DRIP
ANY-WAY...
OUCH!
THAT WAS A TOUGH ONE!
I DID IT!
I GOT A WESTERN SHINMA!!
STRETCH
YEAH!

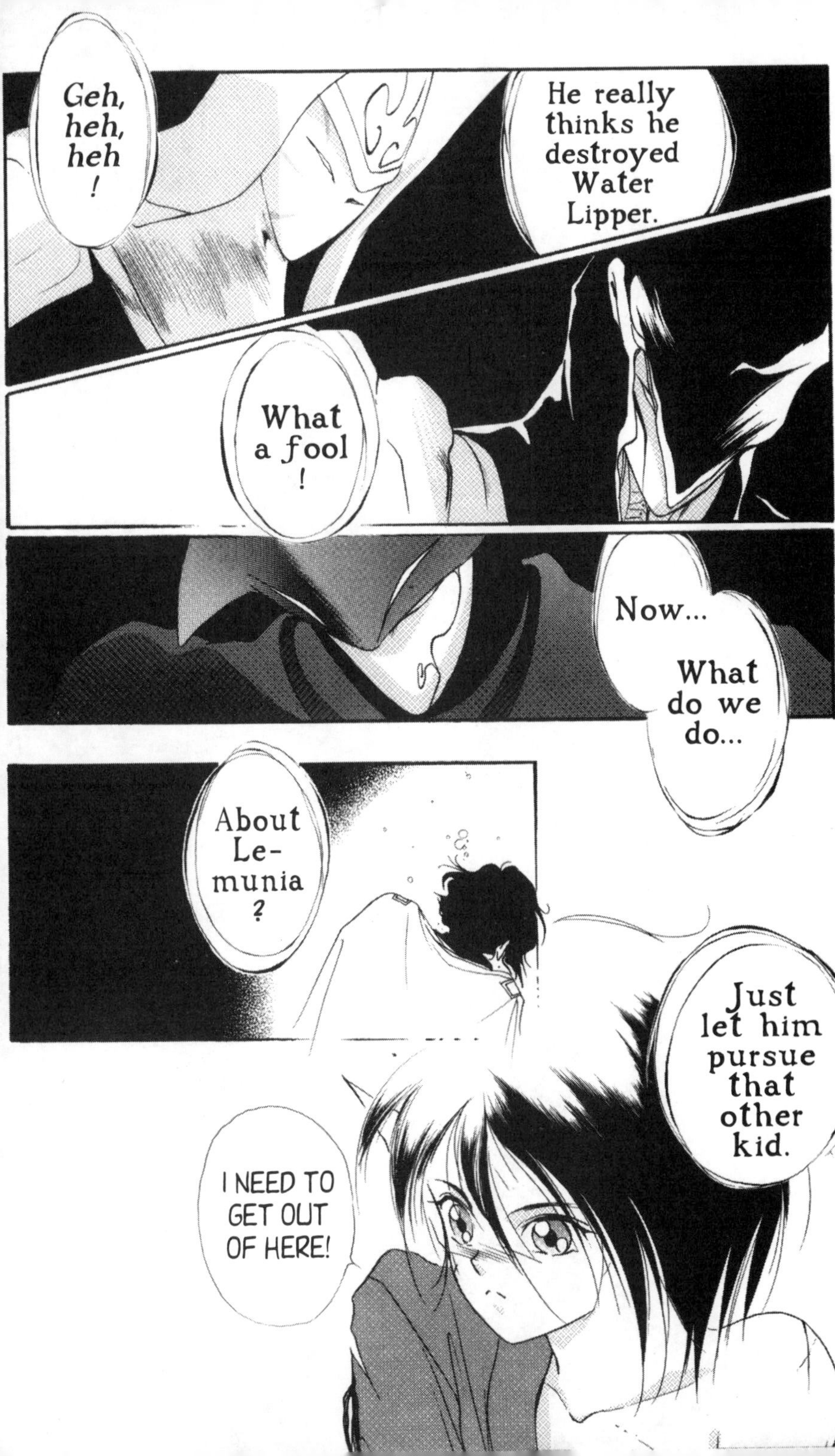
He really thinks he destroyed Water Lipper.
Geh, heh, heh!
What a fool!
Now...
What do we do...
About Le-munia?
Just let him pursue that other kid.
I NEED TO GET OUT OF HERE!

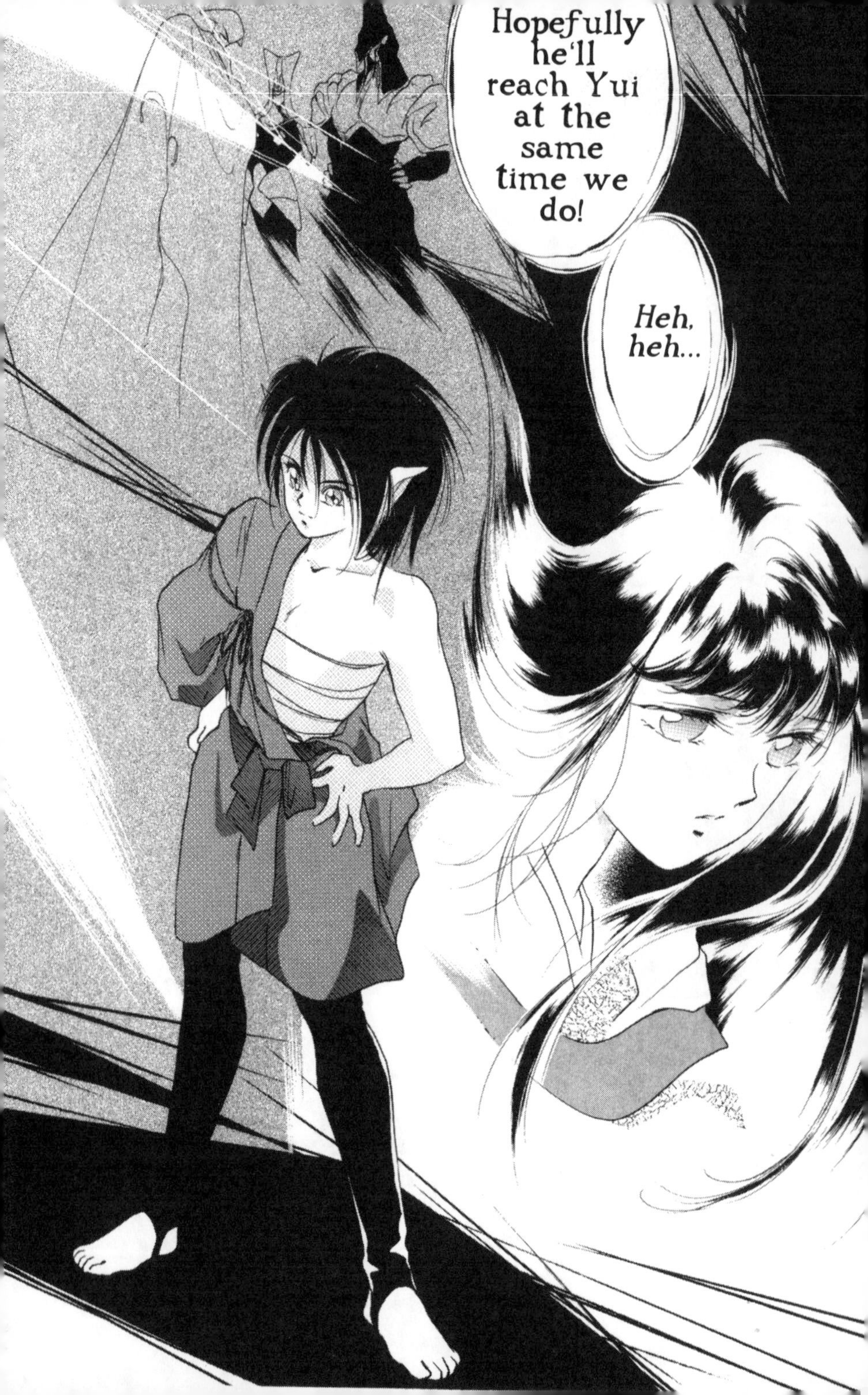
Hopefully he'll reach Yui at the same time we do!
Heh, heh...

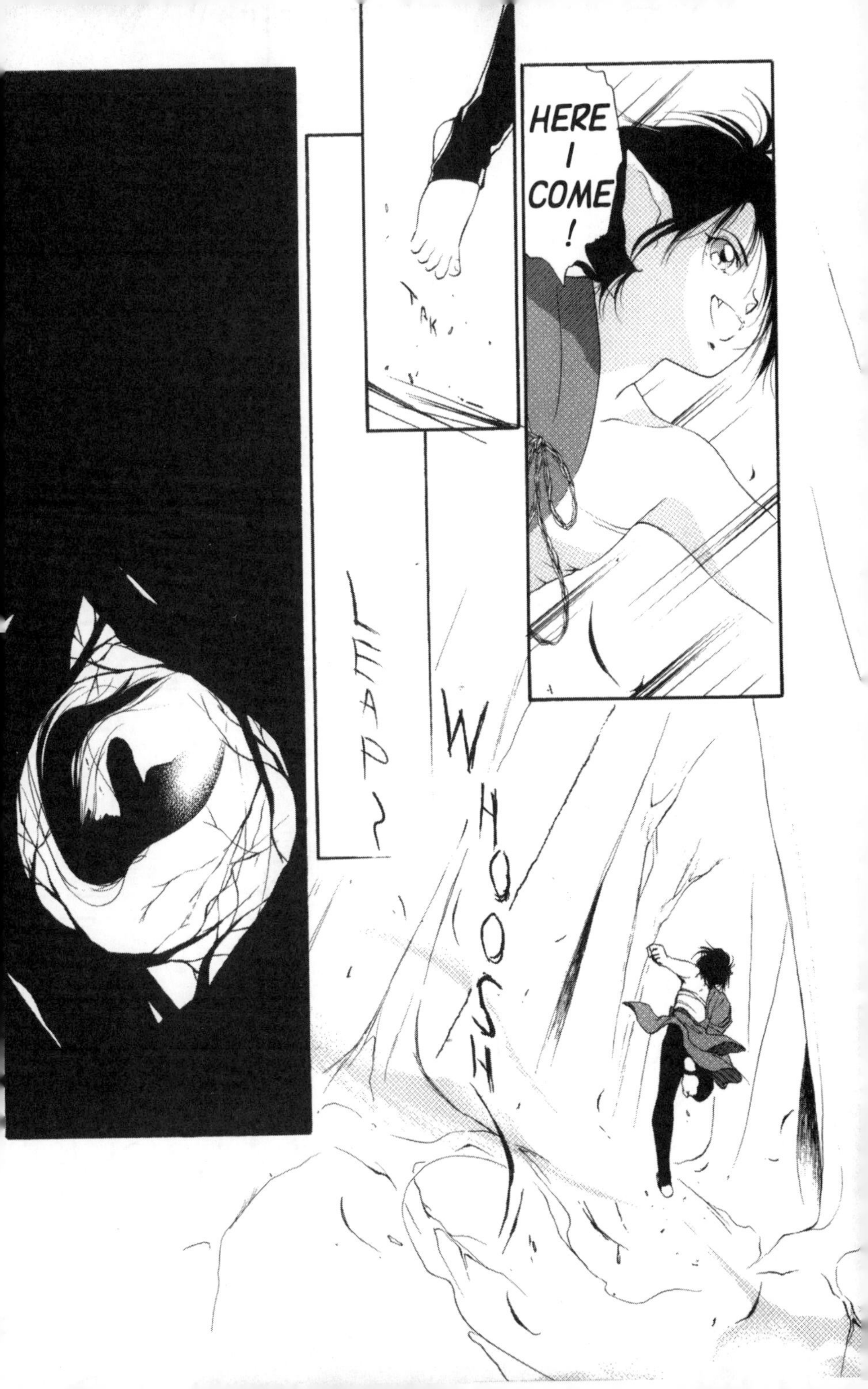
HERE I COME!
TAK
LEAP
WHOOSH

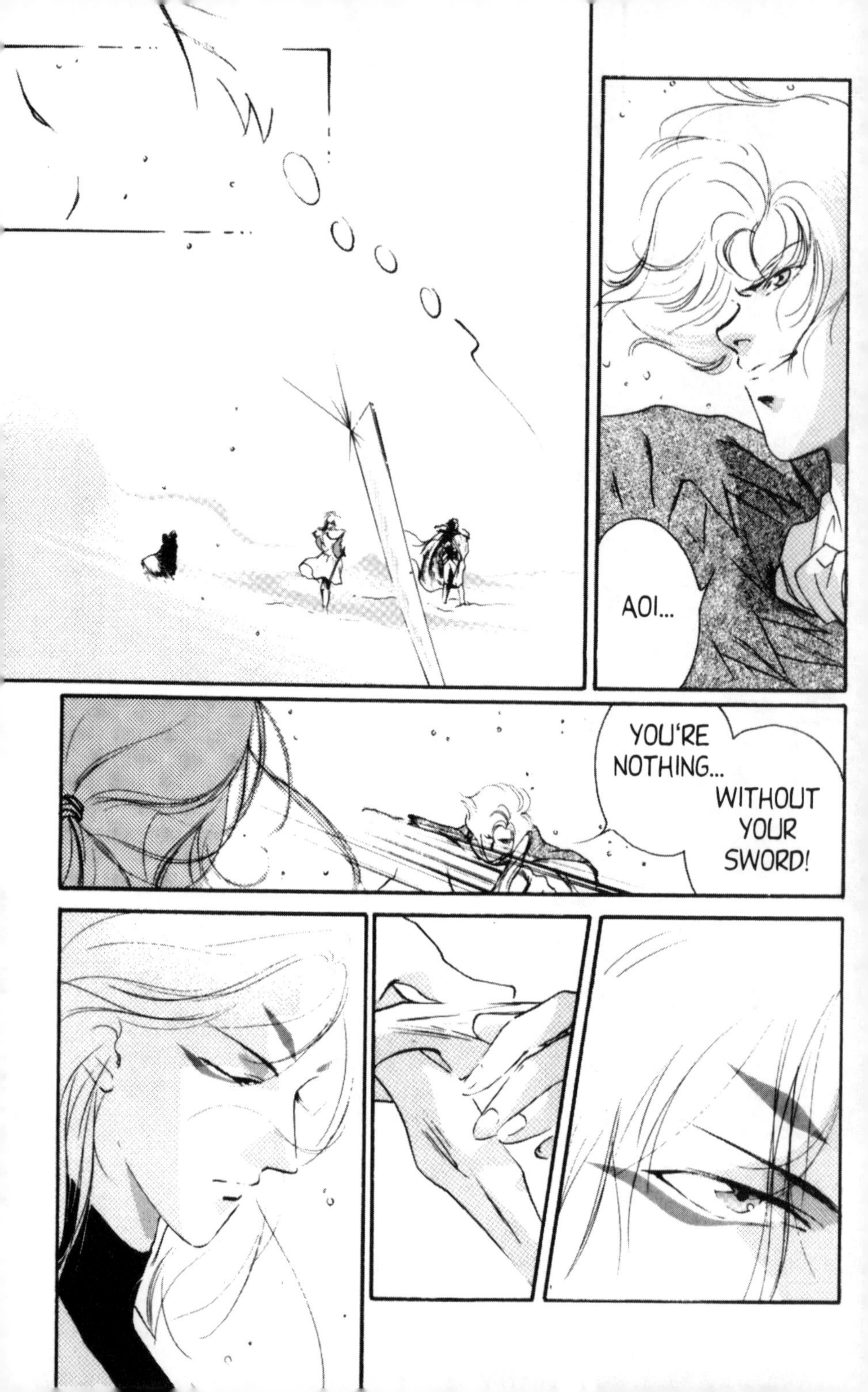
AOI...
YOU'RE NOTHING... WITHOUT YOUR SWORD!

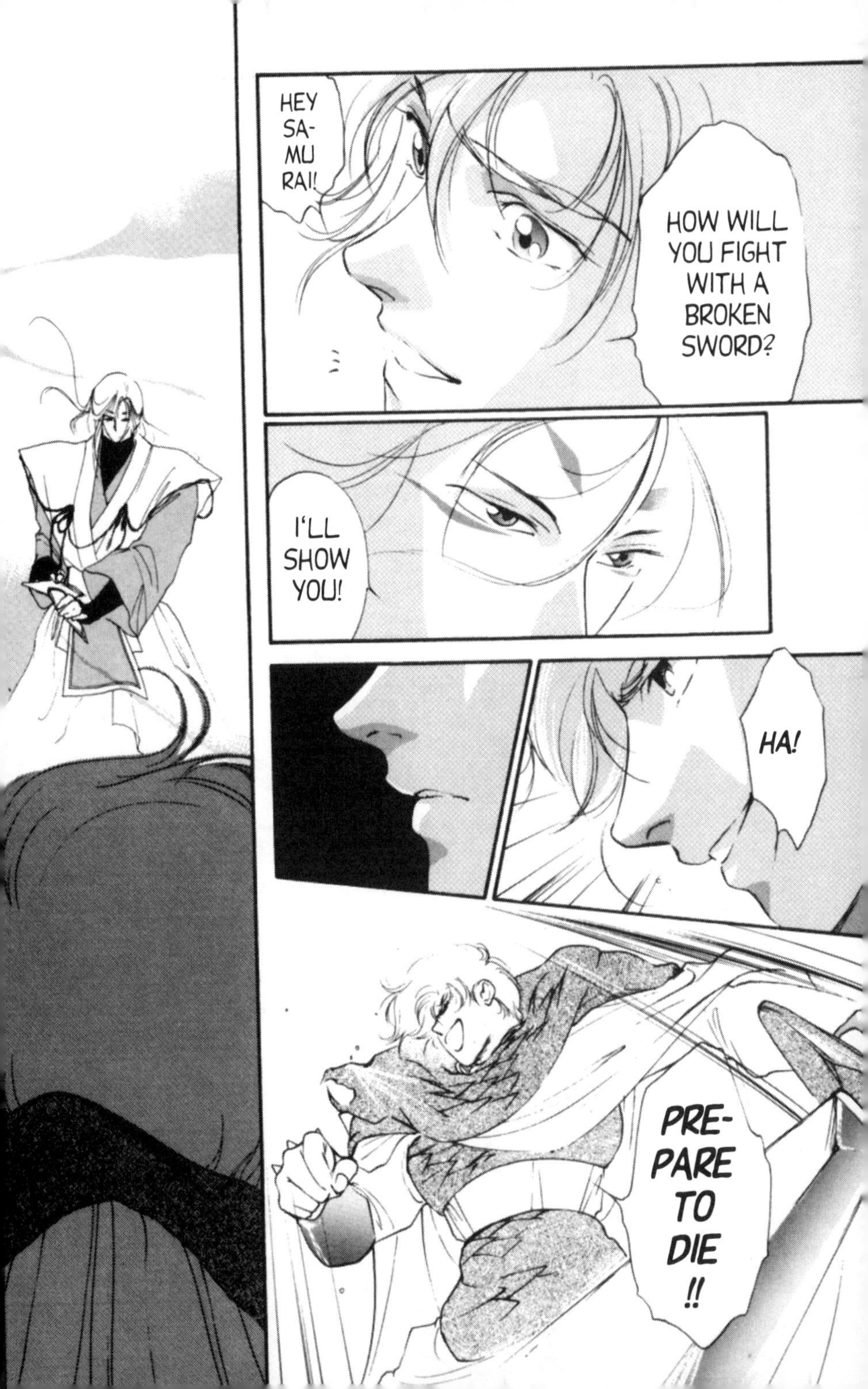
HEY SAMURAI!
HOW WILL YOU FIGHT WITH A BROKEN SWORD?
I'LL SHOW YOU!
HA!
PREPARE TO DIE!!

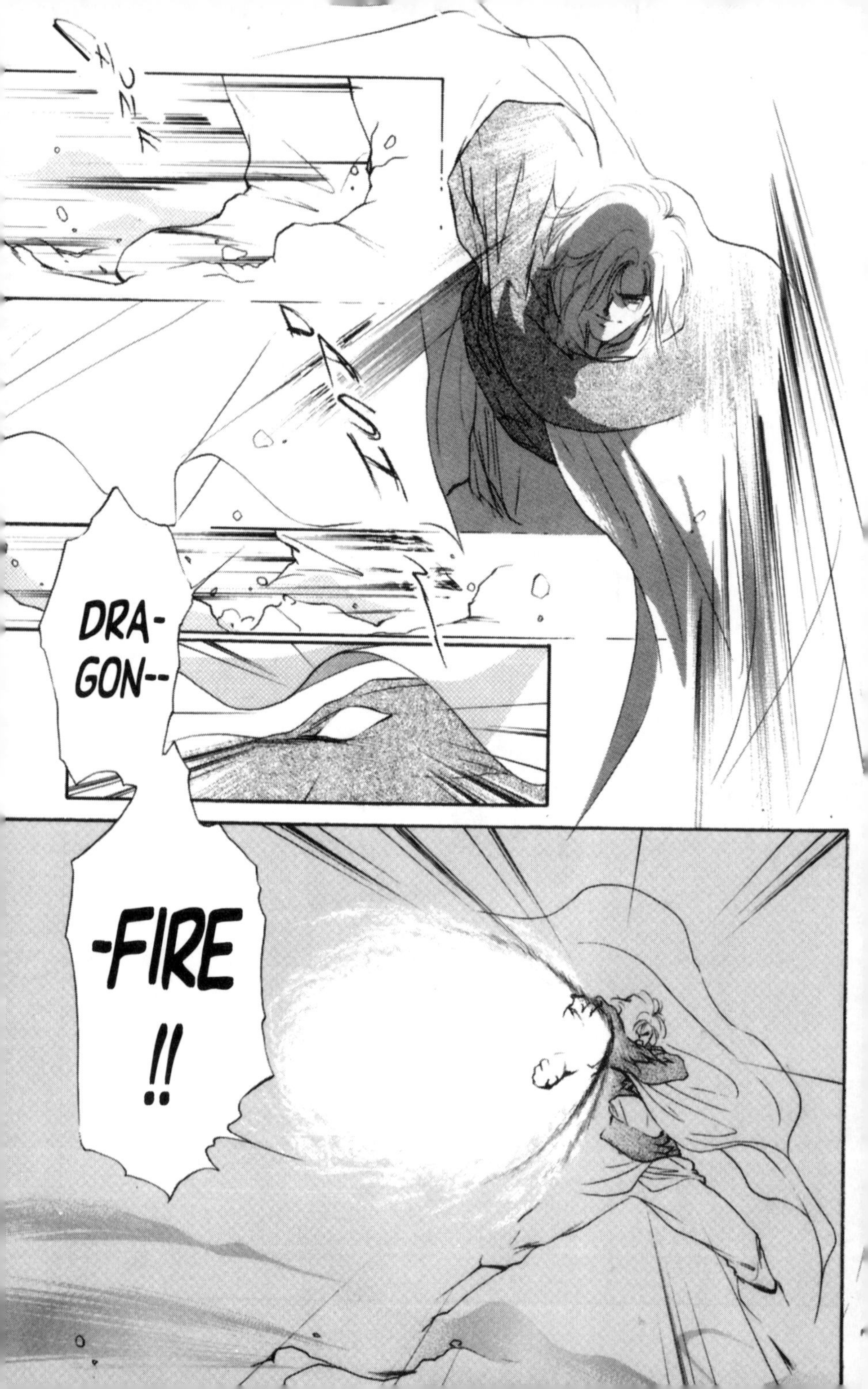
CHUNK
DRA-GON--
-FIRE !!

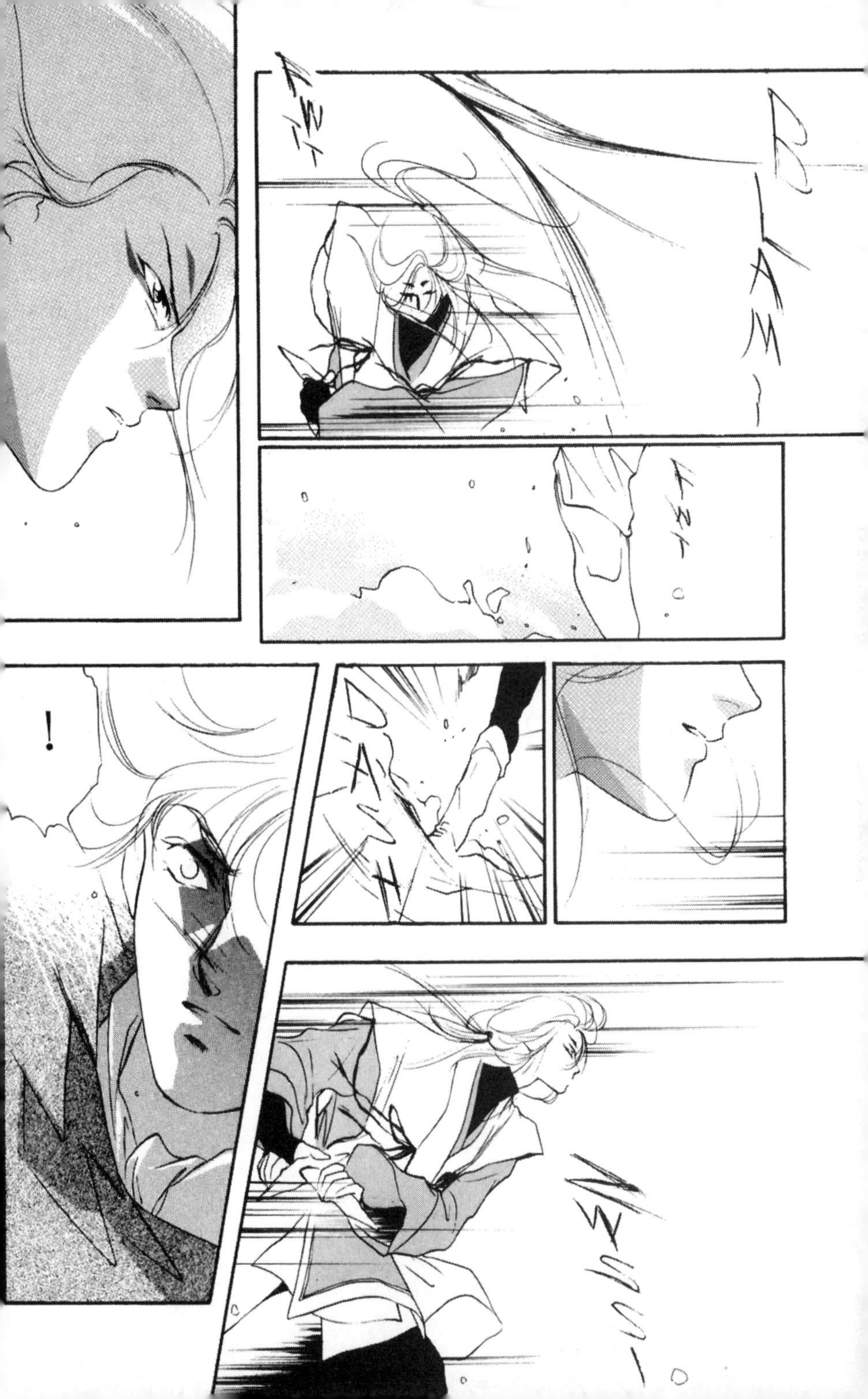
!

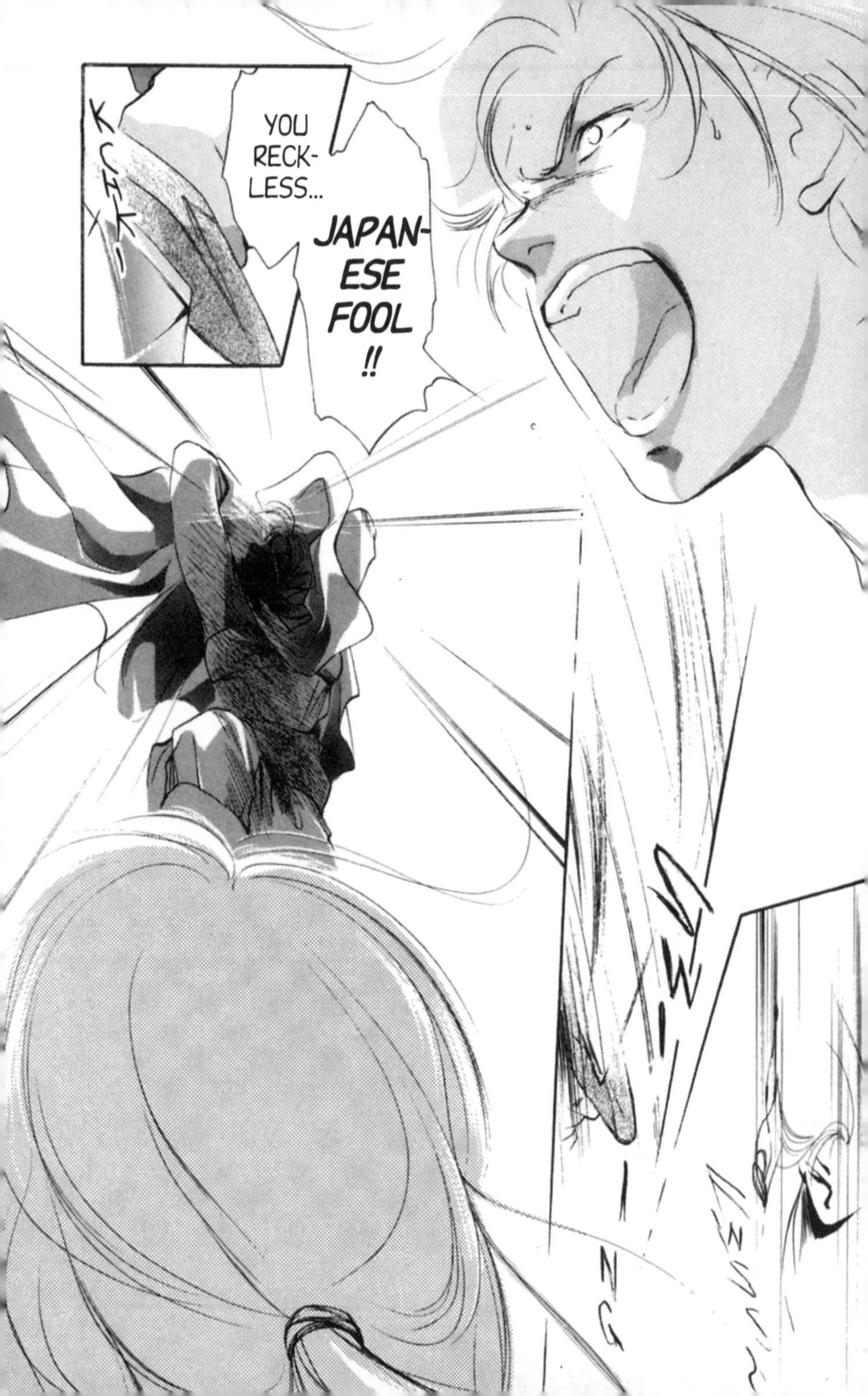

YOU RECK-LESS...
JAPAN-ESE FOOL !!
KCHK!
SWIIING

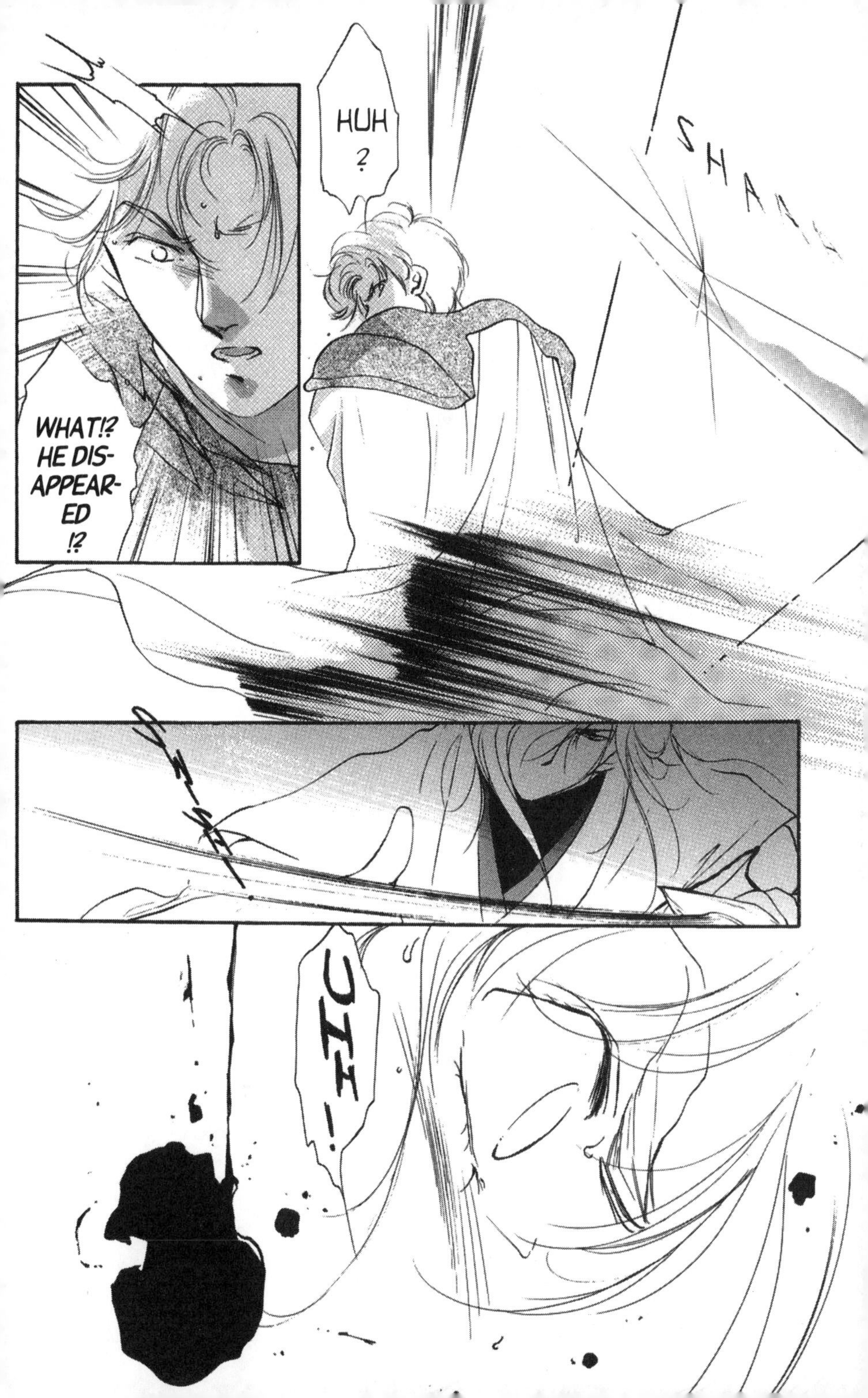
SHAN
HUH ?
WHAT!? HE DIS-APPEARED !?
UHH!

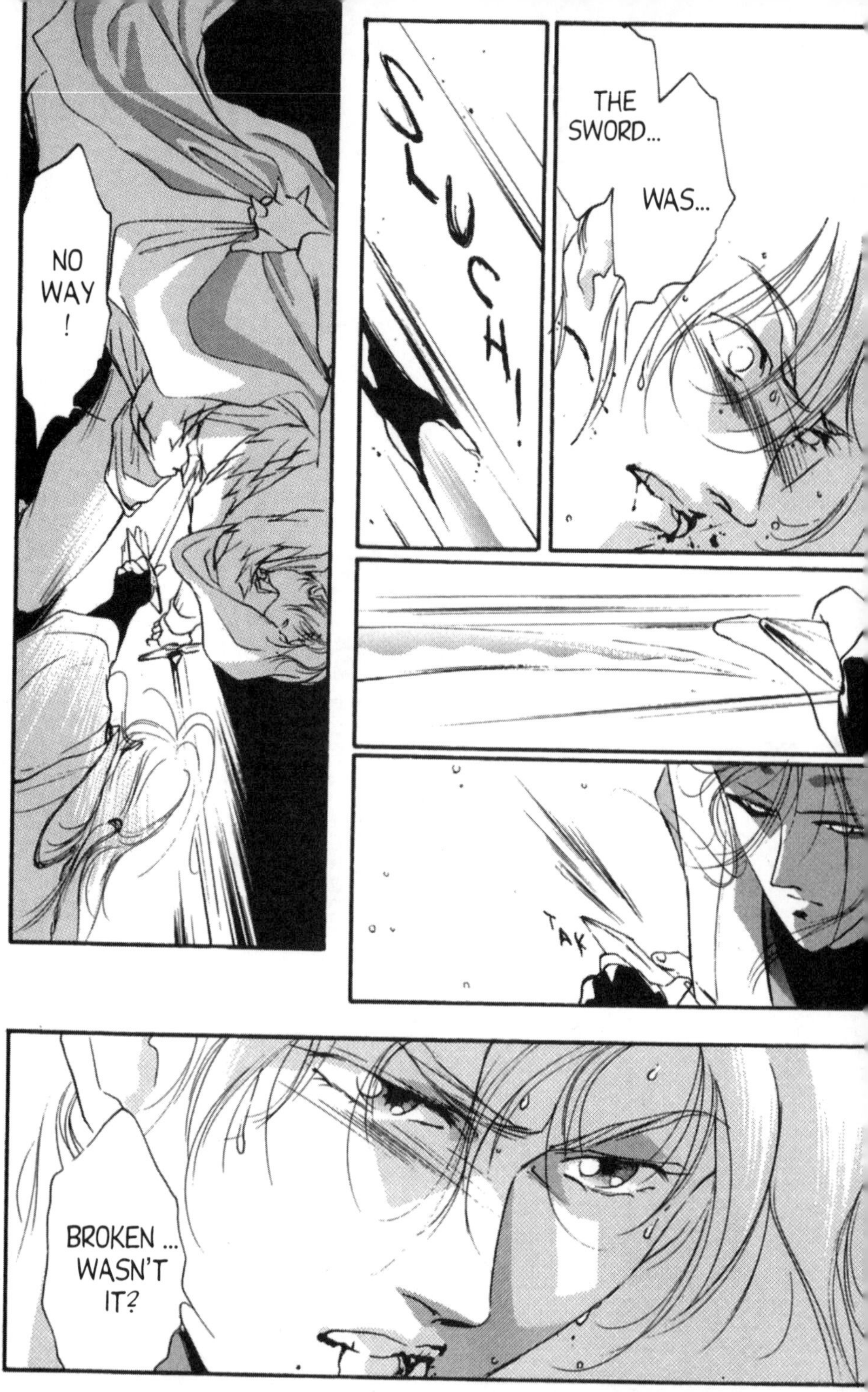
THE SWORD...
WAS...
SLUCH!
NO WAY!
TAK
BROKEN ... WASN'T IT?

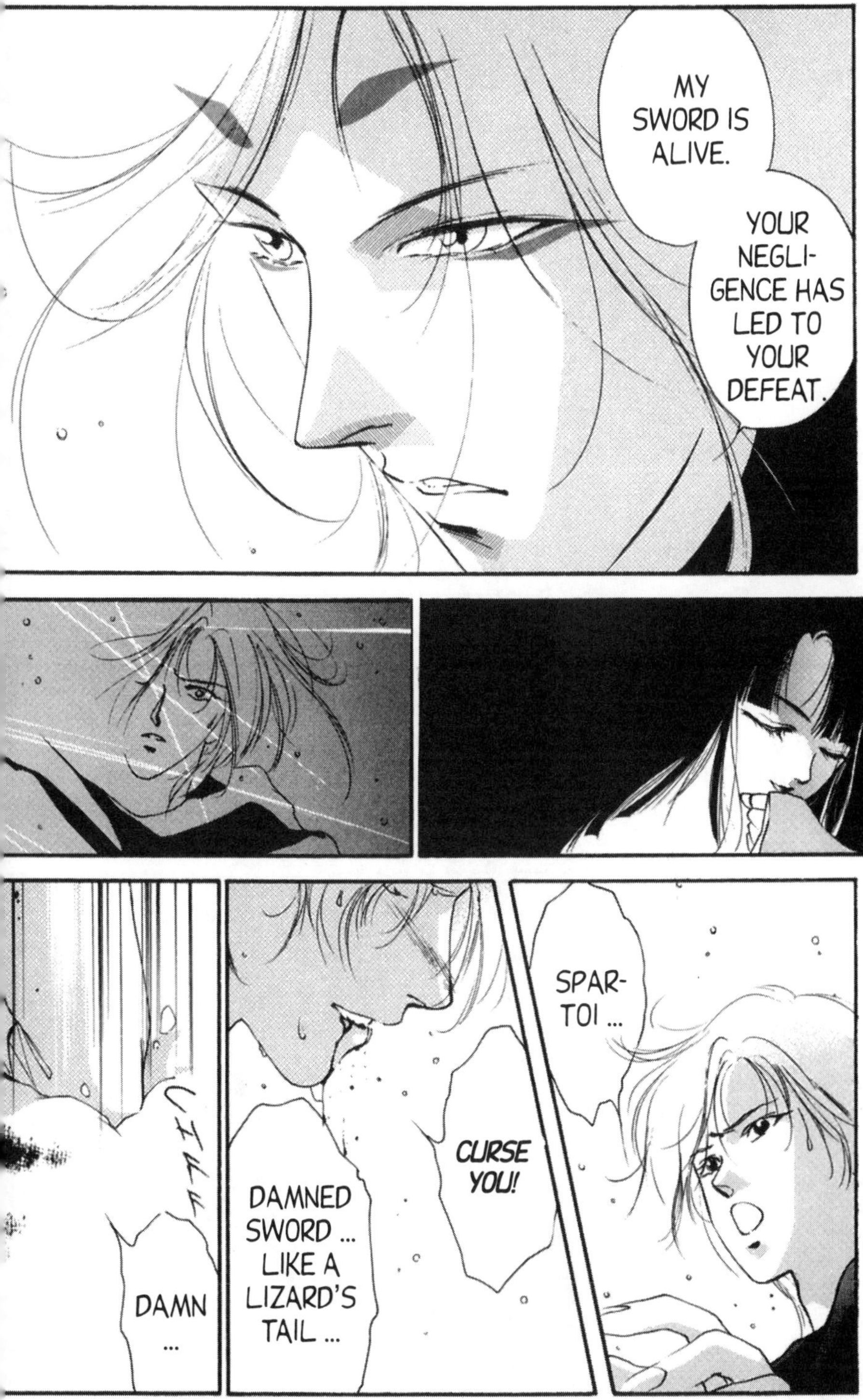
MY SWORD IS ALIVE.
YOUR NEGLI-GENCE HAS LED TO YOUR DEFEAT.
SPAR-TOI ...
CURSE YOU!
DAMNED SWORD ... LIKE A LIZARD'S TAIL ...
DAMN ...

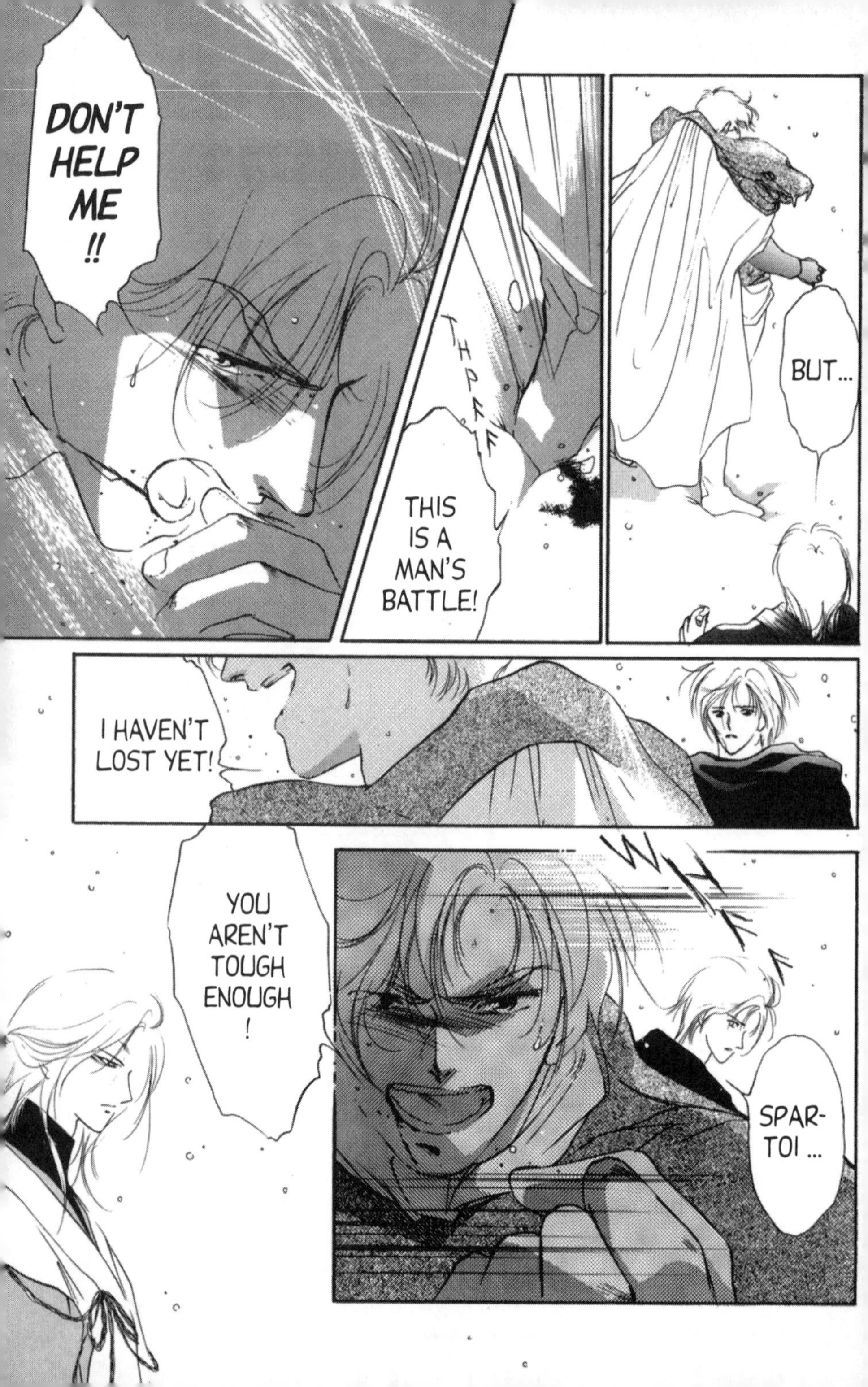
DON'T HELP ME !!
THPFFF
THIS IS A MAN'S BATTLE!
BUT...
I HAVEN'T LOST YET!
WHAM
SPAR-TOI ...
YOU AREN'T TOUGH ENOUGH !

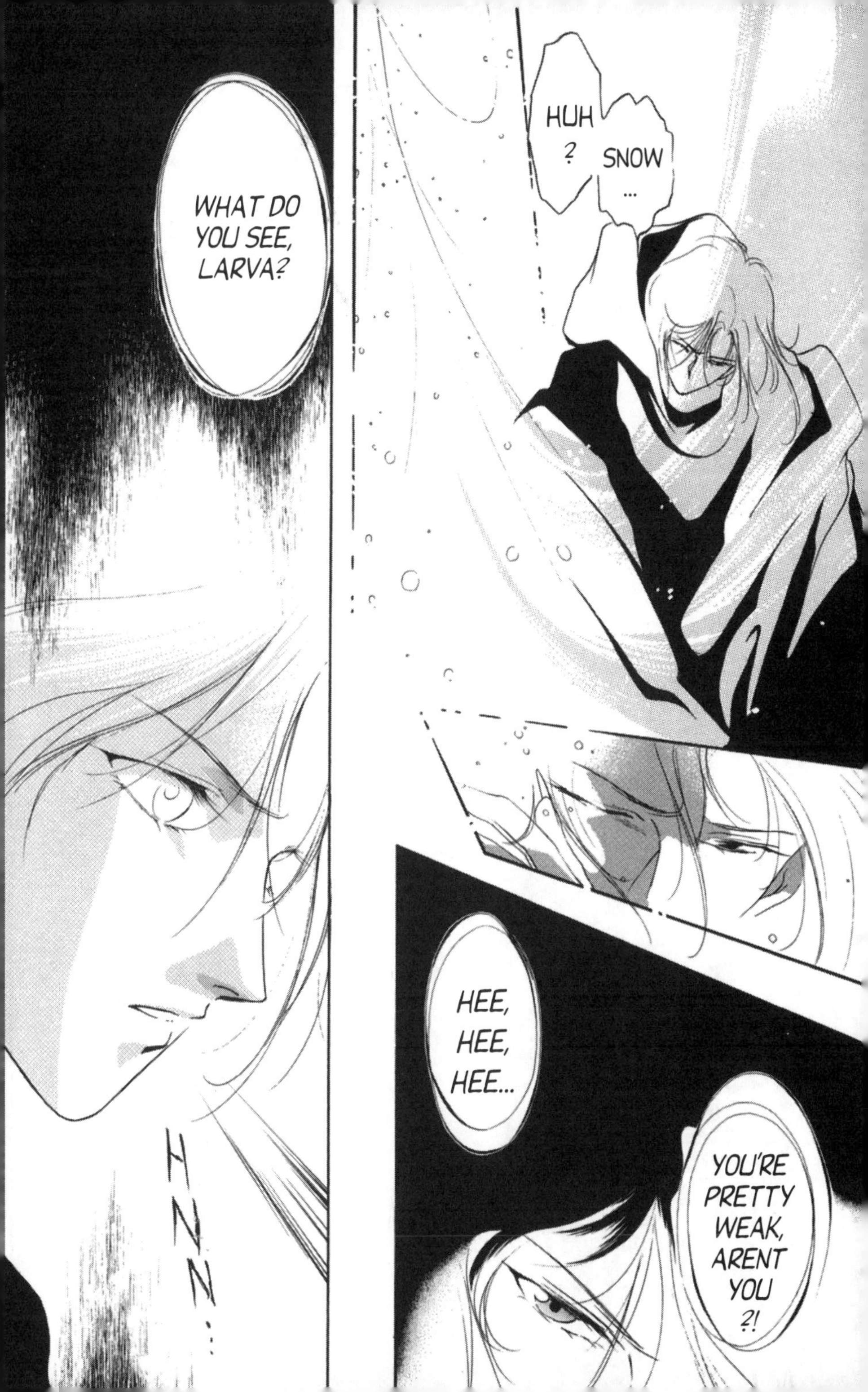
HUH?
SNOW...
YOU'RE PRETTY WEAK, ARENT YOU?!
HEE, HEE, HEE...
WHAT DO YOU SEE, LARVA?
HNN...

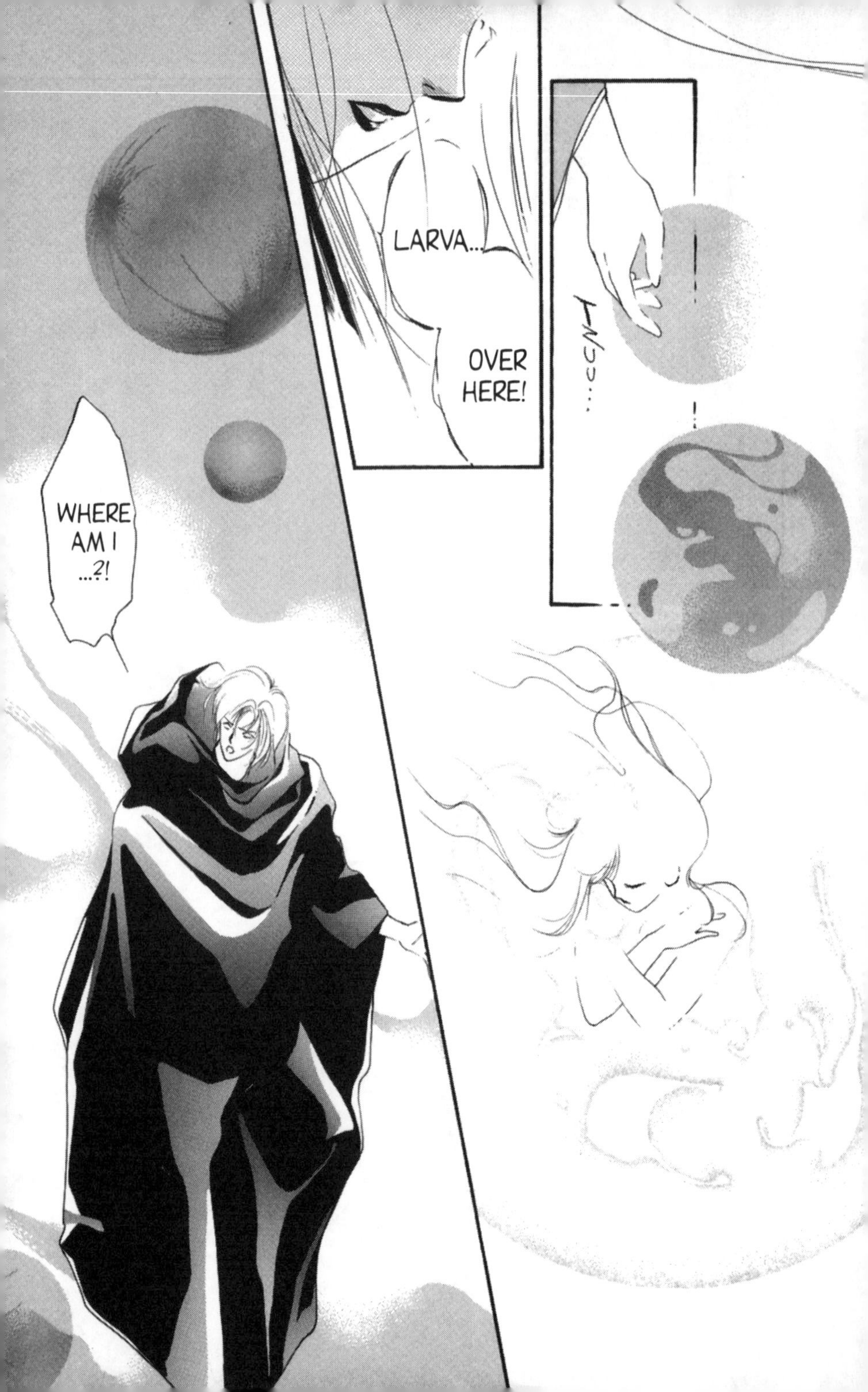
LARVA...
OVER HERE!
WHERE AM I ...?!

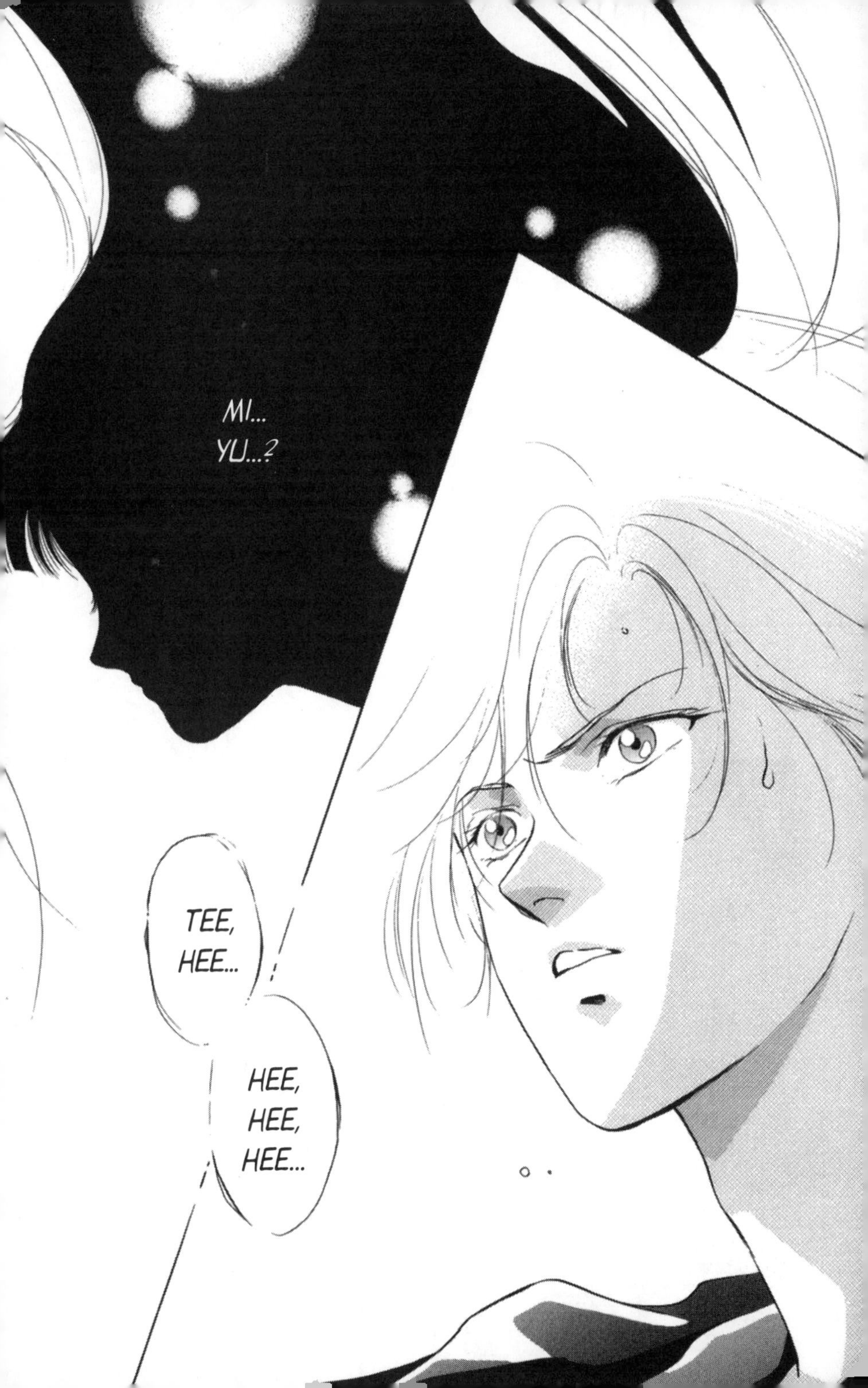
MI...
YU...?
TEE,
HEE...
HEE,
HEE,
HEE...

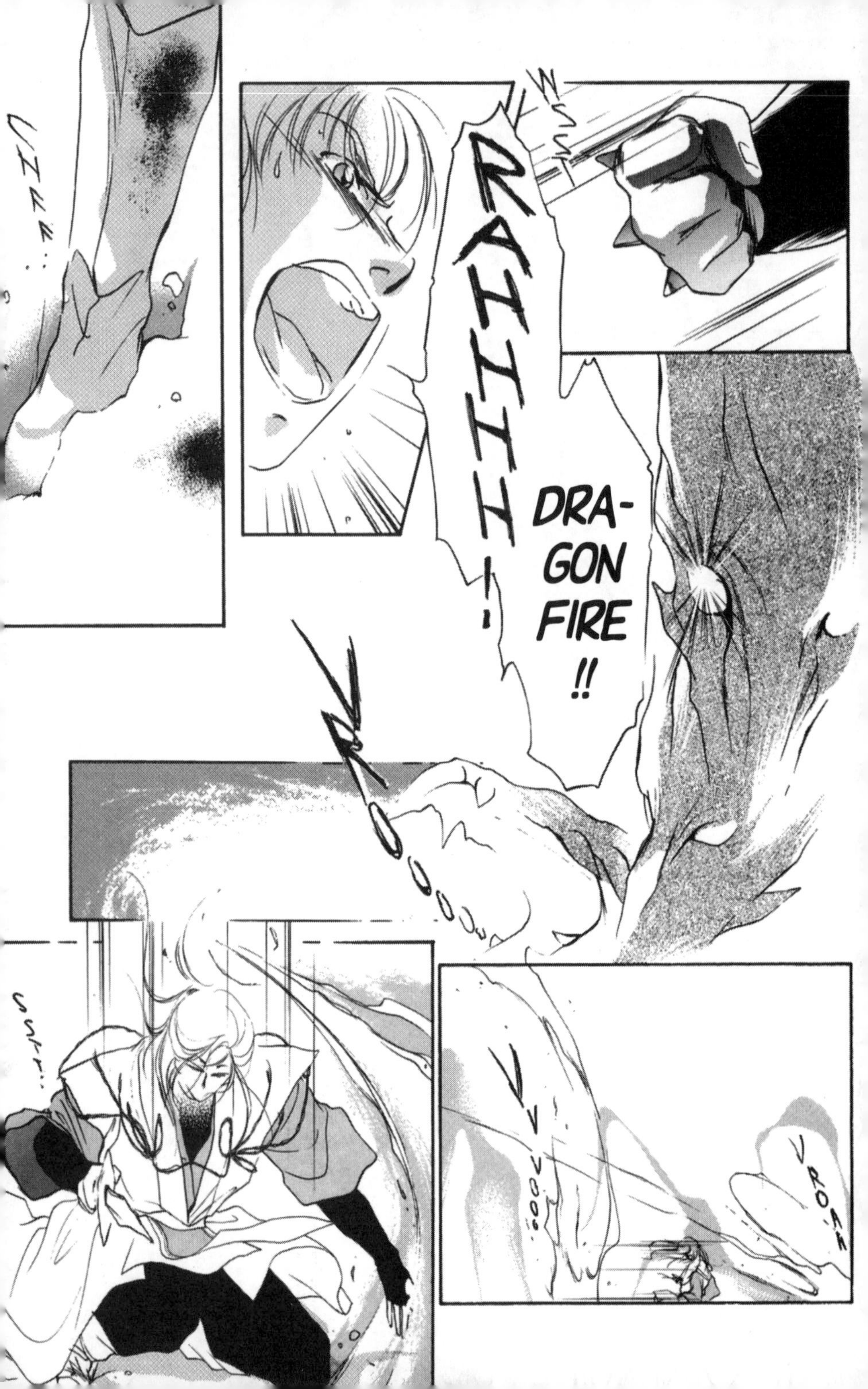
RAHHH!!
DRA-
GON
FIRE
!!

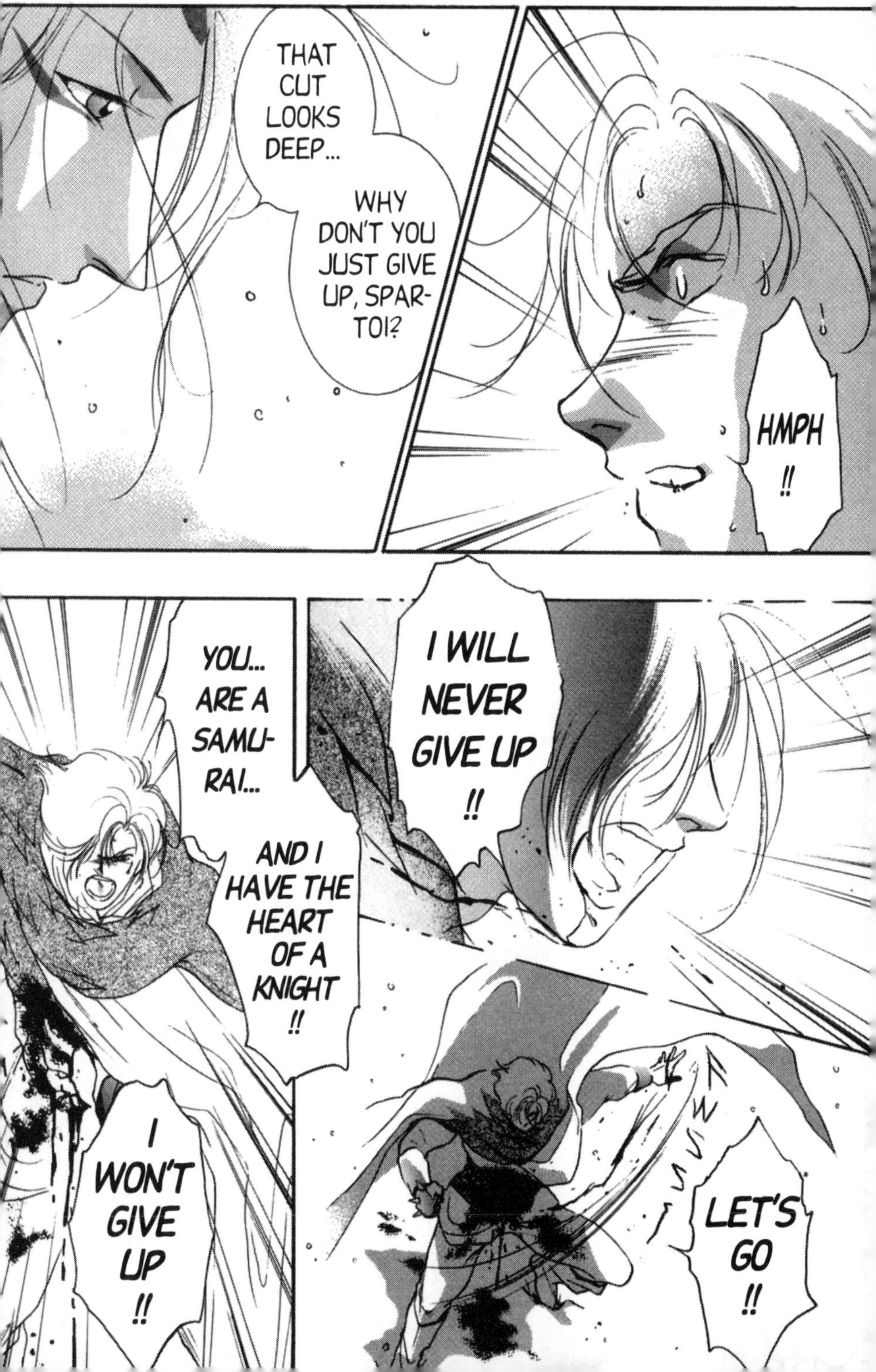
THAT CUT LOOKS DEEP...
WHY DON'T YOU JUST GIVE UP, SPAR-TOI?
HMPH !!
YOU... ARE A SAMU-RAI...
AND I HAVE THE HEART OF A KNIGHT !!
I WILL NEVER GIVE UP !!
I WON'T GIVE UP !!
LET'S GO !!

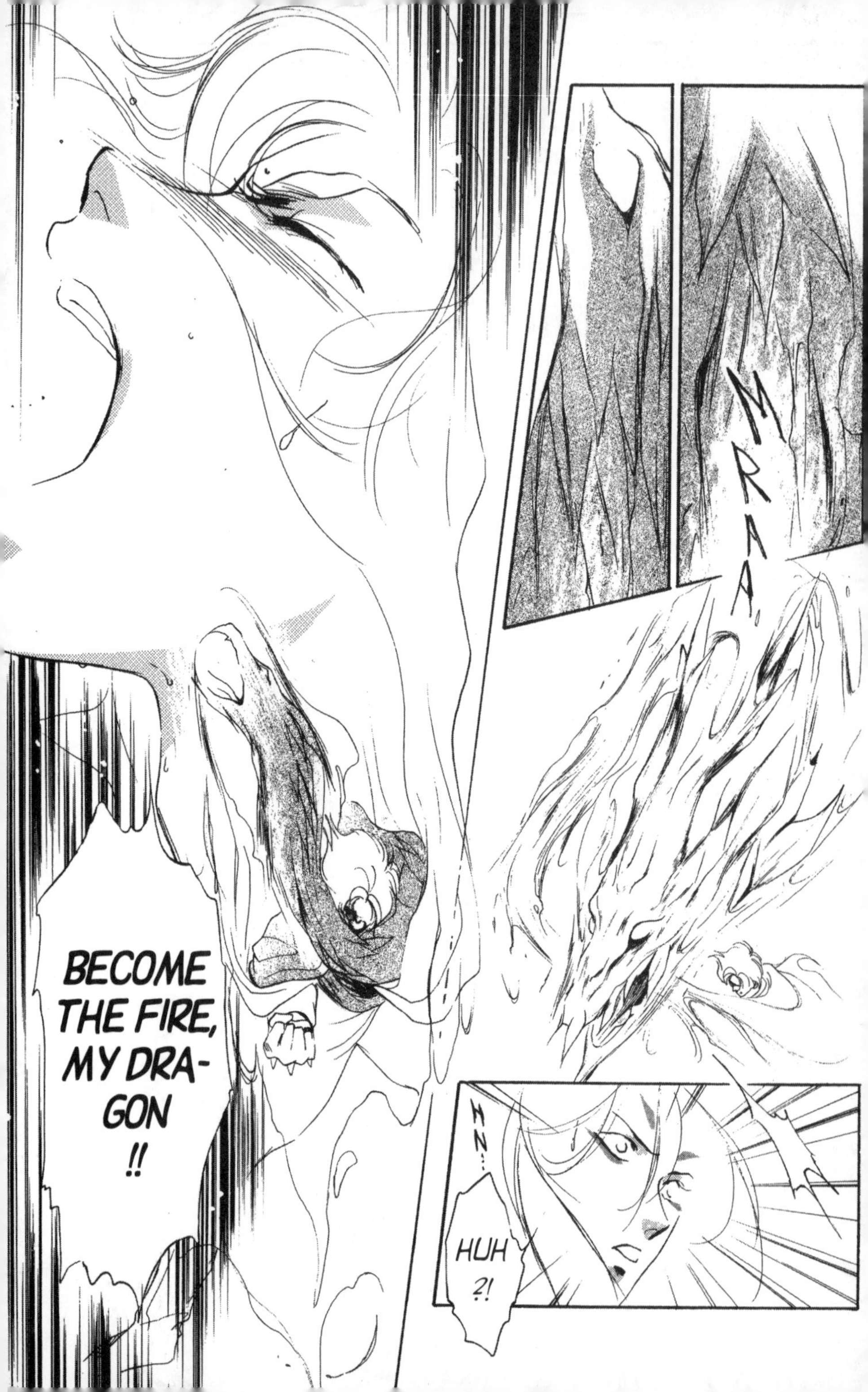

MRAA
BECOME THE FIRE, MY DRA-GON !!
HN...
HUH ?!

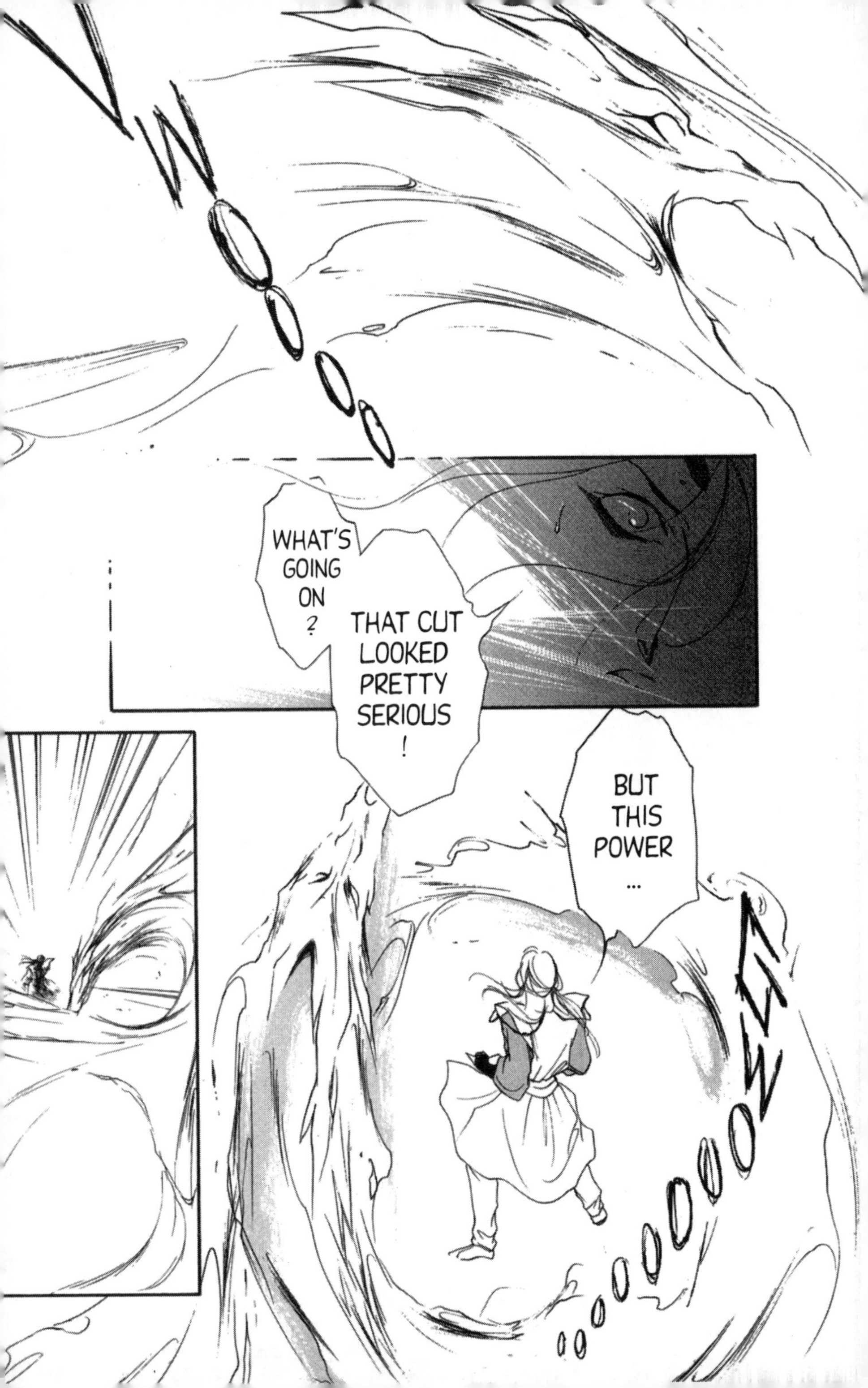
VWOOOO
WHAT'S GOING ON?
THAT CUT LOOKED PRETTY SERIOUS!
BUT THIS POWER...

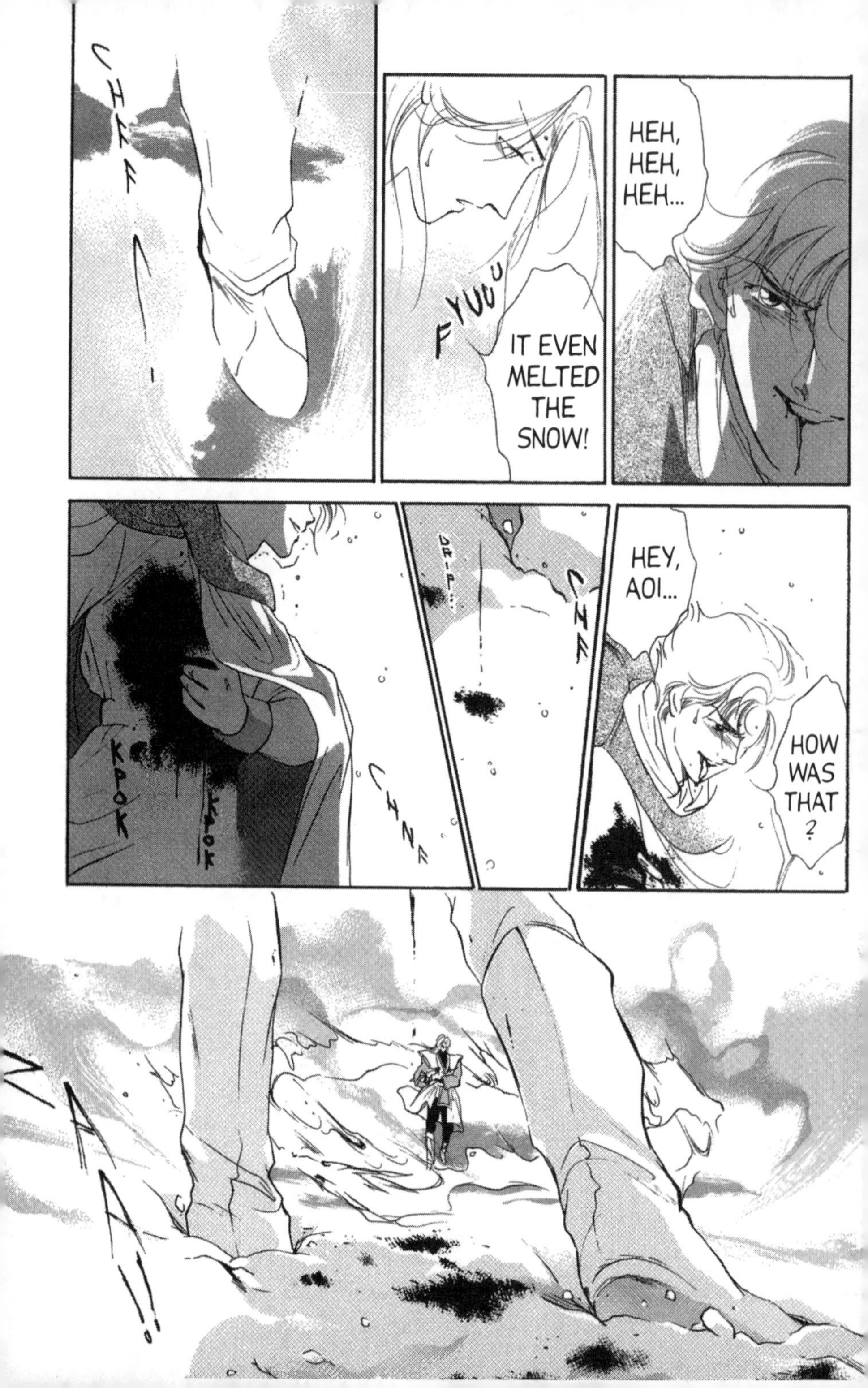
HEH, HEH, HEH...
FYUUU
IT EVEN MELTED THE SNOW!
CHFF
HEY, AOI...
HOW WAS THAT?
DRIP...
CHF
CHNF
KPOK
KPOK
NAA!!

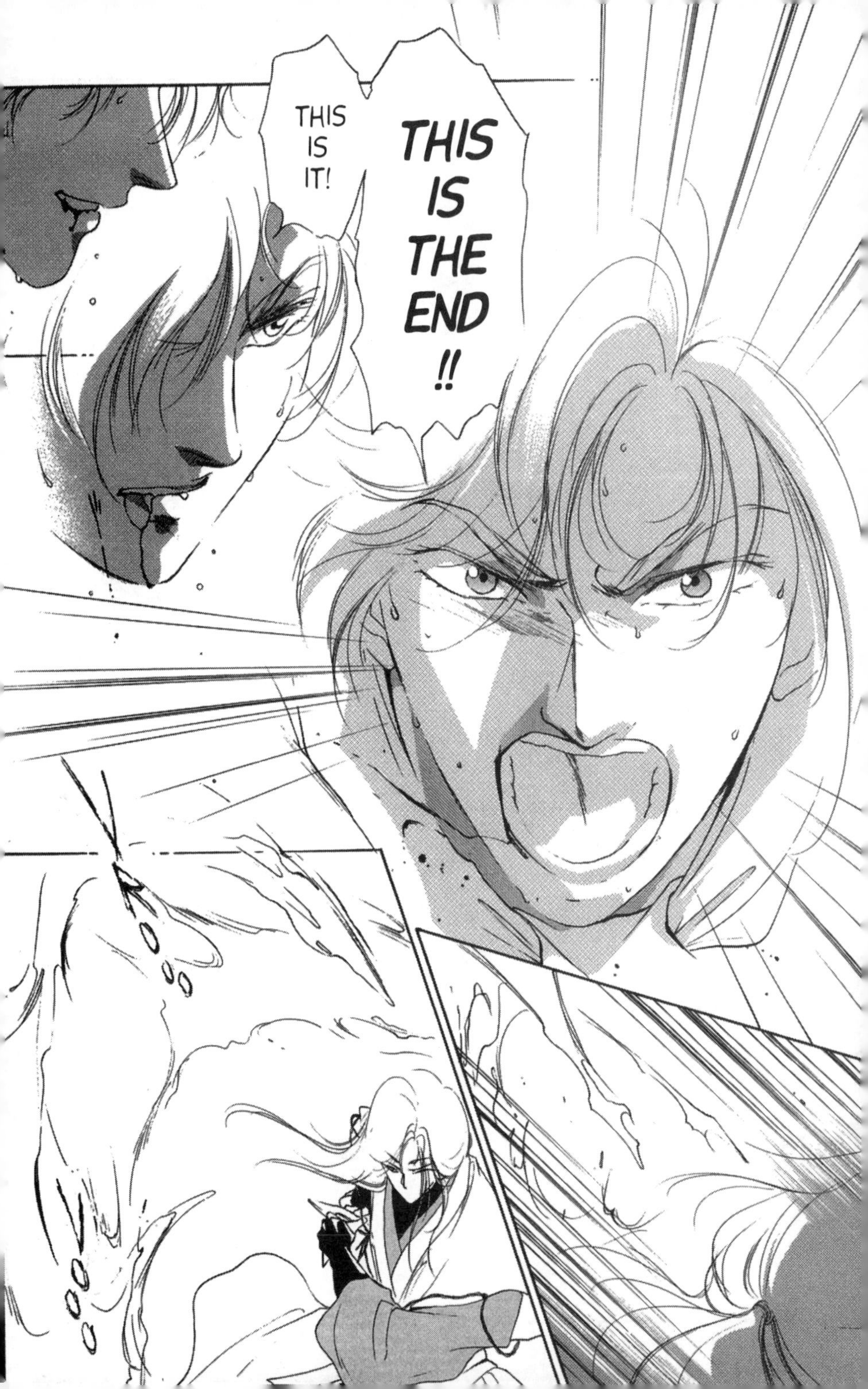
THIS IS IT!
THIS IS THE END !!

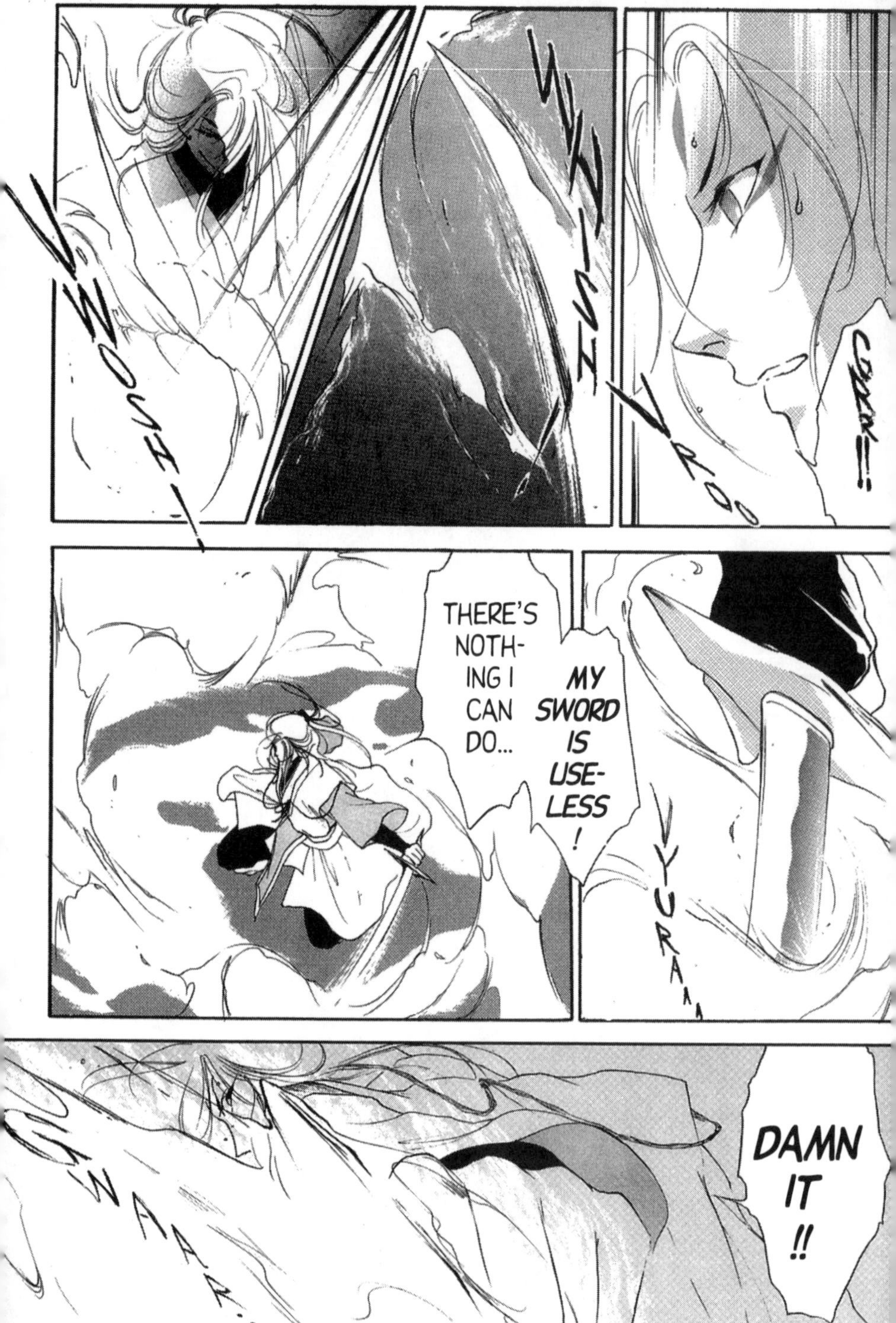

THERE'S NOTHING I CAN DO...
MY SWORD IS USELESS!
YURAAA
DAMN IT!!

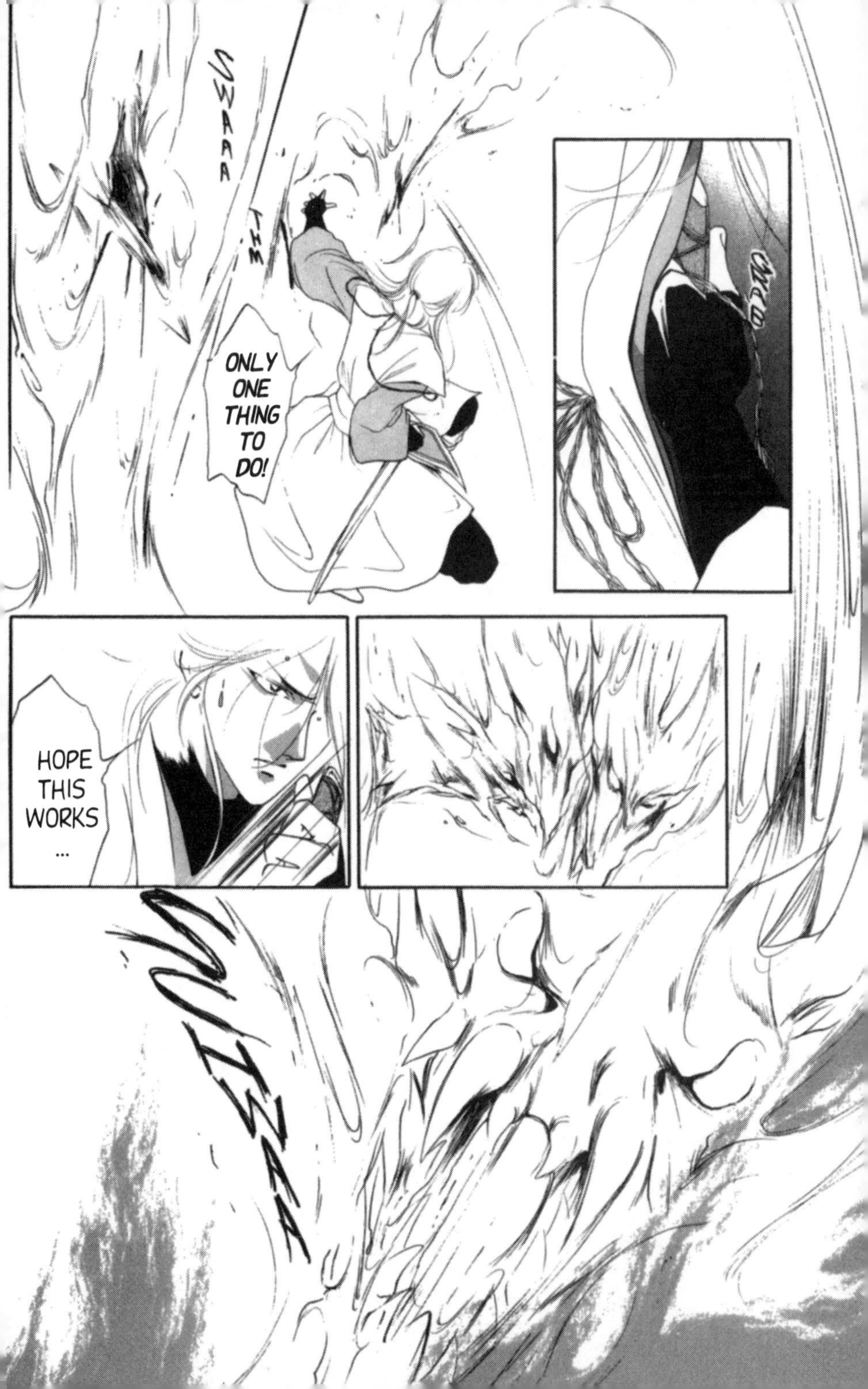
SWAAA
THM
ONLY ONE THING TO DO!
HOPE THIS WORKS ...

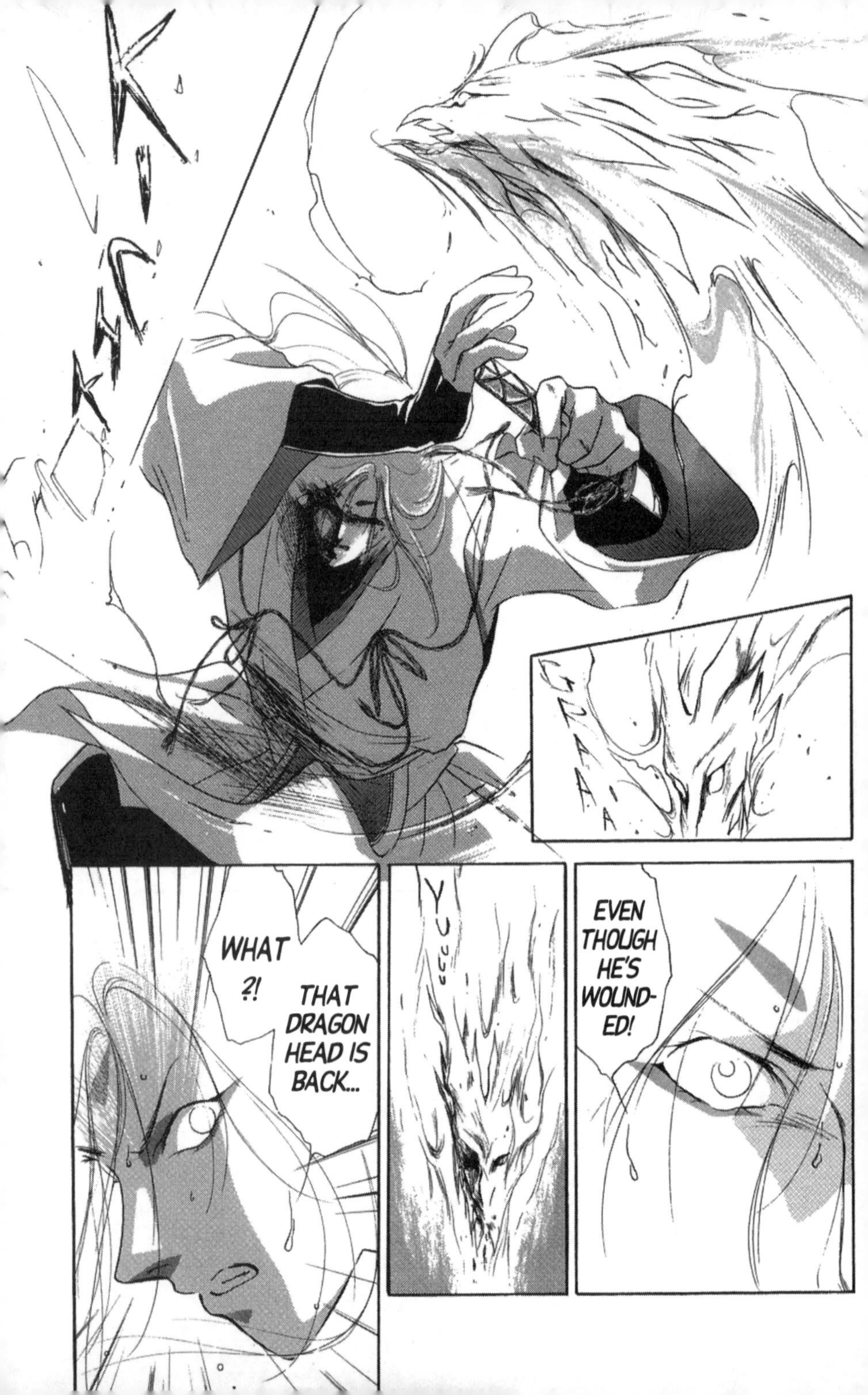

KRAKK
GUAAAA
EVEN THOUGH HE'S WOUND-ED!
YUUUU
WHAT?!
THAT DRAGON HEAD IS BACK...

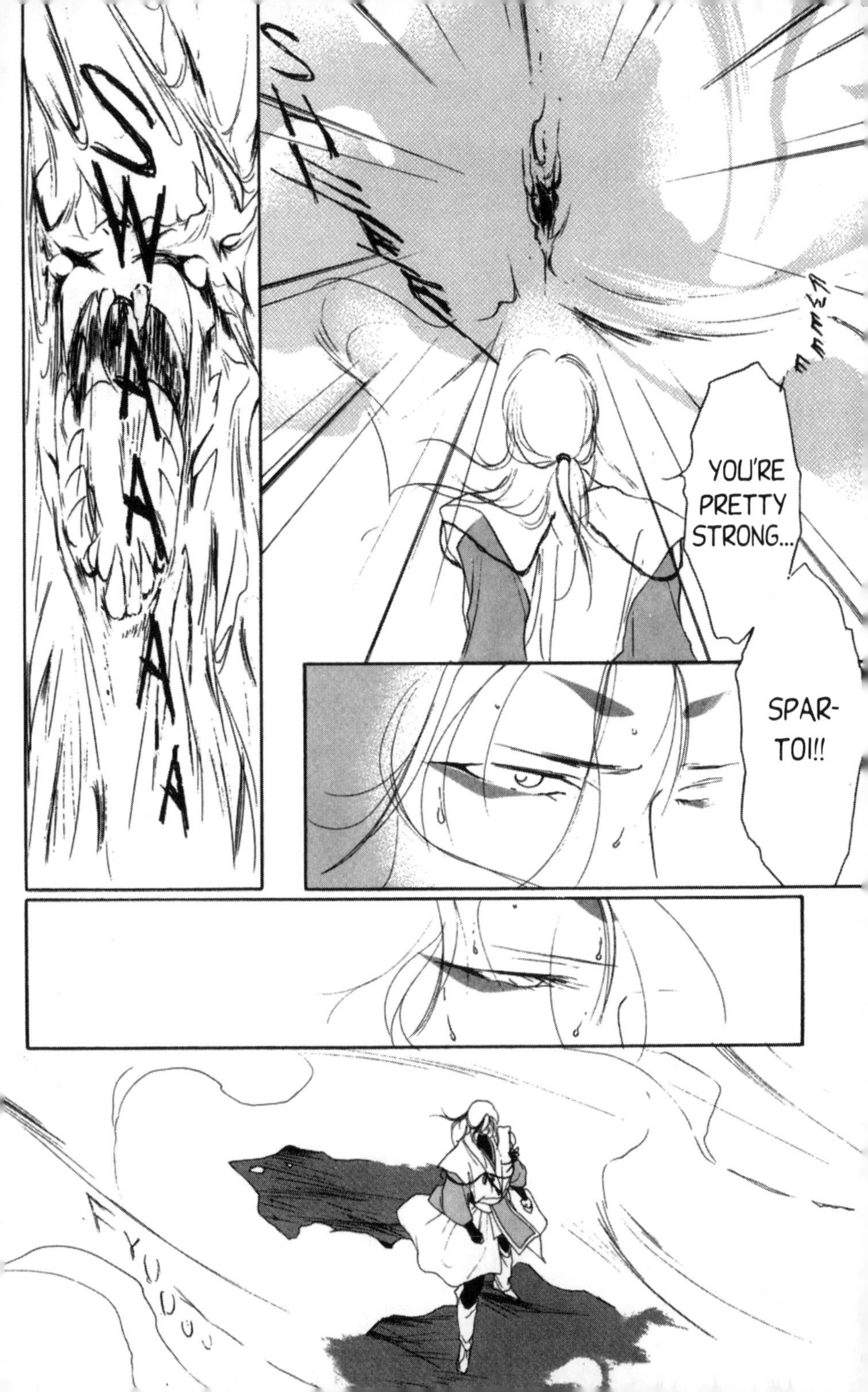
YOU'RE PRETTY STRONG...
SPAR-
TOI!!

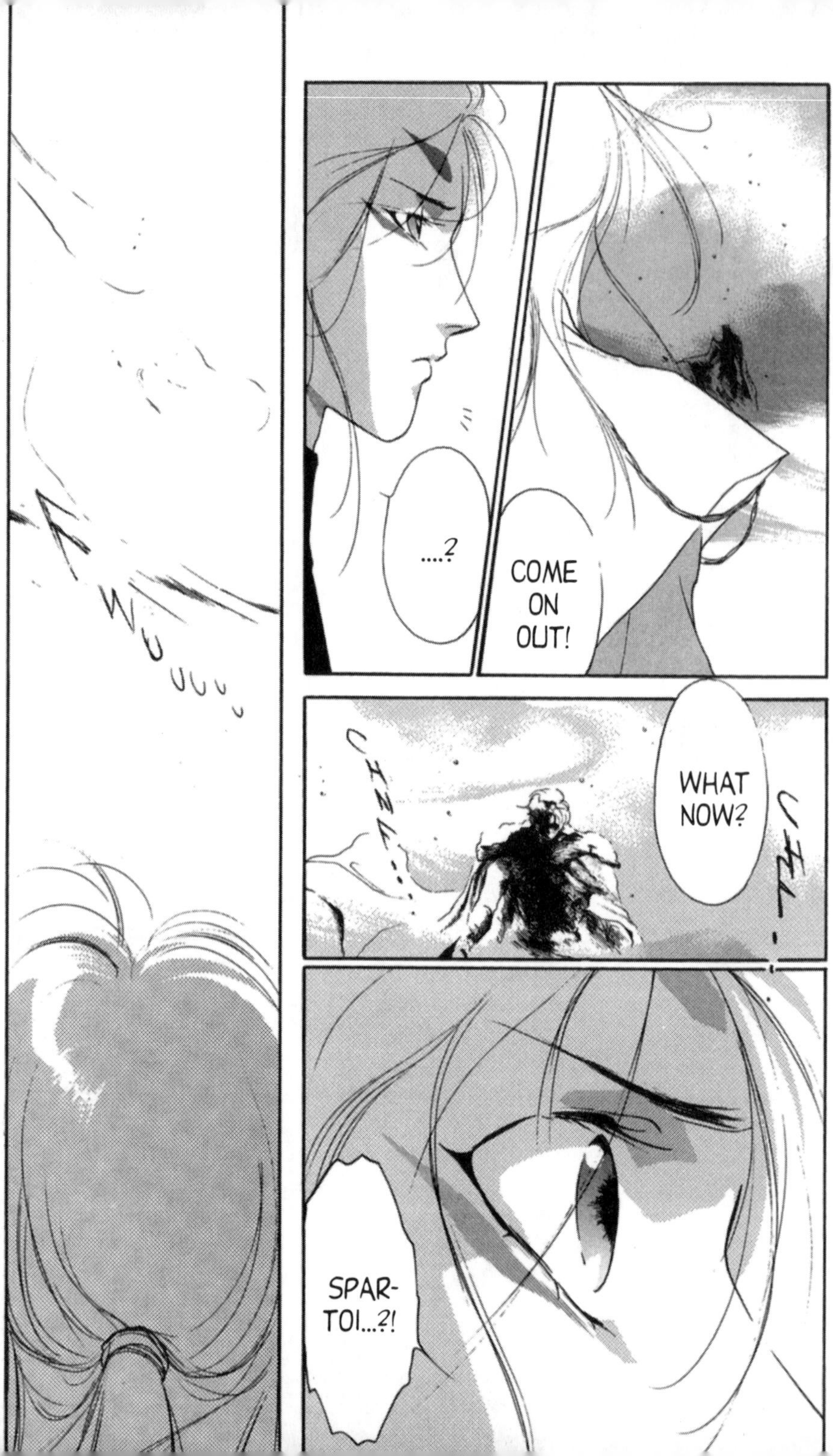
COME ON OUT!
....?
WHAT NOW?
SPAR-TOI...?!

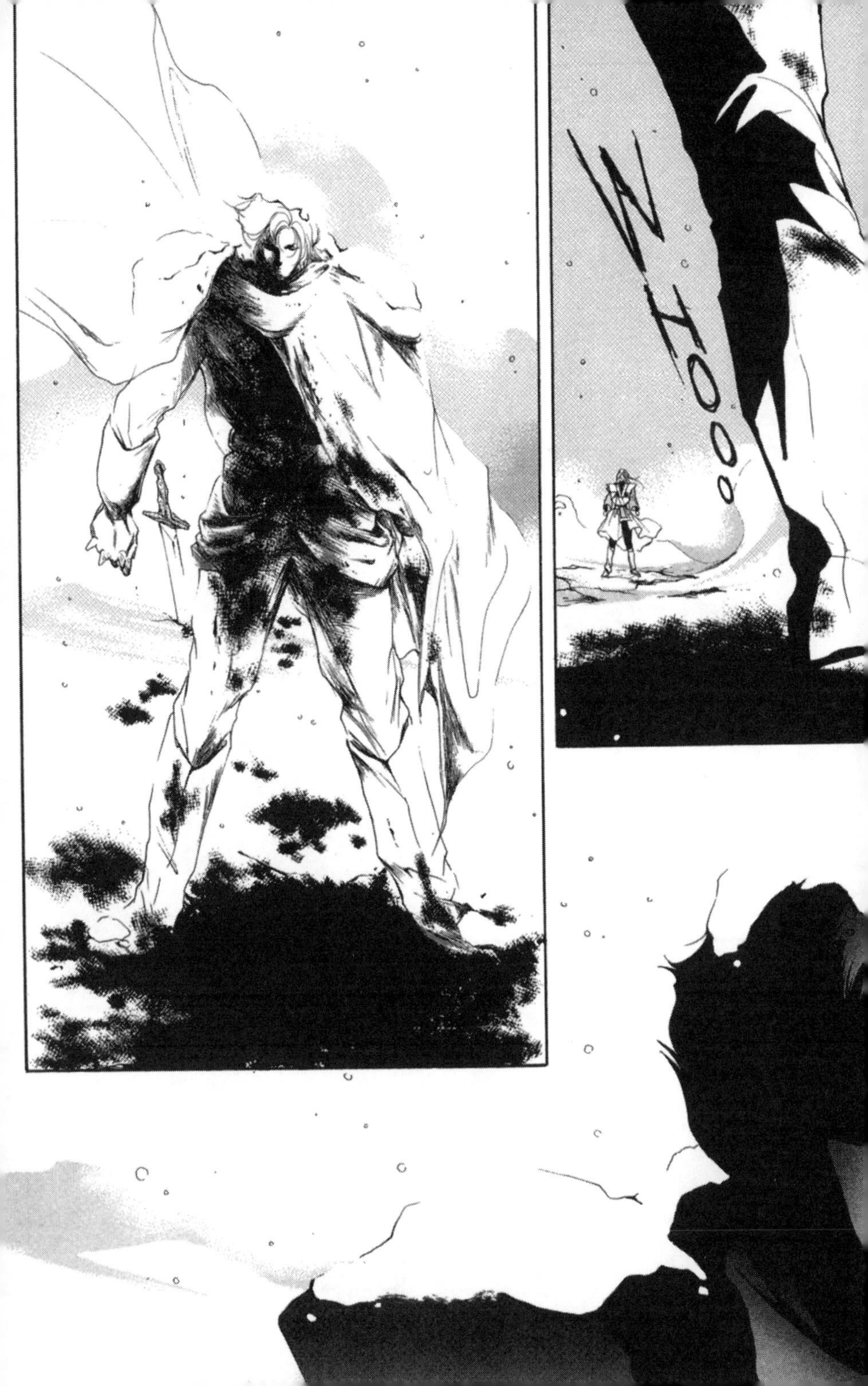
ZHOOOO

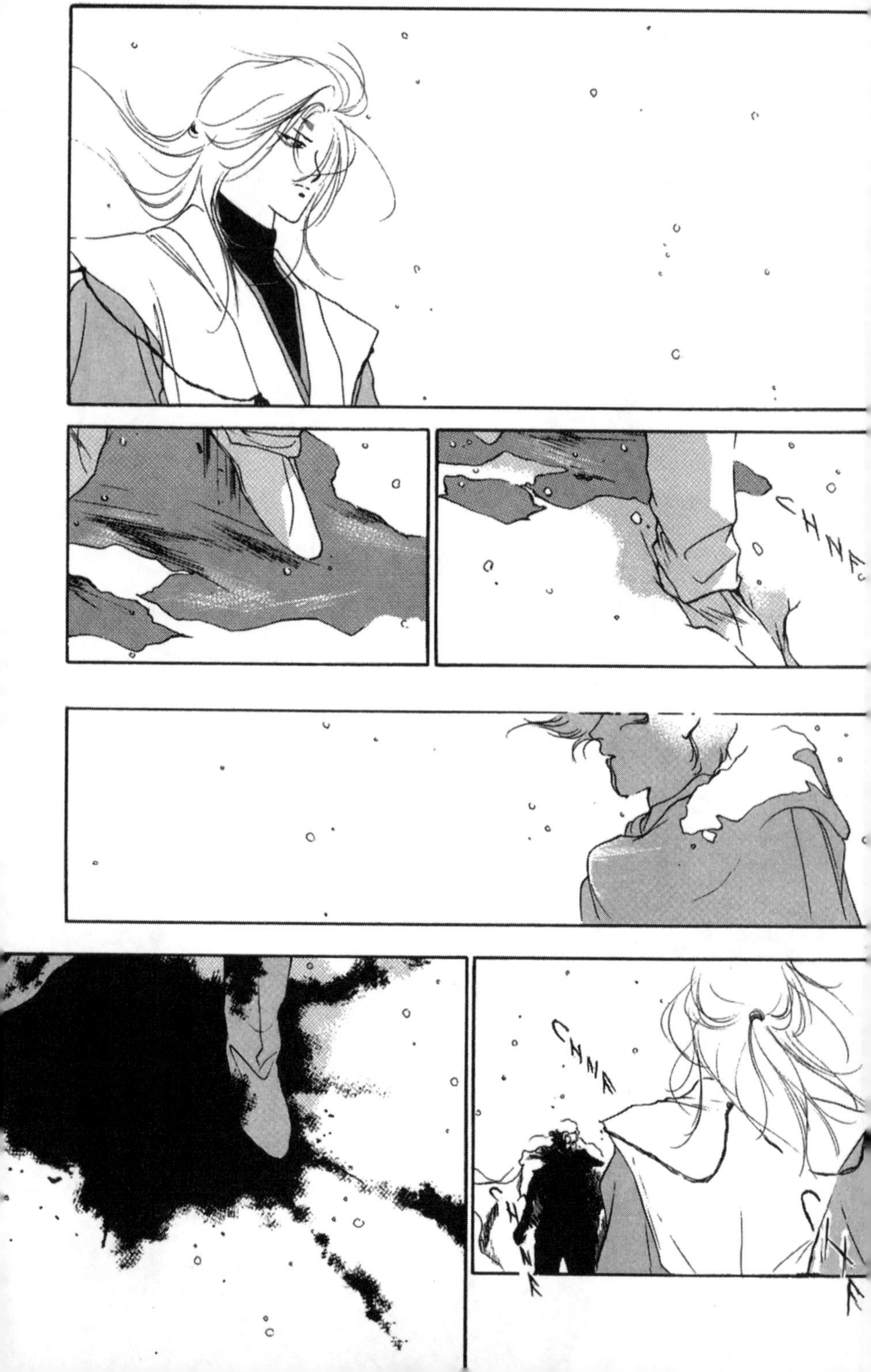
CHNK
CHNK
CHNK
CHNK

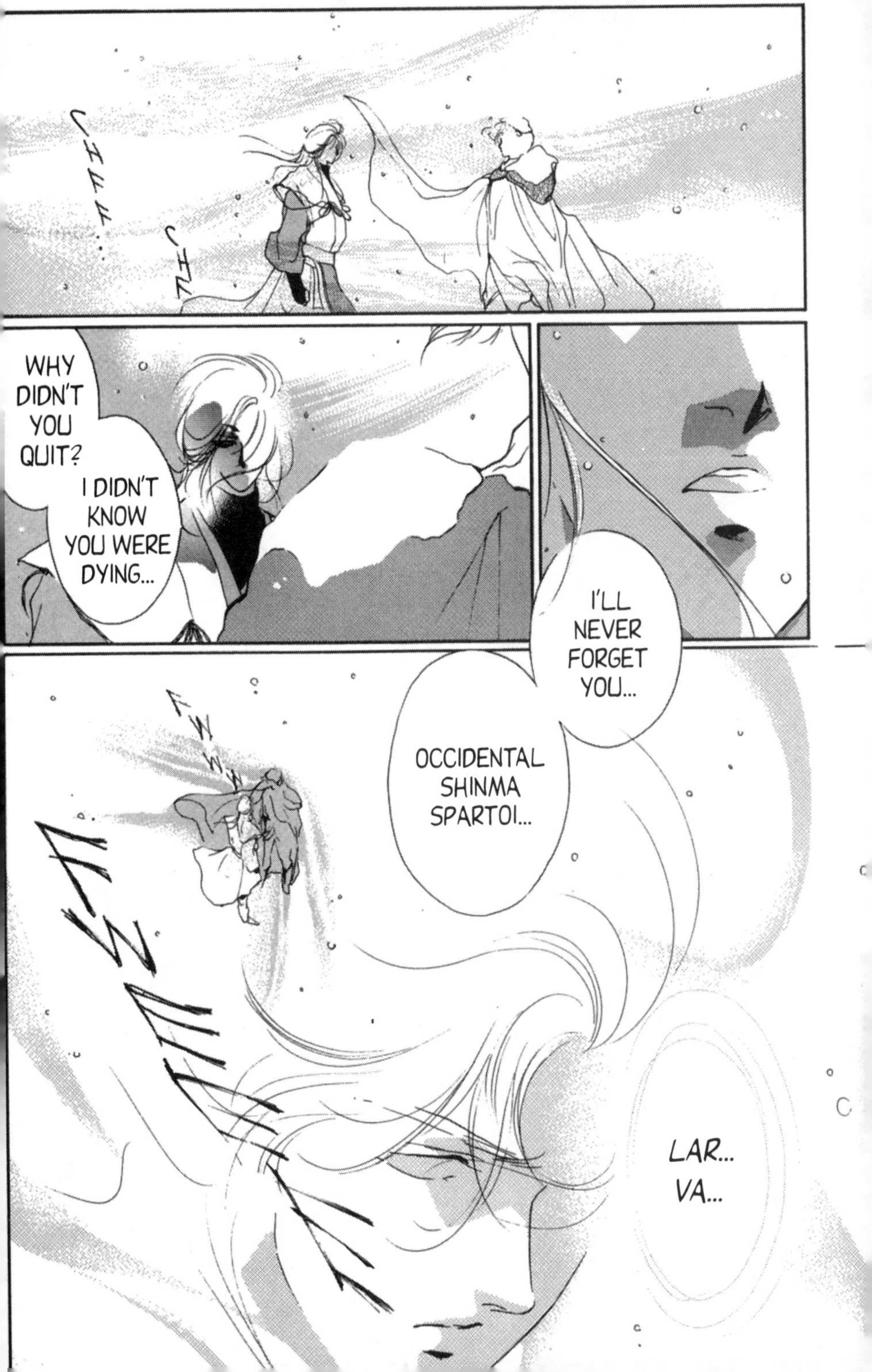
WHY DIDN'T YOU QUIT?
I DIDN'T KNOW YOU WERE DYING...
I'LL NEVER FORGET YOU...
OCCIDENTAL SHINMA SPARTOI...
LAR... VA...

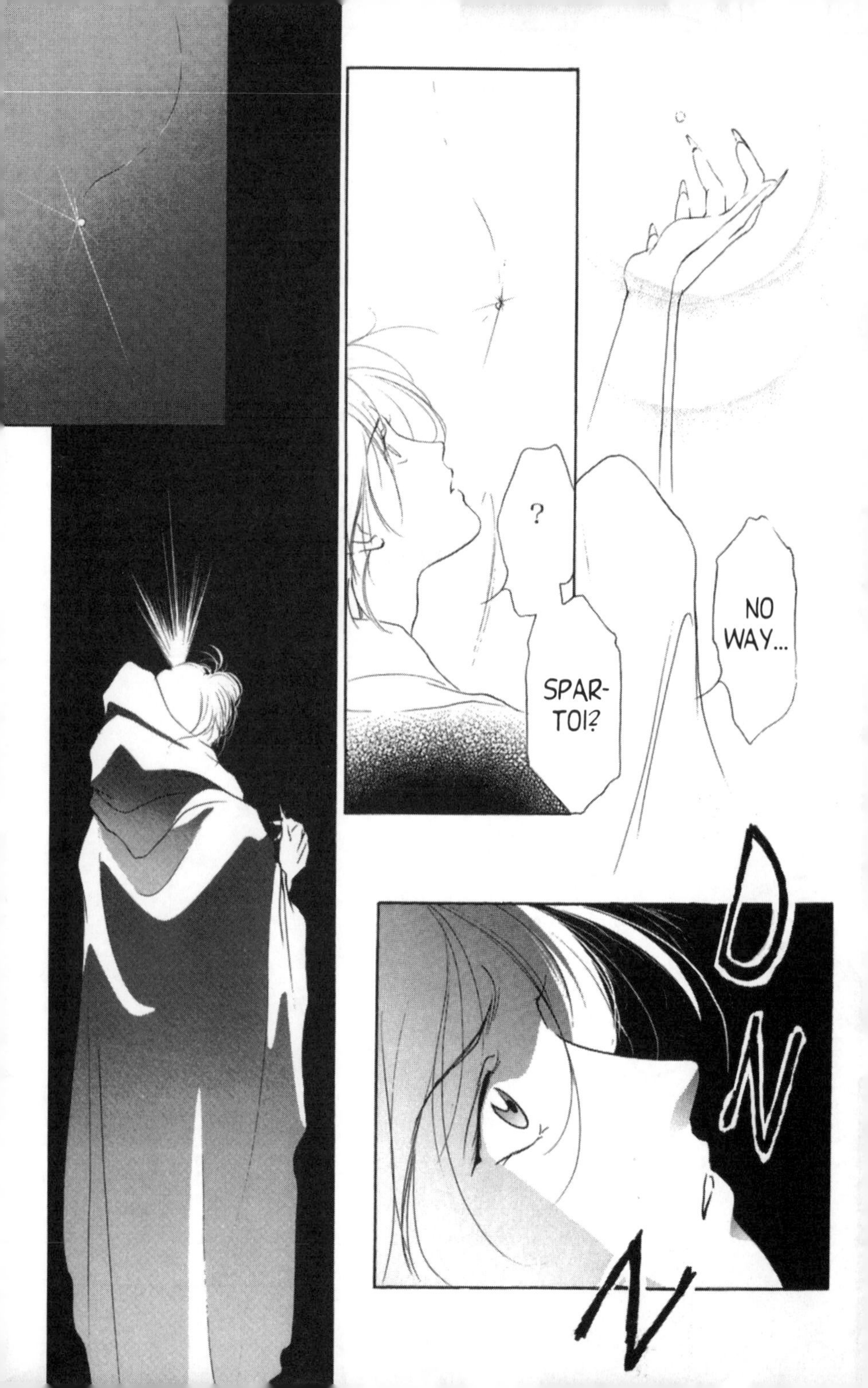
NO WAY...
SPAR-TOI?
?
DNN

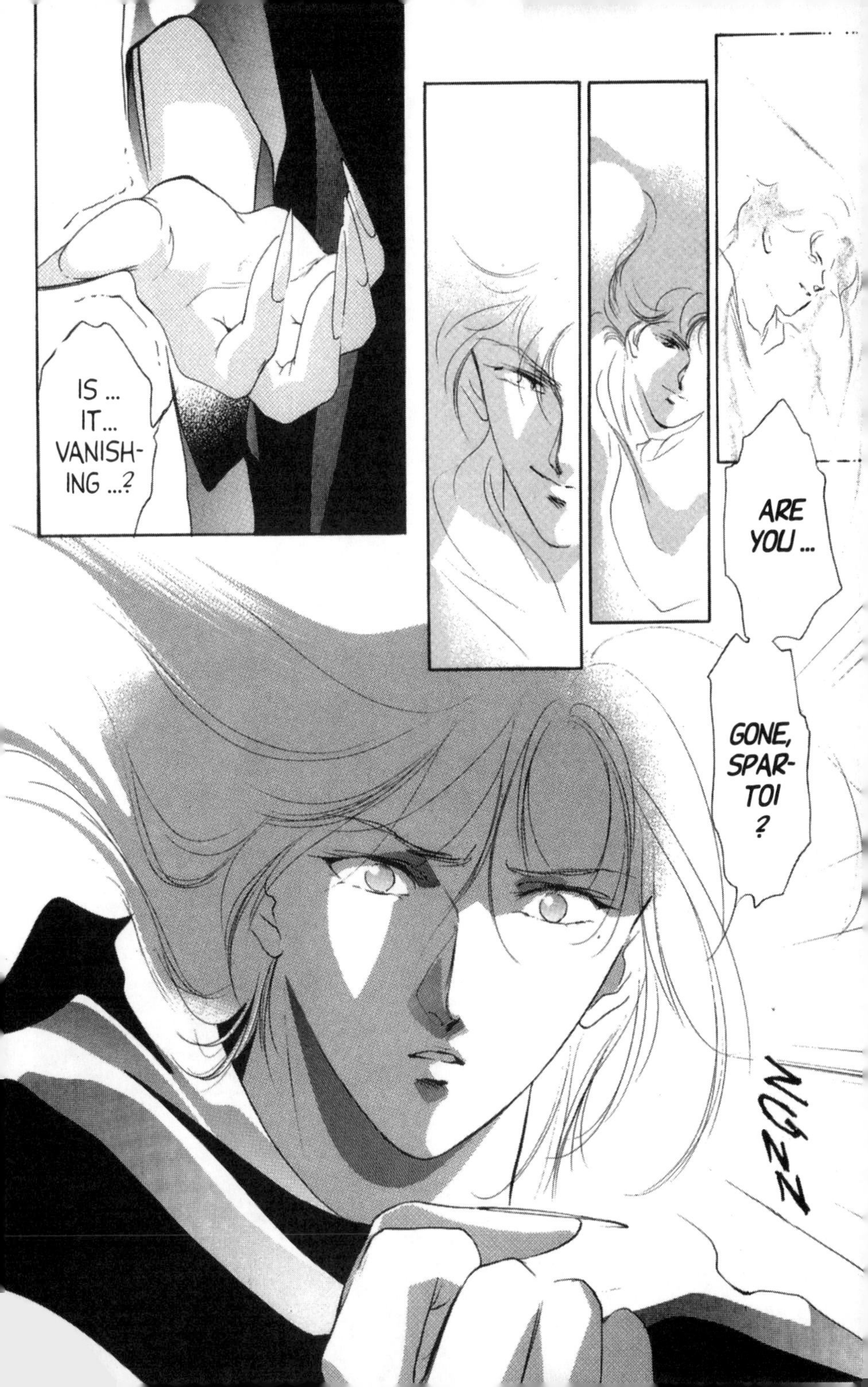
IS ... IT... VANISH- ING ...?
ARE YOU ...
GONE, SPAR- TOI ?

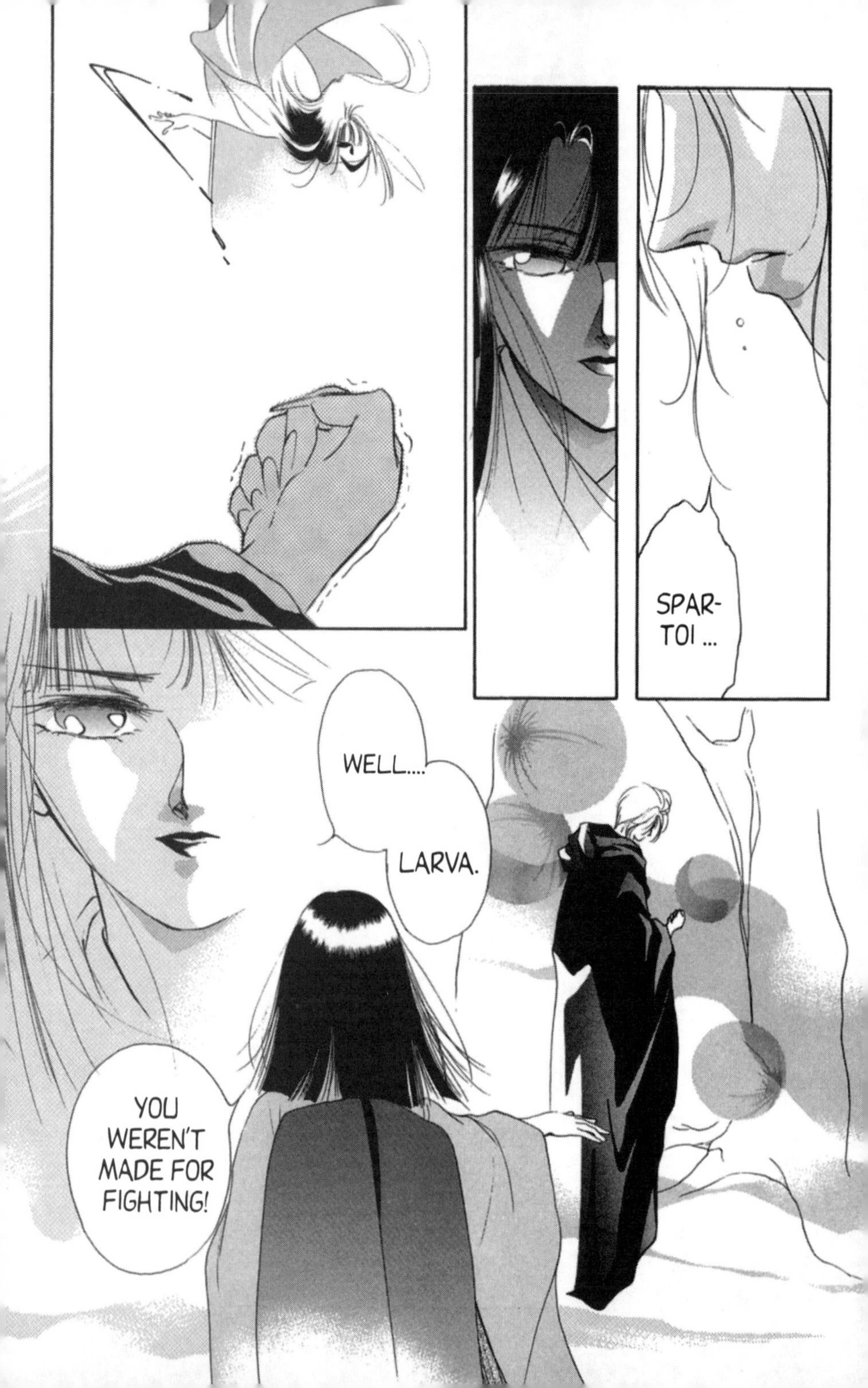
SPAR-TOI ...
WELL....
LARVA.
YOU WEREN'T MADE FOR FIGHTING!

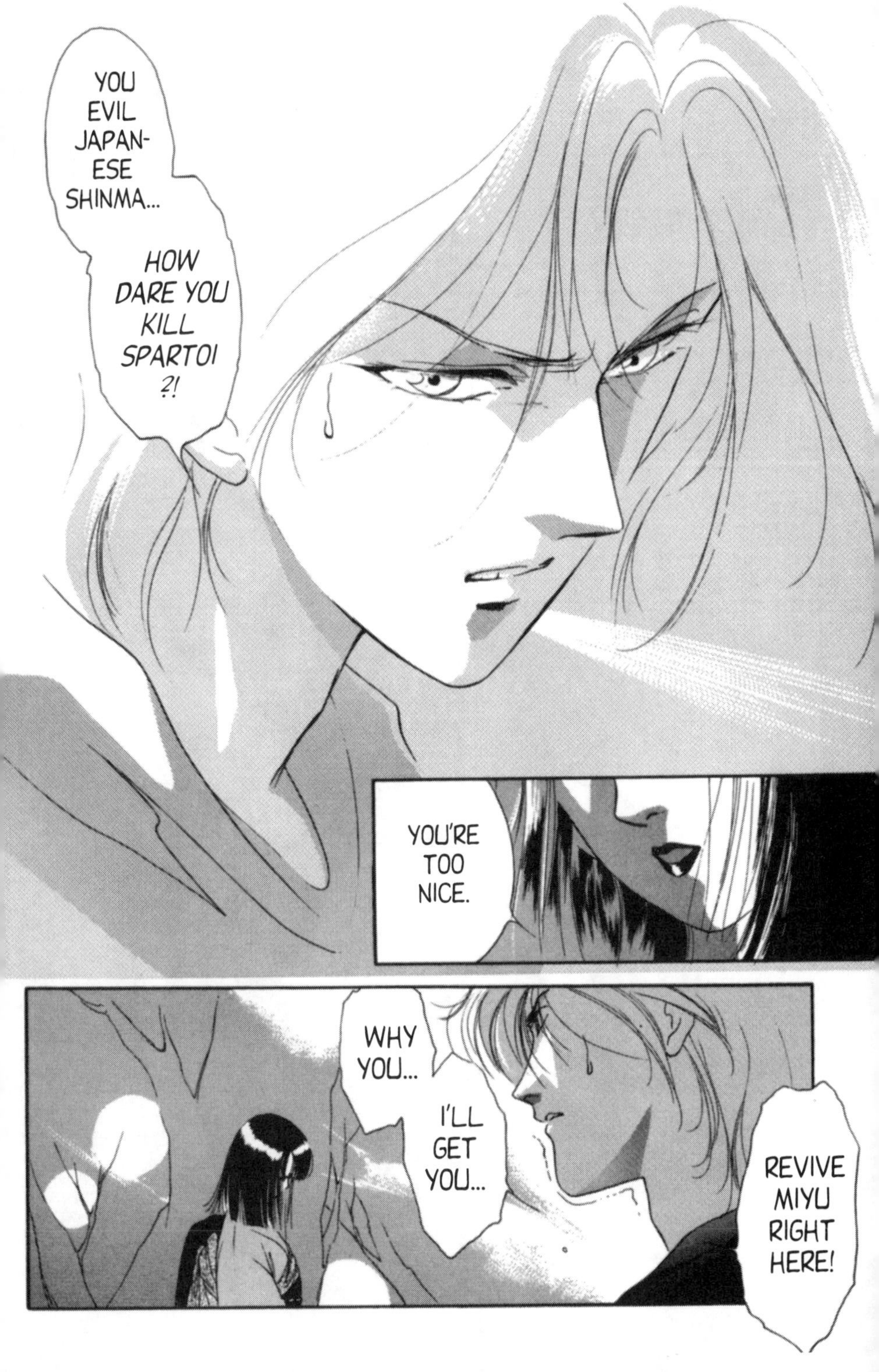
YOU EVIL JAPAN-ESE SHINMA...
HOW DARE YOU KILL SPARTOI ?!
YOU'RE TOO NICE.
WHY YOU...
I'LL GET YOU...
REVIVE MIYU RIGHT HERE!

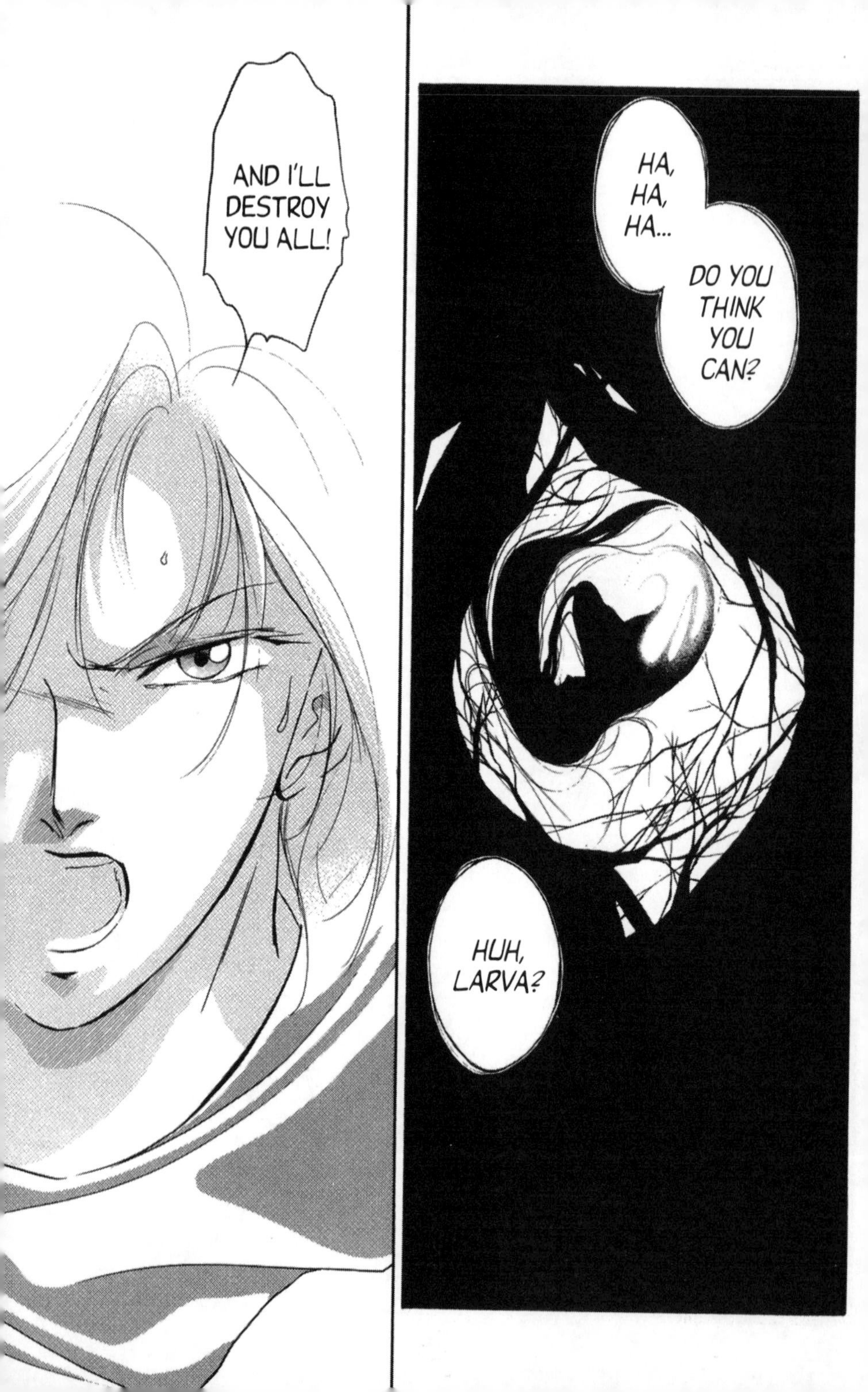
AND I'LL DESTROY YOU ALL!
HA, HA, HA...
DO YOU THINK YOU CAN?
HUH, LARVA?

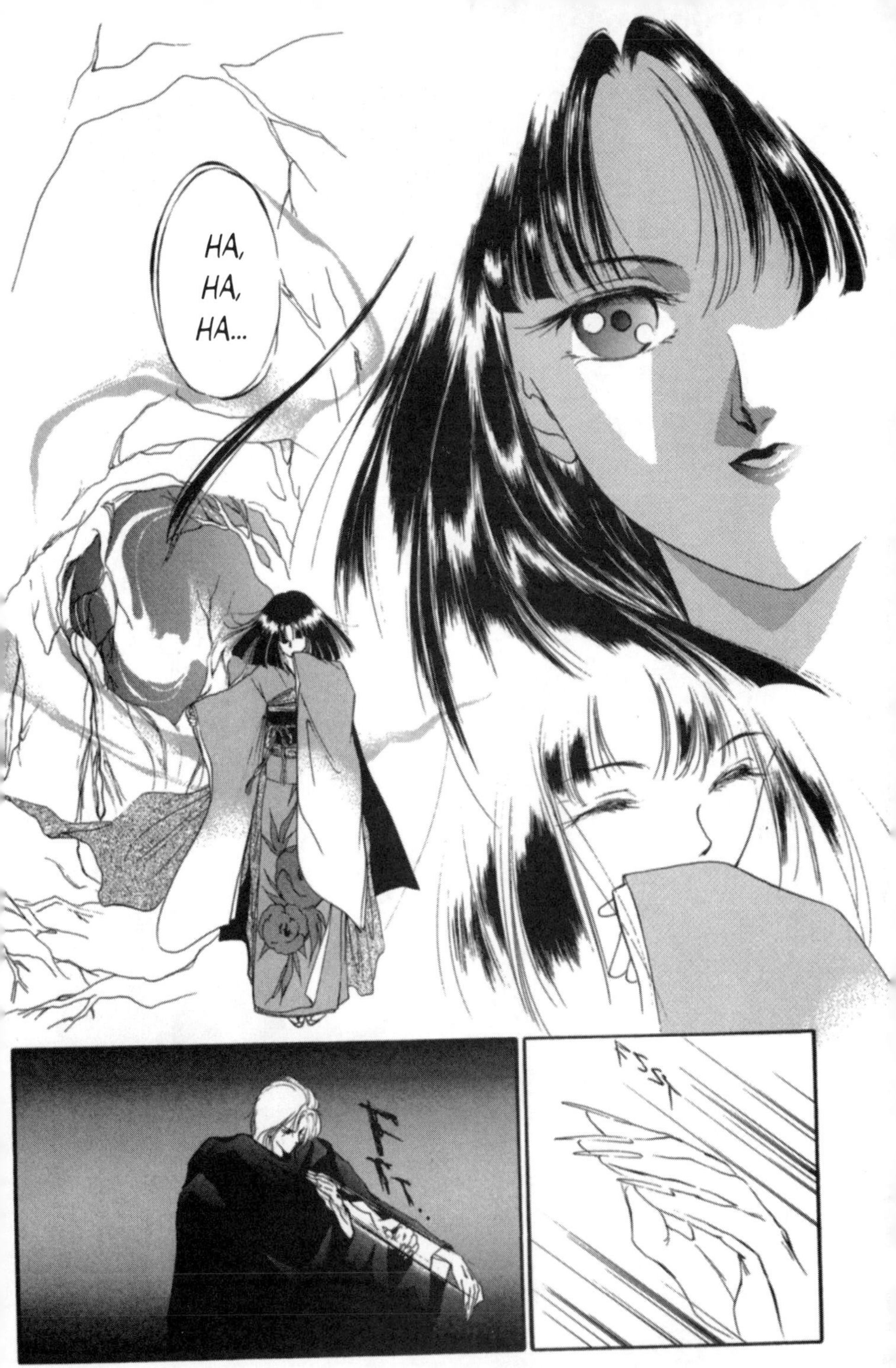
HA, HA, HA...
FSST
FFFT...

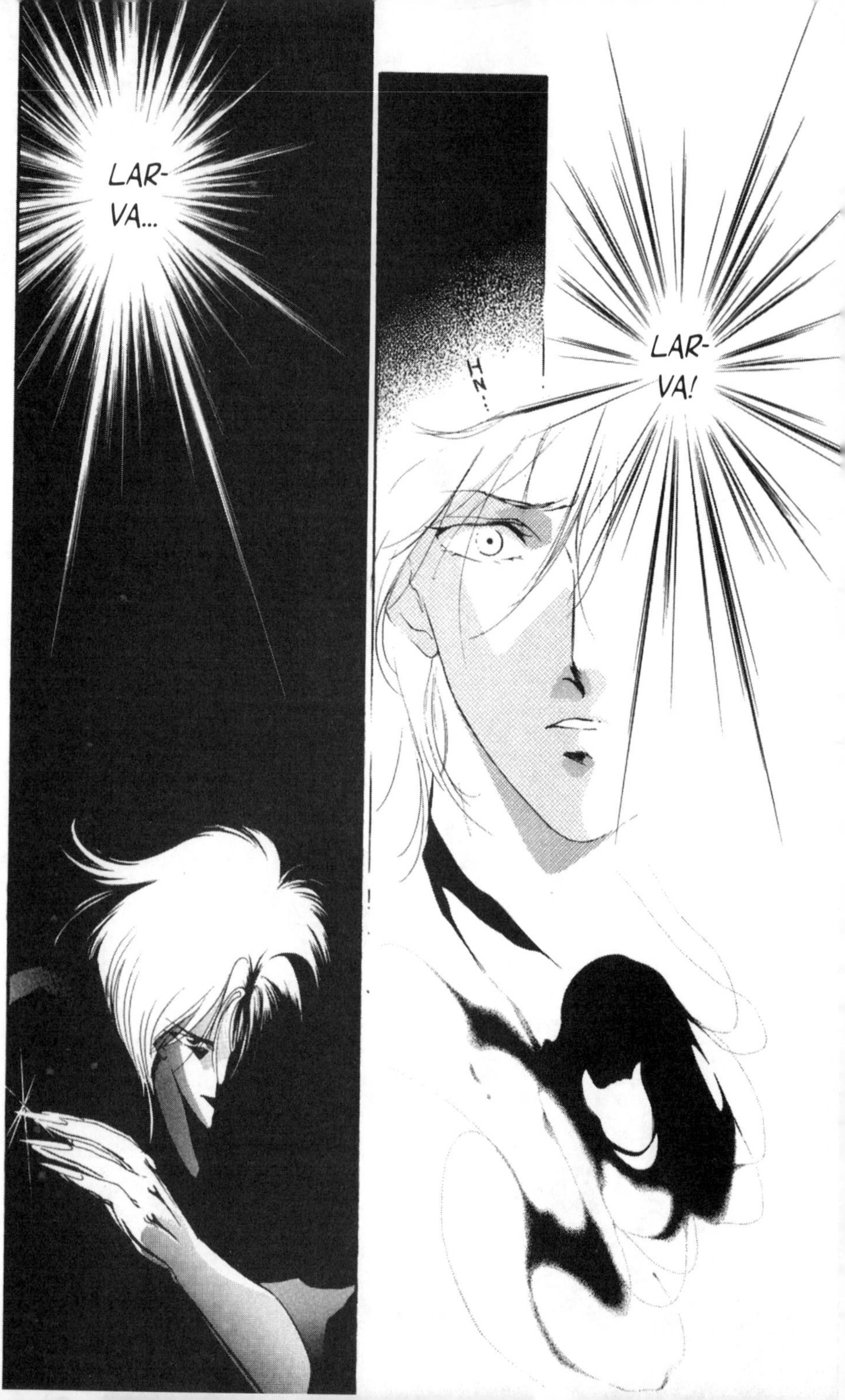
HN...
LAR-VA!
LAR-VA...

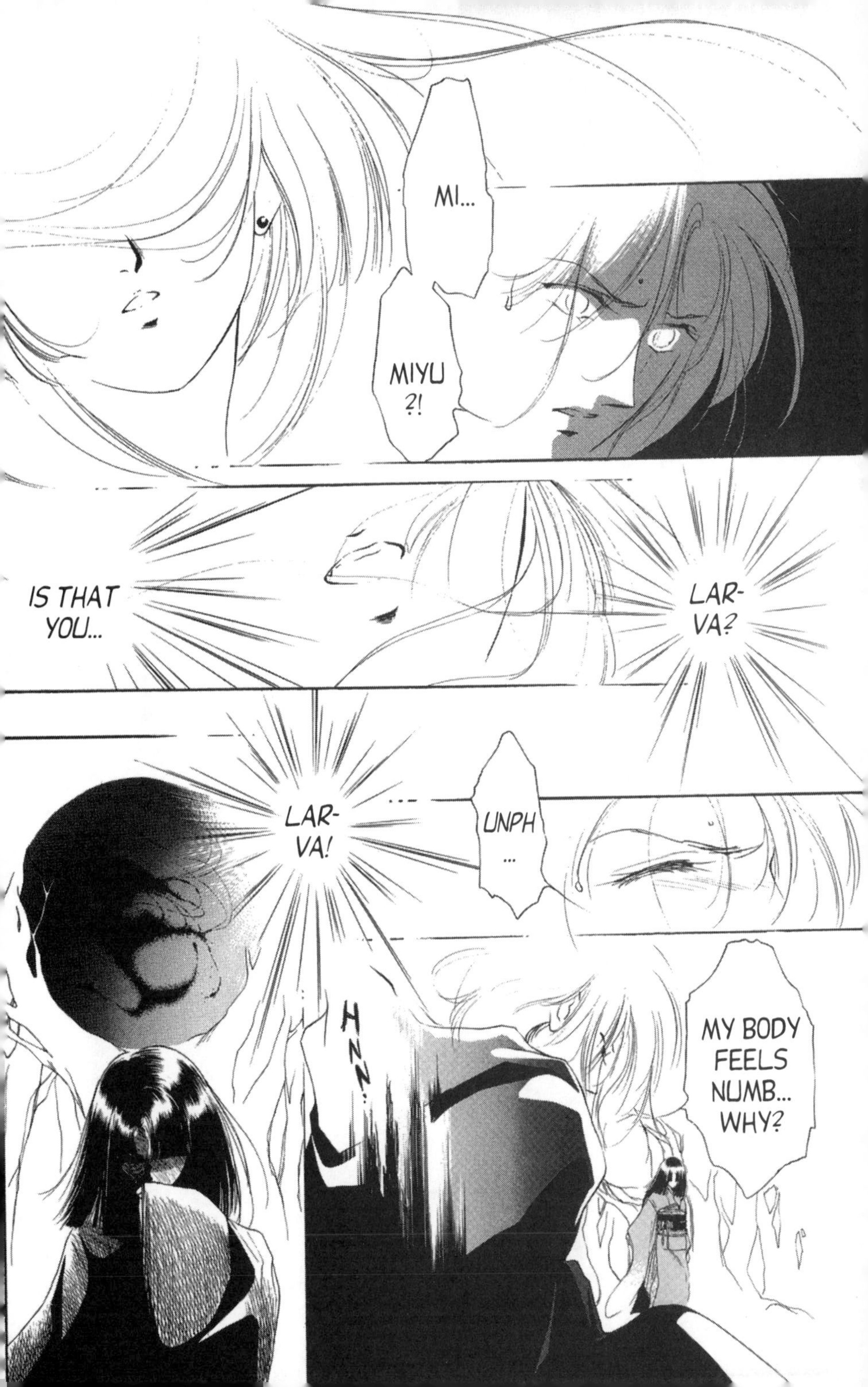
MI...
MIYU ?!
LAR-VA?
IS THAT YOU...
UNPH ...
LAR-VA!
MY BODY FEELS NUMB... WHY?
HNN...

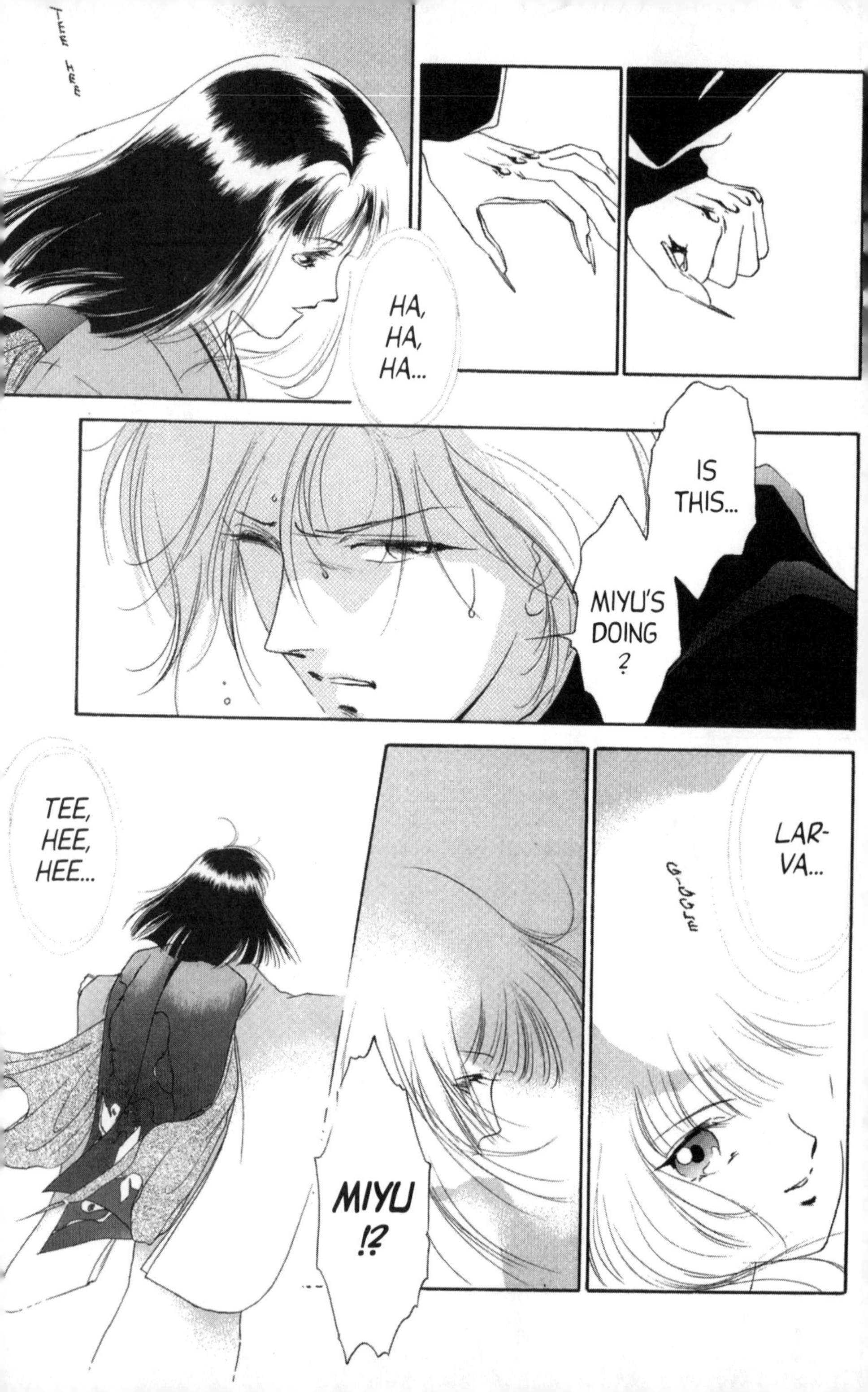
TEE HEE
HA, HA, HA...
IS THIS...
MIYU'S DOING?
LAR-VA...
MIYU!?
TEE, HEE, HEE...

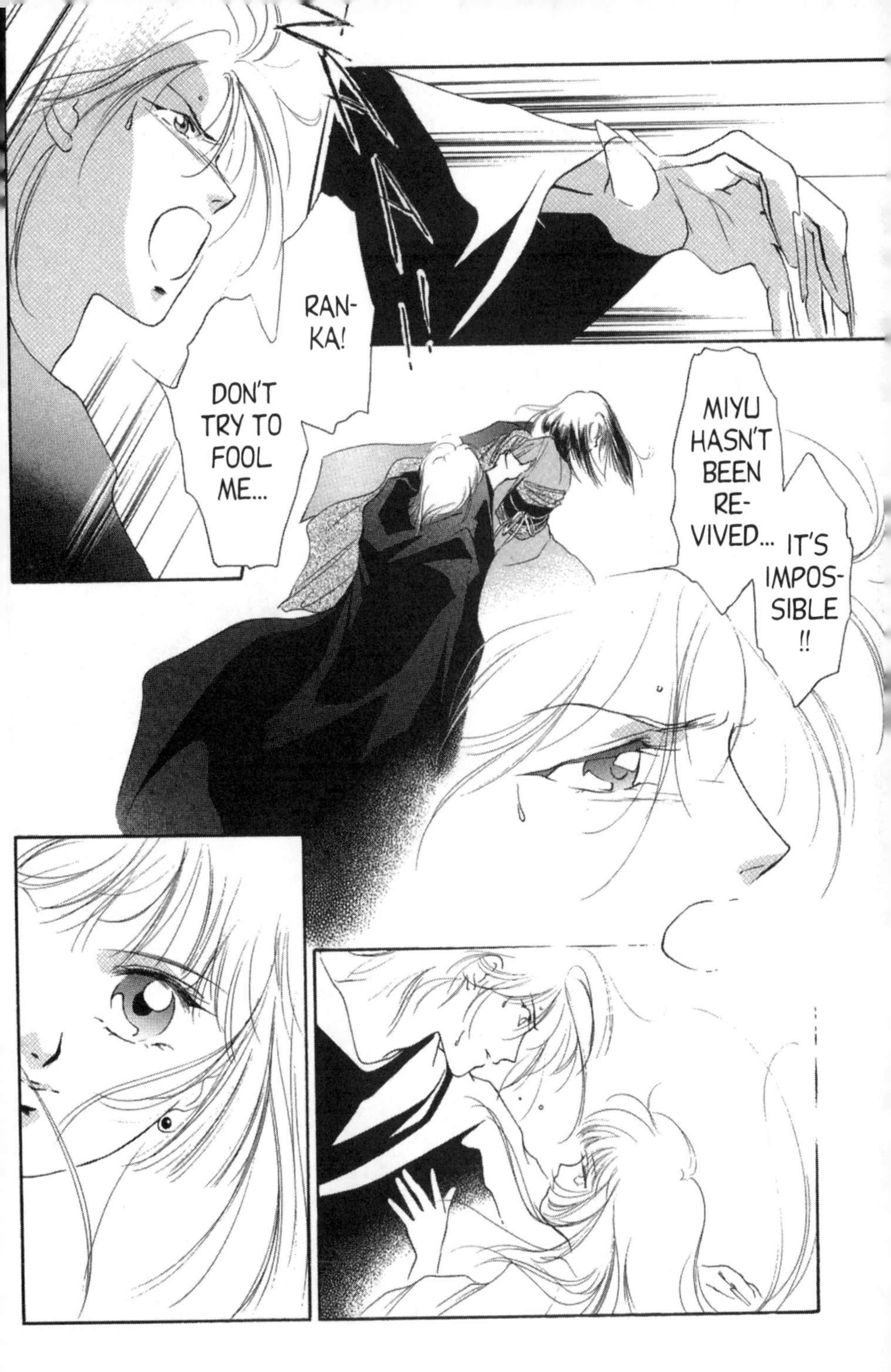
RAN-KA!
MIYU HASN'T BEEN RE-VIVED...
IT'S IMPOSSIBLE!!
DON'T TRY TO FOOL ME...

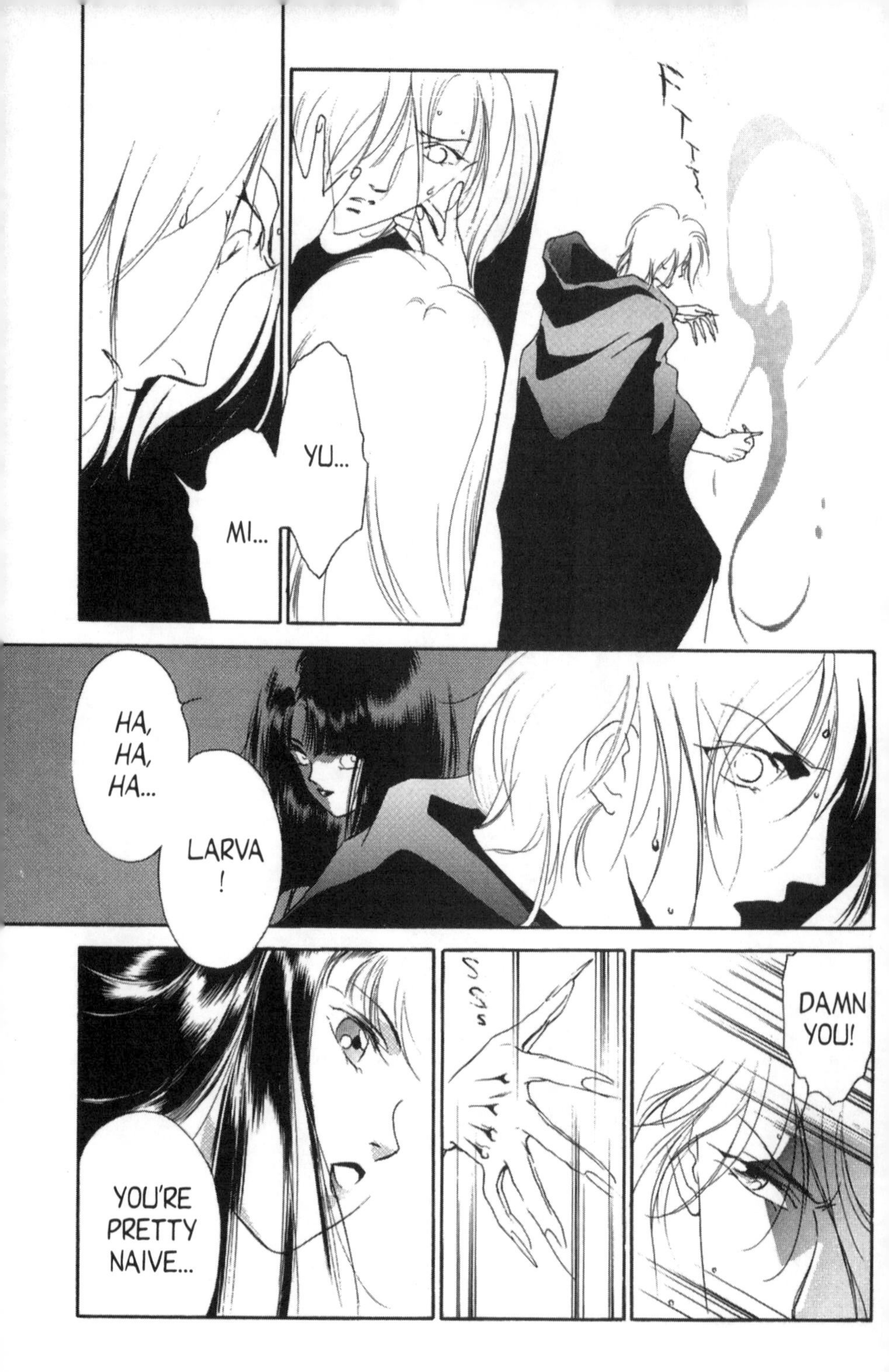
YU...
MI...
HA, HA, HA...
LARVA!
DAMN YOU!
YOU'RE PRETTY NAIVE...

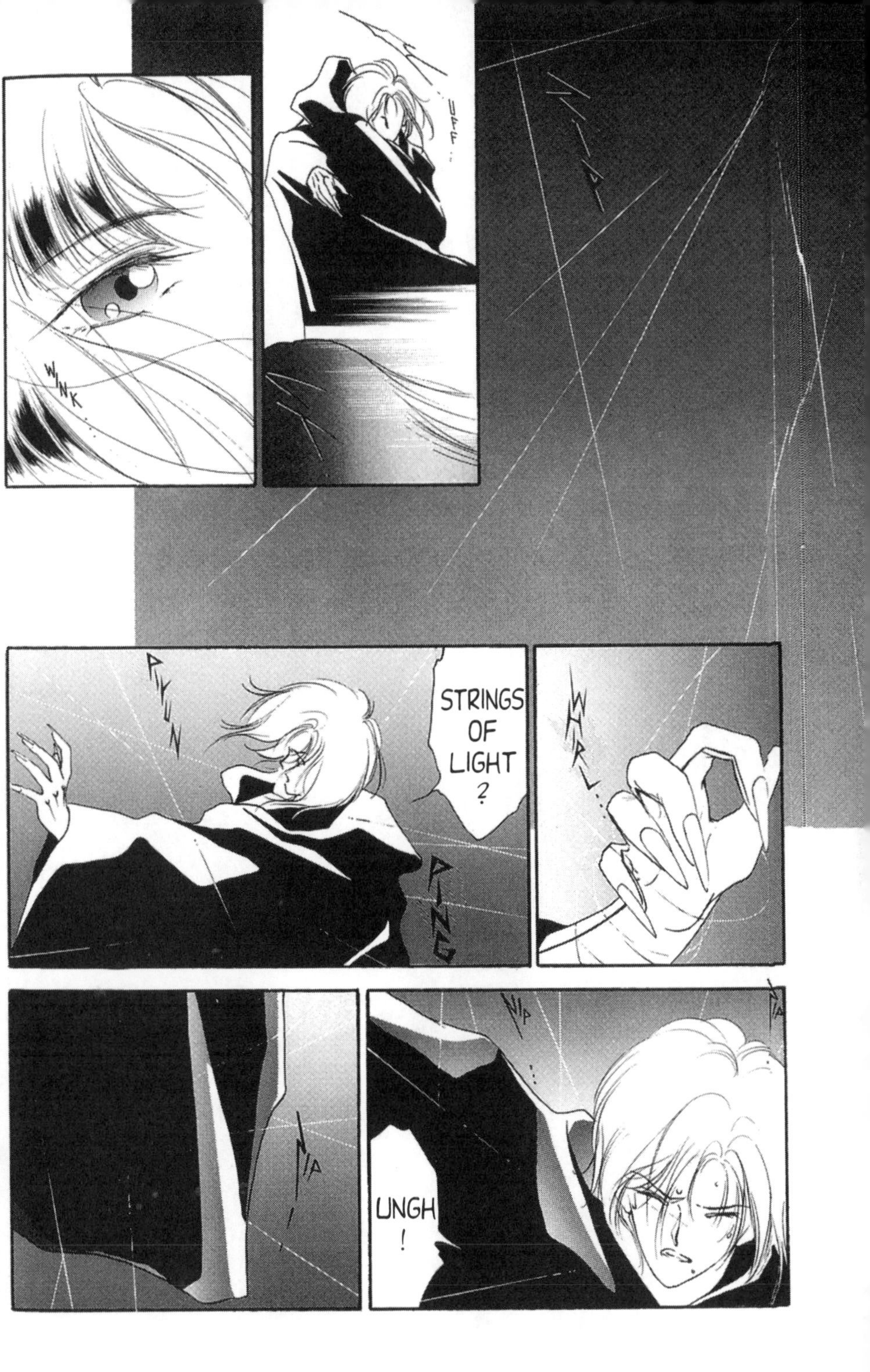
UFF...
WINK
WHIRL...
STRINGS OF LIGHT?
PING
PIYUN
NIP
UNGH!

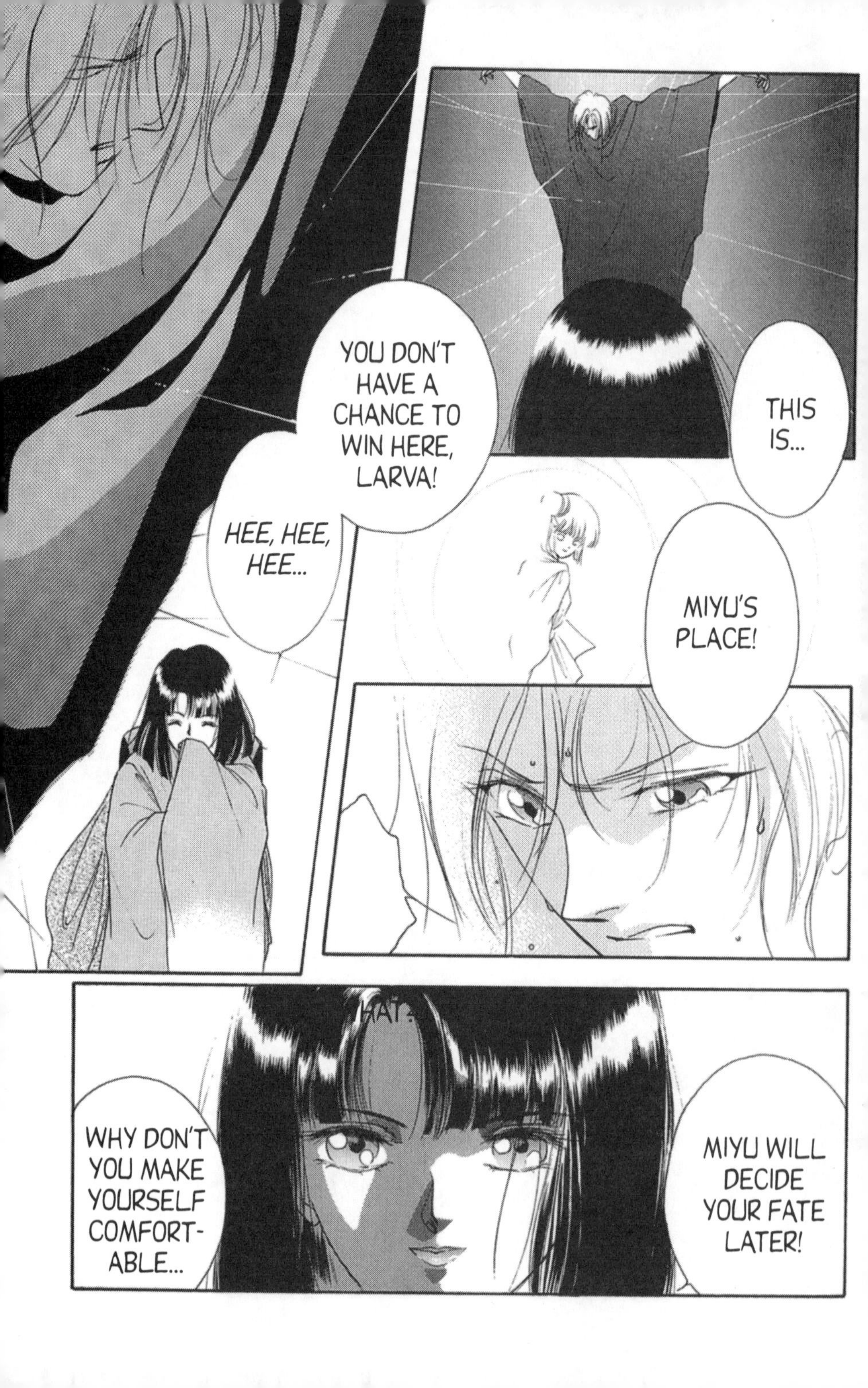
THIS IS...
MIYU'S PLACE!
YOU DON'T HAVE A CHANCE TO WIN HERE, LARVA!
HEE, HEE, HEE...
MIYU WILL DECIDE YOUR FATE LATER!
WHY DON'T YOU MAKE YOURSELF COMFORT-ABLE...

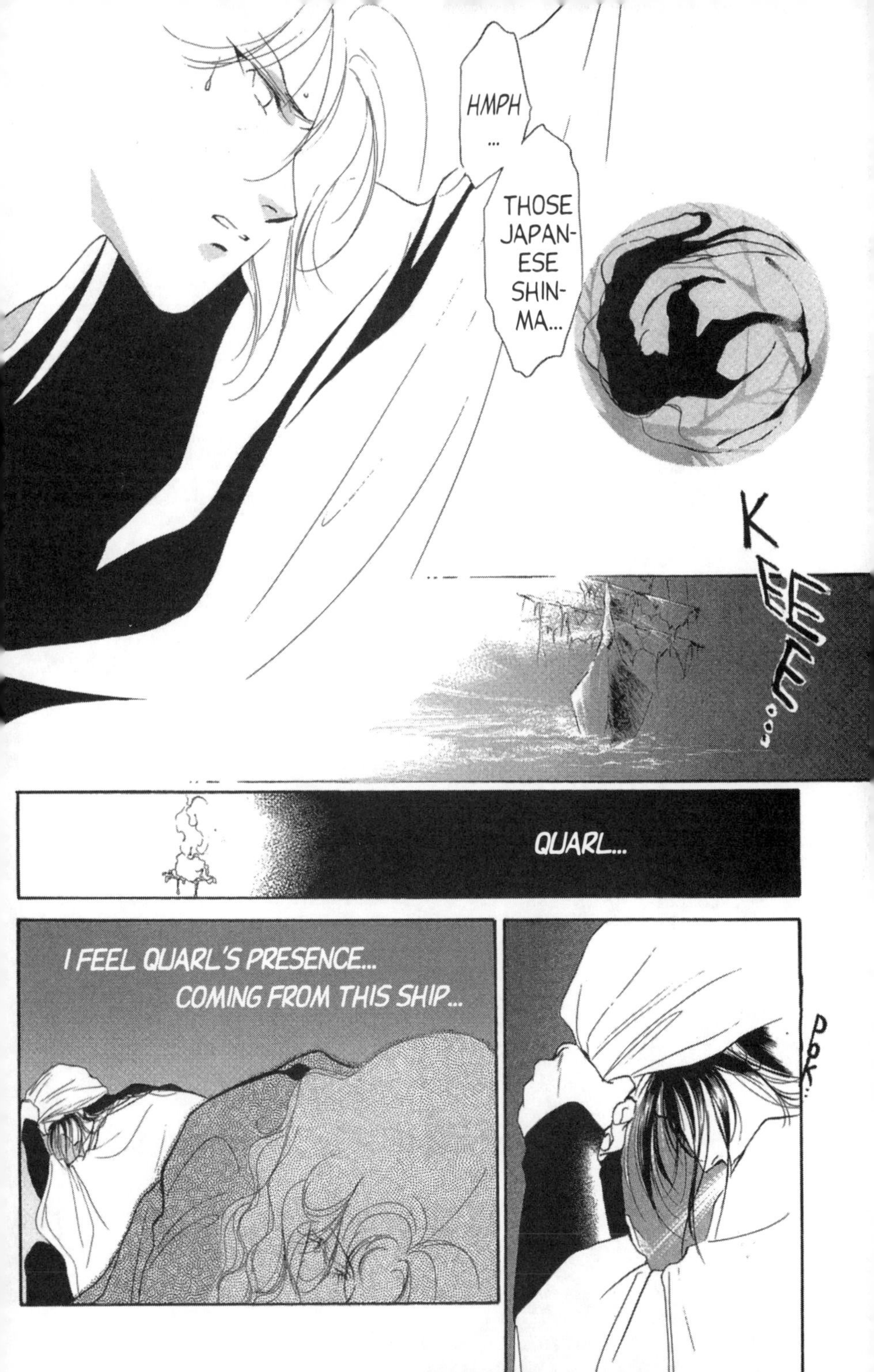
HMPH
...
THOSE JAPAN-ESE SHIN-MA...
KEEEE...
QUARL...
I FEEL QUARL'S PRESENCE...
COMING FROM THIS SHIP...
POK...

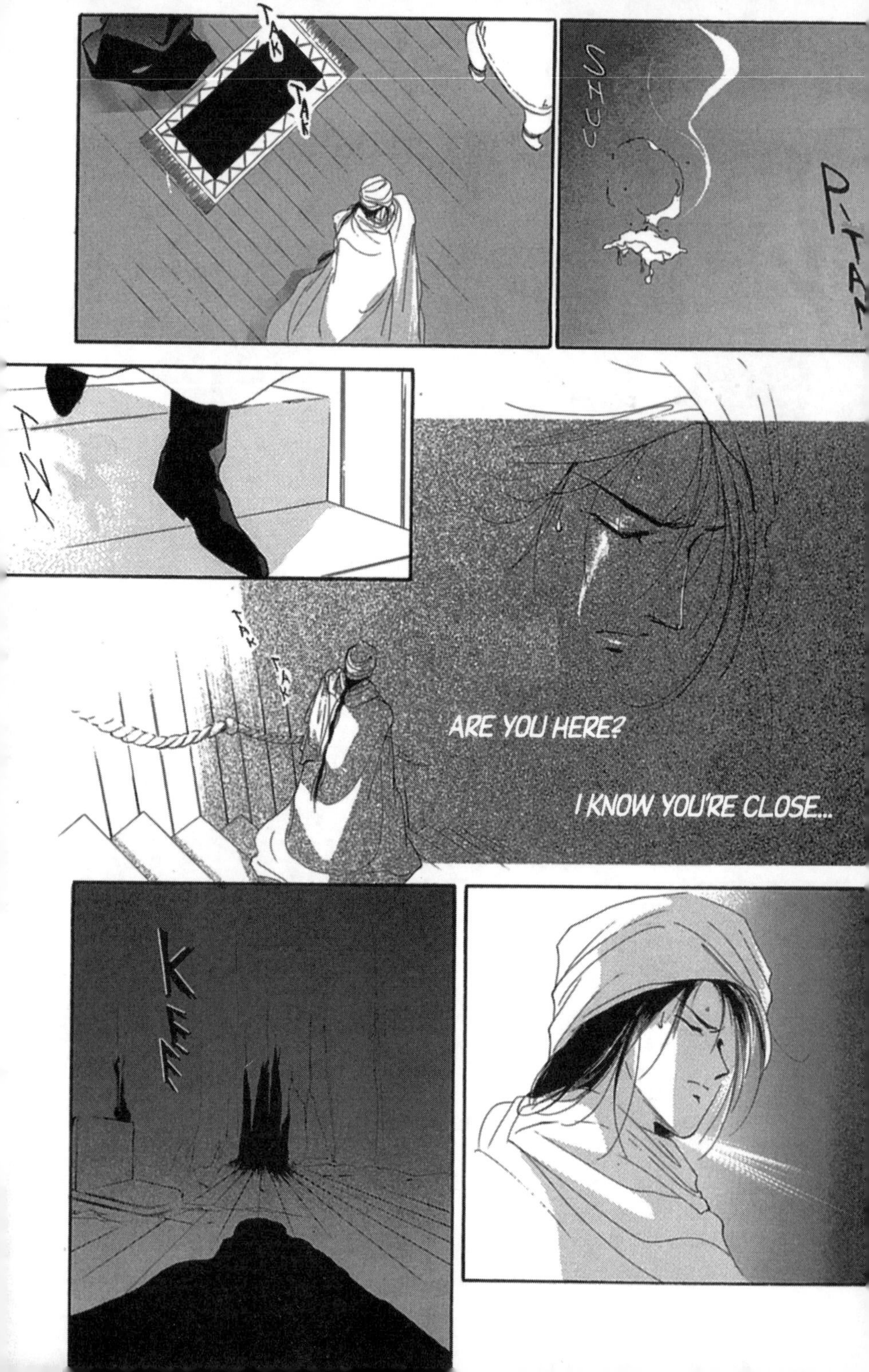
TAK TAK
SHUU
PITAN
TANK
TAK TAK
ARE YOU HERE?
I KNOW YOU'RE CLOSE...
KEEE

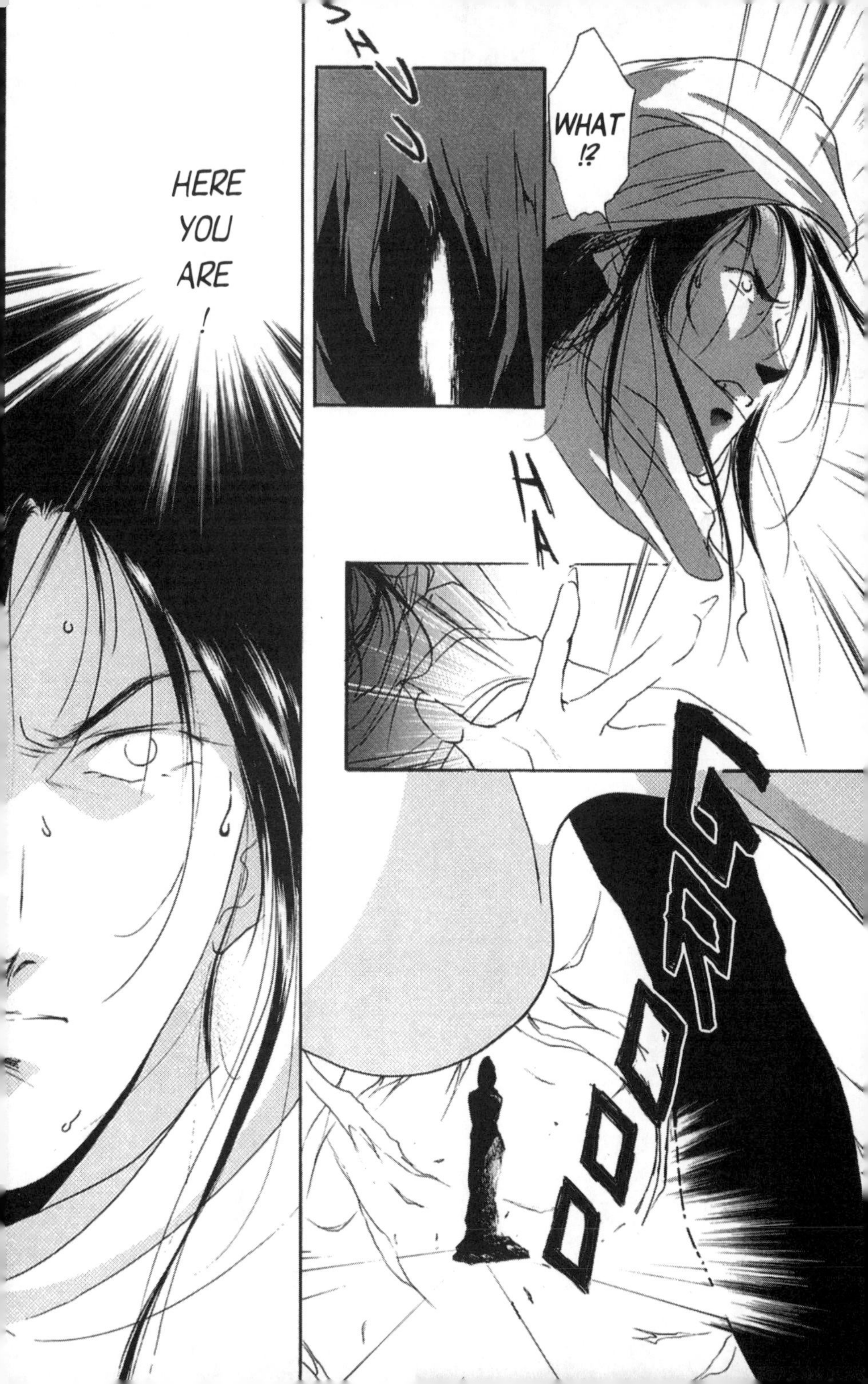
WHAT !?
HA
HERE YOU ARE !

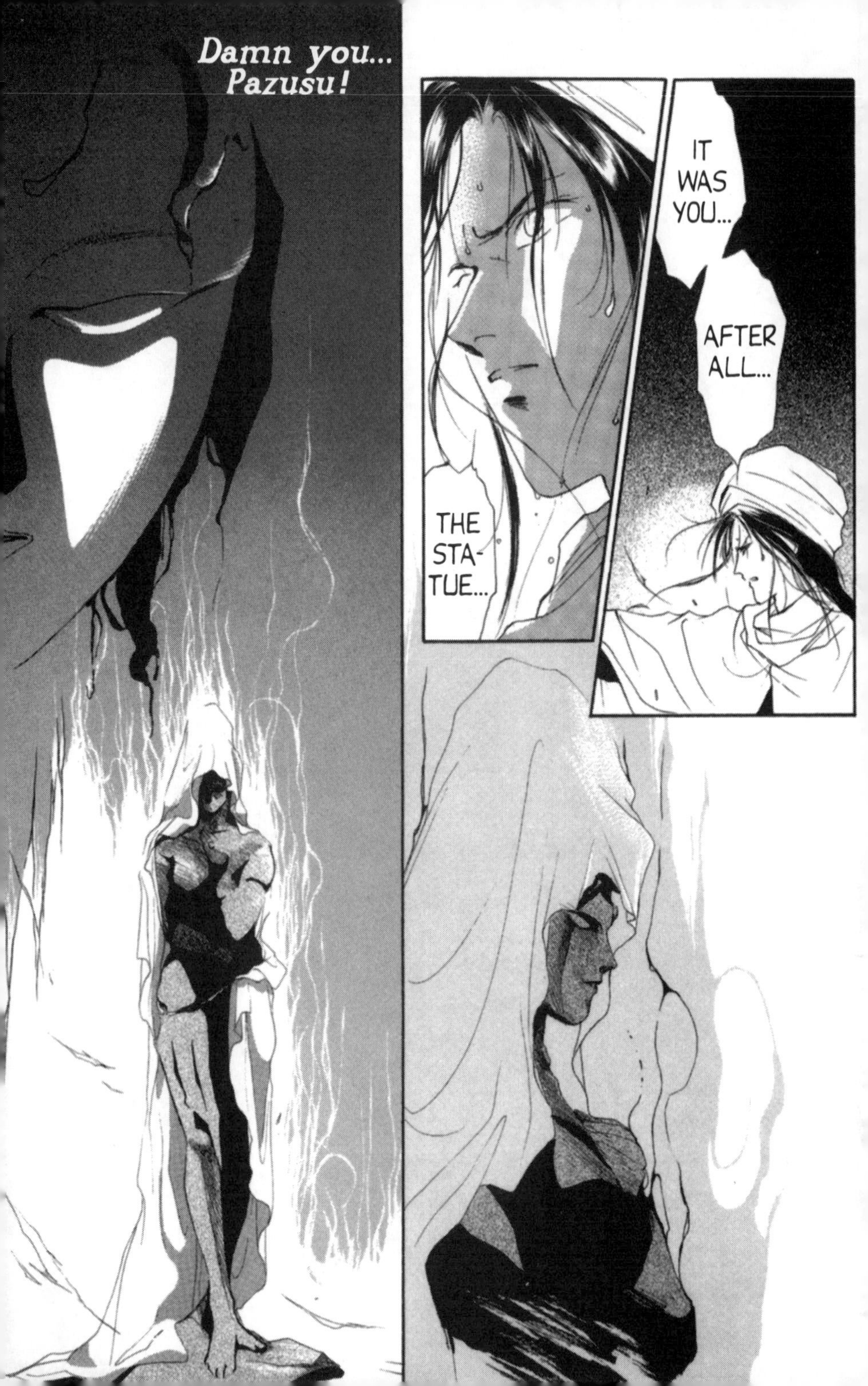

IT WAS YOU...
AFTER ALL...
THE STATUE...
Damn you... Pazusu!

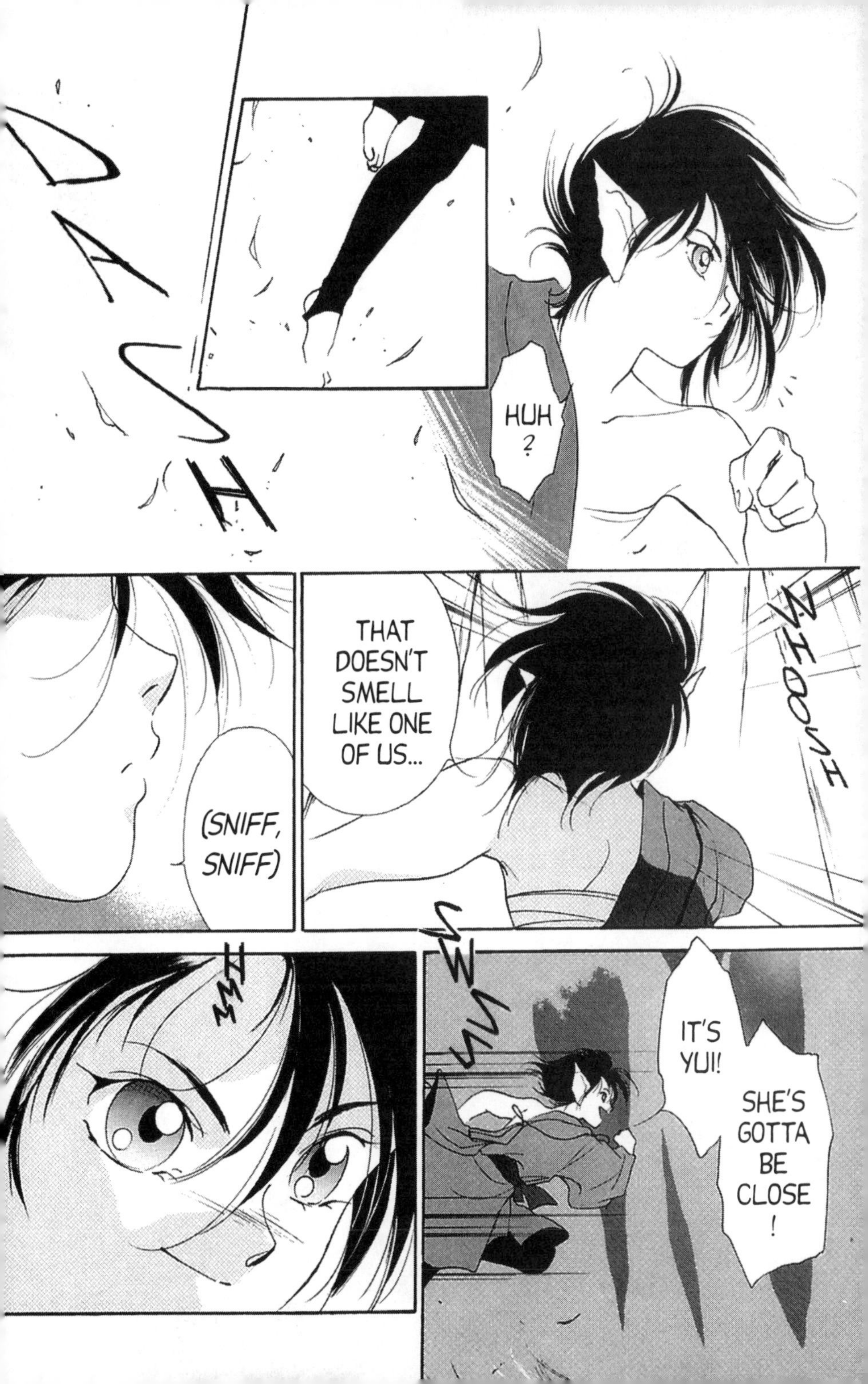
CRASH
HUH?
THAT DOESN'T SMELL LIKE ONE OF US...
(SNIFF, SNIFF)
IT'S YUI!
SHE'S GOTTA BE CLOSE!

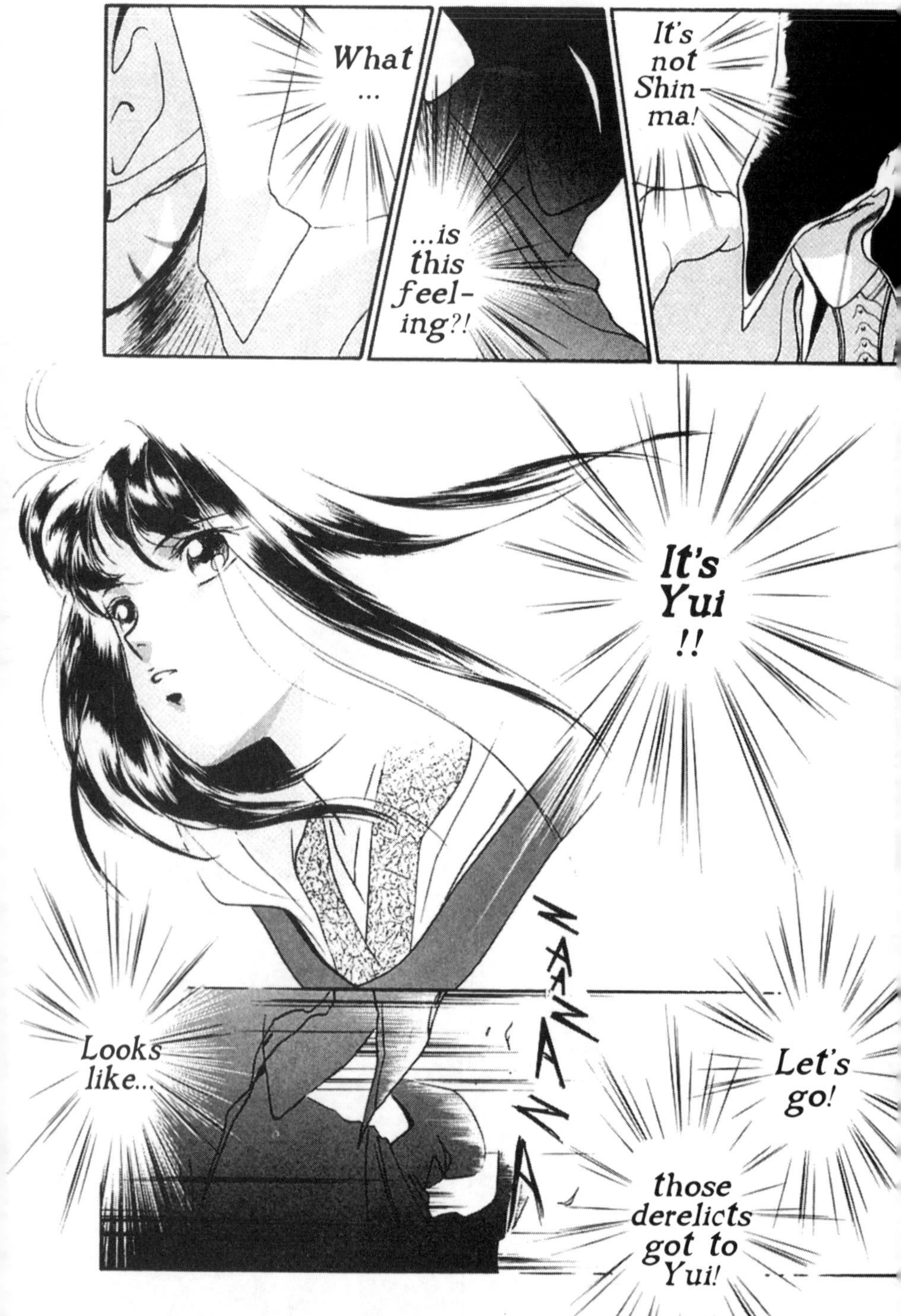
What ...
...is this feeling?!
It's not Shin-ma!
It's Yui !!
Looks like...
those derelicts got to Yui!
Let's go!

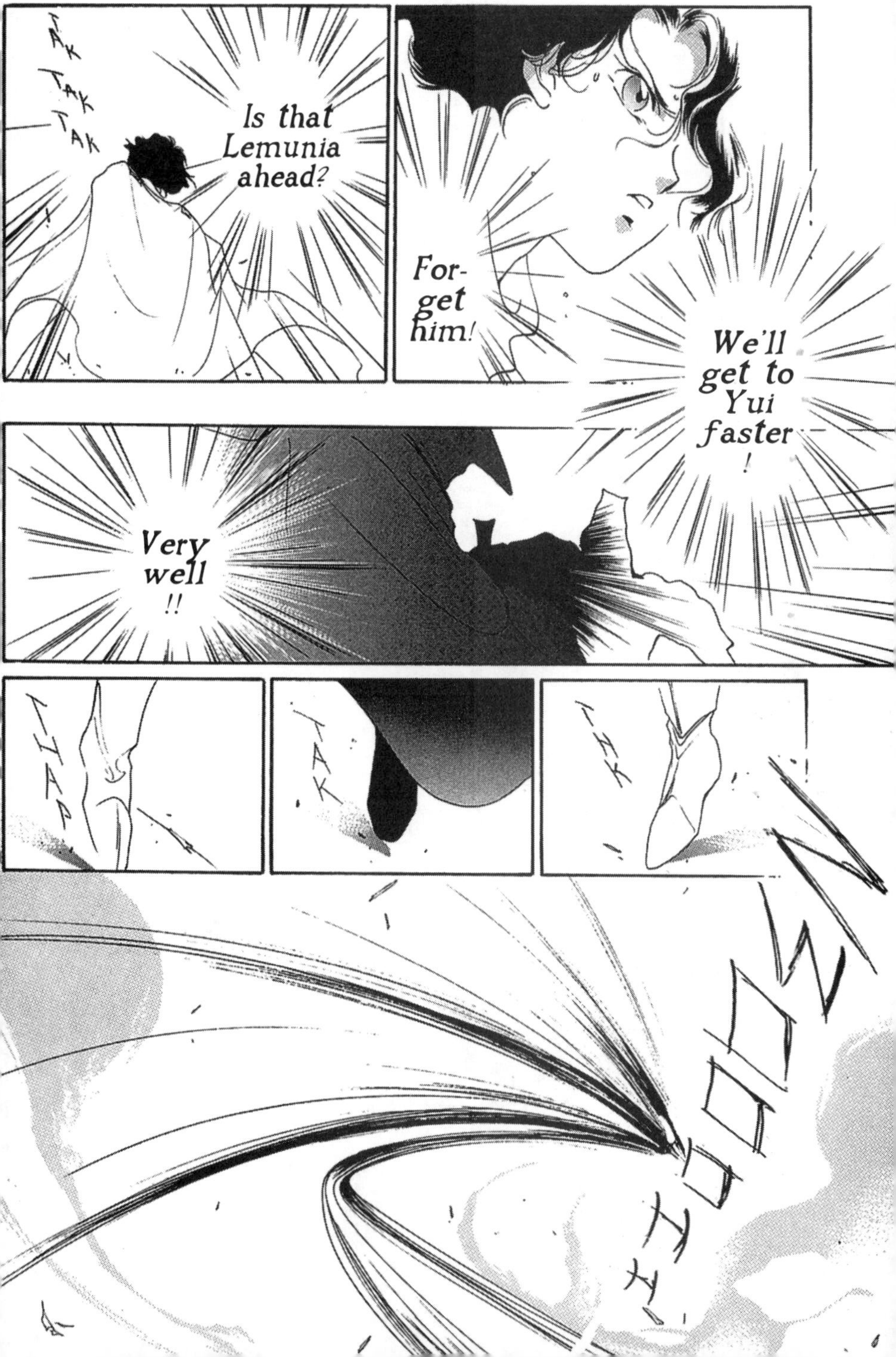

TAK TAK TAK
Is that Lemunia ahead?
For-get him!
We'll get to Yui faster!
Very well!!
THAP
TAK
THK

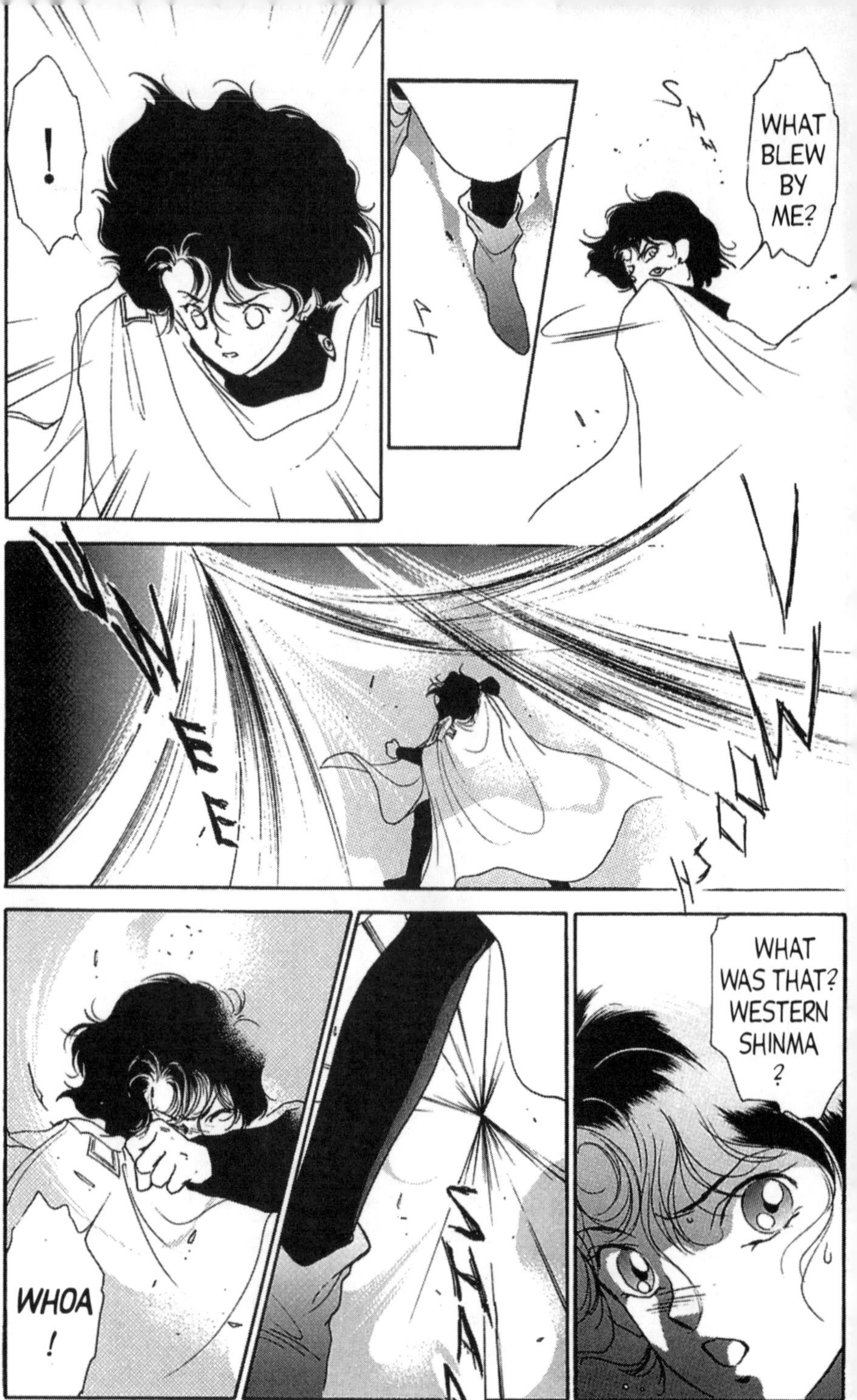
!
WHAT BLEW BY ME?
WHOA!
WHAT WAS THAT? WESTERN SHINMA?

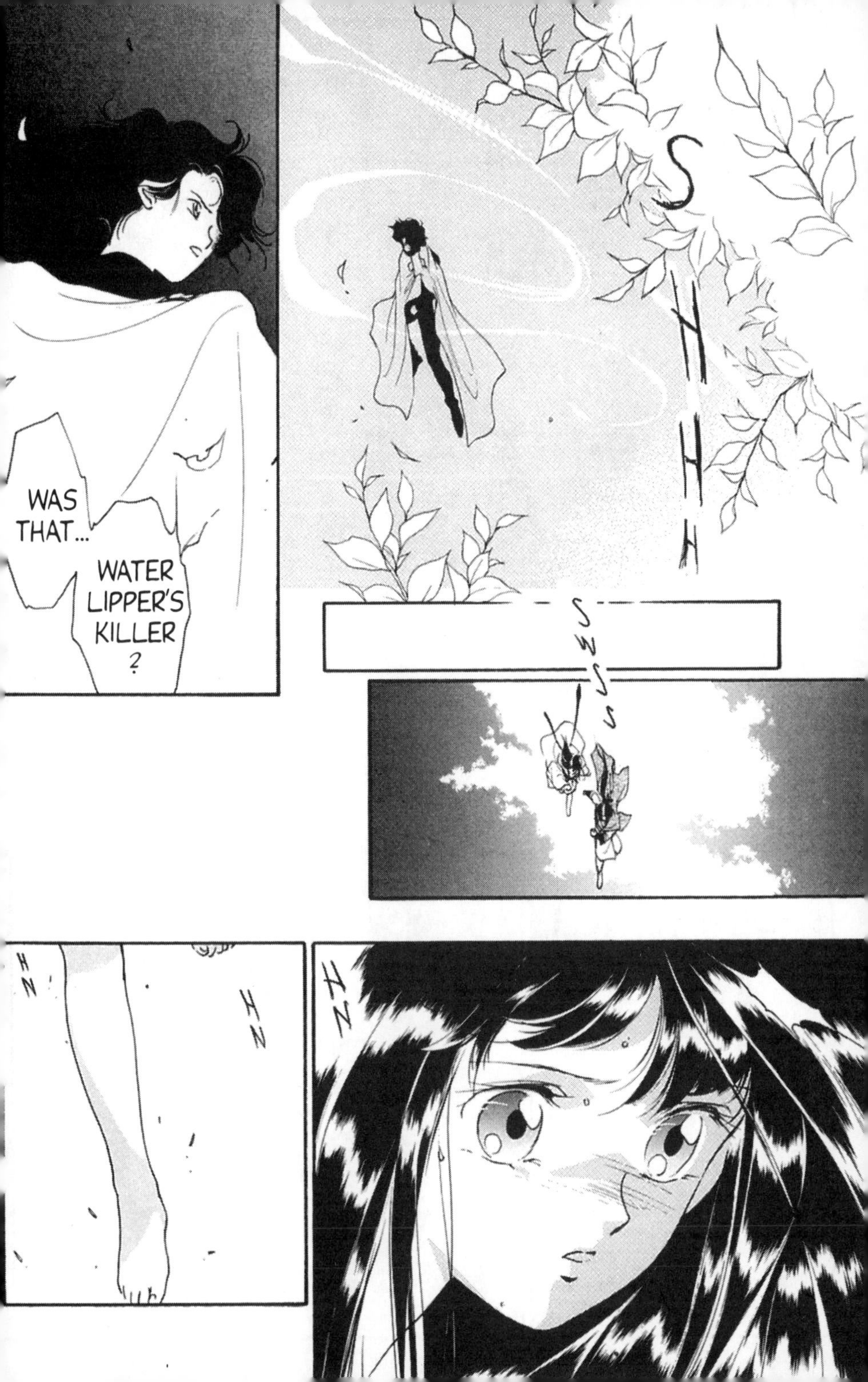
SHHHH
WAS THAT...
WATER LIPPER'S KILLER?
SWSSS
HN
HN
HN

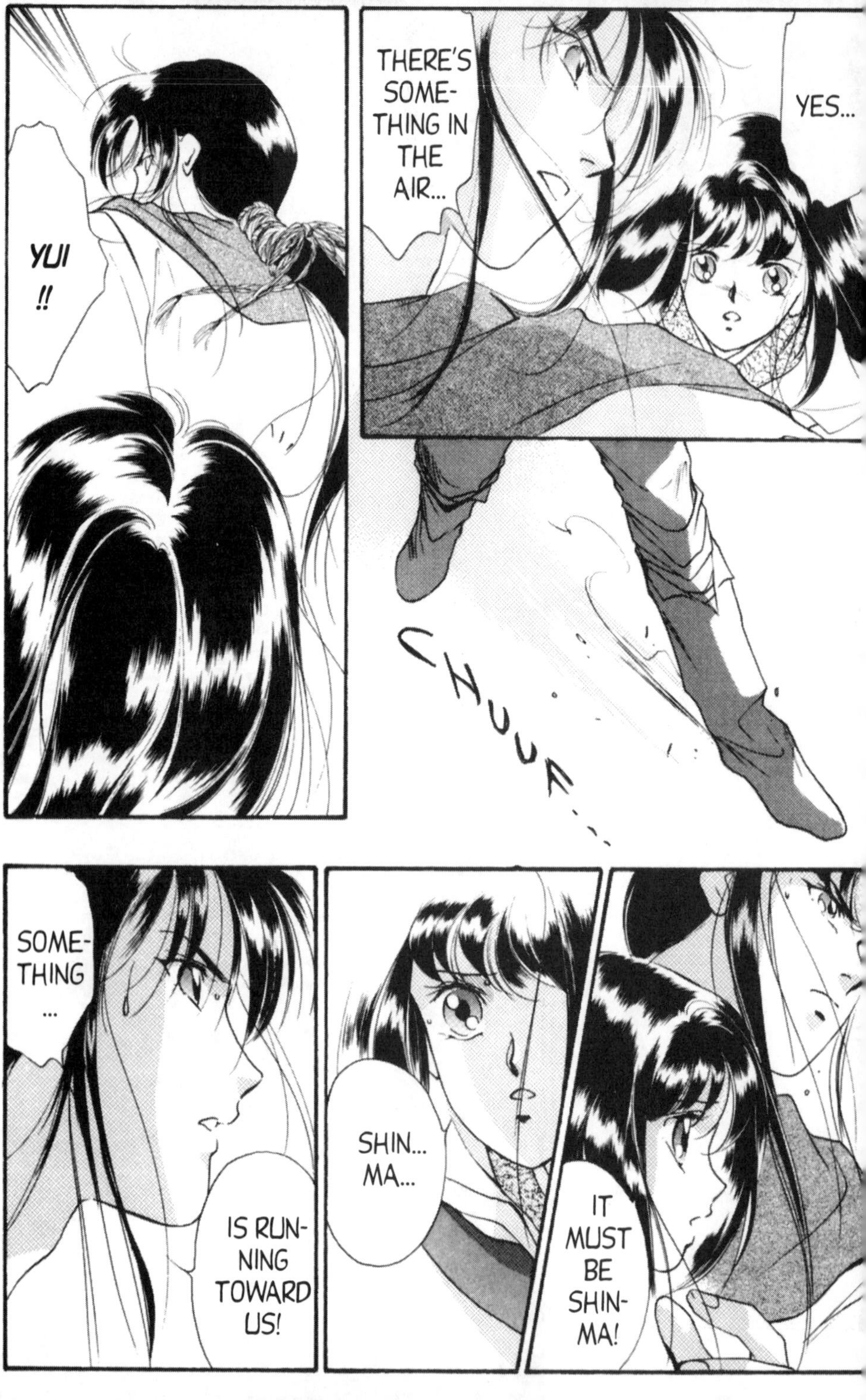
YES...
THERE'S SOME-THING IN THE AIR...
YUI !!
CHUUR...
IT MUST BE SHIN-MA!
SHIN... MA...
SOME-THING ...
IS RUN-NING TOWARD US!

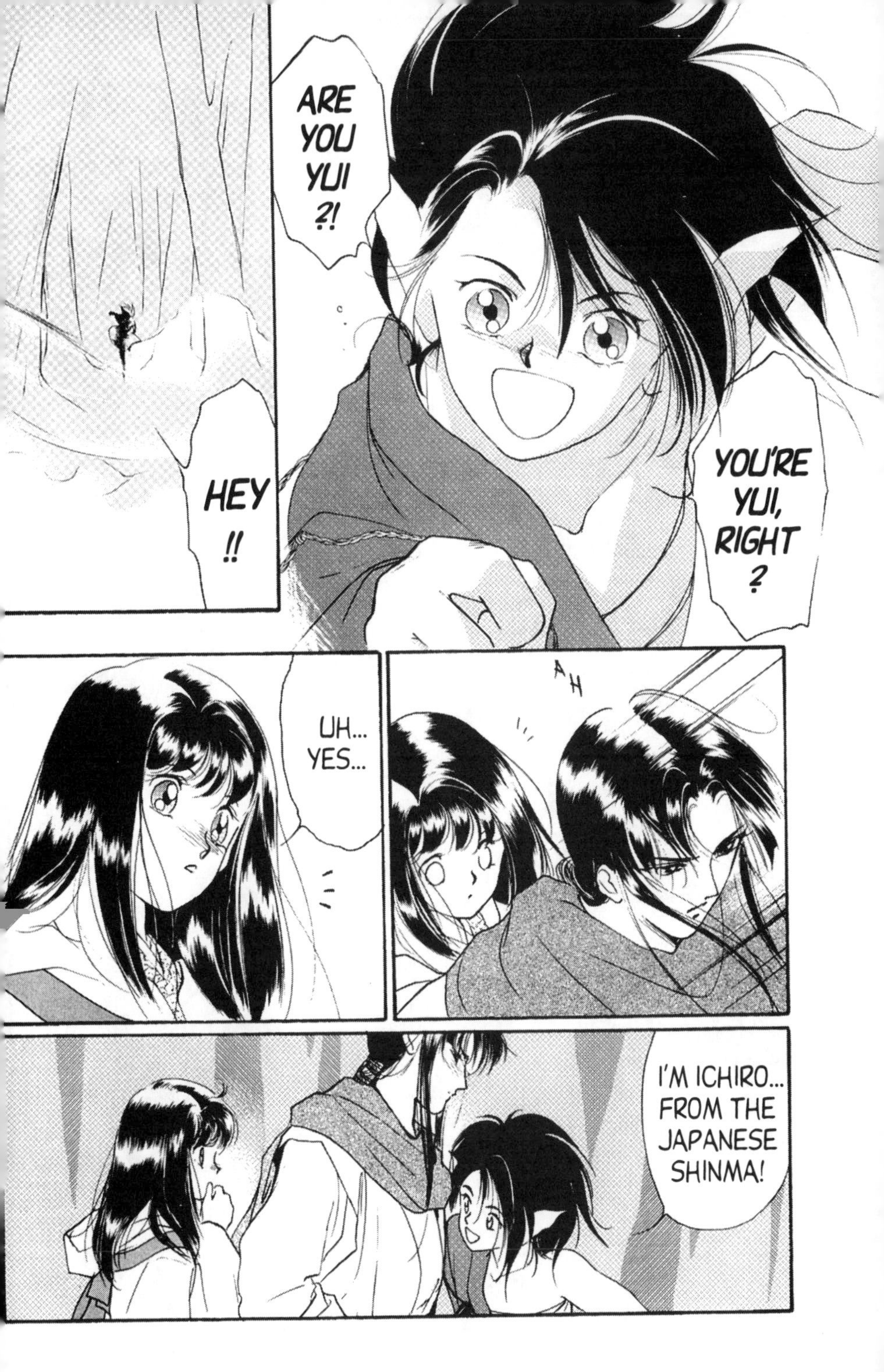
HEY !!
ARE YOU YUI ?!
YOU'RE YUI, RIGHT ?
UH... YES...
AH
I'M ICHIRO... FROM THE JAPANESE SHINMA!

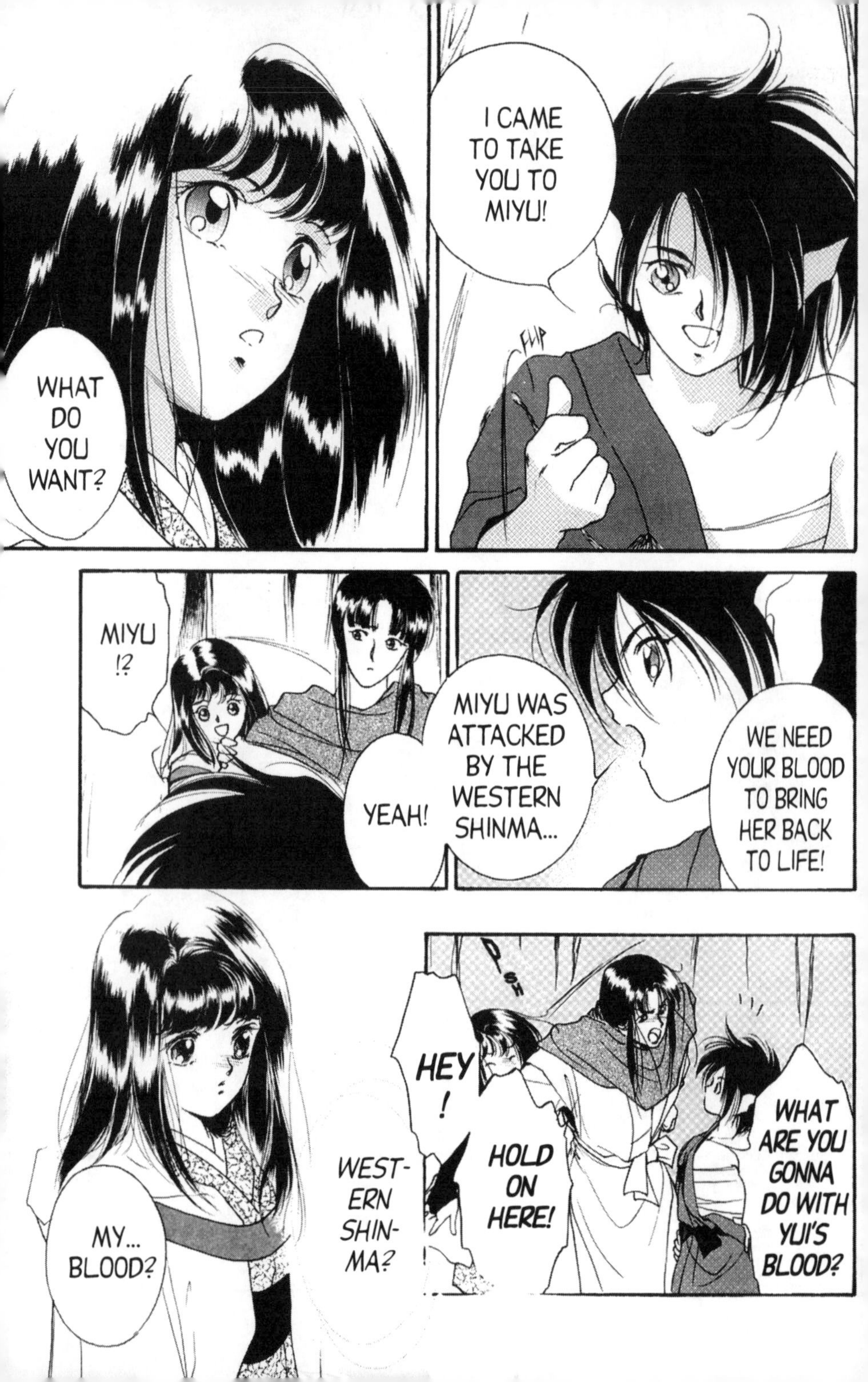
WHAT DO YOU WANT?
I CAME TO TAKE YOU TO MIYU!
FLIP
MIYU !?
YEAH!
MIYU WAS ATTACKED BY THE WESTERN SHINMA...
WE NEED YOUR BLOOD TO BRING HER BACK TO LIFE!
MY... BLOOD?
WEST-ERN SHIN-MA?
HEY !
HOLD ON HERE!
WHAT ARE YOU GONNA DO WITH YUI'S BLOOD?

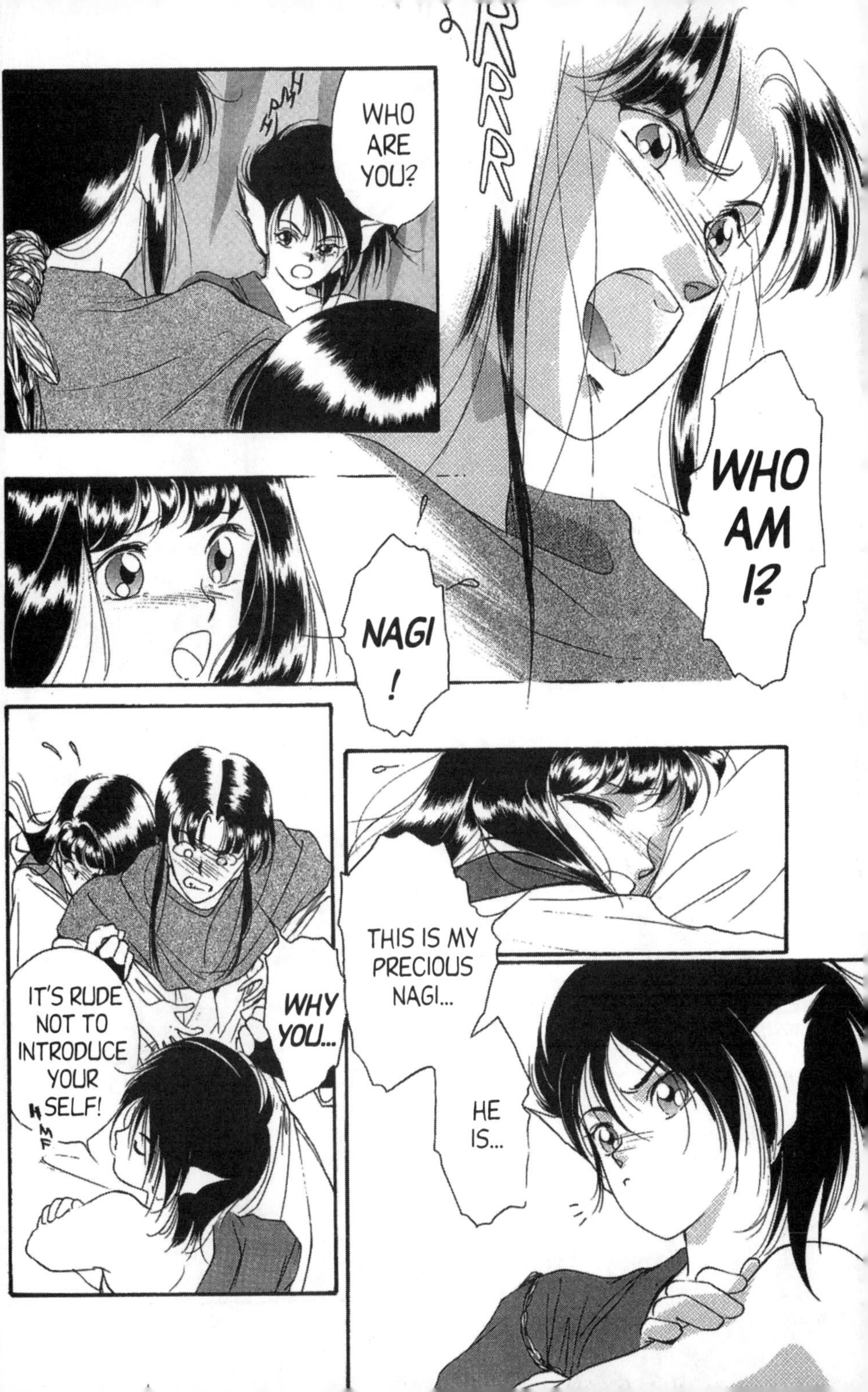
RRRR
WHO AM I?
WHO ARE YOU?
NAGI !
THIS IS MY PRECIOUS NAGI...
HE IS...
WHY YOU...
IT'S RUDE NOT TO INTRODUCE YOUR SELF!
HMF

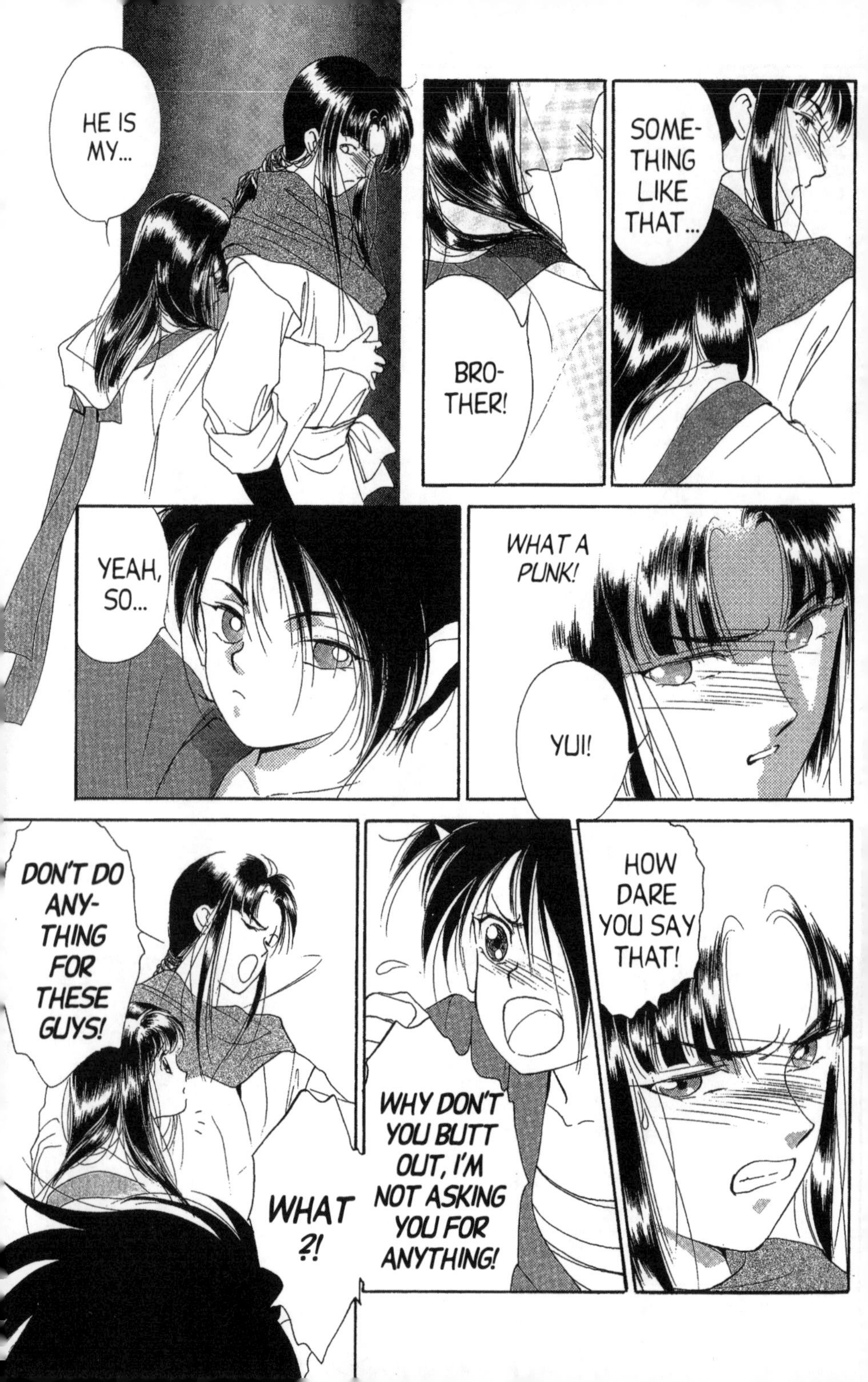
HE IS MY...
BRO-THER!
SOME-THING LIKE THAT...
YEAH, SO...
WHAT A PUNK!
YUI!
DON'T DO ANY-THING FOR THESE GUYS!
WHAT ?!
HOW DARE YOU SAY THAT!
WHY DON'T YOU BUTT OUT, I'M NOT ASKING YOU FOR ANYTHING!

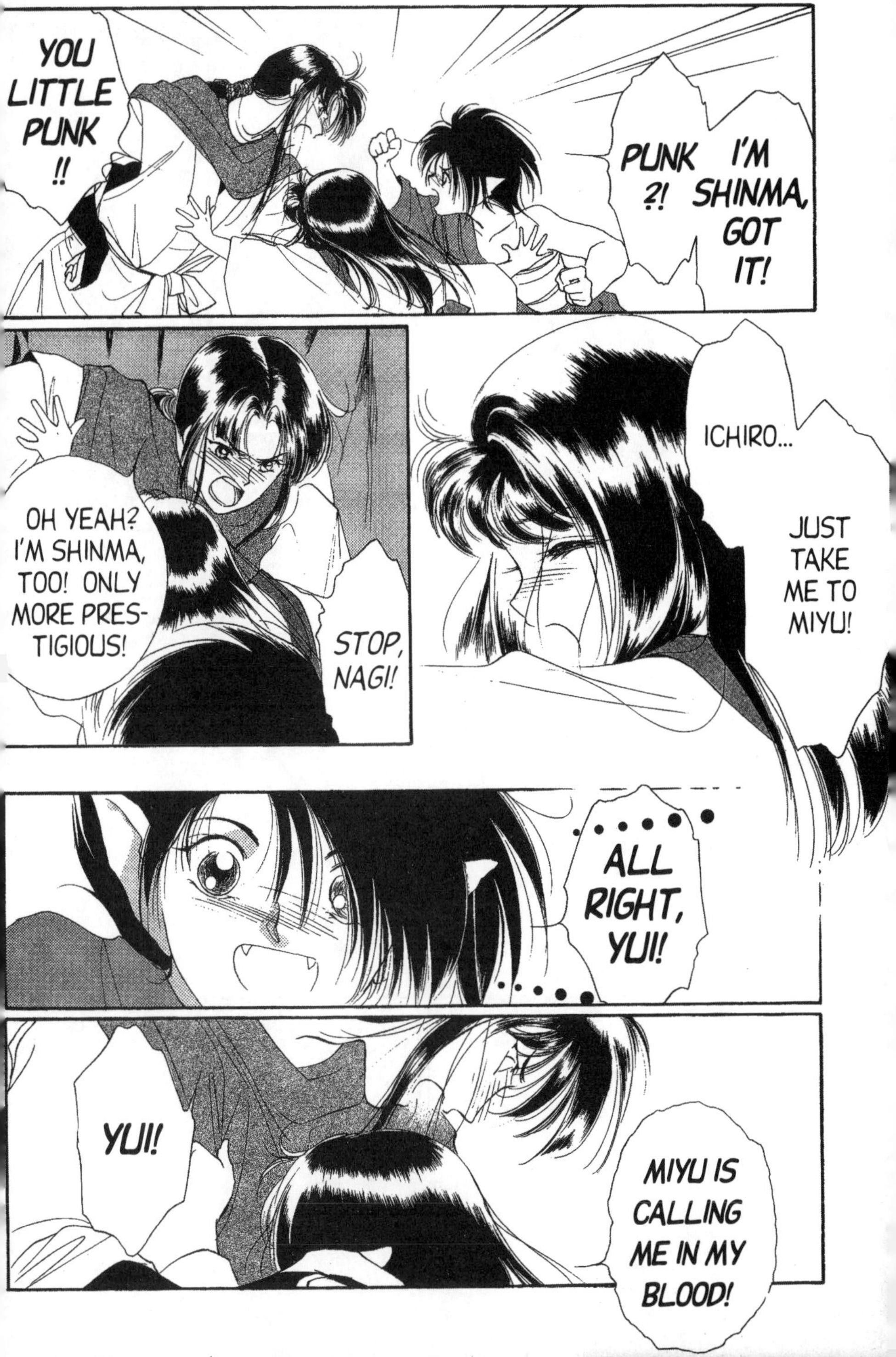
YOU LITTLE PUNK !!
PUNK ?!
I'M SHINMA, GOT IT!
OH YEAH? I'M SHINMA, TOO! ONLY MORE PRES-TIGIOUS!
STOP, NAGI!
ICHIRO...
JUST TAKE ME TO MIYU!
......ALL RIGHT, YUI!.....
YUI!
MIYU IS CALLING ME IN MY BLOOD!

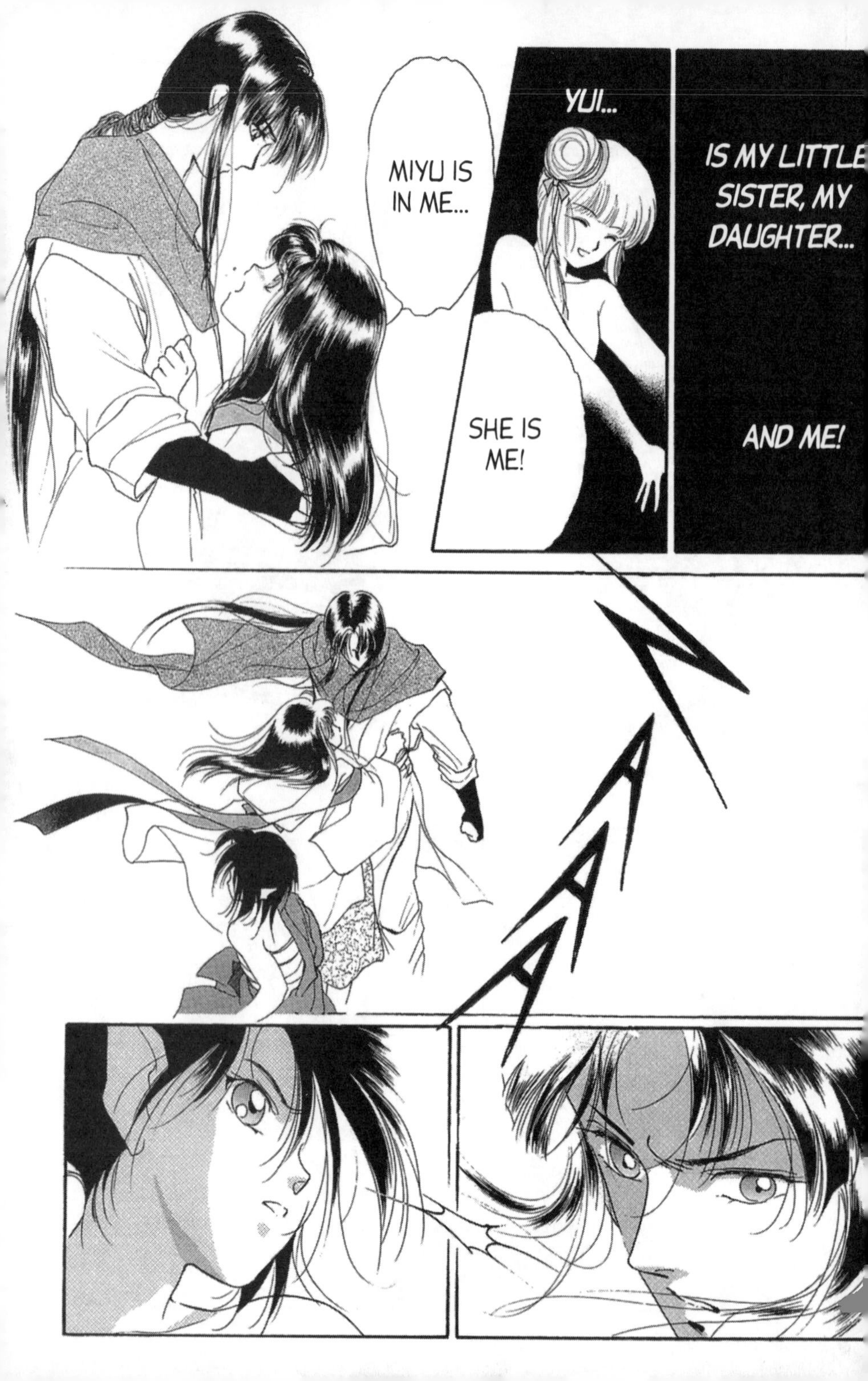
IS MY LITTLE SISTER, MY DAUGHTER...
AND ME!
YUI...
MIYU IS IN ME...
SHE IS ME!
ZAAAAA

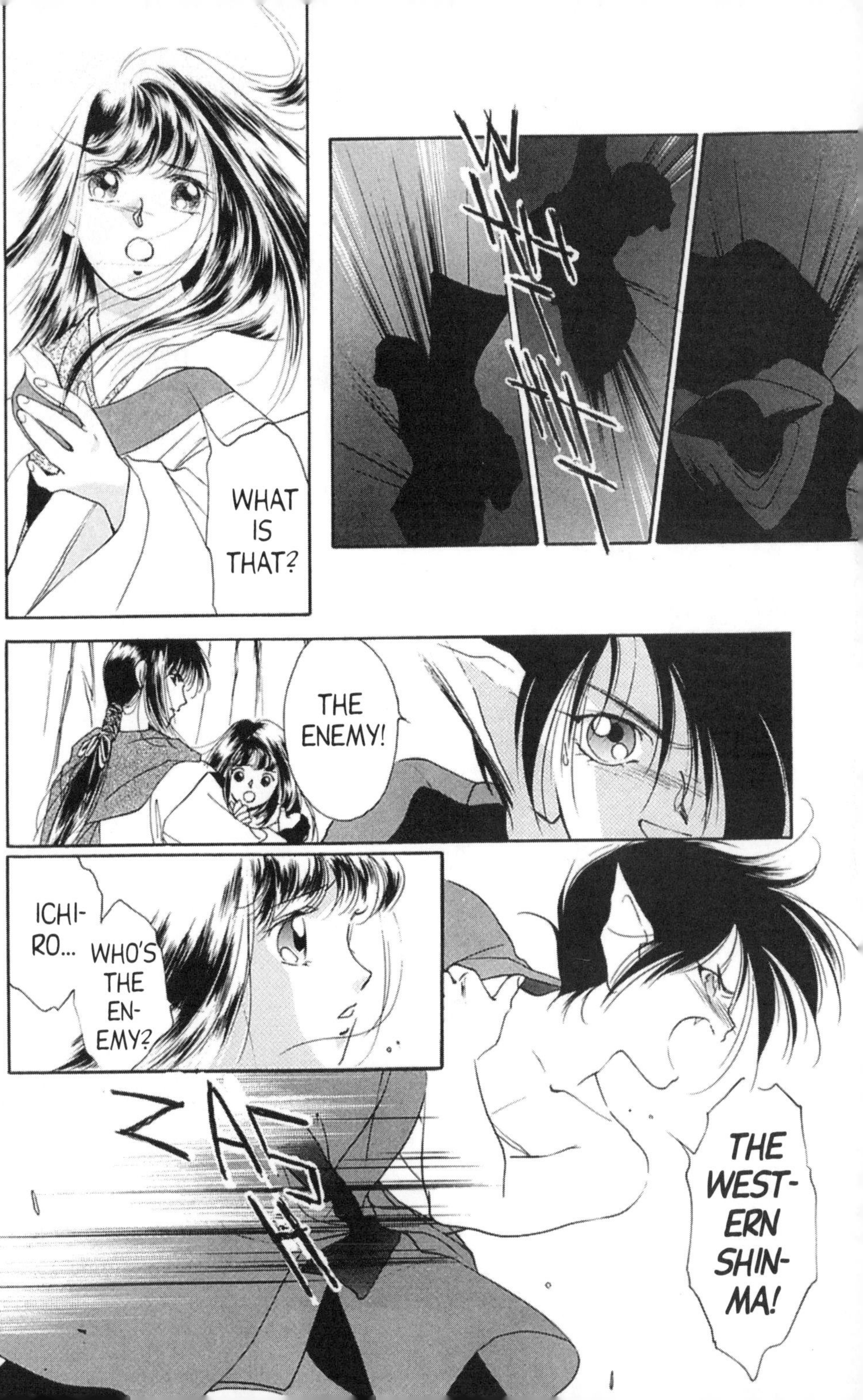
WHAT IS THAT?
THE ENEMY!
ICHIRO...
WHO'S THE ENEMY?
THE WESTERN SHINMA!

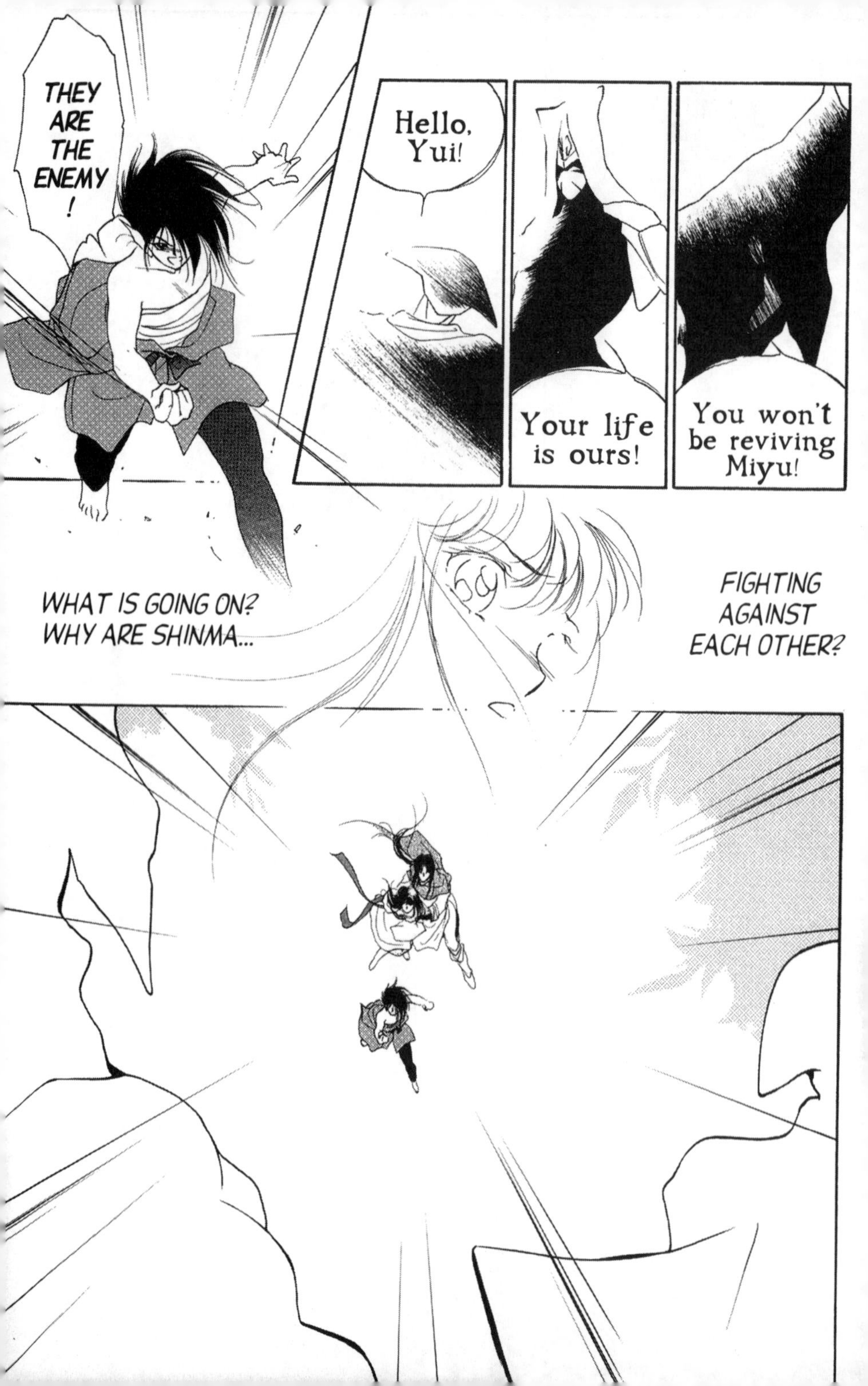
THEY ARE THE ENEMY!
Hello, Yui!
Your life is ours!
You won't be reviving Miyu!
WHAT IS GOING ON? WHY ARE SHINMA...
FIGHTING AGAINST EACH OTHER?

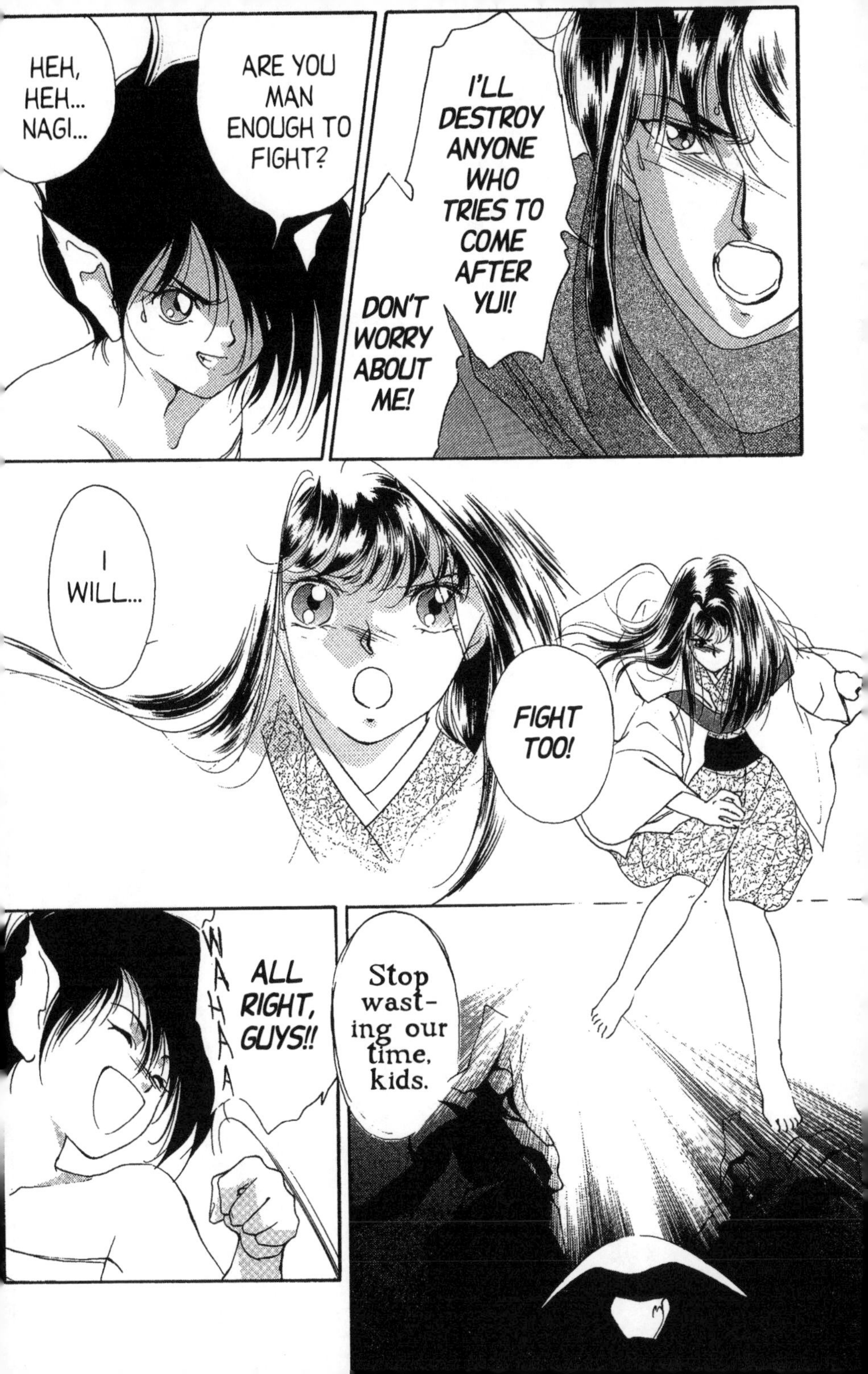
HEH, HEH... NAGI...
ARE YOU MAN ENOUGH TO FIGHT?
I'LL DESTROY ANYONE WHO TRIES TO COME AFTER YUI!
DON'T WORRY ABOUT ME!
I WILL...
FIGHT TOO!
WAHAAA
ALL RIGHT, GUYS!!
Stop wast-ing our time, kids.

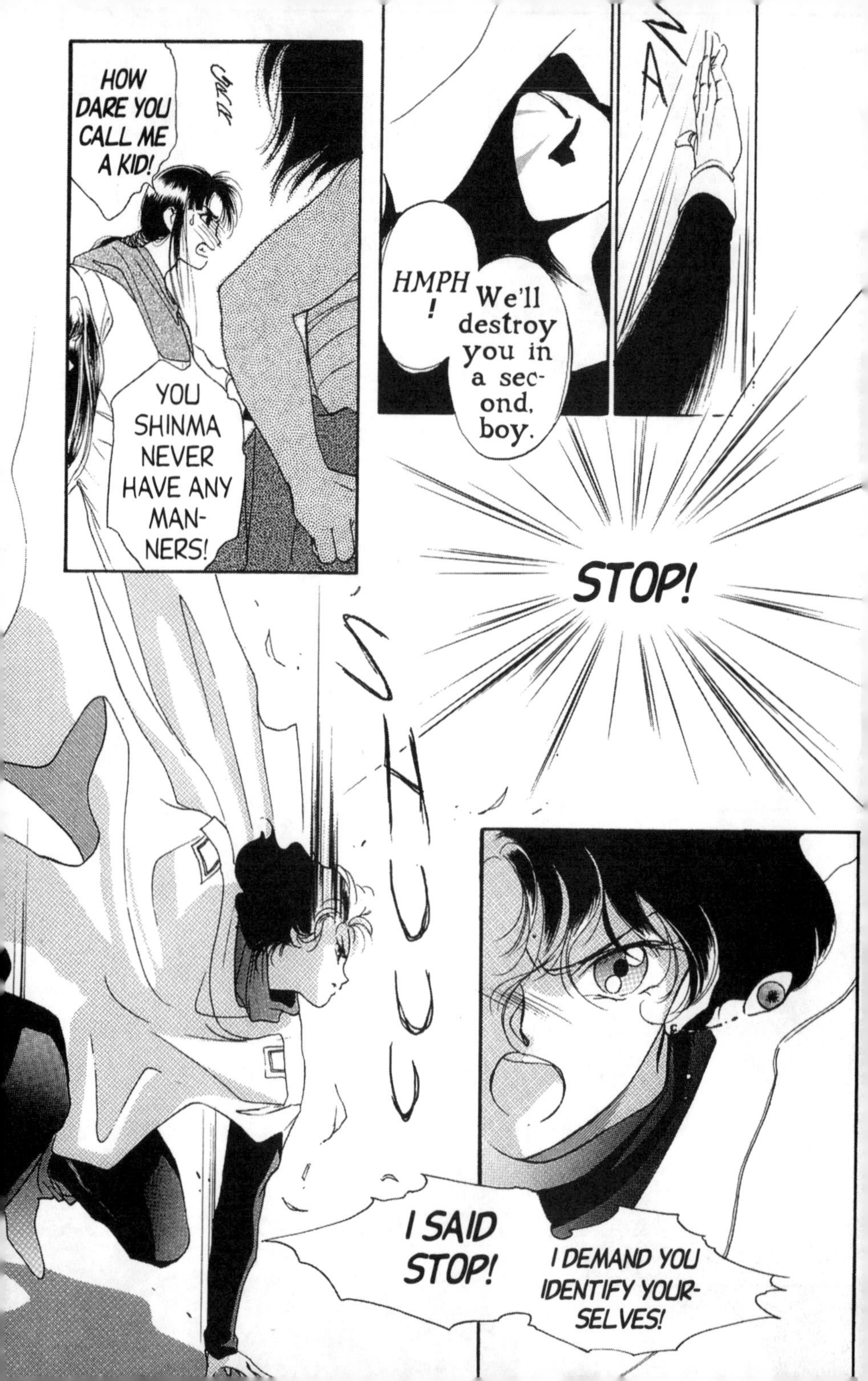

HOW DARE YOU CALL ME A KID!
YOU SHINMA NEVER HAVE ANY MAN-NERS!
HMPH!
We'll destroy you in a sec-ond, boy.
STOP!
I SAID STOP!
I DEMAND YOU IDENTIFY YOUR-SELVES!

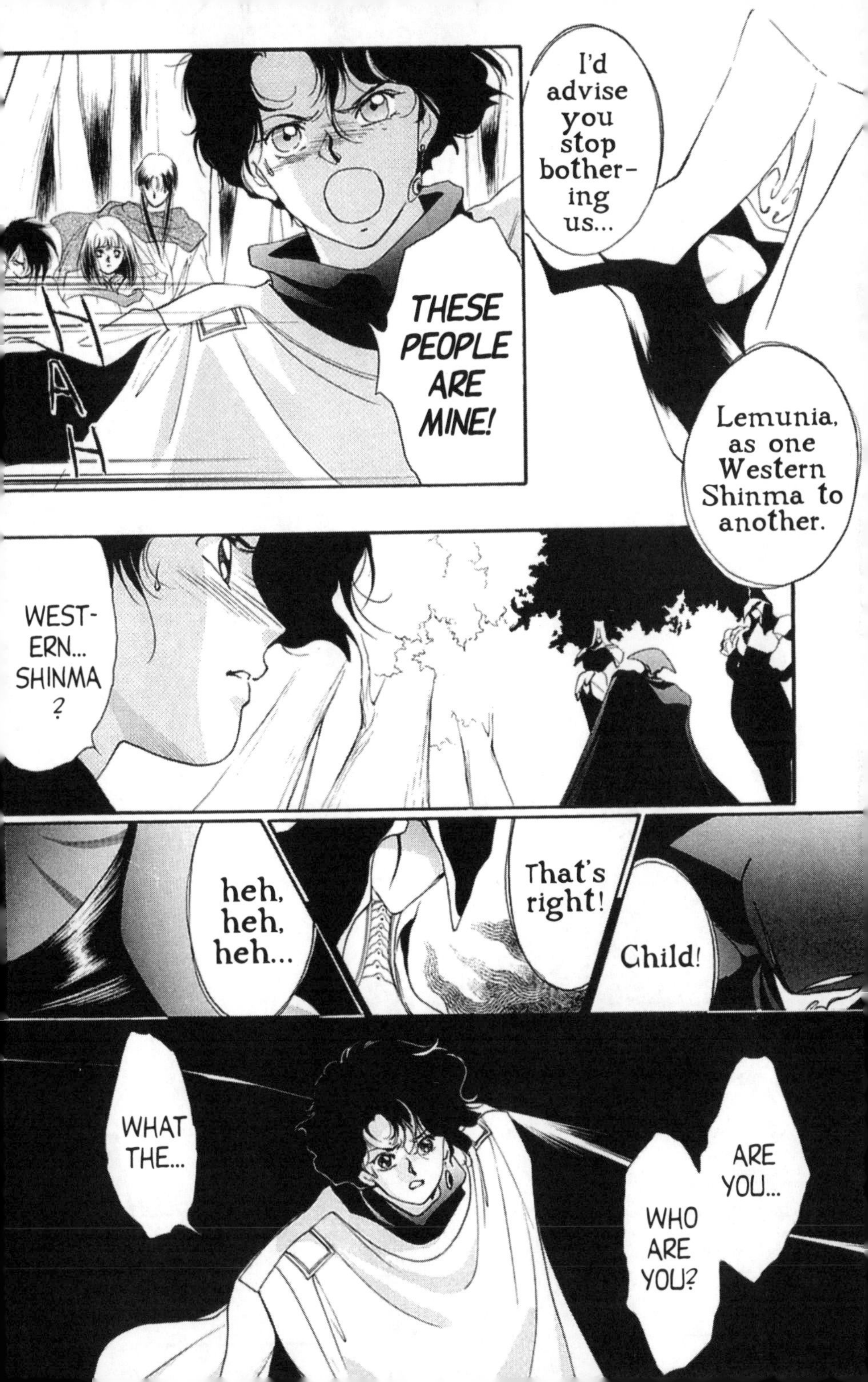
THESE PEOPLE ARE MINE!
I'd advise you stop bothering us...
Lemunia, as one Western Shinma to another.
WESTERN... SHINMA?
heh, heh, heh...
That's right!
Child!
WHAT THE...
ARE YOU...
WHO ARE YOU?

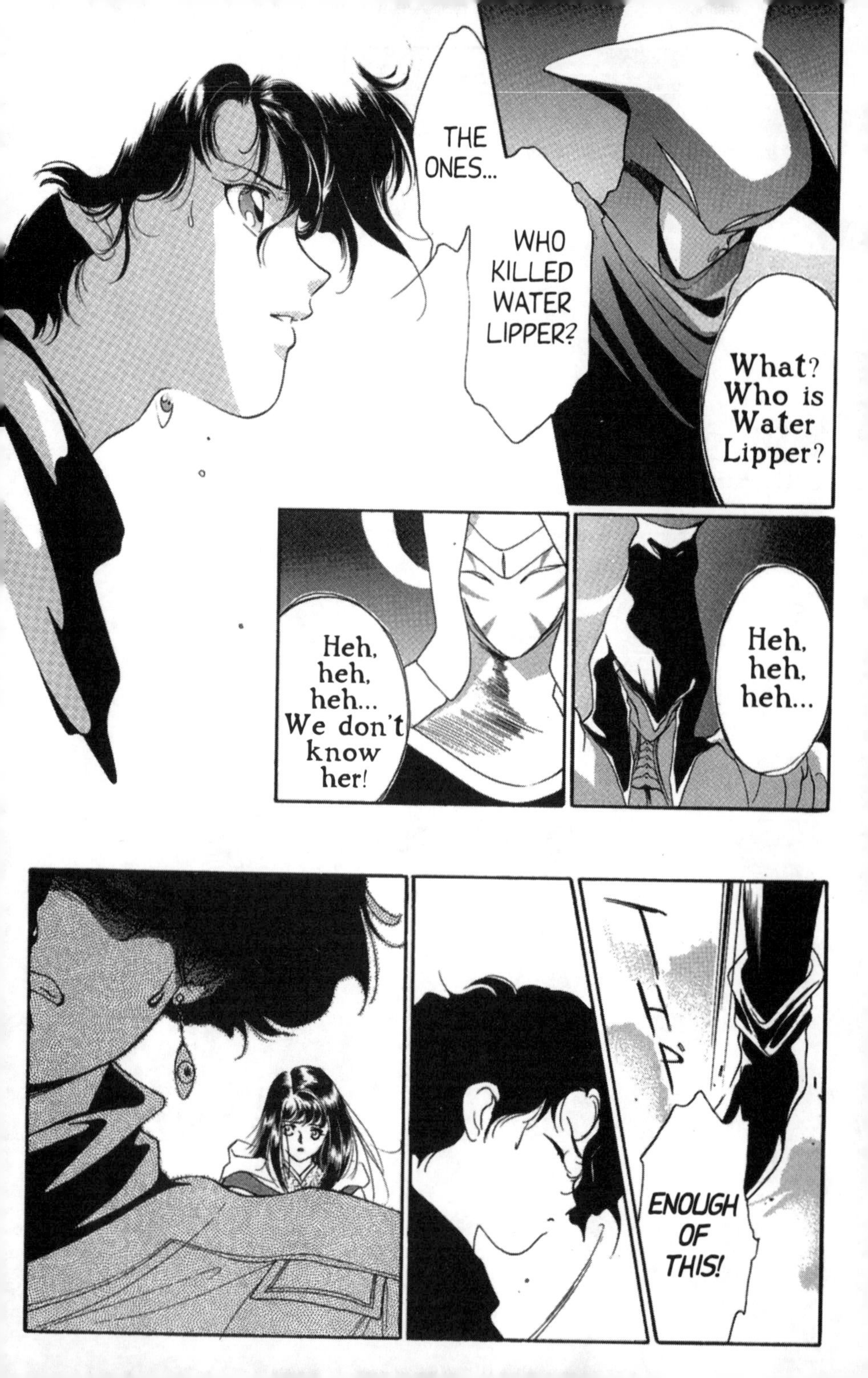

THE ONES...
WHO KILLED WATER LIPPER?
What? Who is Water Lipper?
Heh, heh, heh...
Heh, heh, heh... We don't know her!
ENOUGH OF THIS!

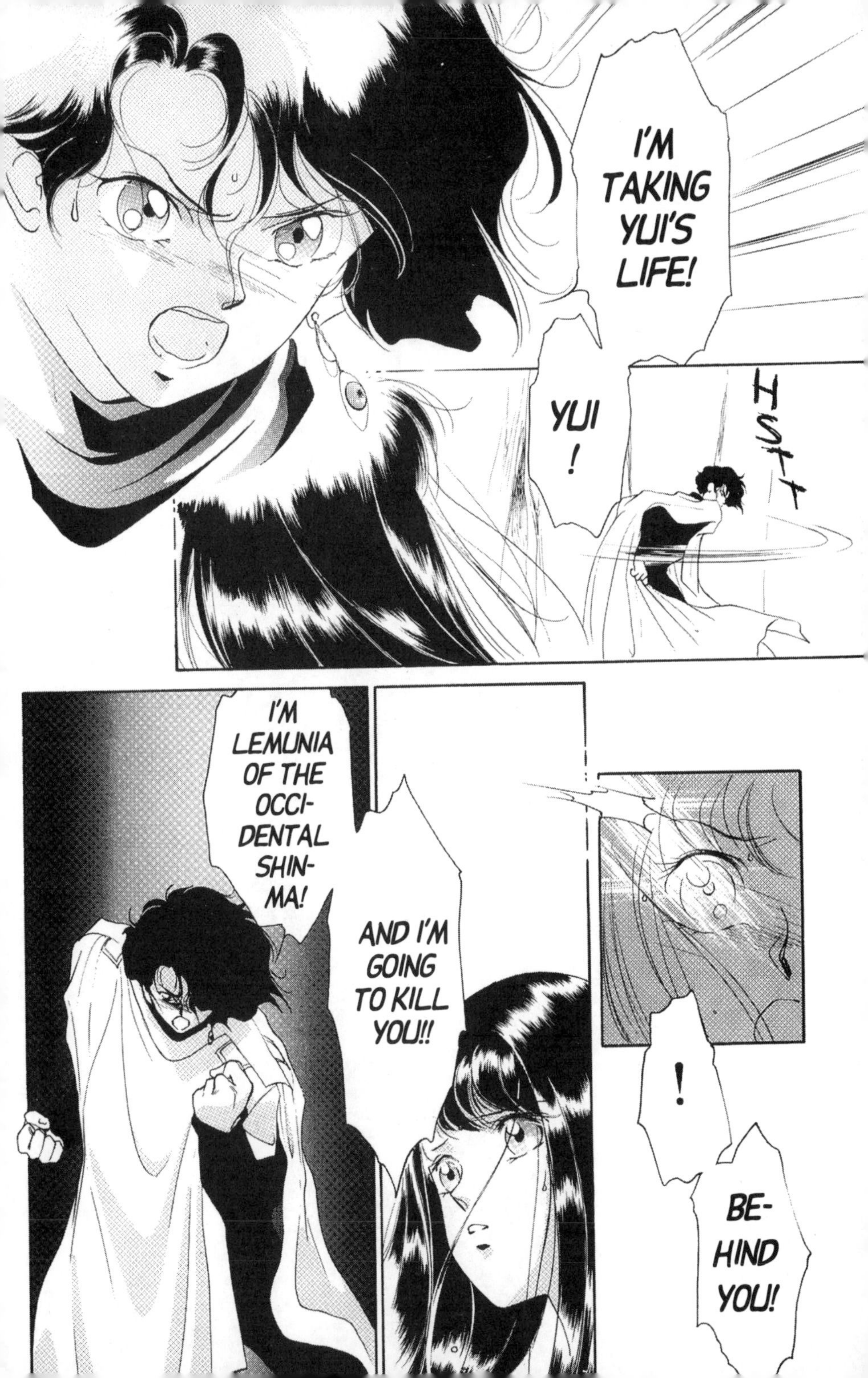
I'M TAKING YUI'S LIFE!
YUI!
HSTT
I'M LEMUNIA OF THE OCCI-DENTAL SHIN-MA!
AND I'M GOING TO KILL YOU!!
!
BE-HIND YOU!

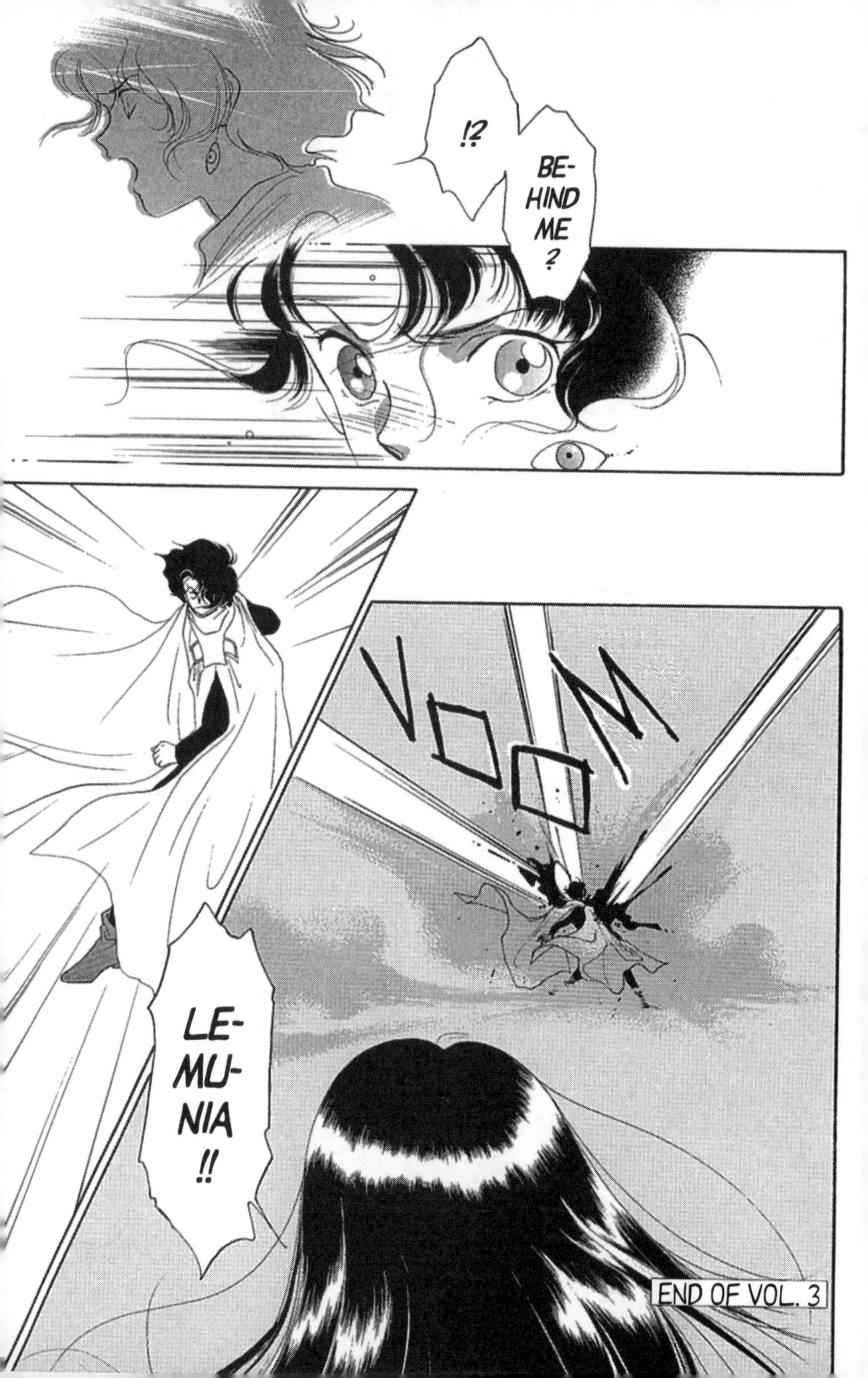

!?
BE-HIND ME?
VOOM
LE-MU-NIA!!
END OF VOL. 3

新吸血姫美夕外伝

一狼勝負!

SIDE STORY OF
NEW VAMPIRE MIYU:

ICHIRO'S ADVENTURE!

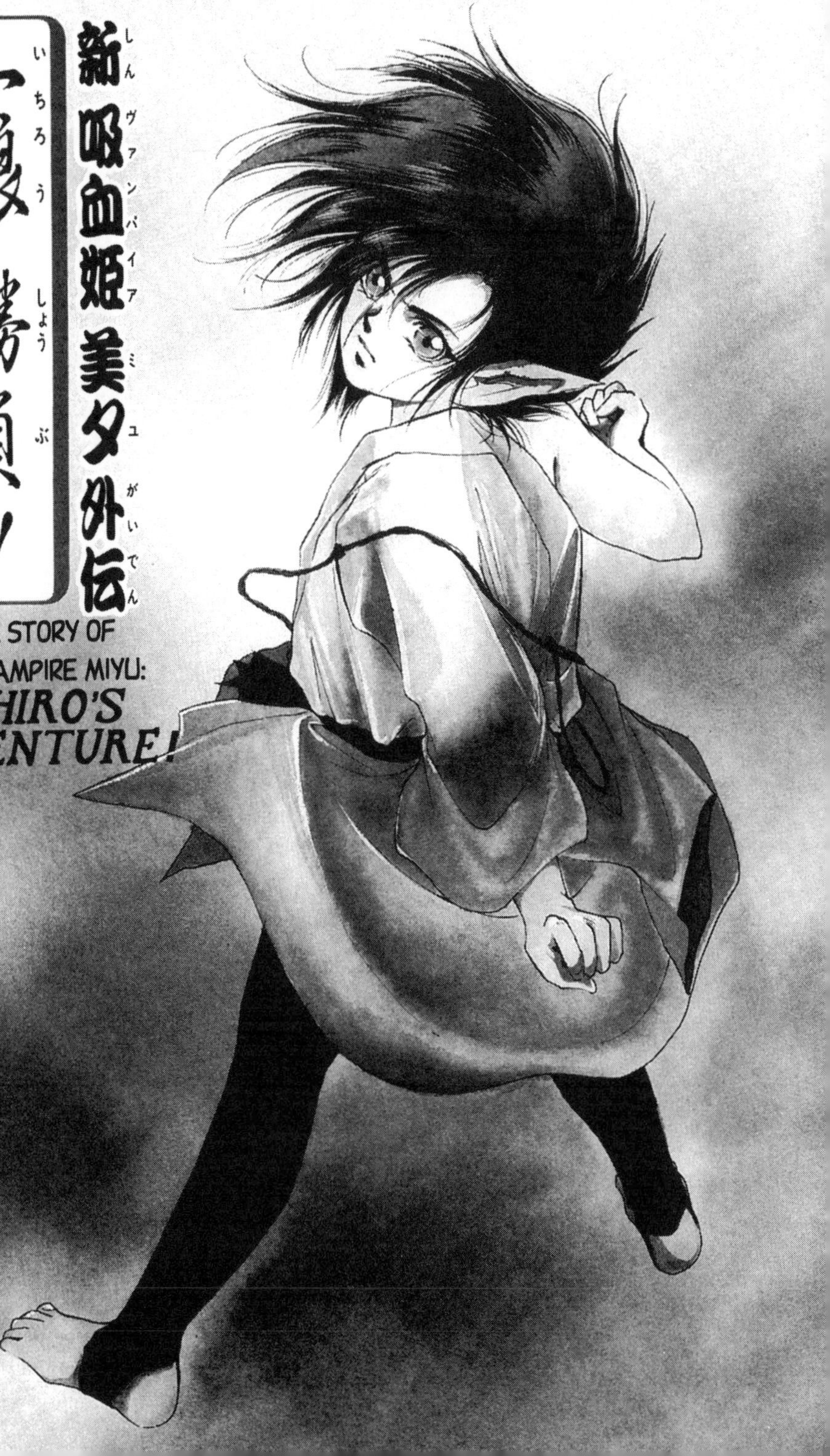

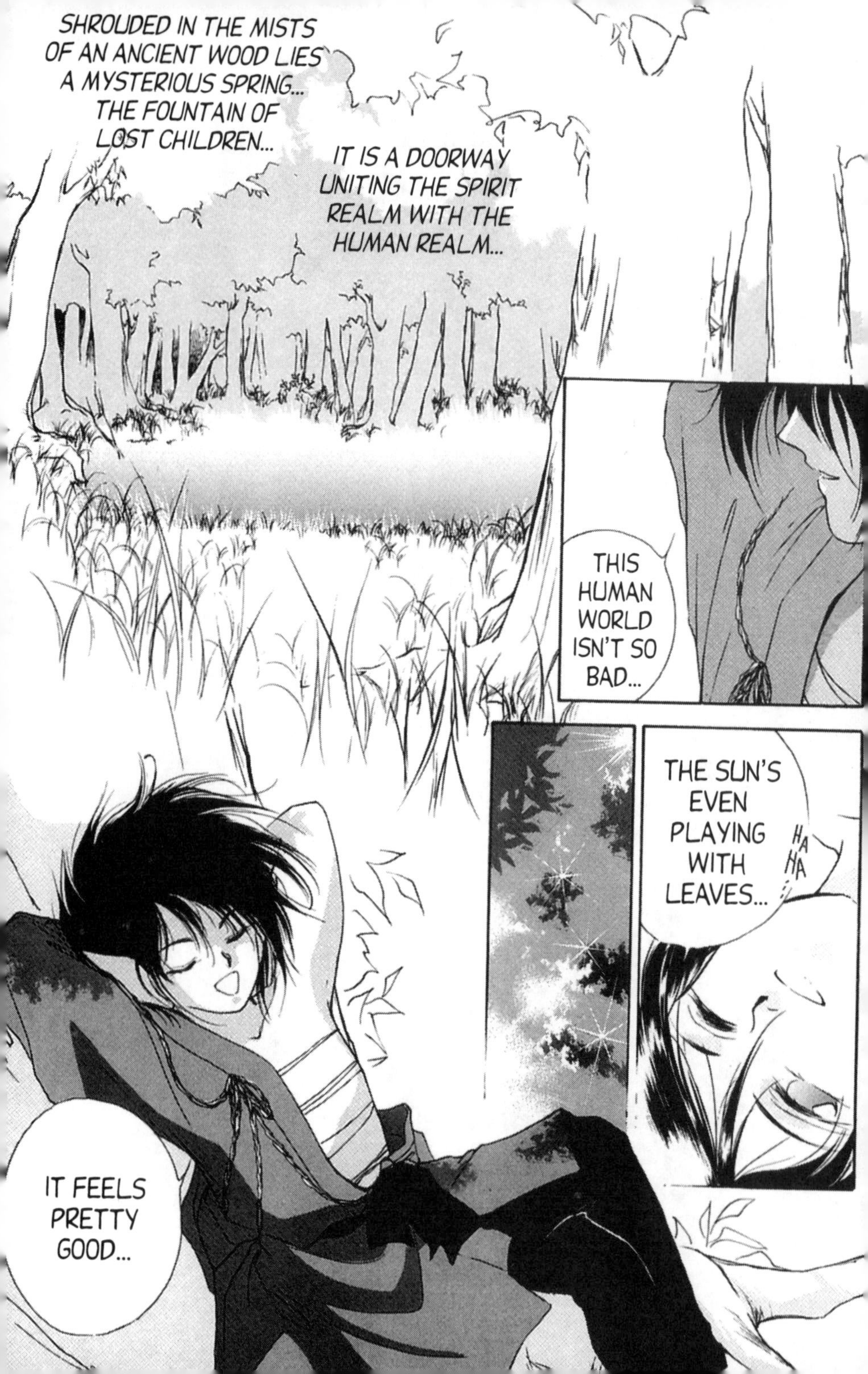
SHROUDED IN THE MISTS OF AN ANCIENT WOOD LIES A MYSTERIOUS SPRING... THE FOUNTAIN OF LOST CHILDREN...
IT IS A DOORWAY UNITING THE SPIRIT REALM WITH THE HUMAN REALM...
THIS HUMAN WORLD ISN'T SO BAD...
THE SUN'S EVEN PLAYING WITH LEAVES...
HA HA
IT FEELS PRETTY GOOD...

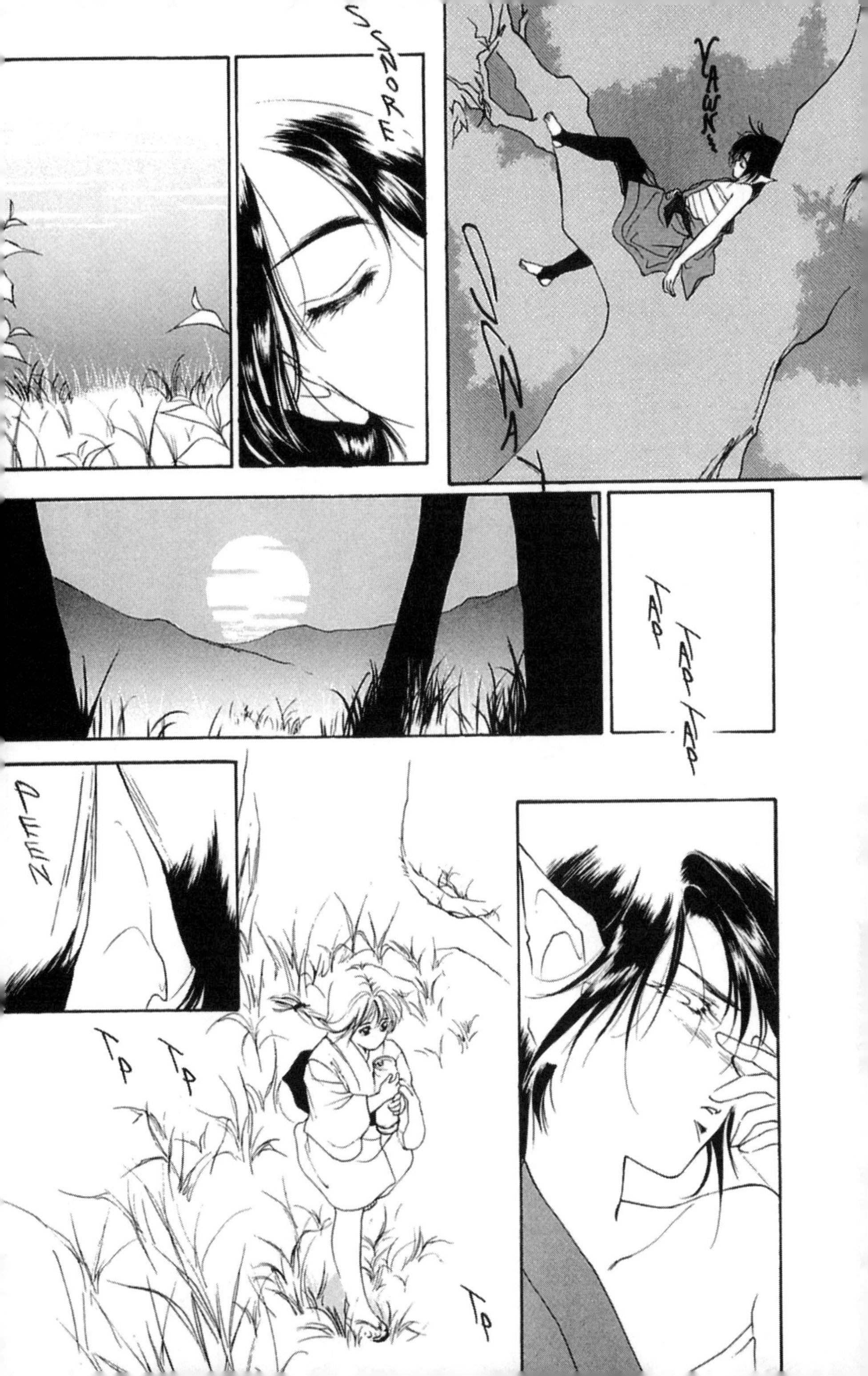

YAWN...
SSSNORE
TAP TAP TAP TAP
TP TP
TP

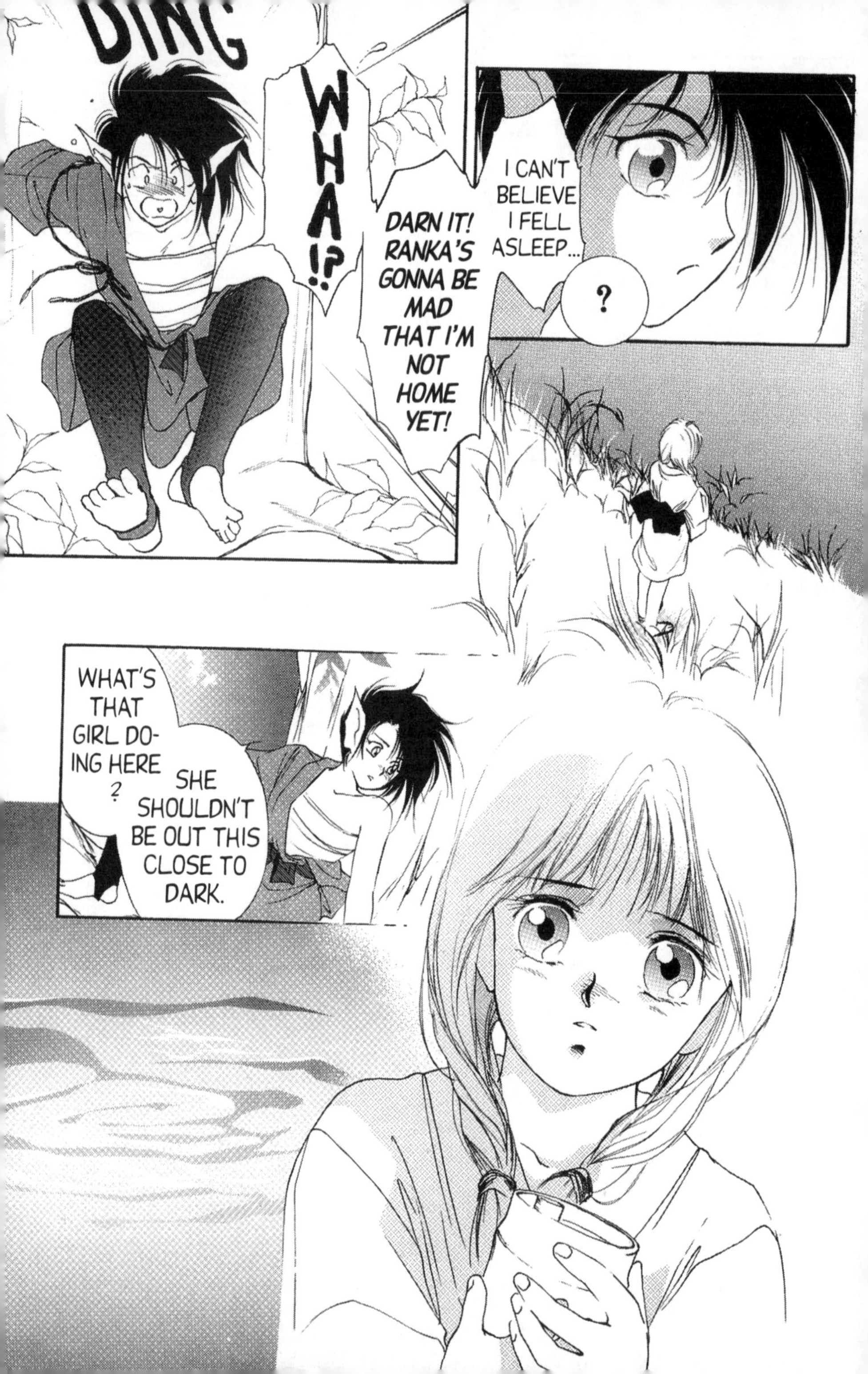
DING
WHA!?
DARN IT! RANKA'S GONNA BE MAD THAT I'M NOT HOME YET!
I CAN'T BELIEVE I FELL ASLEEP...
?
WHAT'S THAT GIRL DO-ING HERE?
SHE SHOULDN'T BE OUT THIS CLOSE TO DARK.

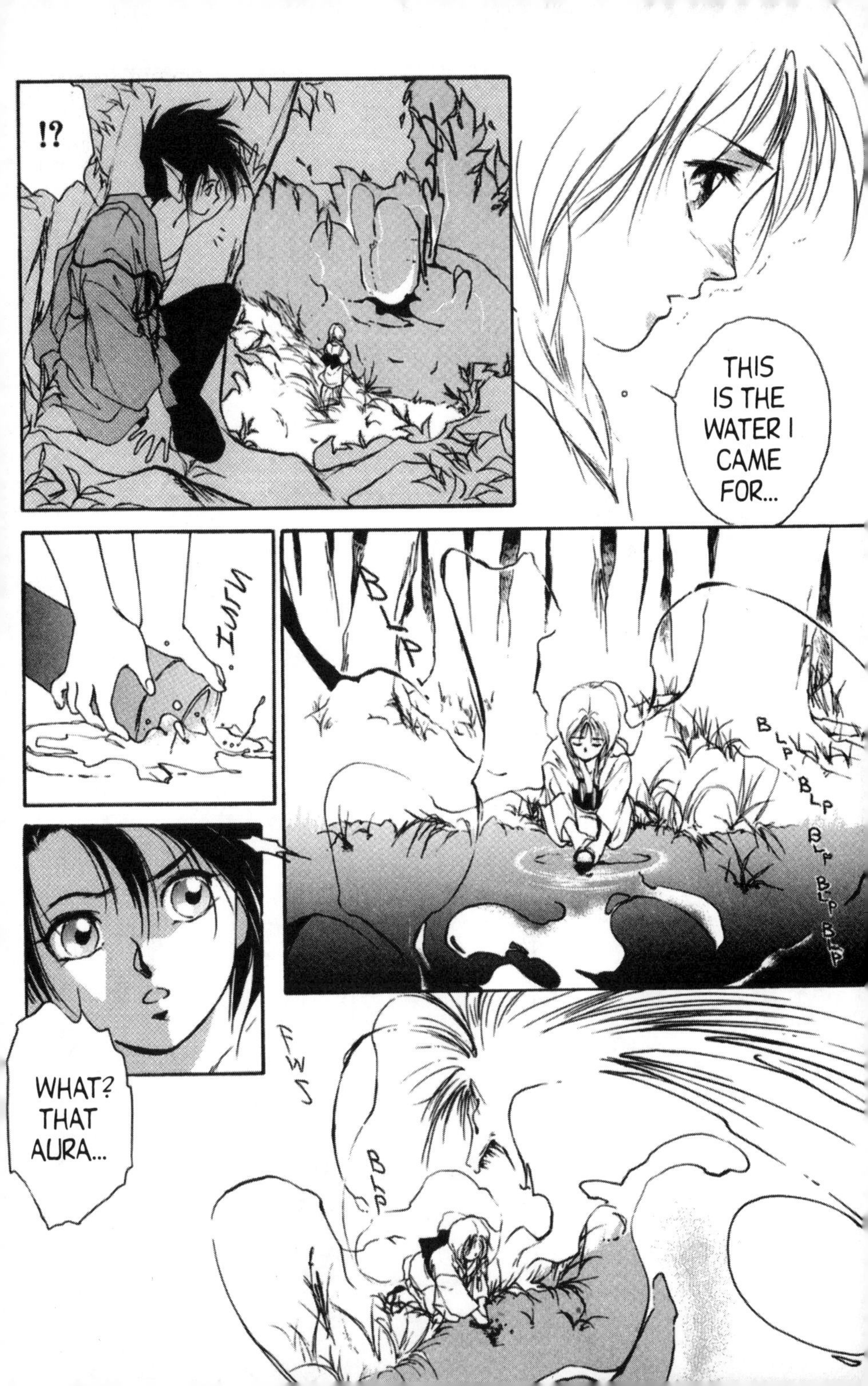
THIS IS THE WATER I CAME FOR...
!?
BLP
BLP BLP BLP BLP BLP BLP
WHAT? THAT AURA...
FWS
BLP

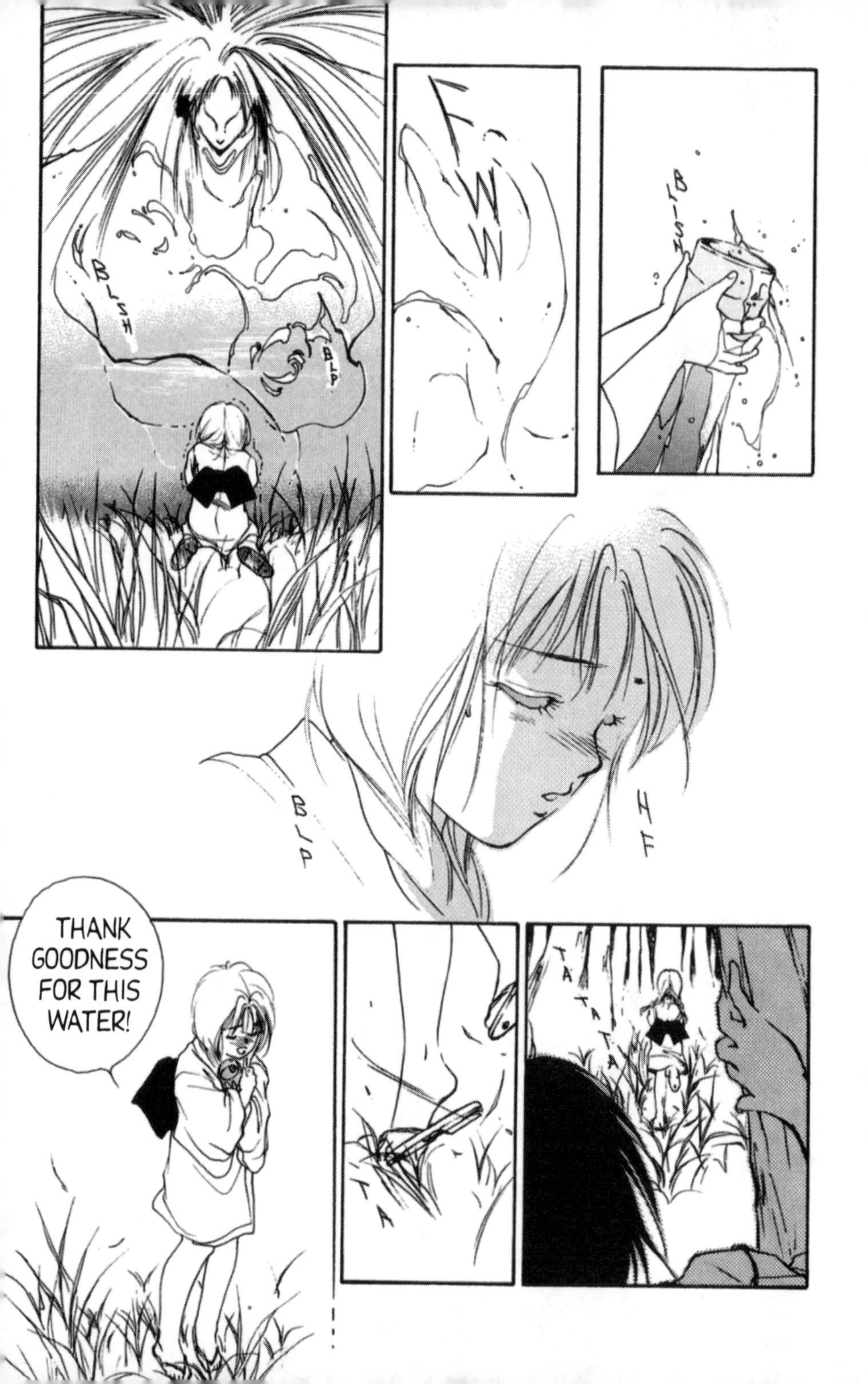
BLSH
BLP
BLP
HF
THANK GOODNESS FOR THIS WATER!
TA
TA TA TA

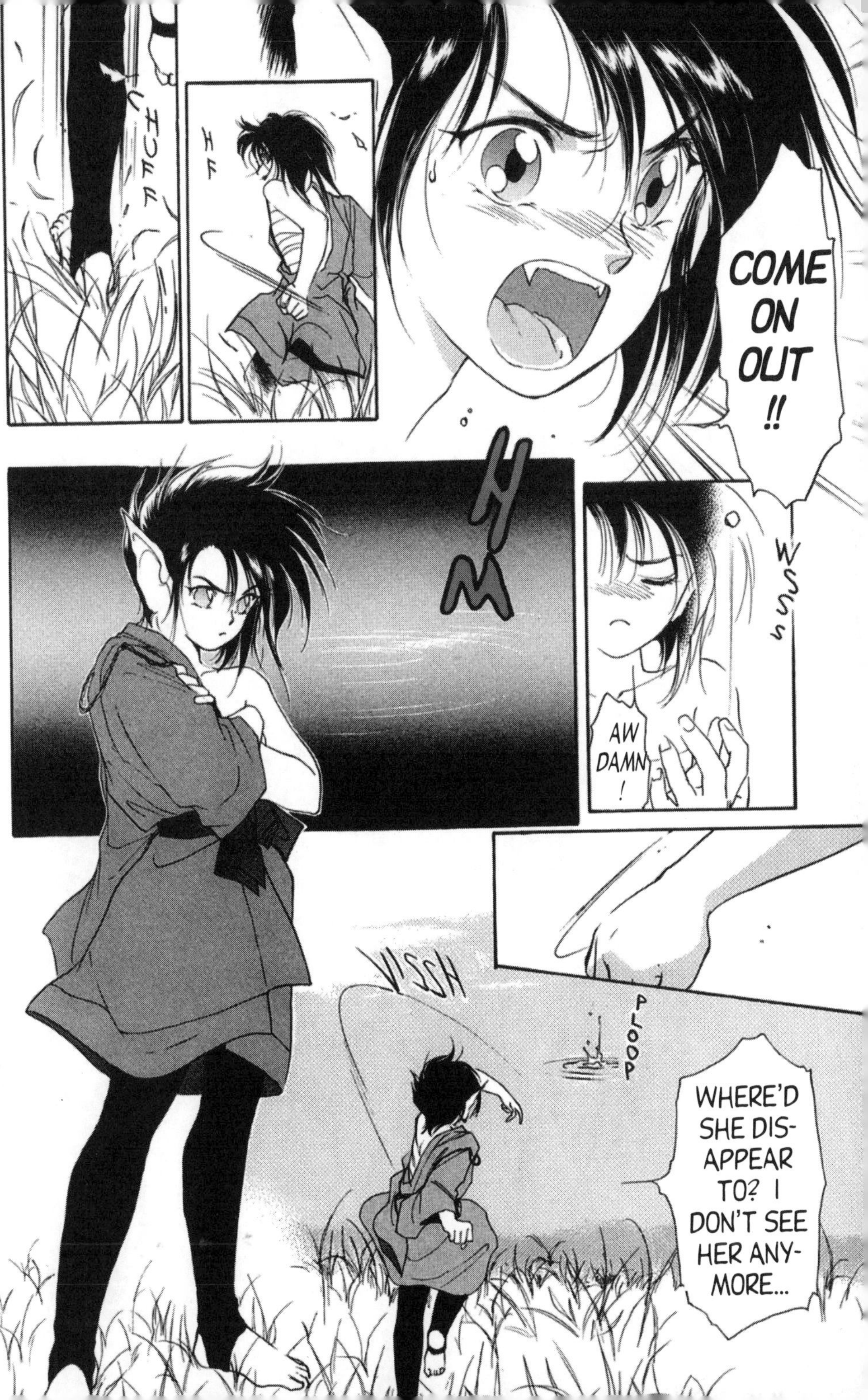
COME ON OUT !!
HF
CHUFF
HM
WSSS
AW DAMN !
PLOOP
HSSH
WHERE'D SHE DIS-APPEAR TO? I DON'T SEE HER ANY-MORE...

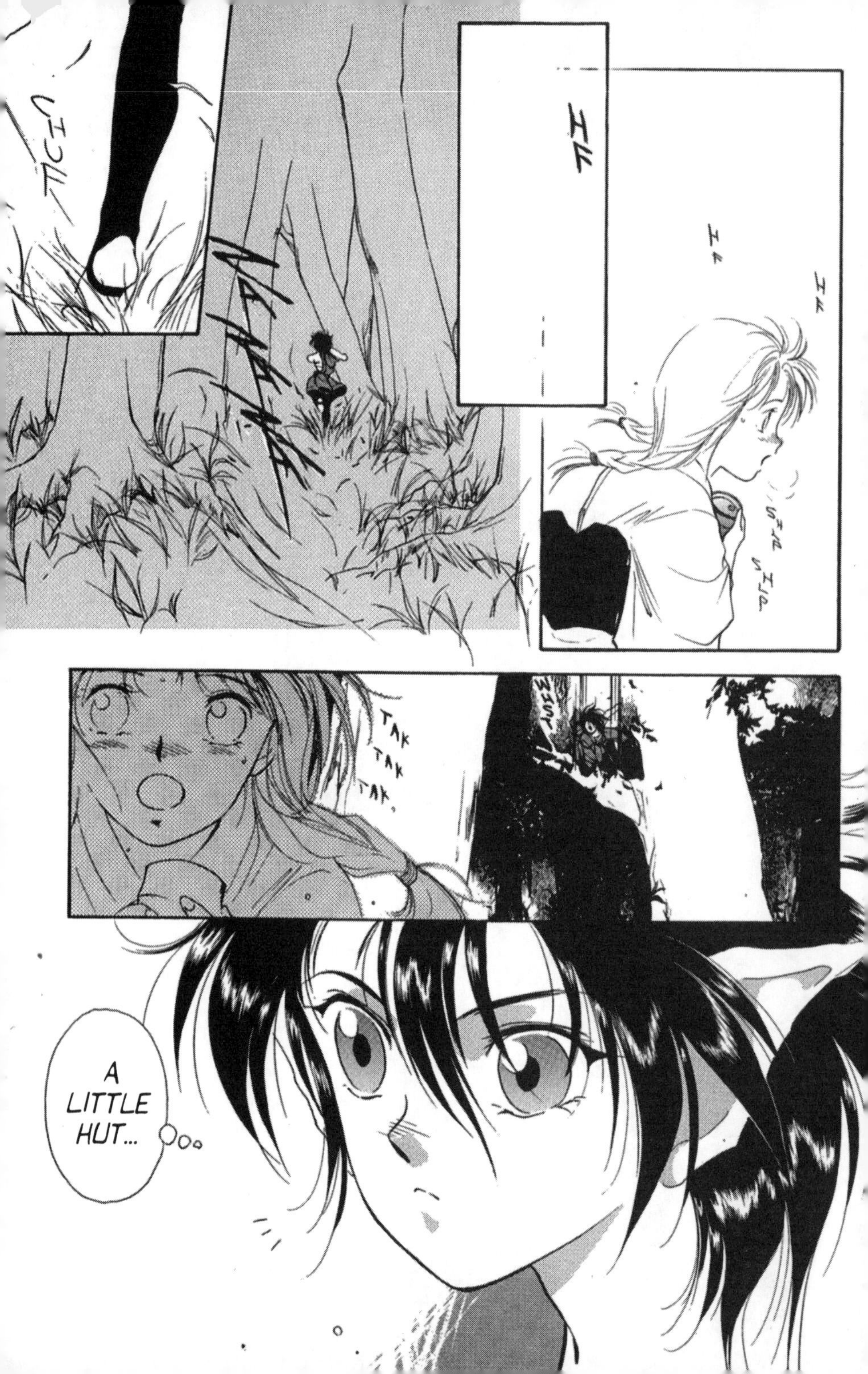
HF
HA
HA
SHP
SHP
CHCL
TAK
TAK
TAK
WHST
A LITTLE HUT...

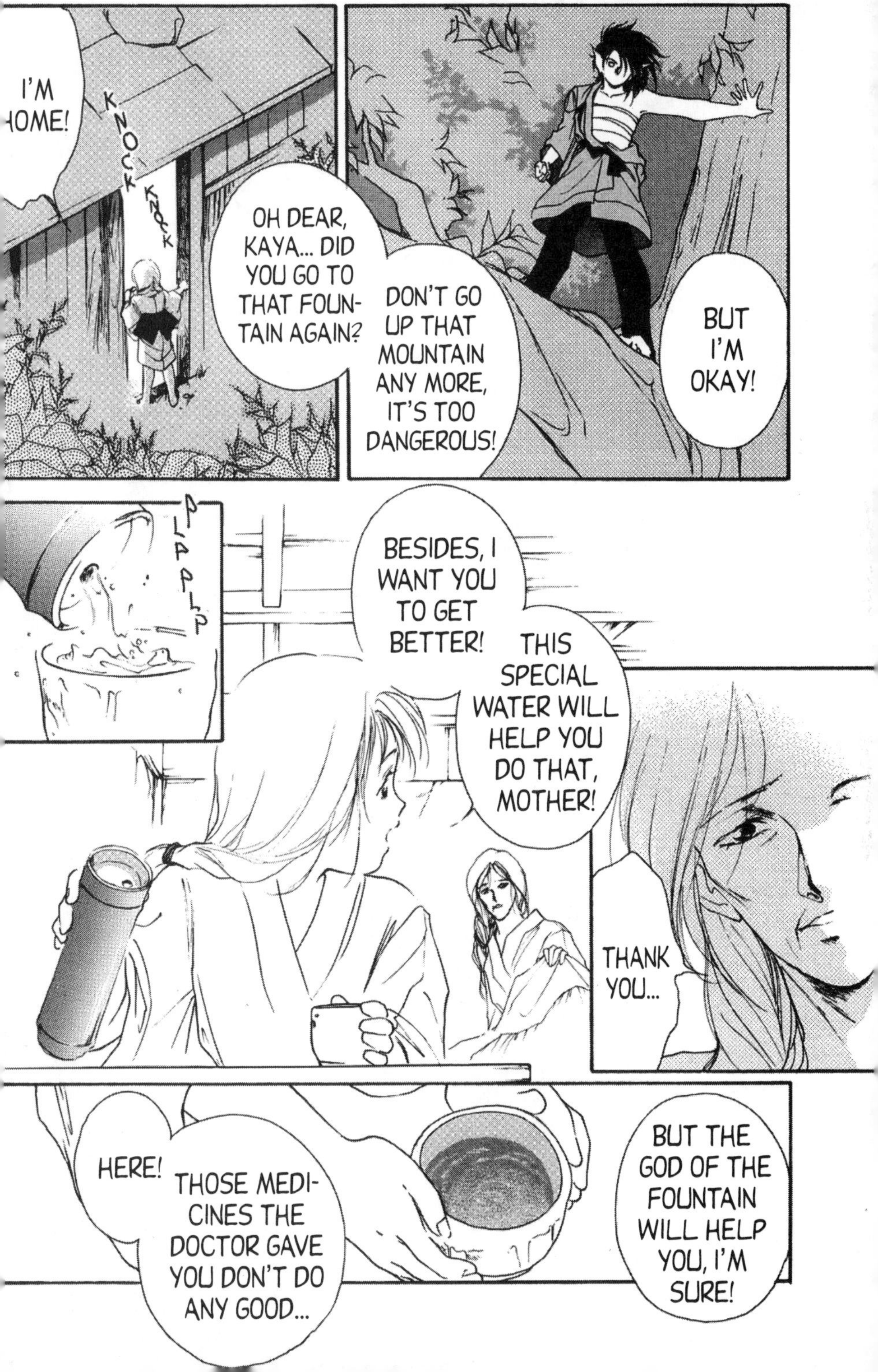
I'M HOME!
KNOCK KNOCK
OH DEAR, KAYA... DID YOU GO TO THAT FOUN-TAIN AGAIN?
DON'T GO UP THAT MOUNTAIN ANY MORE, IT'S TOO DANGEROUS!
BUT I'M OKAY!
PLIP PLIP
BESIDES, I WANT YOU TO GET BETTER!
THIS SPECIAL WATER WILL HELP YOU DO THAT, MOTHER!
THANK YOU...
HERE!
THOSE MEDI-CINES THE DOCTOR GAVE YOU DON'T DO ANY GOOD...
BUT THE GOD OF THE FOUNTAIN WILL HELP YOU, I'M SURE!

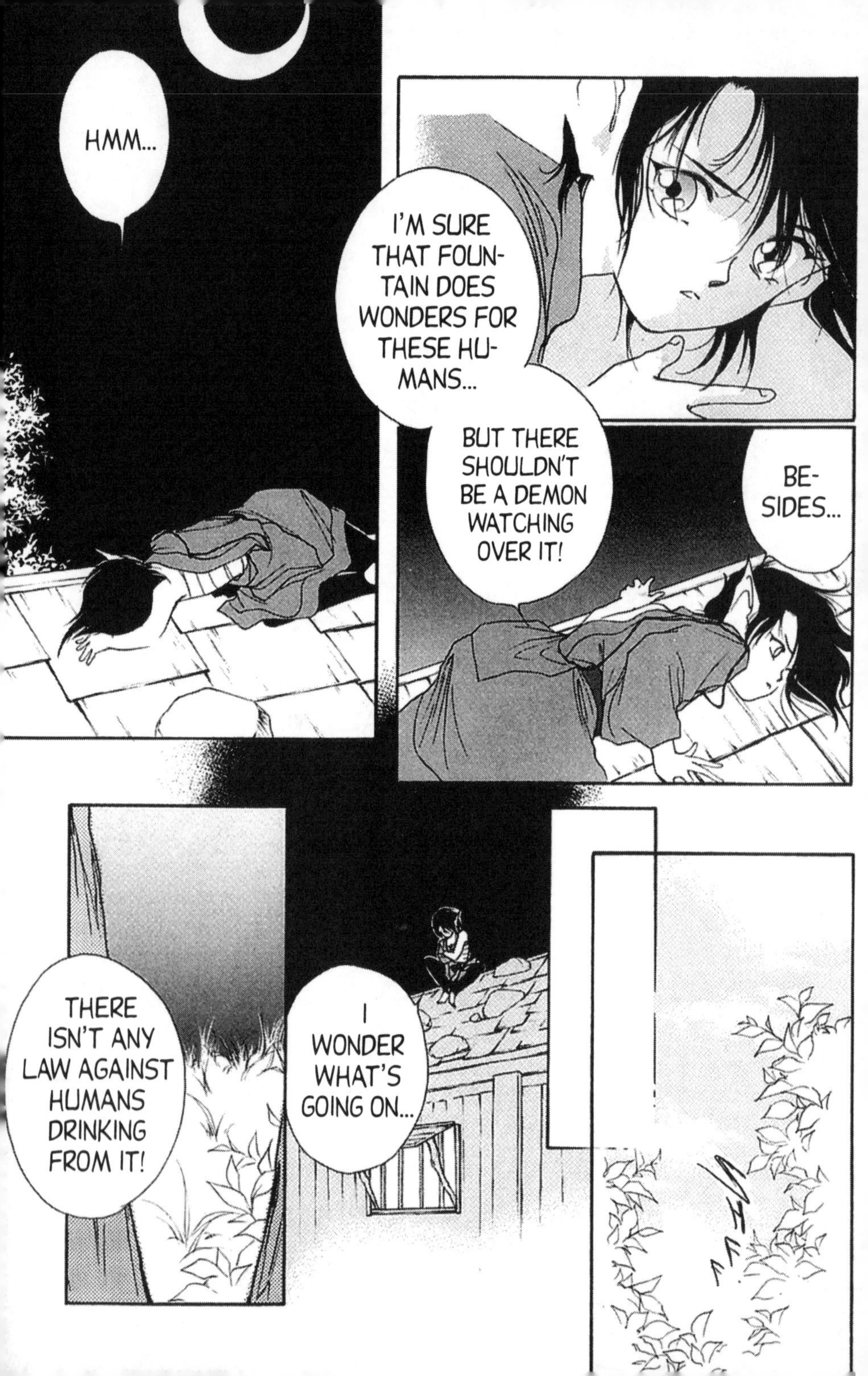
HMM...
I'M SURE THAT FOUN-TAIN DOES WONDERS FOR THESE HU-MANS...
BUT THERE SHOULDN'T BE A DEMON WATCHING OVER IT!
BE-SIDES...
THERE ISN'T ANY LAW AGAINST HUMANS DRINKING FROM IT!
I WONDER WHAT'S GOING ON...

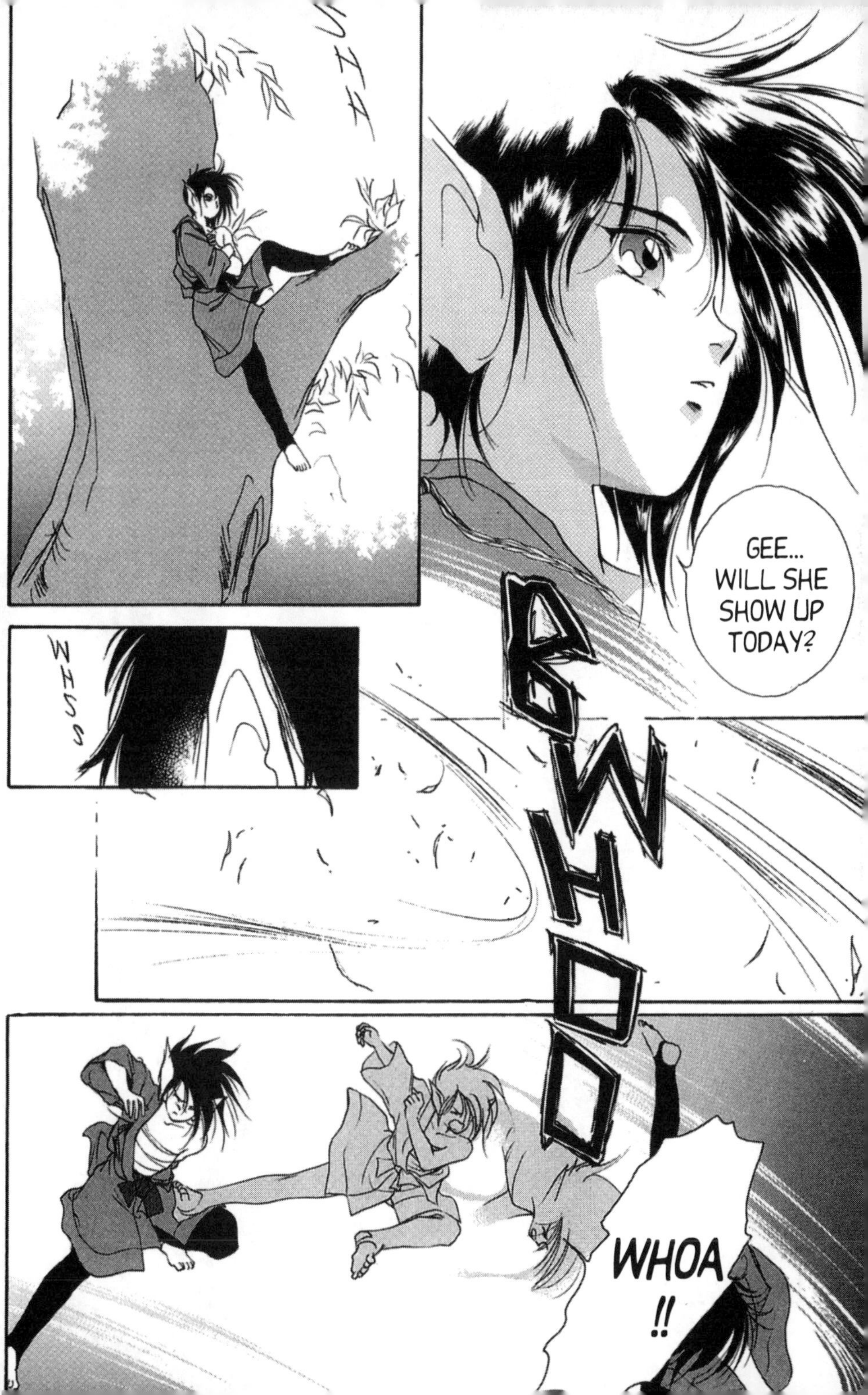
GEE... WILL SHE SHOW UP TODAY?
SHH
WHSS
BWHOOD
WHOA !!

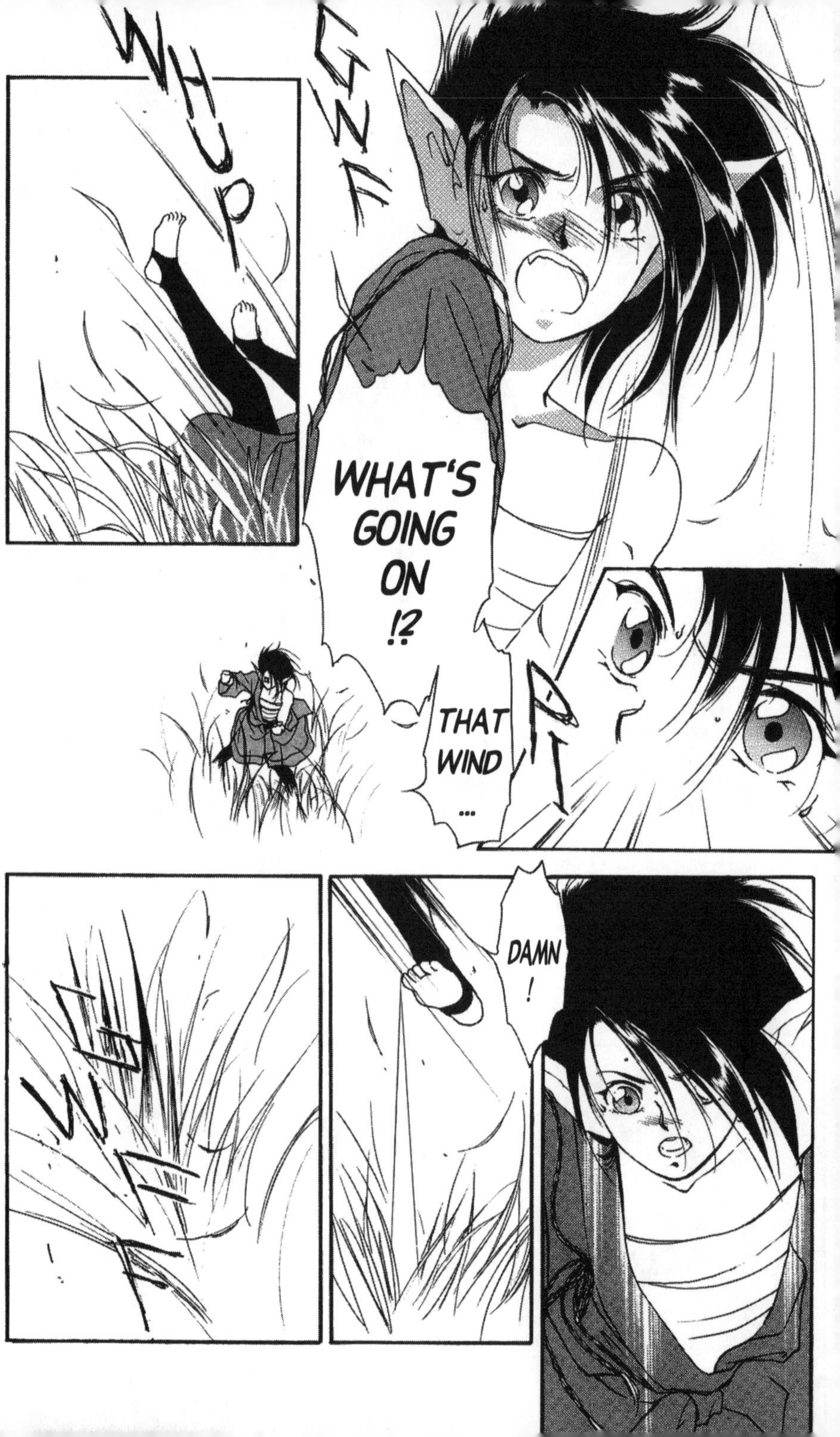
GWF
WHUP
WHAT'S GOING ON !?
THAT WIND ...
DAMN !

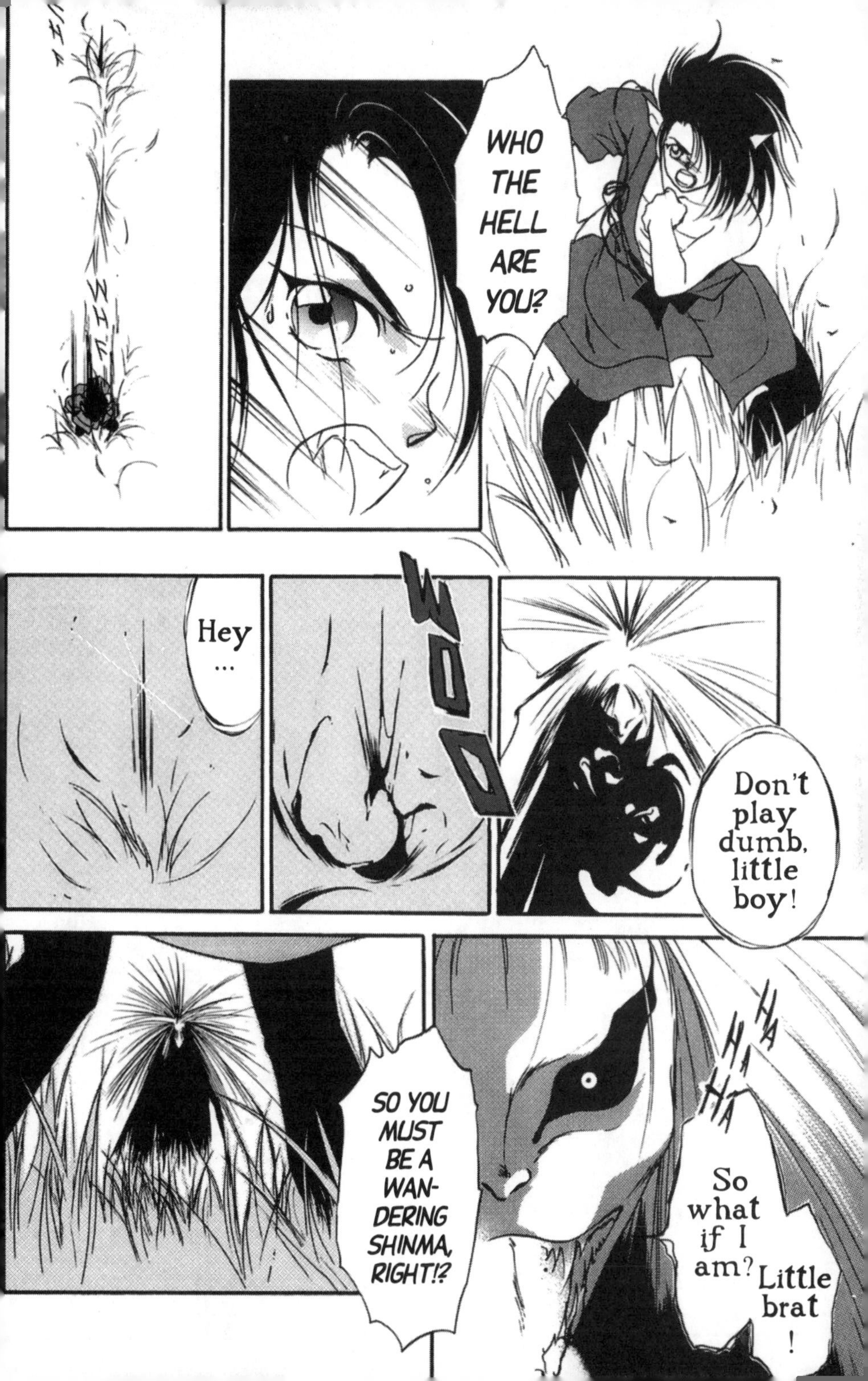
WHO THE HELL ARE YOU?
Don't play dumb, little boy!
Hey ...
HA HA HA HA
So what if I am? Little brat !
SO YOU MUST BE A WAN-DERING SHINMA, RIGHT!?

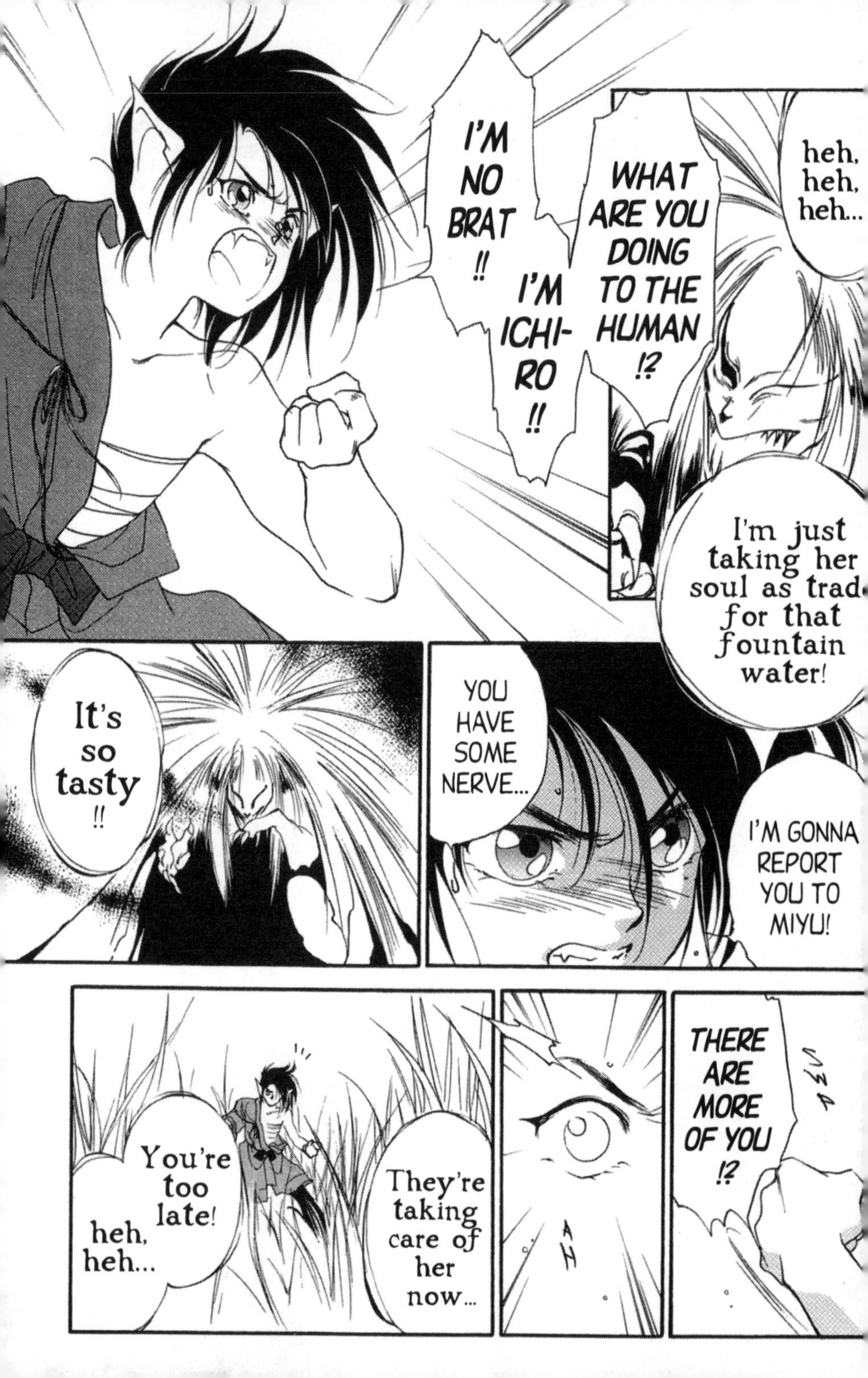
heh, heh, heh...
WHAT ARE YOU DOING TO THE HUMAN !?
I'M ICHI-RO !!
I'M NO BRAT !!
I'm just taking her soul as trad for that fountain water!
I'M GONNA REPORT YOU TO MIYU!
YOU HAVE SOME NERVE...
It's so tasty !!
THERE ARE MORE OF YOU !?
AH
They're taking care of her now...
You're too late! heh, heh...

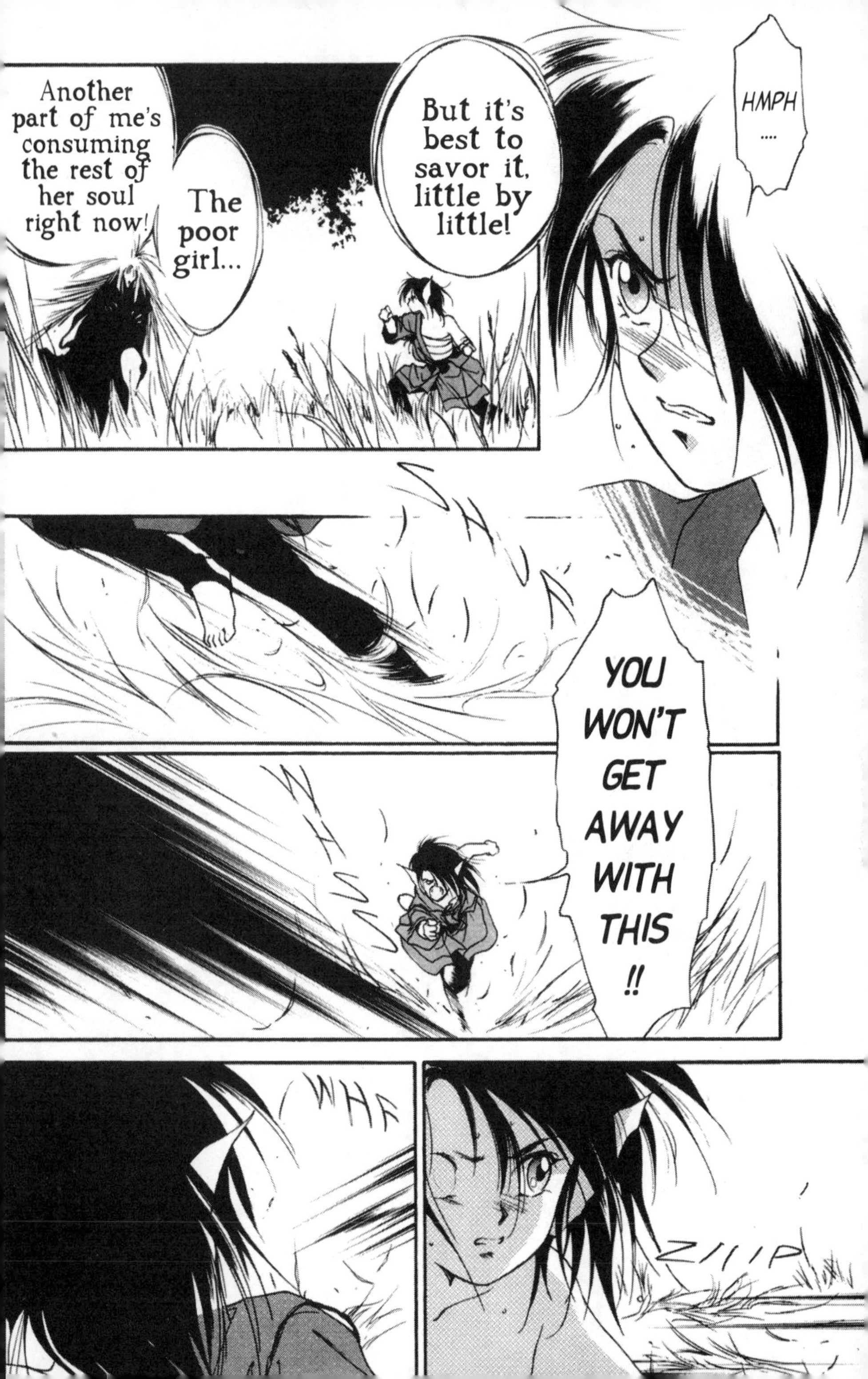

Another part of me's consuming the rest of her soul right now!
The poor girl...
But it's best to savor it, little by little!
HMPH ....
YOU WON'T GET AWAY WITH THIS !!
WHF
ZIIIP

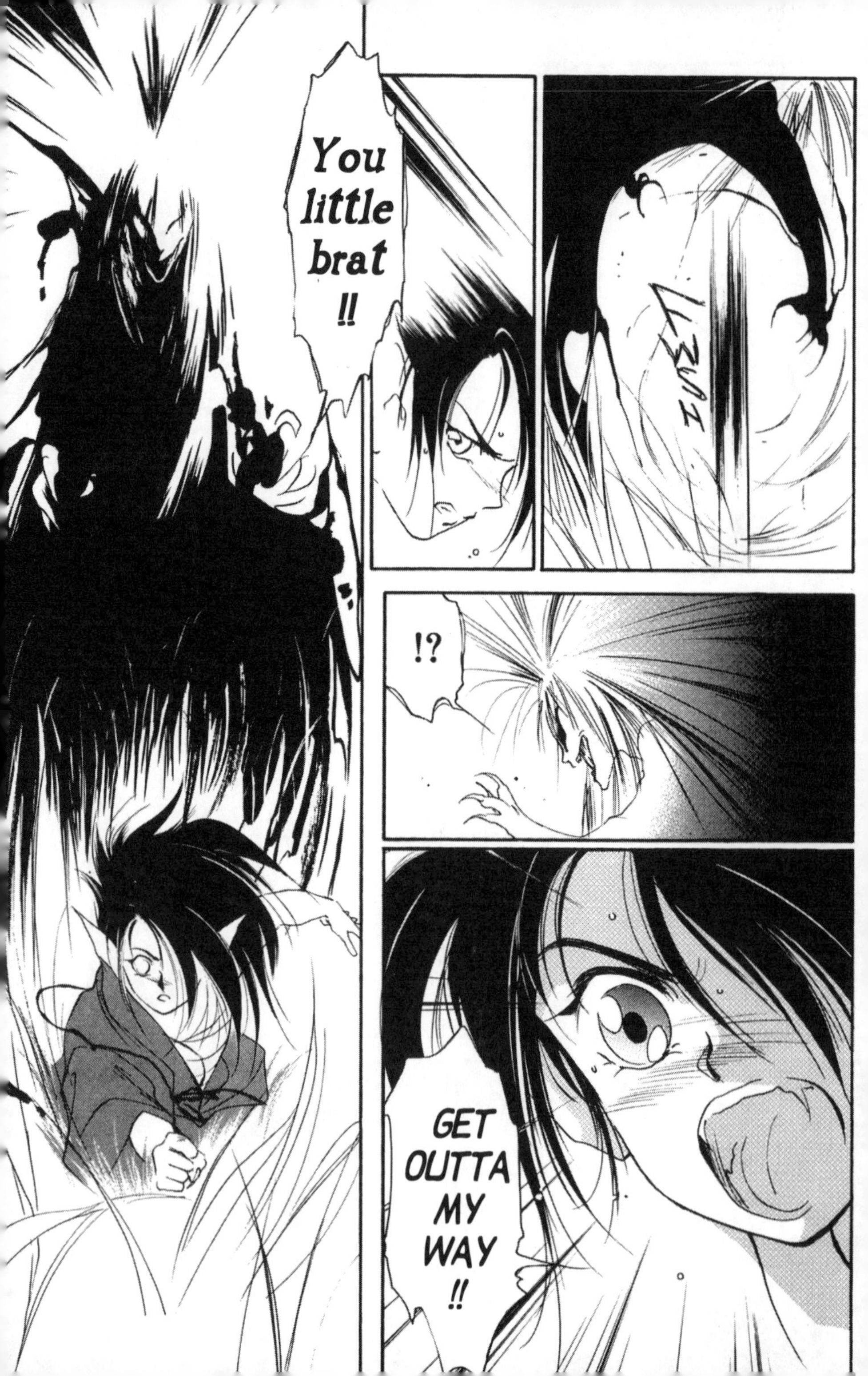
You little brat !!
!?
GET OUTTA MY WAY !!

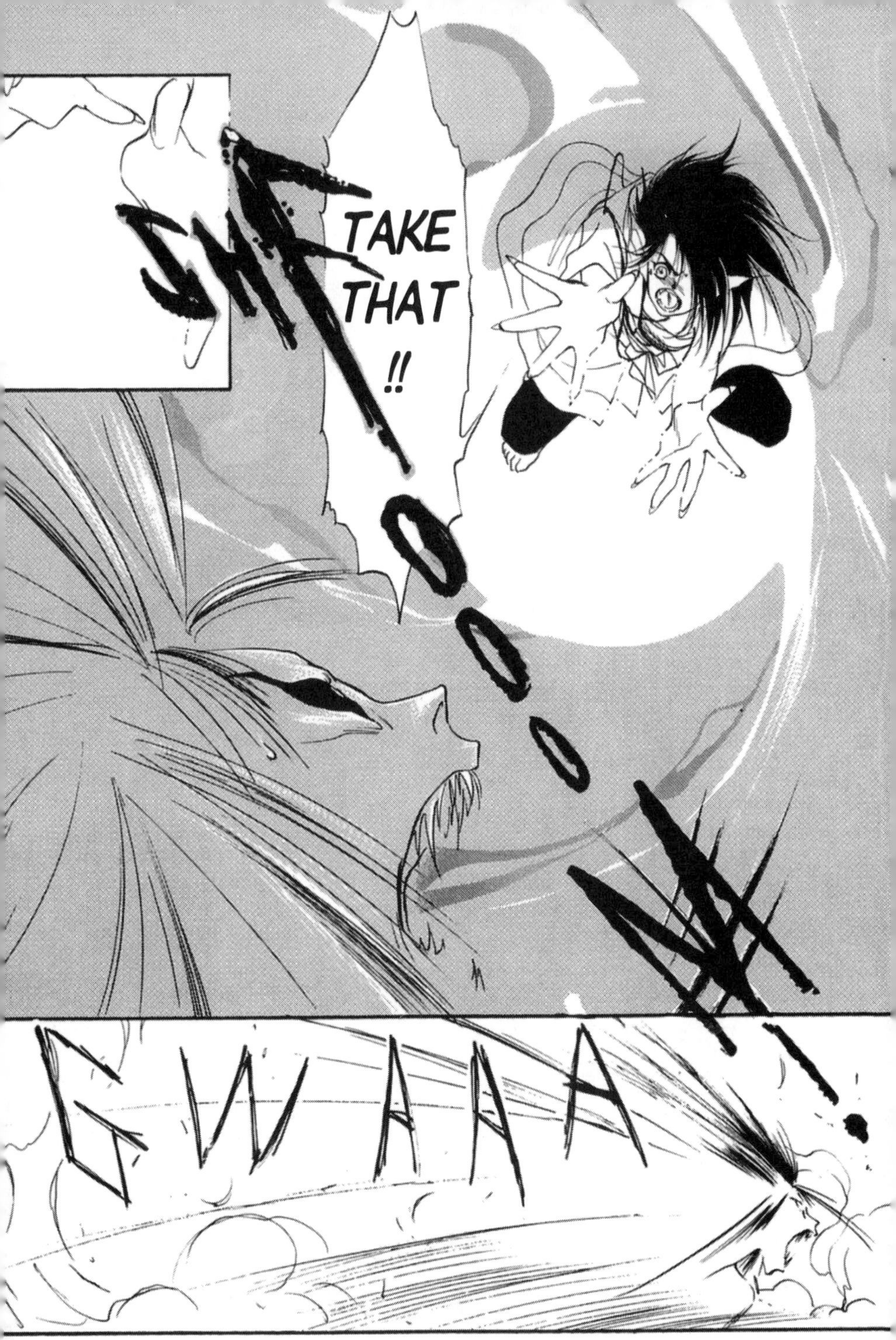
SHF
TAKE THAT !!
OOOOOM
GWAAA !!

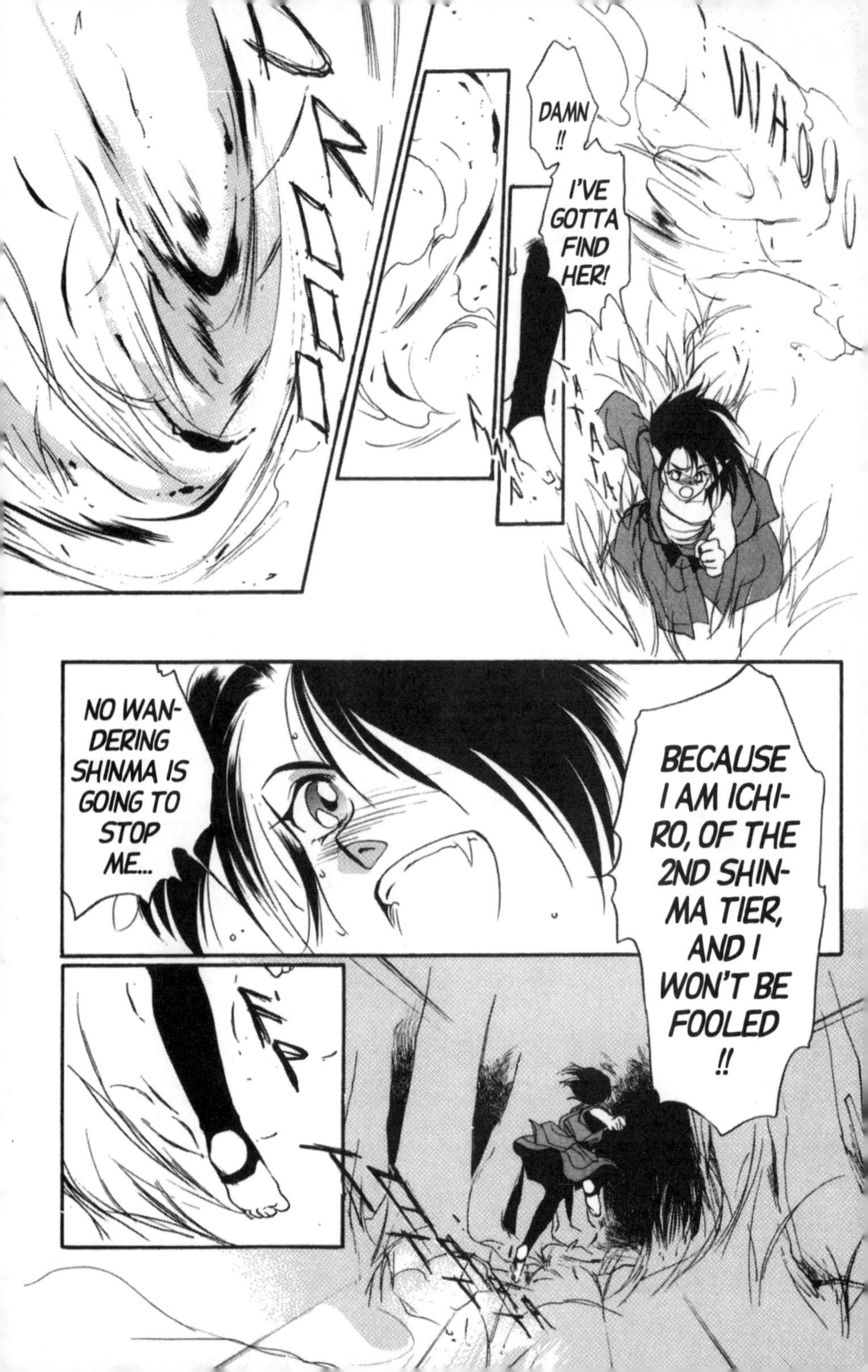
DAMN !!
I'VE GOTTA FIND HER!
NO WAN-DERING SHINMA IS GOING TO STOP ME...
BECAUSE I AM ICHI-RO, OF THE 2ND SHIN-MA TIER, AND I WON'T BE FOOLED !!

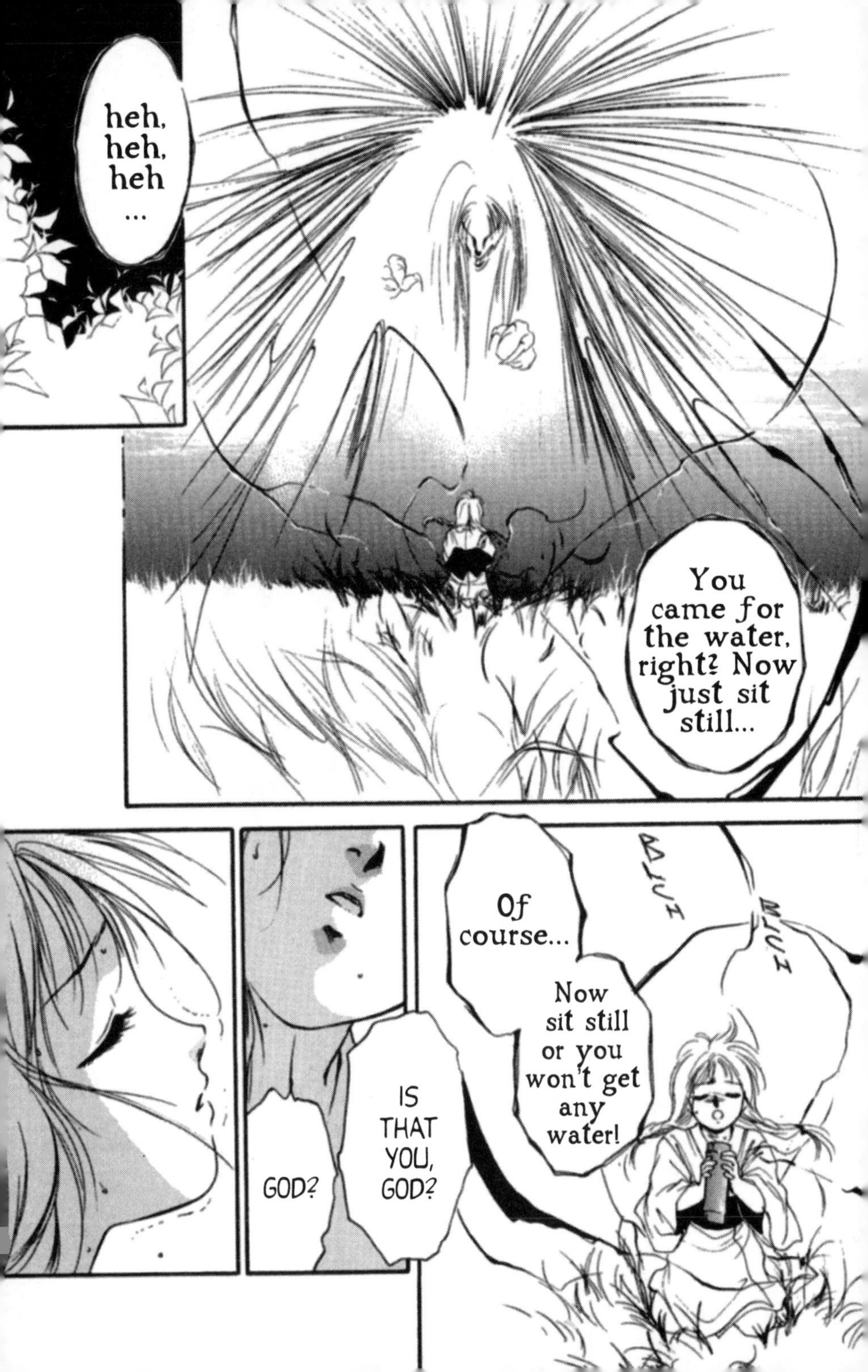
heh, heh, heh ...
You came for the water, right? Now just sit still...
GOD?
IS THAT YOU, GOD?
Of course...
Now sit still or you won't get any water!

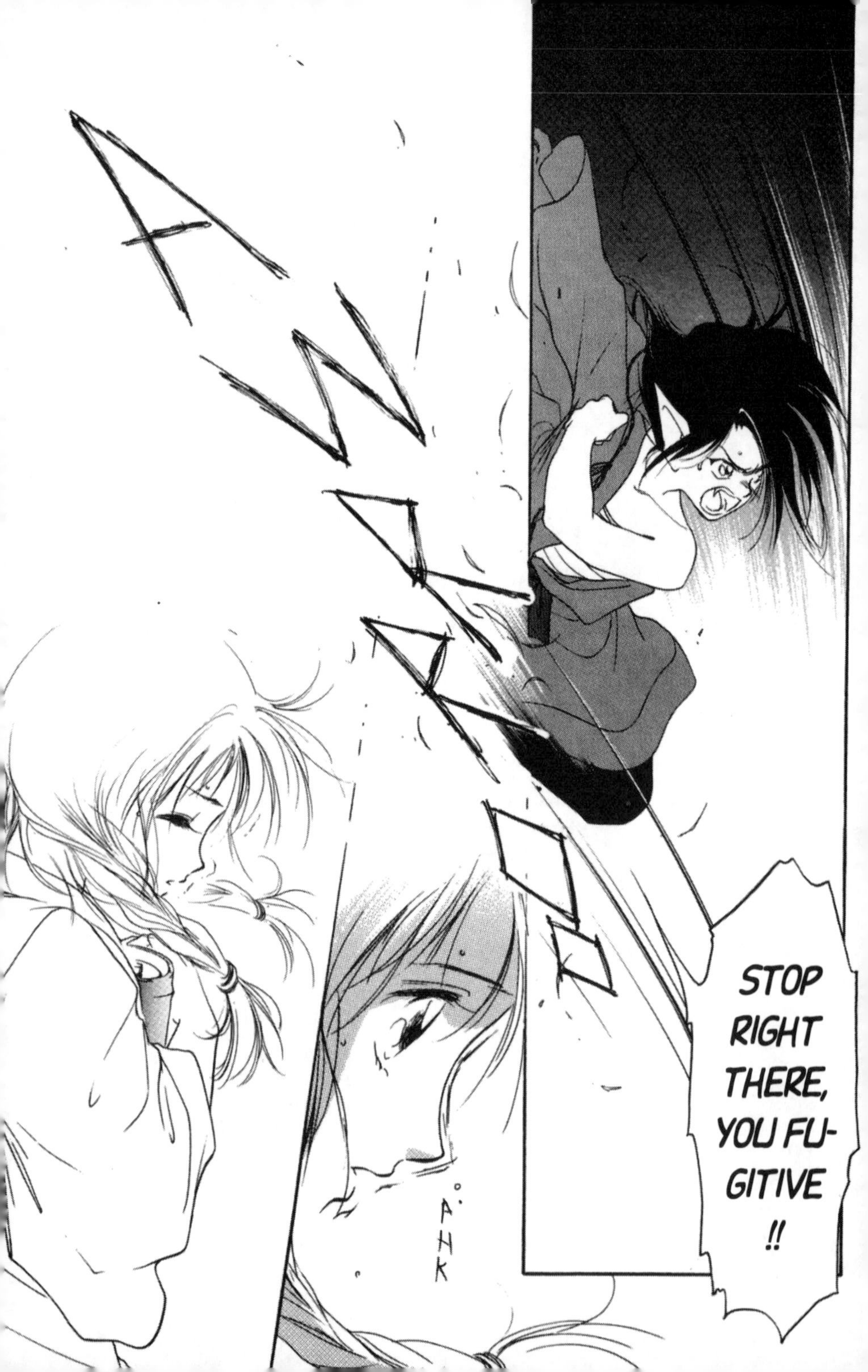
STOP RIGHT THERE, YOU FU-GITIVE !!
AHK

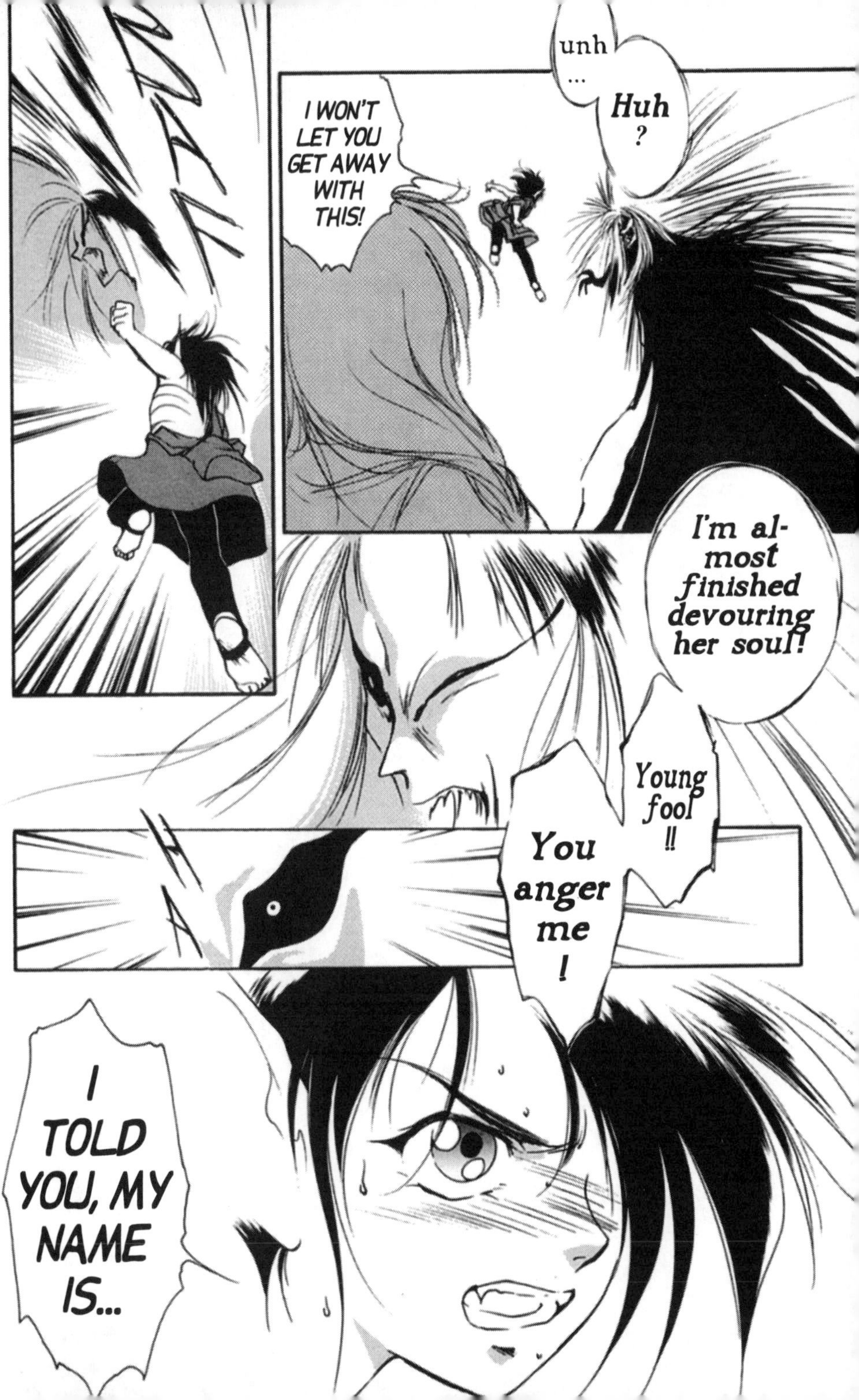
unh ... Huh ?
I WON'T LET YOU GET AWAY WITH THIS!
I'm al-most finished devouring her soul!
Young fool !!
You anger me !
I TOLD YOU, MY NAME IS...

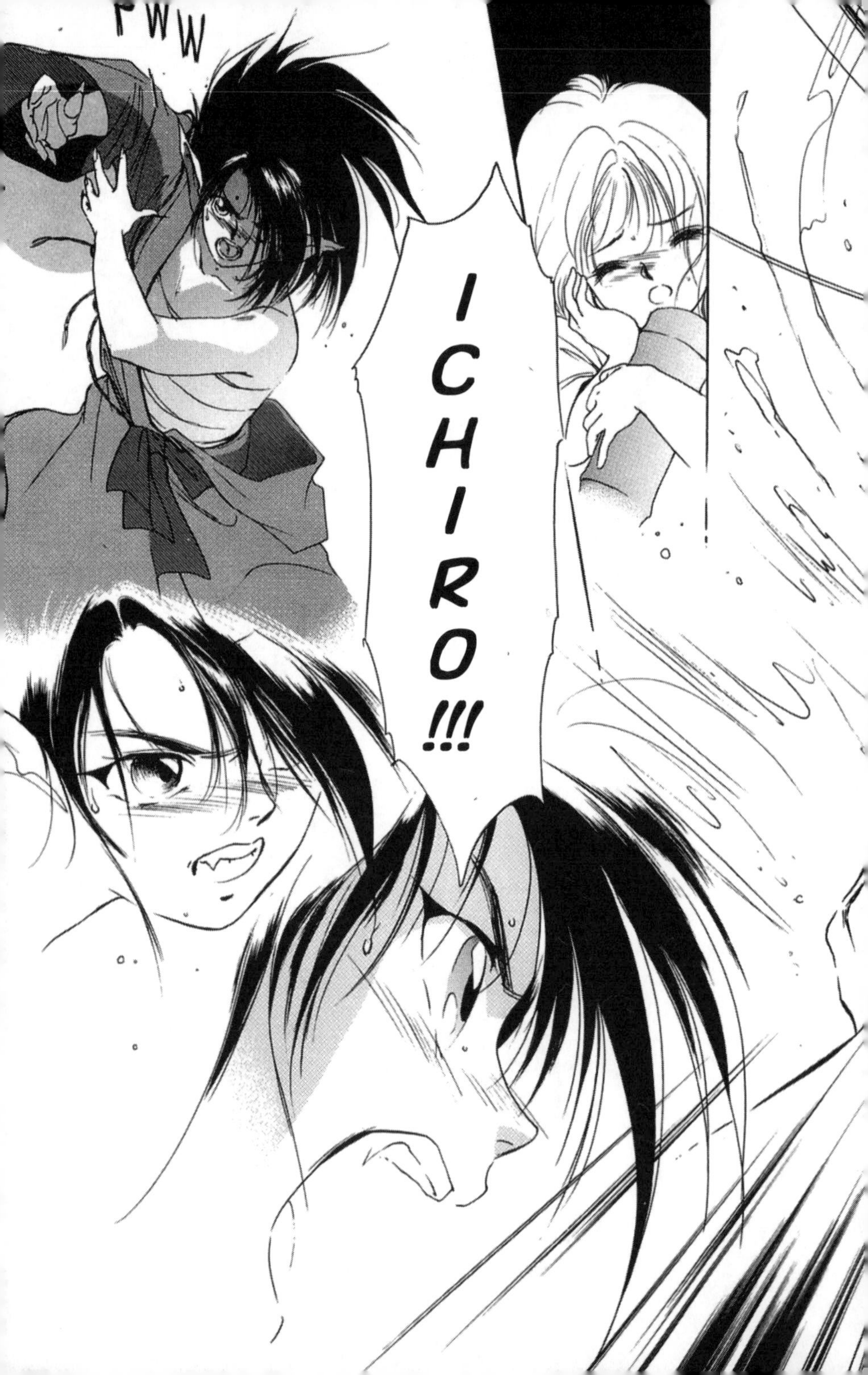
ICHIRO!!!
FWW

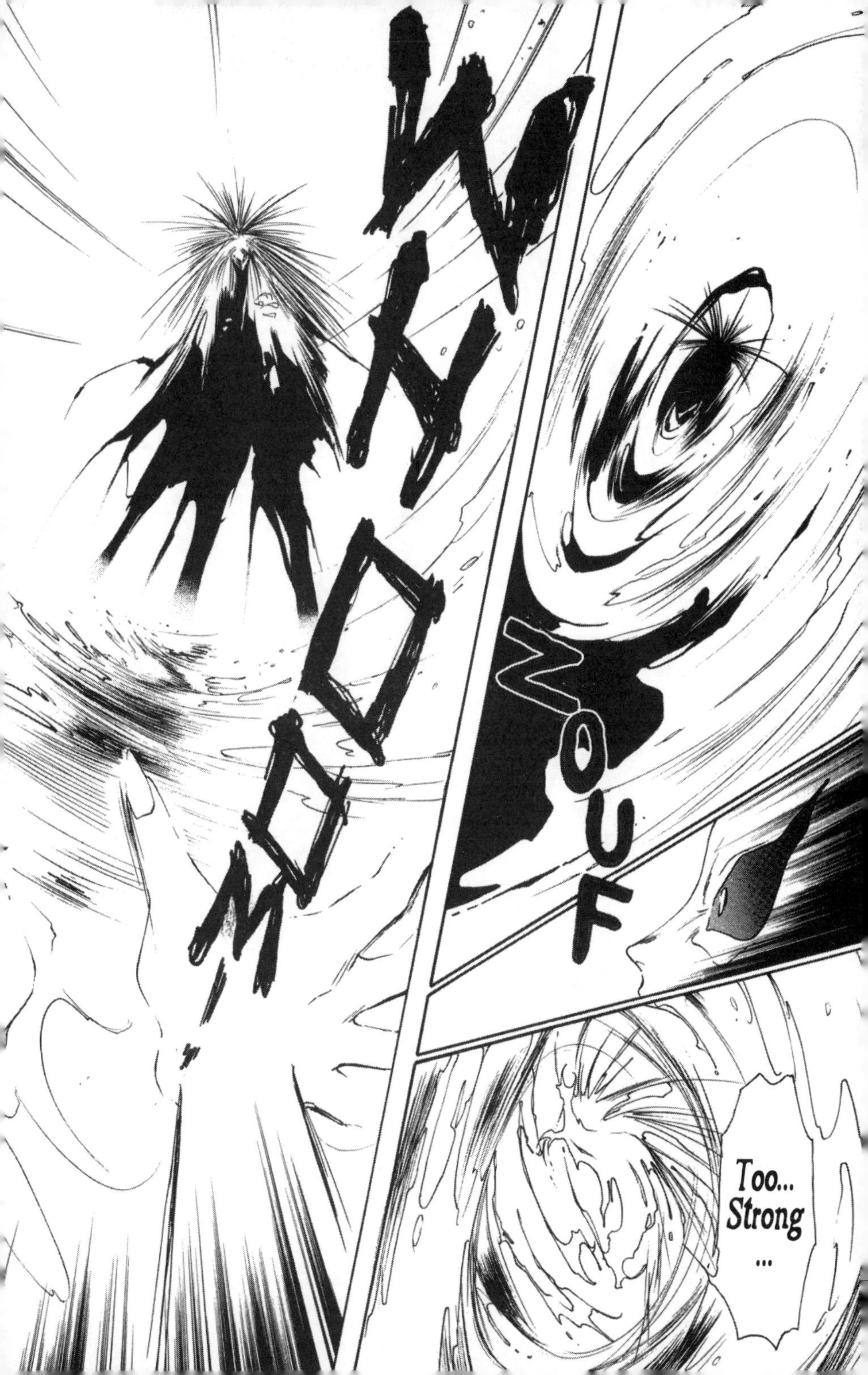
WHOOOM
NOUF
Too... Strong ...

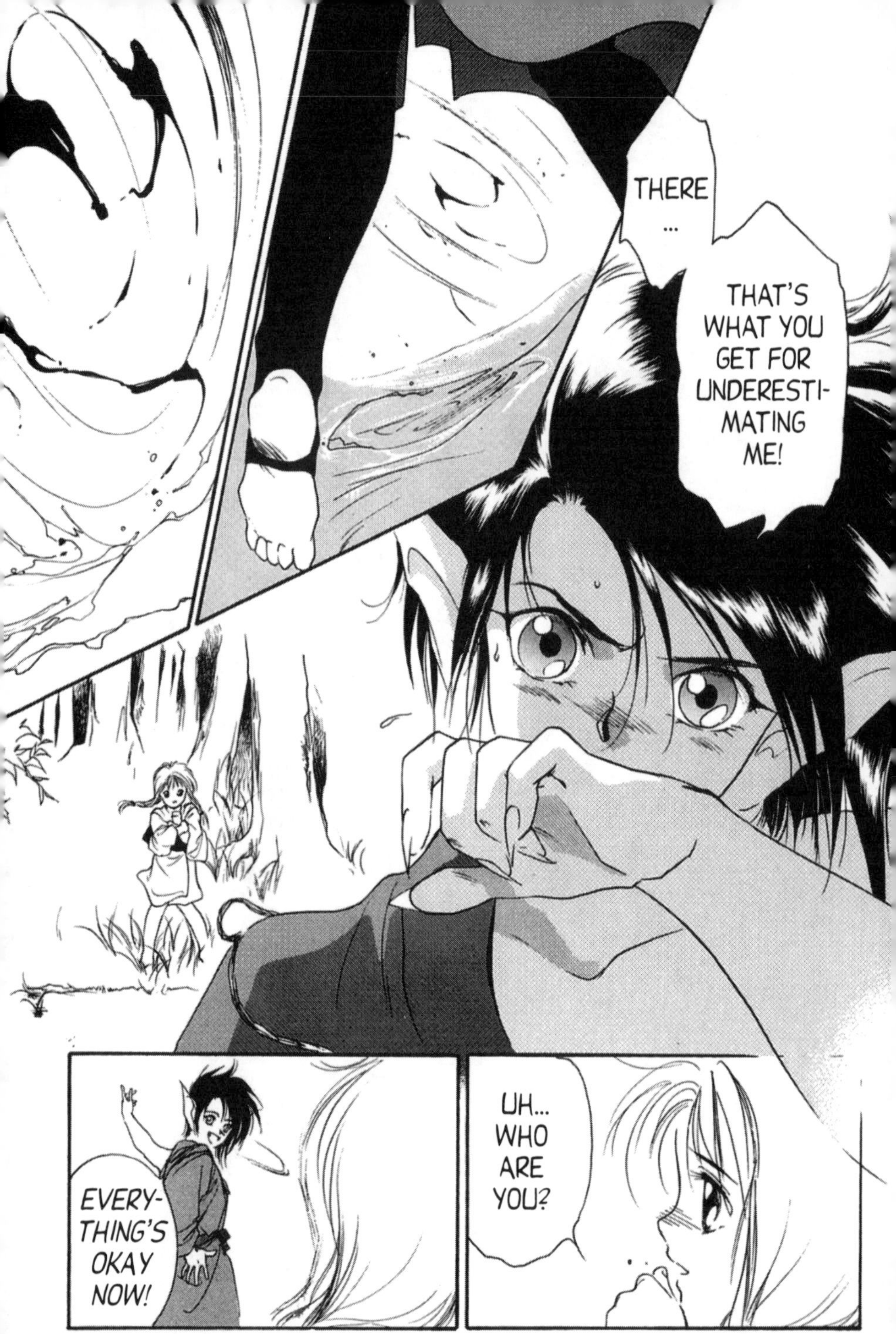
THERE ...
THAT'S WHAT YOU GET FOR UNDERESTI- MATING ME!
UH... WHO ARE YOU?
EVERY- THING'S OKAY NOW!

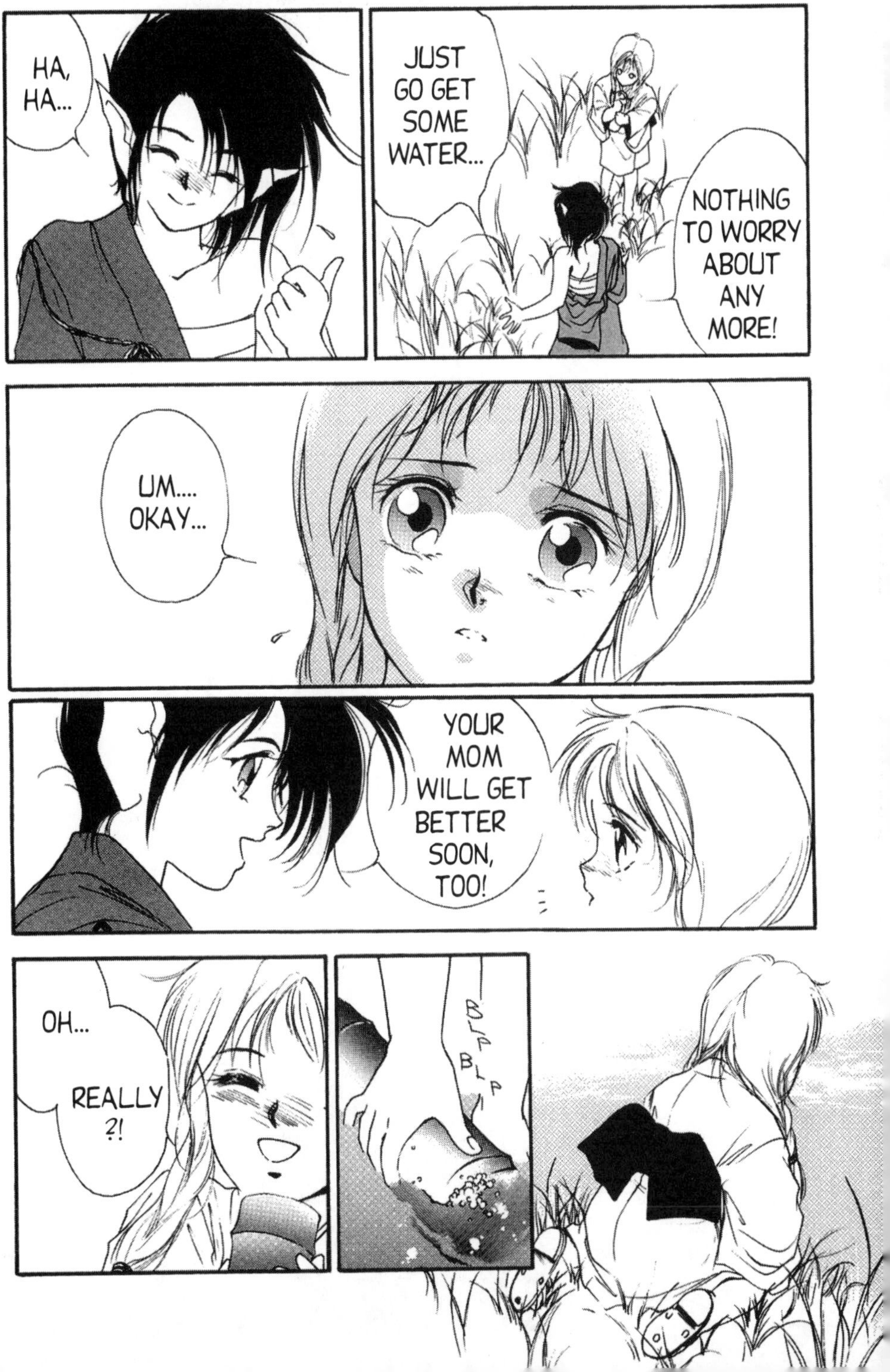

HA, HA...
JUST GO GET SOME WATER...
NOTHING TO WORRY ABOUT ANY MORE!
UM.... OKAY...
YOUR MOM WILL GET BETTER SOON, TOO!
OH... REALLY ?!
BLP BLP

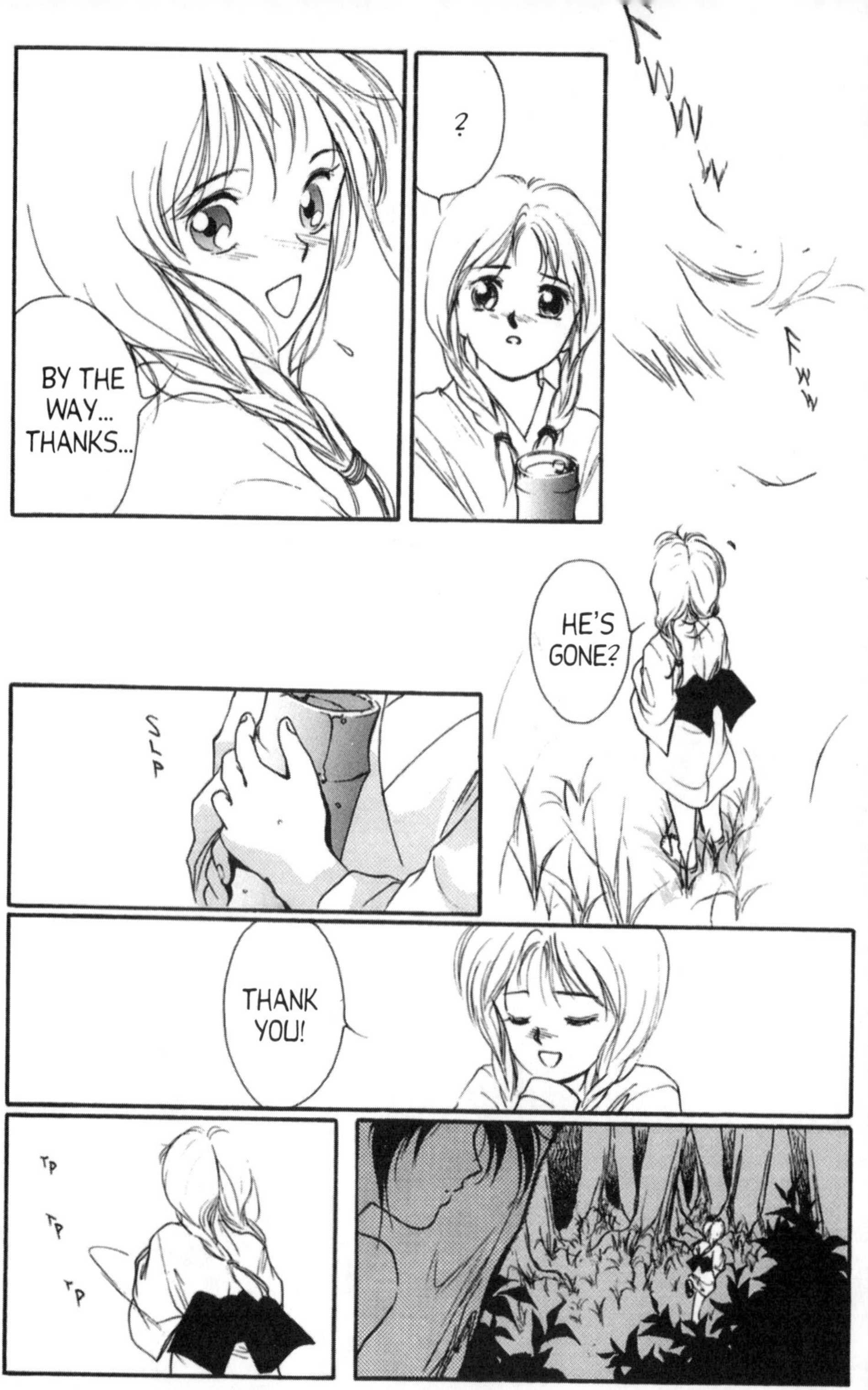

BY THE WAY... THANKS...
?
FWW
HE'S GONE?
SLIP
THANK YOU!
TP
TP
TP

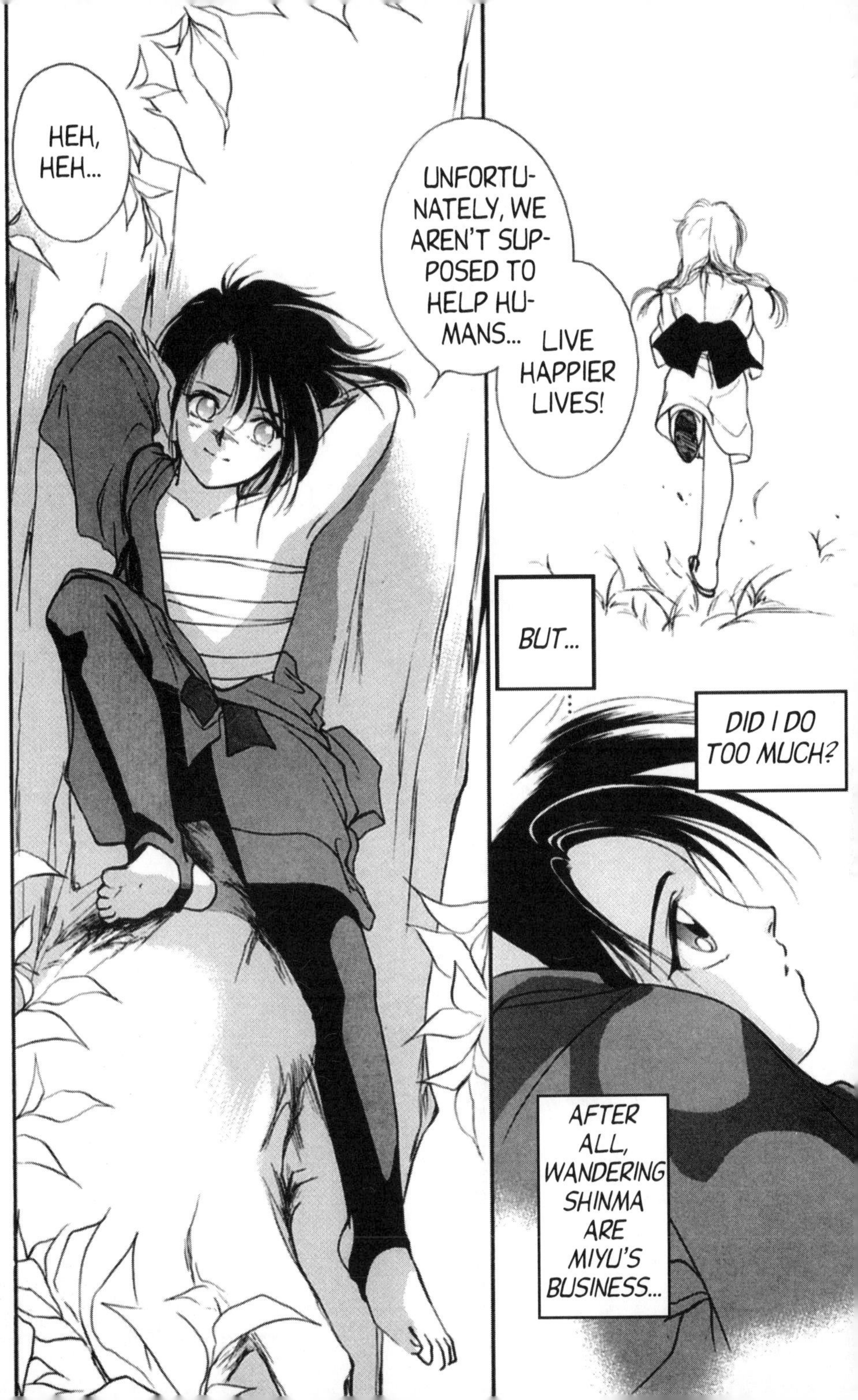
HEH, HEH...
UNFORTU-NATELY, WE AREN'T SUP-POSED TO HELP HU-MANS...
LIVE HAPPIER LIVES!
BUT...
DID I DO TOO MUCH?
AFTER ALL, WANDERING SHINMA ARE MIYU'S BUSINESS...

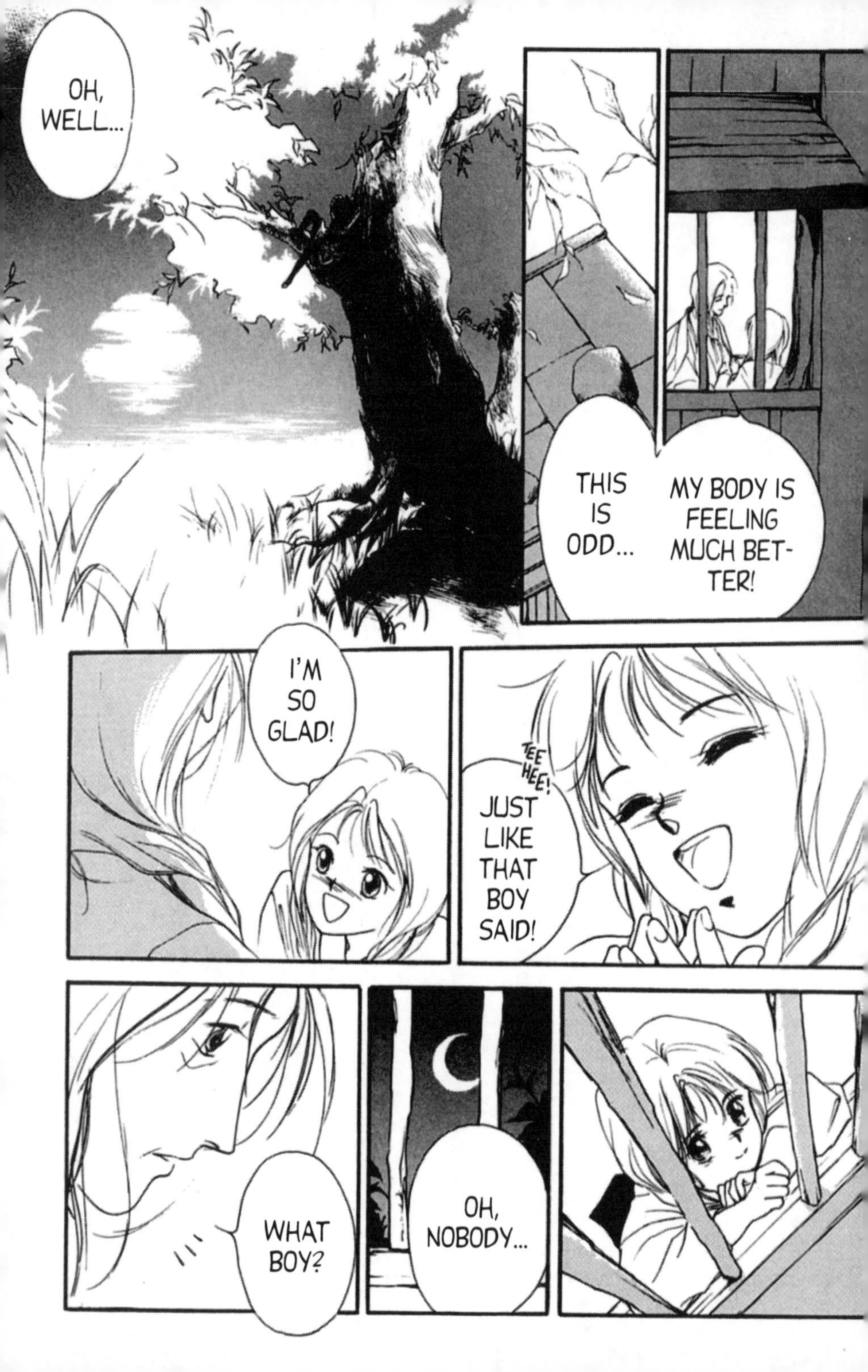
OH, WELL...
THIS IS ODD...
MY BODY IS FEELING MUCH BET-TER!
I'M SO GLAD!
TEE HEE!
JUST LIKE THAT BOY SAID!
WHAT BOY?
OH, NOBODY...

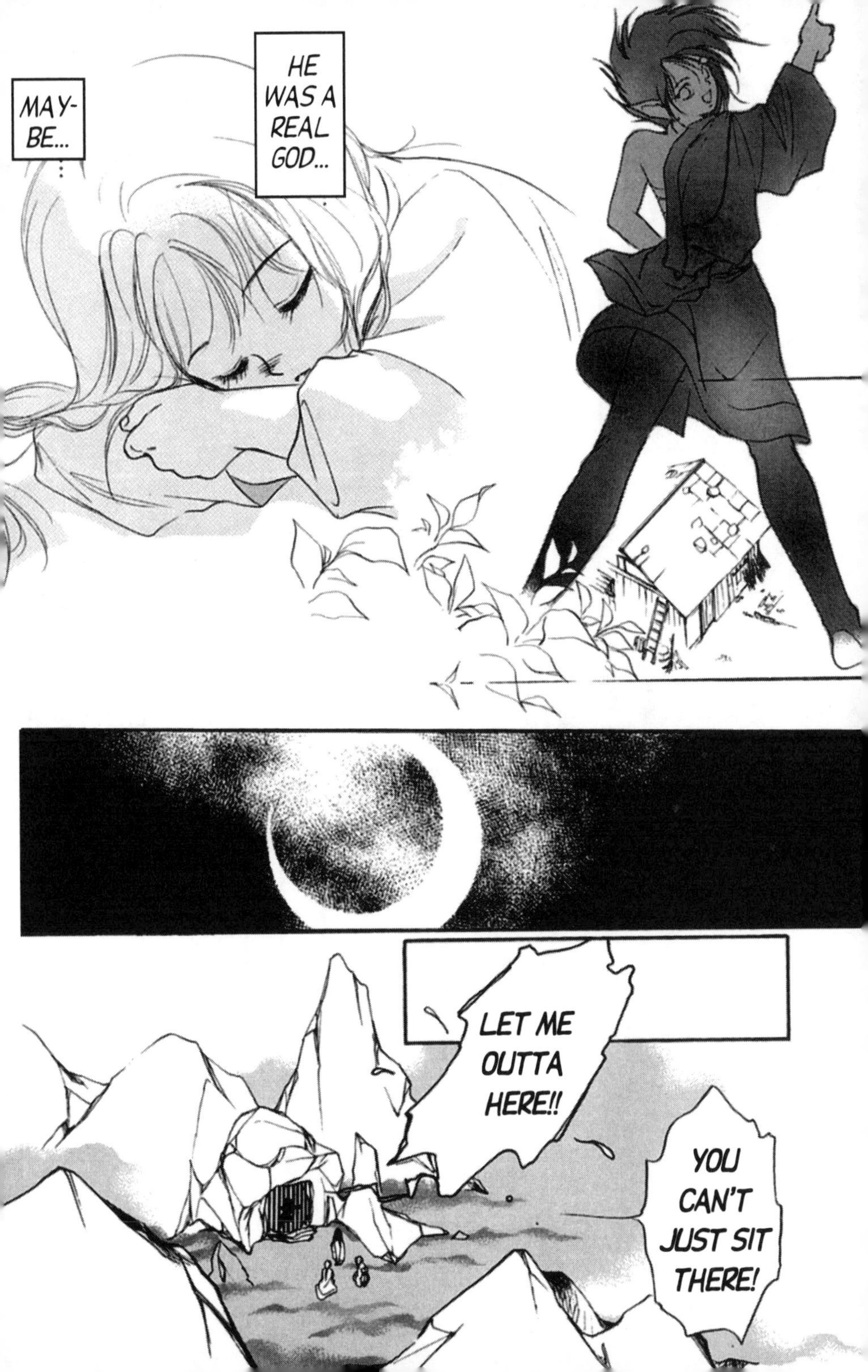
HE WAS A REAL GOD...
MAY-BE...
LET ME OUTTA HERE!!
YOU CAN'T JUST SIT THERE!

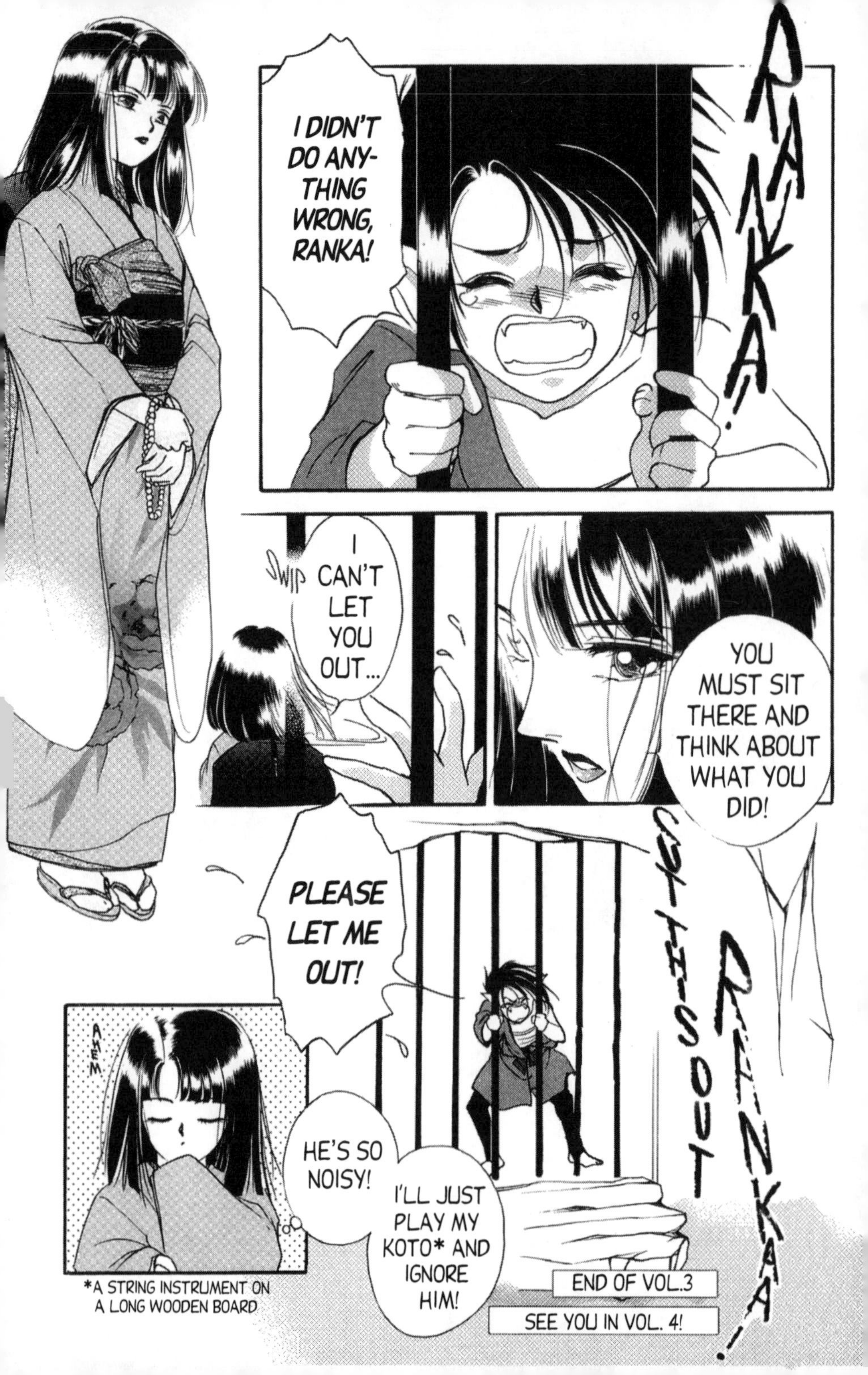
RANKA!
I DIDN'T DO ANYTHING WRONG, RANKA!
YOU MUST SIT THERE AND THINK ABOUT WHAT YOU DID!
SWIP
I CAN'T LET YOU OUT...
RANKAA...!
CAN'T LET HIS OUT
PLEASE LET ME OUT!
AHEM
HE'S SO NOISY!
I'LL JUST PLAY MY KOTO* AND IGNORE HIM!
END OF VOL.3
SEE YOU IN VOL. 4!
*A STRING INSTRUMENT ON A LONG WOODEN BOARD

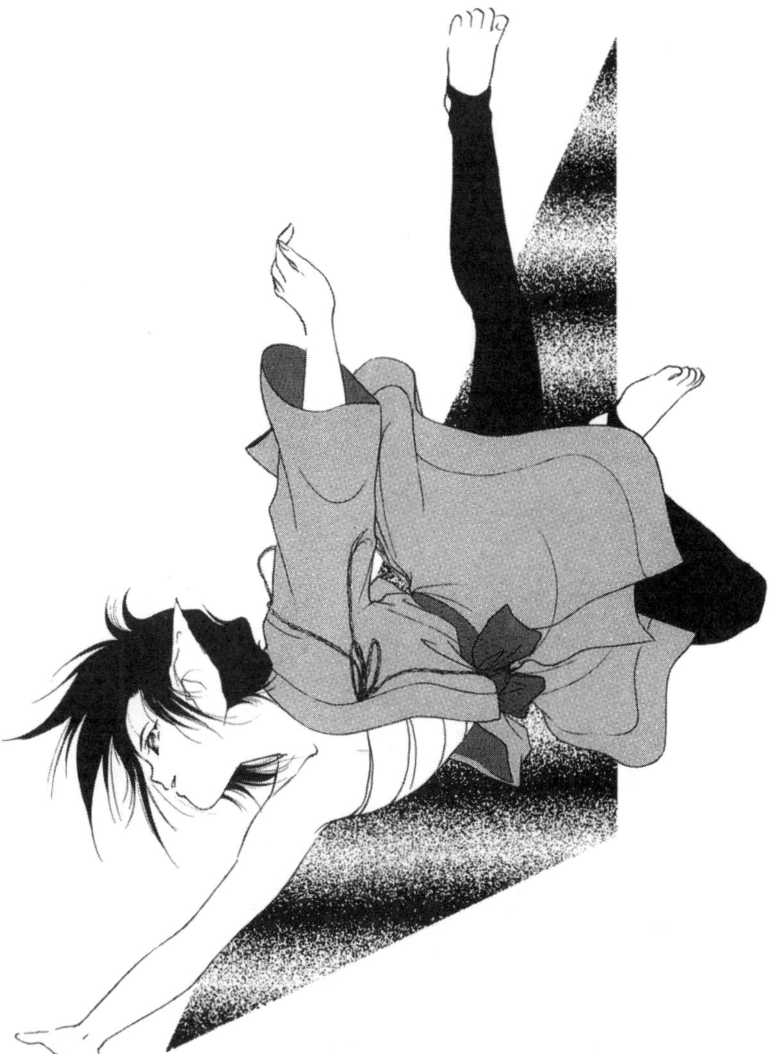